CONTINGENT CITIZENS

CONTINGENT CITIZENS

SHIFTING PERCEPTIONS OF LATTER-DAY SAINTS IN AMERICAN POLITICAL CULTURE

EDITED BY SPENCER W. MCBRIDE, BRENT M. ROGERS, AND KEITH A. EREKSON

CORNELL UNIVERSITY PRESS
Ithaca and London

First published 2020 by Cornell University Press

Library of Congress Cataloging-in-Publication Data

Names: McBride, Spencer W., editor. | Rogers, Brent M., editor. | Erekson, Keith A., editor. | Jortner, Adam Joseph. Some little necromancy.
Title: Contingent citizens : shifting perceptions of Latter-day Saints in American political culture / edited by Spencer W. McBride, Brent M. Rogers, and Keith A. Erekson.
Description: Ithaca : Cornell University Press, 2020. | Includes bibliographical references and index.
Identifiers: LCCN 2019037679 (print) | LCCN 2019037680 (ebook) | ISBN 9781501716737 (hardcover) | ISBN 9781501749544 (paperback) | ISBN 9781501716744 (pdf) | ISBN 9781501716751 (ebook)
Subjects: LCSH: Church of Jesus Christ of Latter-day Saints—Political activity—History. | Church of Jesus Christ of Latter-day Saints—Public opinion—History. | Mormons—Political activity—History. | Mormons—Public opinion—History. | Political culture—United States—History. | Public opinion—United States—History.
Classification: LCC BX8643.P6 C66 2020 (print) | LCC BX8643.P6 (ebook) | DDC 289.3/73—dc23
LC record available at https://lccn.loc.gov/2019037679
LC ebook record available at https://lccn.loc.gov/2019037680

Contents

PREFACE

The Church of Jesus Christ of Latter-day Saints and its members reveal a peculiar irony in the history of the United States. Joseph Smith founded the church in 1830 as American society was undergoing a dramatic democratization that extended to the country's political system. The Latter-day Saints and their religious beliefs arose in a fledgling American democracy, yet Americans have frequently struggled to determine the place of Latter-day Saints in that political system. In a country that celebrates itself as a bastion of freedom, Americans' use of mob violence, civic decrees, and legal prohibitions reveal a public tension over the extent to which Americans should tolerate the civic participation of their Latter-day Saint neighbors.

In this book, we explore the different ways politicians, lawmakers, and the general public perceived the place of the Church of Jesus Christ of Latter-day Saints and its members in American political culture throughout the nineteenth and twentieth centuries. Indeed, historians have long acknowledged the difficulty Americans have experienced in deciding where Latter-day Saints belong in the country's political realm. In terms of rights and identity, this difficulty has often resulted in American Latter-day Saints existing on an ambiguous plane somewhere between citizens and foreigners.

Whereas many scholars have focused on the ambiguous status of Latter-day Saints and their experience in certain historical events or as a lens through which to view particular moments of the American past, we track and examine the evolution of this phenomenon over a period of nearly two centuries.[1] The book comprises chapters that demonstrate the endurance and evolution of this American political problem; they reveal that, while the level of acceptance Latter-day Saints experienced varied over time, the feeling that they were not quite fully American prevailed. This theme lies at the heart of the book.

However, the characterization of Latter-day Saints in American political culture is not limited to questions of their peculiarity. In addition to exploring the persistent difficulty of Americans to determine the place of their Latter-day Saint countrymen in the political sphere, we suggest additional ways of conceptualizing the relationship. How does the question of Latter-day Saints' full participation in the American political system inform larger conversations about the role of religious authority and voter mobilization in a democracy? What if we viewed the history of Latter-day Saints in American politics as it relates to the country's ongoing struggle to determine the proper parameters of power and sovereignty? How does the otherness of American Latter-day Saints complicate narratives of American unity and nationalism? Does the Latter-day Saint story help bridge narratives of American political history that are typically broken in their continuity by the Civil War?

Such questions do not dismiss the importance of the ambiguous status of Latter-day Saints in American politics, but they complicate it. They bring the Latter-day Saints more fully into the central narratives of American history. They connect a particular form of religious discrimination to presidential politics, questions of sovereignty, women's rights, westward expansion and migration, geopolitics, and twentieth-century culture wars. Thus, the stories in this book transcend the narrow category of Mormon history and speak to broader patterns in the history of American politics. Beyond describing the plight of a religious subset of the American public, we use the history of that subset to illuminate larger trends in the evolution of American political culture.

It is important to recognize that the Latter-day Saints were not passive victims in the debates over their place in American political culture. Discontent with systemic discrimination, they engaged in local, state, and federal politics to protect their communities and to reform society in a way that preserved their full citizenship rights. As several of the chapters reveal, Latter-day Saints created a populist presidential campaign, repeatedly sought self-government through statehood, and protected their communities from state-sponsored violence through controversial declarations of martial law. They also concentrated their agricultural enterprises to exert greater influence on regional and national economies, and, in the 1970s and 1980s, mobilized voters in the contentious national campaigns surrounding the Equal Rights Amendment.

Still, as a religious minority, Latter-day Saints in the United States ultimately had to rely on those in the country's political mainstream to advocate for them. The extent to which they could exercise their full set of rights as citizens was dependent on the attitudes of non-Mormons in power. However, when the country's Latter-day Saint population became the focus of political speeches, editorials, and propaganda, Americans were talking about more than the "Mormon question." They were often talking about the inherent fragility of democracy and used the Latter-day Saints as a convenient encapsulation of its perceived threats. For instance, in the nineteenth century, concerns about Latter-day Saints voting as a bloc coincided with similar fears regarding Catholic Americans and how these religious groups represented a "foreign" threat to the republic. This anti-Mormon and anti-Catholic rhetoric—this fear of foreign intervention in American elections—coincided with drastically increased political participation by average Americans that threatened the societal control of elite men. In another instance, many Americans opposed Utah statehood over four decades on the basis that the Latter-day Saints were unfit for self-government because of the practice of plural marriage and their acceptance of certain theocratic principles. However, beneath the statehood question and the claims of unfitness for self-rule lay broader concerns about the limits of popular sovereignty in the United States within the context of rapid territorial expansion and a shift in the country's demographics amid a rise in immigration.

Americans have long been conditioned to believe that their democracy is in peril, in part because it usually is. The country's founders recognized that government by the people could quickly give way to either anarchy in the hands of unruly masses or tyranny in the hands of a demagogue. The potential for such self-destruction was woven into the very fabric of democracy. As John Adams observed in 1814: "There never was a Democracy Yet, that did not commit suicide."[2] Vigilance is vital. However, as demonstrated in the chapters that follow, this ever-present fear of democracy's demise often exacerbated extant prejudices against religious minority groups, including the Latter-day Saints.

The chapters in this book are not comprehensive in their coverage of the myriad roles of Latter-day Saints in American history, nor are they presented in chronological order. Instead, they are organized in three parts that emphasize different conceptual categorizations. Each part commences with a brief introduction to the chapters therein. After an introduction exploring the ways in which the Latter-day Saint experience was exceptional and the ways that it was typical in the history of the United States, Part I explores the concepts of authority and mobilization, as evidenced in the use of political rhetoric that appealed to the fear of tyranny, the mobilization of voters in support of Joseph Smith's presidential candidacy, and the organizing of Mormon women in opposition to the Equal Rights Amendment. Part II employs the concepts of power and sovereignty to understand Mormons' participation in frontier violence, their exercise of martial law, the threat to seize part of the continent in the mid-nineteenth century, and the practice of blending political and economic power in the early twentieth century. Part III probes the ways that Mormons engaged conversations about unity and nationalism by serving as a substitute for discussions of slavery in antebellum America, identity and allegiance in the nineteenth century, mainstream Americanism during the Cold War, and political realignments during the late twentieth-century culture wars.

Acknowledgments

This book benefited from the support of several people not listed in the table of contents. We thank the Church History Department of The Church of Jesus Christ of Latter-day Saints for sponsoring and hosting the symposium in which the ideas in this book were first expressed and debated. The leadership of the department, Steven E. Snow, Reid L. Neilson, and Matthew J. Grow, enthusiastically facilitated the event. Lis Allen played a vital role in managing the symposium's arrangements, and Mike Henry and Brian Warburton of the Church History Library arranged for a display of relevant archival documents at that event.

The chapters in this book were improved by comments and questions from several individuals who attended the symposium or suggested revisions on subsequent drafts. For this we thank Mason Allred, Bart Atkin, Christopher Blythe, Josh Bullough, Brian Cannon, Gerrit Dirkmaat, David Grua, Steven Harper, Steve Hepworth, Natalie Johnson, Christopher Jones, Jeffrey Mahas, Scott Marianno, Monroe McBride, Colleen McDannell, Steve Olsen, Tyson Reeder, Michelle Sayers, John Sillito, Lisa Olsen Tait, Jeff Thompson, Jordan Watkins, and Jed Woodworth. We also thank our editor at Cornell University Press, Michael McGandy, who helped this project take shape from its earliest stages and the fantastic team at the press who have guided the manuscript through the production process. We also express our gratitude to Joseph Stuart who created the book's index.

Of course, our families have been the constant supporters of our historic endeavors. Keith remains ever grateful for the *non*contingent support of Carolyn, Emily, Alyse, Haley, and Lyndie. Brent especially wishes to acknowledge the sacrifice, encouragement, and love of his family, Ashley, Keagan, Makinsey, and Braxton Rogers, during the development and production of this book. Spencer similarly thanks his wife, Lindsay, and their children, Erik, Laney, Joshua, and Thomas, who inspire him.

A Note on Style

The church founded by Joseph Smith in 1830 was called the Church of Christ. In 1834 the name changed to the Church of the Latter Day Saints. Then, in 1838, the church adopted the name the Church of Jesus Christ of Latter-day Saints. While this has remained the church's official name since 1838, throughout its history the church has been alternately referred to as the Mormon Church or the LDS Church. The term "Mormon" has also been used to refer to other individuals, institutions, and practices that trace their origins to Joseph Smith. In this book we use the official name of the church as the first reference in each chapter and use "the church" as a shortened reference thereafter. When referring to church members, we use "Latter-day Saints," "Saints," and "Mormons" interchangeably. We also use "Mormon" or "Mormons" in proper nouns, historical context, and quotations from historical sources.

CONTINGENT CITIZENS

Introduction

Not Exceptional, Typical, or Americanized: The Latter-day Saint Experience with American Politics

Keith A. Erekson

Since its beginnings in western New York in the 1830s, the Church of Jesus Christ of Latter-day Saints has prompted commentary and controversy about its place on the American political and cultural landscape. One surprising consensus among frequently disparate viewpoints has been the assertion of exceptionalism, whether for the church as a religious institution, or for Latter-day Saints as individuals and a collective people, or for the faith's belief system and culture. Advocates for the faith call out peculiar doctrinal beliefs as evidence for being God's chosen people and distinct inheritors of the early Judeo-Christian tradition. Antagonists have emphasized the group's particular strangeness as grounds for its being a unique threat worthy of federal regulation, or at least a good laugh on Broadway. Analysts resort to exceptional language when attempting to classify a Christian faith that is neither Catholic nor Protestant, a New World religion rooted in both Old Testament tradition and the arid realities of the American West, or a body of voters who are fixedly conservative with marked divergence from fellow Republicans. As apt as the question of Latter-day Saint exceptionalism may seem to certain moments of the church's history, it is an overly simplistic construct that is ill-suited to capturing the complexity surrounding perceptions of the Saints in American political culture.

We can move beyond the concept of exceptionalism by seeing the Latter-day Saint political experience more broadly in nineteenth- and twentieth-century American political and cultural history. In so doing, we find that three other conditions more persuasively describe the contours of the experience—the potential for democratic mobilization, the exercise of actual political power, and the relationship to a fragile national unity. Because Latter-day Saints organized into a community led by a prophet with authority to direct their obedience and action, the movement has always harbored an ability to mobilize political support within the American democratic system. When church leaders exercised this authority—to endorse candidates, to seek legal protection, to back causes—the latent threat of mass mobilization became manifest as political power and sovereignty, whether through a city charter in Illinois or territorial status in the American West. By exercising political power in a pluralistic society, the Saints entered cultural conversations about unity and nationalism. The concepts of authority and mobilization, power and sovereignty, and unity and nationalism thus provide ways of situating the experience of this religious group within wider American contexts.

In addition to questioning the construct of exceptionalism, I also challenge the prevailing narrative about the church's political participation—the so-called Americanization theory—which posits that Latter-day Saints have grown less exceptional and more typical over time, the result of conscientious decisions to abandon polygamy in the 1890s and move into the political mainstream in the twentieth century.

Like other Americans, Latter-day Saints and their political experience have been both swept up and shaped by national political debates about slavery, Manifest Destiny, popular sovereignty, civil religion, and equal rights. The discourse of past eras has clearly invoked religious-sounding themes and topics—superstition, fanaticism, polygamy, persecution, family—but the topics and the debates involve other, more widely applicable stakes. And while there are certainly exceptional aspects of the church's experience in American politics, the general picture reveals tensions that are common among other religious minorities (including Catholics, Jews, Quakers, and Shakers) that have sought equal treatment under American law, equal participation in the American political system, and a place at the American cultural table.

In this introduction, I probe the limits of the debate between exceptionalism and typicality, and critique the conventional wisdom of the Americanization theory. I also provide a new outline of Latter-day Saint history framed within American politics that foregrounds Latter-day Saints' potential and actual exercise of power and the impact of that power on discussions of national unity.

Moving beyond the Exceptional and the Typical

Latter-day Saint historical actors, their contemporaries, and their historians (apologetic, antagonistic, and analytical) have regularly employed a language of peculiarity. As R. Laurence Moore observed nearly four decades ago, this language has tended to benefit all proponents: "Most everyone who wrote about Joseph Smith's church, and above all this included Mormons themselves, asserted that Mormons were not like other Americans" and "all parties discovered reasons to stress not what Mormons had in common with other Americans, which was a great deal, but what they did not have in common."[1]

Believers employed claims of exceptionalism as doctrinal evidence for truth claims. Missionaries taught that beliefs about modern prophets, new scripture, and restored ecclesiastical authority underscored the church's position as "the only true and living church." At the same time, opponents of the movement garnered the most attention and raised the most support when painting the faith as a terribly unique threat—strangely un-Christian beliefs, a startlingly oppressive system of plural marriage, a singularly corrupt theocracy that merged religious and political authority. A variety of commentators and scholars have also identified the faith as the quintessential American religion. Not only did it originate in the United States, its rapid growth can in many ways be attributed to the democratization of American society in an era when the country experienced a rise in and tepid acceptance of religious pluralism. Such language persists in modern political discourse. The political scientists David E. Campbell, John C. Green, and J. Quin Monson have recently shown that twenty-first-century Saints view themselves as an ethnoreligious subculture distinct from wider American and American Christian cultures (especially evangelicals), a view that informs both insider political behavior and outsider perceptions.[2]

But we should not be too distracted by the rhetoric of the debate's participants. The historian Daniel Walker Howe recently stated that, while some features of the faith and its history make it seem unique—scripture, polygamy, continuing revelation—it displays characteristics that are far more characteristic of the times and place of its origin. For example, like fellow compatriots, nineteenth-century Saints espoused freedom of religion, pluralism, democracy, temperance, abolition, Manifest Destiny, and faith in progress.

Like their fellow religionists, they preached restorationism and millennialism, participated in the Second Great Awakening, and worked to establish a utopian community. And, like other Americans, they blended religion and politics. "Although Americans prided themselves on their individualism, in practice they readily followed revivalist preachers, joined associations both civil and religious, and enlisted in cooperative utopias," Howe noted. "They took a lively interest in civil affairs and voted en masse along with their neighbors. The Latter-day Saints participated in such undertakings characteristic of antebellum America, and their leaders displayed an effective understanding of that culture."[3] In his summary of nineteenth-century economic practices, the historical economist Leonard J. Arrington remarked that, "despite their assertions of 'peculiarity,' much of what was done by the Mormons was truly American."[4] The line between peculiar and typical cannot be so neatly drawn.

Even the act of asserting uniqueness is part of a larger cultural framework. Philip Barlow places Latter-day Saint claims of being a uniquely chosen people in a chosen land within the civil religious framework of American exceptionalism that traces back to John Winthrop's city on a hill, Abraham Lincoln's last best hope on earth, and modern visions of national superiority. R. Laurence Moore made a similar observation upon reviewing the relationship between mainline Protestantism and so-called fringe groups—Latter-day Saints, Catholics, Jews, Christian Scientists, Jehovah's Witnesses, and Pentecostals: "[They] have all maintained a sense of separation from mainstream culture while advancing a very solid claim to be typically American." Indeed, "one way of becoming American was to invent oneself out of a sense of opposition."[5] In other words, in claiming to be exceptional, Latter-day Saint actors are also being typically American.

The literature on polygamy in the American political landscape serves to illustrate a more helpful approach. If there were a single, defining difference for the faith, perhaps it would be the practice of polygamy. After all, the topic drew national attention and became the stated basis for federal intervention in the 1880s. And yet, as Moore pointed out, the majority of Saints did not practice polygamy and many of them found it distasteful. Unlike their portrayals in popular literature, practitioners rarely exhibited lascivious behavior and organized opposition to the church occurred in Missouri of the 1830s before the practice was publicly proclaimed. Nevertheless, in the late nineteenth and early twentieth centuries, the question of polygamy drew outsized attention in popular literature and political commentary.

In more recent years, however, new analysts have seen through the debate about a religion and its marriage practices to the wider political, cultural, and historical contexts. Sarah Barringer Gordon skillfully demonstrated the way that Republican politicians used polygamy as a legally equivalent substitute for slavery—by arguing for federal power to break up the domestic institution of polygamy they sought to establish a precedent by which to break up the Southerners' purportedly domestic institution of slavery. Southern Democrats did not fall for the ruse and defended polygamy until they seceded from the Union (the first antipolygamy legislation was passed, significantly, the next year in 1862). After the Civil War, opposition to the church played out along sectional lines and Patrick Mason has demonstrated the ways in which shared dislike of the Saints served as a unifying balm between the North and the South. Spencer Fluhman found in the debates of the same era a larger question about what counted as religion, while Christine Talbot saw them as "a contest over the very meaning of Americanness." Indeed, "the Mormon question became a national question," Talbot concluded, "because Mormons occupied a western territory and exercised real political power."[6] Within a generation of scholarship, our understanding of the national debate about polygamy moved from seeing the Saints as unique and isolated to understanding the controversy within wider postbellum political concerns—concerns not about specific religious practices, but about the exercise of power within a fragile national political alliance.

As illustrated with the case of polygamy, the discussion of Latter-day Saints in American politics has frequently served as a substitute for talking about something larger than the persons or the faith. How does an antislavery politician try to move against slavery under the gag rule? How do Northerners and Southerners find common cause after a civil war? How do Americans make sense of the rapid social transformations brought on by urbanization, immigration, and the diversification of the national populace? They did so, in part, by using the church as a substitute. Americans raised similar concerns about a host of other groups, from Catholics to Native Americans to secessionists. Thus, in the American political arena, Latter-day Saints have not posed unique challenges to a majority-Protestant America. Rather, they have served as a useful projection for fears and anxieties about other—larger, less-defined, more threatening—developments. Examining the political history of the faith enables historians to more fully discuss American identity, questions of sovereignty, and matters of federal power.

Contextualizing the Americanization Theory

To question the peculiarity and typicality of the Latter-day Saint religious experience challenges one of the most commonly accepted frameworks for telling the church's history. Analysts with disciplinary backgrounds in sociology, history, and political science have proffered variations of an idea that the church began as a radical, outsider group in the nineteenth century and then became respectable—even model American—in the twentieth century through processes variously called Americanization, assimilation, or domestication. The Americanization theory draws on the work of Max Weber and other sociologists of new religious movements. In sociological terms, the "sect" became a "church," the new religious movement went mainstream. In a sentence, the sociologist Armand Mauss summarizes "the theory (such as it is) that the unpopular Mormon movement, having failed in a desperate nineteenth-century struggle for religious and political autonomy, finally achieved success and respectability in North America by abandoning its most offensive practices and deliberately pursuing a policy of assimilation with the surrounding American culture."[7]

In the case of the Latter-day Saints, the standard story line delineates how, for more than half a century after the Civil War, they were forced—by federal troops, antipolygamy legislation, and the requirements of statehood—to backtrack and abandon polygamy, theocratic government, and collectivist economic experiments. After a climactic confrontation between 1887 and 1907, the Saints quickly abandoned their original identity and essential practices so that they might deliberately and purposefully become, in the words of the journalists Richard and Joan Ostling, "regarded as model Americans by the time World War I arrived." The rest of the twentieth century is seen simply as the falling of dominoes initiated by the lost battle over polygamy: patriotic participation in World War I, implementation of a model welfare system during the Great Depression, an eventual and complete embrace of civil rights and American capitalism, all resulting in a monolithic conservative bloc of citizens who, by the 1980s, in the words of Harold Bloom, had "'out-American[ed]' all other Americans." The 2012 nomination of the grandson of polygamists (Mitt Romney) by the once-antipolygamy Republication Party has been used to illustrate the dramatic turn of public opinion. Reviewing more than forty years of economic, political, cultural, institutional, theological, and rhetorical histories, Mauss found this "American thesis" to be so "implicit in much of the extant literature" that it "has become the conventional wisdom."[8] Four decades of near scholarly consensus, however, is only the least of several reasons to reconsider the Americanization thesis.

The Americanization or church-sect model can be challenged on both logical and historical grounds. First, because of its roots in early twentieth-century social science, the thesis bears the implicit but fallacious assumption that America and the mainstream can somehow be held constant in the historical petri dish while objective analysts scrutinize the changes in the church. It is certainly true that the faith underwent a dramatic transition between the 1880s and 1920s, however, during the same period the United States also witnessed rapid and bewildering transformations in industrialization, urbanization, politics, foreign policy, global military engagements, and domestic race relations. The same federal government that passed, enforced, and declared the constitutionality of antipolygamy legislation also excluded Chinese immigrants, confiscated Native American lands, and established Jim Crow segregation. Both the Latter-day Saints and their fellow Americans were changing in ways that shaped their mutual interaction profoundly, a point substantially lost in the Americanization model.[9] As a result, the interconnected changes between religious and political history constitute an essential subject that has largely been obscured by the emphasis on a monotone story of Mormon assimilation into mainstream America.

Second, the simplistic tidiness of the Americanization theory is frequently muddied by historical realities that become more apparent when viewed in a broad chronological frame rather than in a single event. For example, Kathleen Flake largely distills the American accommodation of the faith into the four-year Senate investigation of the first Latter-day Saints elected to the nation's highest legislative body to find the Senate articulating "the political terms by which increasingly diverse religions would be recognized and accommodated in America for the remainder of the century." But the doctrinal transformations she cites began as many as three decades earlier than 1904–5, and the adaptations she identifies originated more widely and developed more slowly than her brief theoretical time line allows. Similarly, analysis of more recent political opinion polling has revealed that twenty-first-century Latter-day Saint voters are more conservative than Republicans on questions of gender roles and individual welfare while simultaneously more likely to approve of abortion and immigration, leading to a conclusion that the Saints behave like light—"just as light has the properties of both a particle and a wave, so are Mormons best understood as being simultaneously in the mainstream and on the fringes of American society." Similar rhetorical contortions are devised to explain how Mormons "present an anomaly to this pattern," or how Mormons represent a "perplexing riddle," a "paradox," or an "enigma."[10]

Third, the Americanization thesis establishes a framework for viewing Latter-day Saint political history as a transition between polarized extremes. Commentators wonder how public perception could transform from a nineteenth century in which Mormons were criticized, jailed, expelled, killed, targeted by the Republican Party, demonized by reformers, mobilized against by the federal army, legislated against by the US Congress, and disenfranchised by the Supreme Court to a twenty-first century in which Latter-day Saint Americans run for president, lead the Senate, participate in state politics, manage global corporations, compete in professional sports, and entertain millions on television and the silver screen.

If the Americanization theory downplays transformations in the broader United States, subjugates disparate details that do not fit its tidy model, and tends toward polarized analysis, it might be worth asking why it has so long endured in the scholarship on the church's history. Beginning in the 1950s, scholars within and outside of the faith tradition began to pay increasing attention to the church, its people, and its history. As a generation of new social historians rebelled against the political consensus history of the 1940s and 1950s, a cohort of new Mormon historians adopted the Americanization rhetoric in a push to professionalize the study of a new Mormon history. The new historians succeeded chiefly in adding a professionalized layer to the decades-old fault lines between critics and apologists.[11] For the new scholarly apologists, the invocation of Max Weber and objective social science methods strengthened the claims of neutrality and respectability of the findings. But the model also appealed to new critics of the faith—whether antagonistic outsiders or estranged insiders—because it rests on a distinction between Joseph Smith's religious practice of the 1840s and practices of the twentieth century. Opponents used the model to highlight the hypocrisy of historical changes while alienated insiders could simultaneously express their devotion to Joseph Smith and their disaffection with modern church practice.

Thus, the Americanization theory has explored the question of the church in America in a way that locates an answer in the changes *within* the faith—Latter-day Saints believe in revelation that permits their doctrine to evolve according to prophetic seers or pressing needs, or they have simply abandoned their beliefs to accommodate the sect within an unchanging mainstream American society. Is it not time to move beyond seers and sects? Without denying the obvious observation that the church has changed over time, can we not also ask how both America and Americans changed during the same time period? Is it possible that church and state simultaneously influenced each other? Can we reconceptualize the Saints' political experience so as to uncover and explore all the ways that Joseph Smith's supporters, critics, and country have changed *together* over the past two centuries?

Reframing American Politics

If we view the experience of the Latter-day Saints beyond frameworks focused solely on their exceptionalism or as a case study in assimilation, there are opportunities to see how the church and its history contributed to broader transformations in American politics, culture, and history. As developed through this volume, the concepts of authority and mobilization, power and sovereignty, and unity and nationalism provide loci around which to take another look at the Saints' engagement with American politics and culture. Because the church organized Americans into an institution characterized by geographical community building, it bore political implications from the outset. In a democracy, the organization of any community—whether as a political party, church, or civic group—raises the possibility for authoritarian control and mass mobilization through bloc voting and collective action. As the Latter-day Saint movement grew, its leaders turned such potential into power, first in local politics in New York, Ohio, and Missouri, but eventually in regional politics in the American West, and national politics in a fractured republic on both the brink of and return from civil war.

During the church's first generation, the consolidation of potential and actual power revolved around the person of Joseph Smith. Within the context of the Second Great Awakening, the young man in his late teens and early twenties began to speak of angelic visitations and an ancient record on golden plates that he translated and published in 1830 as The Book of Mormon. That same year, Smith organized a church in western New York that soon moved to Ohio and then established a second center in western Missouri. Missionaries called on converts to renounce their past faiths and physically relocate to gather in preparation for the apocalyptic troubles of the last days.[12] Thus, within only a year or two, the movement had assembled components that could either fan the faith of adherents or the fears of adversaries—a prophet bearing a message from God for modern times, a message that mingled an ethereal otherworld with the pragmatic present, and a body of believers willing to obey that message at personal cost and sacrifice.

The potential for an organized political threat faced its first organized political opposition in Missouri in 1833. Two decades before the concept of popular sovereignty would lead to bloodshed in Kansas and Nebraska, it found expression in local vigilante actions on the Missouri frontier. After Smith named Jackson County, Missouri, as the central Mormon gathering place, converts of primarily New England origin flooded into a community of primarily southern origin. As the county's Latter-day Saint population grew and its disposition to trade and vote together became evident, the earlier settlers of the county organized to expel them, "peaceably if we can, forcibly if we must." The Missouri legislature offered a solution for peace by establishing a new county for Latter-day Saint settlers. Ironically, this solution transformed the potential for church influence into actual political power by creating a new jurisdiction dominated by church interests. Five years passed before Latter-day Saints filled their county. In 1838, the governor of Missouri ordered all Saints to leave the state under threat of "extermination," a threat that state and local militias proved willing to enforce. Latter-day Saints would spend the ensuing decade moving their appeals for redress through state and national legislative, executive, and judicial processes. Their descendants would spend generations remembering their personal suffering and collective loss.[13]

The political lessons learned by the Saints in Missouri were applied throughout the nineteenth century as the movement grew in size and moved geographical locations. Having both tasted political power and desired a greater ability to protect themselves and their property, Latter-day Saints secured from the Illinois legislature a strong charter for the city of Nauvoo, which they would raise on the eastern bank of the Mississippi River. Here, the American line between church and state appeared to outsiders to vanish as Smith added mayor and general of the local militia to his title, taught more openly about personal consecration and communal order, and secretly instituted plural marriage. The potential for political mobilization again took concrete form as Smith reemphasized the concept of geographic gathering, as missionaries drew converts from England and Northern Europe who arrived as potential Illinois voters. In one election, the Saints' vote swung overnight from Whig to Democrat. Smith soon presented himself as a candidate for the US presidency in 1844, but within months he was assassinated and within years his followers would repeat the cycle.

The Latter-day Saint experience with American politics demonstrates continuities across the nineteenth century. The Civil War did not mark a dramatic change in their political participation, but rather it reveals continuities in the experience that translated from a Midwestern to a national context. The fragility of democracy in Missouri and Illinois reflected the larger instability that characterized antebellum national politics. By claiming, settling, and developing a major portion of the American Intermountain West, Latter-day Saints demonstrated their ability to mobilize voters into a relationship of power that influenced the unity of the nation. The Saints' request for statehood came in the midst of tenuous national slavery politics that resulted in the creation of the Utah territory in 1850 and a civil war in 1861. Mormon plural marriage—openly preached after 1852—served as a surrogate for public debates about slavery and then as a target of Protestant reform through unprecedented federal power in an era that witnessed Chinese exclusion, Indian removal, and the formalization of Jim Crow segregation. The exercise of political power occurred within larger story lines about the meaning of Americanness and what constituted threats to a fragile national unity.[14]

During the later years of the nineteenth century, the scope of Saints' political participation escalated from local to regional to national, while the location moved westward to Utah and then north and south along the Rocky Mountains into Canada and a newer (smaller) Mexico. Again, outsiders—federally appointed officials, miners who first passed through and then settled in the territory, speakers on the moral lecture circuits, legislators in Washington, DC—saw the Saints as a dangerous political faction that mingled church and state. Joseph Smith's successor as church president and prophet, Brigham Young, assumed those two titles, adding governor of the Utah Territory and chief officer of various cooperative economic ventures. For insiders, the desire for autonomy and self-preservation found no resolution in protection from state or federal governments. As with earlier problems in Missouri, the new issues worked through political and legal processes. In the 1890s, the church renounced polygamy, a Utah-based People's Party was dissolved to encourage participation in the nation's two parties of choice (in which insiders aligned primarily with Republicans and outsiders with Democrats), the church sold business interests, Latter-day Saint children began to attend public schools, and Utah received statehood.

Though the times and places and details changed, certain continuities of practice and perception nevertheless persisted. Though the church president no longer held an executive political office, individual Latter-day Saints sought and won offices to which they brought their worldview and values. For three decades, the state of Utah split its senators between Saints and outsiders (until the Seventeenth Amendment mandated direct election). State politics balanced sides between a democratic governor and republican legislature for two-thirds of the twentieth century. The church began a practice of announcing stands on issues, rather than taking sides among political parties. But the threat of political mobilization persisted; even though the Saints voted against church stands on welfare and prohibition in the 1930s, they generally aligned with them on the liquor laws of the 1960s, ERA and abortion in the 1970s, and same-sex marriage in the 1990s and early twenty-first century. Latter-day Saints likewise continued to participate in the exercise of actual political power in presidential cabinets, federal courts of appeals, district courts, and state supreme courts. In 2008 and 2012, the church's belief system colored Mitt Romney's bids for president, though he succeeded in securing the Republican Party's nomination.[15] In the twenty-first century, Latter-day Saint individuals, the institutional church, and the religious worldview continue to demonstrate a potential for political mobilization, actual cases of active exercise of political power, and the centrality of religion in conversations about national unity.

PART I

Authority and Mobilization

Fears of authoritarian mass mobilization pervaded public discourse about the role Mormons should play in American political processes—whether as voters or as officeholders. It was hardly a novel approach. American anti-Catholicism included the long-standing argument of Protestant Christians in Europe that Catholics' devout allegiance to the pope represented a threat of political mobilization by a religious authority whose interests were not necessarily aligned with those of the state. And it was an argument that many Americans readily applied to their Mormon countrymen. The influence that the top Mormon leaders seemed to hold on their followers led some onlookers to envision an unpredictable voting bloc untethered from the interests of the rest of the country. Fear that Mormon leaders would expand their religious authority into the political sphere, whether that potential for mobilization was latent or actively occurring, was invoked at various times and in diverse contexts in the nineteenth and twentieth centuries. The four chapters in Part I explore some of the ways that this fear of Mormon political mobilization influenced American political discourse, and how it often belied a deeper sense of the fragility of the American democratic experiment.

Critics of the Mormons did not always need to explicitly predict the potential for authoritarian control if the religious sect grew in numbers and influence. As Adam Jortner explains in his chapter, the language that many nineteenth-century Protestant Christians used to decry superstition among new religious groups such as the Mormons and the Shakers implied that the adherents of these movements were more susceptible to con men and imposters; superstition was antirepublican. Jortner demonstrates that magic, superstition, and necromancy were not merely derogatory descriptors of the religious beliefs of those outside mainstream Protestant Christianity. They were also political terms, used to designate some groups—including the Mormons—as untrustworthy, unfit for political participation, and a threat to republicanism itself.

In other instances, Americans were more direct in declaring Mormons as unfit for political participation. As Spencer W. McBride demonstrates in his chapter, newspapers throughout the country declined to take Joseph Smith's 1844 presidential campaign seriously. Some wrote off the campaign as a hoax. Others warned that such efforts represented a dangerous attempt to concentrate religious and political authority in one person. Still others used news of Smith's candidacy as an avenue by which to attack long-standing political rivals with no connection to the Mormons. Yet, as McBride observes, public mockery of Joseph Smith and his political ambitions was not mere entertainment to many of these newspapers. It was a subtle strategy intended to discredit Mormon participation in the American political system in the eyes of the undecided—those who were not already sympathetic or critical of Smith and his followers.

Just as many Americans expressed reservations about affording Mormons' full participation in the country's political system, several early Mormon leaders exhibited their own reservations about the direction in which American democracy was heading. As Benjamin E. Park argues in his chapter, mid-nineteenth-century Mormons were convinced that the country's Protestant majority had failed to protect the rights of minority groups and that corrective action was needed. Many American Catholics joined them in this opinion. Park compares the approaches of the two groups and the ways they sought to bring different forms of religious authority into the American political system as a way of redeeming the nation.

These nineteenth-century fears that Mormon leaders could use their religious authority to mobilize their followers as a voting bloc continued into the twentieth century, and in some instances seemed to be realized. Perhaps no situation better encapsulates the connection between Mormon religious authority and the power to mobilize American Mormons than the fight over the Equal Rights Amendment during the 1970s. As Natalie K. Rose shows in her chapter, leaders of the National Organization for Women (NOW) and a number of prominent news outlets named the Church of Jesus Christ of

Latter-day Saints and its impact on the votes of the women in its ranks as a major blow that led to the amendment's defeat. But this did not mean that NOW conceded the support of Mormon women—and the votes of the state of Utah—without a fight. Indeed, after the church came out against the ERA, NOW employed a door-to-door electioneering strategy in Utah—similar to the proselytizing strategy of Mormon missionaries abroad—in the hopes of persuading enough Mormon women to break with the political stance of their church so that Utah might approve the amendment. Rose describes a fascinating episode in American political history in which Mormon women played a deciding role in a national election, and the oft-debated potential of church leaders to direct their followers' political activity took center stage.

CHAPTER 1

"Some Little Necromancy"

Politics, Religion, and the Mormons, 1829–1838

ADAM JORTNER

A new religion emerged in the early United States. It came under severe censure for its leader, whom critics accused of combining religion with prophecy and prophecy with magic, of being a "deluded fanatic," "a false prophet working miracles," and a "fortune-teller."[1] Such beliefs were an obvious front for an effort to seize political power. The faith was "superstition and fanaticism" and bred "clerical as well as secular tyranny," according to one critic.[2] The whole religion, the president of Yale College stated, was a "cloud of religious Dust" making it possible for its practitioners to act "as Spies among us."[3] Later critiques connected their tyranny to their miracles. "Its miracles, visions, revelations, superstitions," were means "by which the elders obtain[ed] unlimited sway over the minds of their subjects."[4] Mobs repeatedly attacked their homes, whipped up by printed accusations that the faith was built of equal parts "infatuation and witchcraft."[5]

The religion, of course, was Shakerism—but its critics from 1781 to 1822 presaged the attacks against Mormonism in the coming years. Critiques lobbed at the Shakers—claims of magic, superstition, slavery, and witchcraft—were hurled at the Mormons, too. In its first decade, the Church of Jesus Christ of Latter-day Saints was labeled "Salem Witchcraft-ism,"[6] "hocus pocus," and "superstition."[7] Mormons were "a gang of impostors" who "know they utter false predictions. They know they cannot work miracles."[8]

One official report indicated that Mormonism "had for its object *Dominion*, and the ultimate subjugation of this State and the Union."[9] Political dissent against Mormonism in its first decade shared with anti-Shakerism an antipathy toward purported superstition and magic, taking such as evidence of a predilection for tyranny. Ann Lee, the Shaker founder, was referred to as a "fortune teller": Joseph Smith Jr. was branded as "very expert in the arts of necromancy."[10]

The propensity for critics to accuse Mormons of superstition and magical practice, and to associate that accusation with an enmity toward republicanism, had a long provenance in the early republic. So-called alternative religions of the early republic routinely faced charges of being both superstitious and dangerous to democracy. Often citizens charged that superstition bred tyranny and violence. Robert McAfee blamed the 1813 Creek War on a false religion deliberately imported to the Old Southwest by the Shawnee Prophet Tenskwatawa: "Having witnessed the powerful effects of fanaticism on the northwestern frontier under the management of that miserable vagabond," he wrote, British agents from Canada had "been careful to inspire some of the Creek worthies with prophetic and miraculous powers."[11] A popular tract denouncing the Cochranite sect in Maine referred to the religion as "quackery" and "religious deception" perpetrated by "an impostor or religious juggler." As a result, the tract explained, "those who are in close communion with him are bound to obey him," and Jacob Cochran "expects to have the United States, [in] the present season, under his control!"[12]

The term "superstition" has sometimes been taken at face value by historians (and by anti-Mormon critics). More recent scholarship has instead insisted that magical practice "was *not* anti-Christian" or have adopted some definition of magic as a halfway house between religion and science.[13] These approaches suggest that when Mormons dabbled in or practiced magic, particularly in the 1820s, they participated in an activity distinct from religion which was nevertheless culturally permissible at the time. Such an approach, however, still holds to the notion that magic was somehow other in early republican religion—an outlier or a disreputable activity distinct from true religion. That view of magic itself derives from the critiques of magic (and Mormonism) as "superstition"—a term with an inchoate but negative definition in the American political imagination of the early republic. Stephen Harper notes that the historiography of early Mormons often assumes this kind of "disorientation" from reports *about* the Mormons.[14] Contemporary critics' distaste for magic and their assumptions that such things were heretical, in addition to modern dichotomies about magic and religion, may have seeped into scholarly discourse. The terminology of the 1820s and 1830s, however, created a much harder and faster distinction between magical practice and religious truth than the actual amorphous forms of religious practice in the Age of Jackson.

"Necromancy" was a political term in early America. So were terms like "magic" and "superstition." They carried the freight of antirepublicanism; to be superstitious was to be open to impostors and con men, who would steal both money and freedom. "Superstitious feelings," warned John C. Calhoun on the floor of the House of Representatives, meant a "fearful retrograde in civilization" and a "dreadful declension toward barbarism."[15] While religion could be pluralistic in Thomas Jefferson's America, superstition could not. The definition of any given religion as a faith or as superstition—as truth or necromancy—was therefore a political act, determining which religions could be trusted and which were unacceptable. In the political parlance of the 1830s, Mormonism fell into the latter category.

It had good company. Repeated efforts were made by mobs, militias, and courts to wipe out new religions in America. Mobs assaulted Shaker communities in 1780, 1781, 1805, 1810, and 1825.[16] In 1784 a town in New Hampshire banned Shakers from settling there, forcing all arriving Shakers to report to an investigating committee.[17] In 1811 and 1812, armed militias assaulted the sacred sites of Prophetstown, Indiana, where Tenskwatawa's new religion had made its capital. Andrew Jackson similarly declared war on the Red Stick movements, insisting that his soldiers "undeceive" their enemies, for "they must be made to know that their prophets are impostors."[18] Jemima Wilkinson, Jacob Cochran, Jacob Osgood, and Nathaniel Wood were all arrested or imprisoned for crimes ranging from blasphemy to treason. These legal imbroglios appear to have worked: Wilkinsonianism, Cochranism, Osgoodism, and the New Israelitism did not survive the nineteenth century.

The political case against Mormonism is only the most famous entry in a longer history of religious prejudice and invective largely forgotten today. The rhetoric against magic and superstition had germinated in Anglo-American thought for decades, and its appearances prior to the publication of the Book of Mormon set the tone for the reception of the Book of Mormon (or at least, for its reception by those who did not embrace the restored gospel). Indeed, in the early years of Mormonism, it was fears of tyranny and superstition (and not polygamy or rumors thereof) that generated political backlash against the Saints. That in turn suggests that the Mormons did not generate the political animus against them by their own actions; they merely inherited it from Shaker, prophet, and Wilkinsonian antecedents. Moreover, it also recommends the need for a reappraisal of the role of "magic" in the genesis of the Mormon faith and the career of Joseph Smith Jr.; if necromancy was a political slur, then not all accusations of Smith as a necromancer should be taken at face value.

American political interest in the terms "superstition" and "magic" had philosophical origins in early modern Europe. During the Reformation, superstition was serious business—not because the term can be used retroactively to describe the beliefs of those Europeans, but because "it was immensely important to contemporaries . . . the very antithesis of true religious worship," as Stuart Clark writes.[19] The use of charms or nonprescribed prayers suggested disbelief in the efficacy of established religion and a violation of the First Commandment. Protestants classed most Catholic observance under the rubric of "superstition," but Catholic theologians denounced popular healings, charms, astrology, and even saying more than the prescribed number of prayers as false belief—superstition.[20] Superstition was a kind of idolatry, and if it ever appeared to work, surely demonic and not divine power had allowed it.

These ideas had obvious importance for early nation-states and other jurisdictions with official churches. If superstition was idolatry, it must be stamped out. But as the Enlightenment pushed the very idea of witchcraft into the category of superstition, justifications and reasoning began to change. As philosophes tried to find ways to avoid repeating the religious bloodbath of the seventeenth century, belief in witches and magic became the problem. In 1653 John Spencer argued that "easy men may be quickly be frighted from such images of straw, as the relations of monsters and strange sights are," turning loyal subjects into zealots for bad causes. Keeping a lid on prodigies and supernatural reports therefore required political intervention, so as to preserve *"the quiet and tranquility of the State."*[21] The English Whig Francis Hutchinson wrote his *Historical Essay Concerning Witchcraft* (1718) in part to suggest that "these Doctrines [on witchcraft] have often been made Party-Causes both in our own and other Nations. One side lays hold of them as Arguments of greater *Faith* and *Orthodoxy*" and "sometimes Governments are shaken, if they oppose their Notions."[22] John Hale reflected on Salem's witch trials in 1700, writing that "there hath been a great deal of innocent blood shed in the christian world . . . in condemning persons for malefick witchcraft," but also that "there have been great sinful neglects in sparing others, who by their divinings about things future, or discovering things secret, as stolen goods" have drawn the curious in by "specious pretences."[23] Monster stories and pretended magic were as bad as false accusations of witchcraft; as his fellow Salem critic Robert Calef wrote, they led to accusations of "imaginary crimes" and hence impeded the true worship of God. True religion required an abandonment of superstition—this time regarding belief in magic and witchcraft themselves.[24]

Yet Spencer, Hale, and Calef were writing about the dangers of superstitious belief within principalities that still possessed an official church. What happened when the principality became a republic? As disestablishment sundered the state's responsibility to monitor religious orthodoxy, the danger of false belief became more firmly political. Superstition lost its religious connotations but it remained a threat to good order. False belief became a monster in itself, a deliberate set of lies and "impostures" invented by hucksters and con men to seize both economic and political power. True republicans, so the argument went, must fear superstition for its ability to whip the multitudes into a frenzy, and thereby extinguish self-government. Belief in magic or witchcraft by anyone made a political crisis for all.

Numerous writers developed this case in the early republic.[25] William Bentley's 1799 *History of Salem* described the 1692 witchcraft panic as an evil "of the public opinion, and not in a court of justice." The "public clamours," Bentley wrote, made "nineteen innocent persons . . . victims of the public credulity."[26] In 1788 a Philadelphia debate claimed that those who believed in witchcraft represented "the prevalence of ignorance and superstition," enforced by "the fury of barbarous enthusiastic multitudes."[27] Even mere fortune-telling and magic could be dangerous, as the Congregationalist stalwart Joseph Lathrop sermonized: "Hearkening to diviners tends, not only to destroy religion, but to dissolve our mutual confidence and subvert our social security. . . . On social, therefore, as well as on religious principles, these diviners ought to be prosecuted rather than encouraged—to be punished rather than patronized." When the Lutheran minister Frederick Quitman discovered that a purported healing charm was nothing more than Latin gobbledygook, he wrote that "government ought to stop such fatal practices, whereby the lives of many are put in jeopardy." After all, it was "the sacred duty of those, who are appointed guardians and teachers of the people . . . to deliver those that were entrusted to my care, from the shameful yoke of superstition, and to help them to the enjoyment of rational liberty."[28]

A corpus of volumes appeared in the early republic with exactly this message. John Greenleaf Whittier cautioned Americans against supernaturalism—"matters beyond and above the conception of [one's] sharpened five senses." For Whittier, supernaturalism was superstition, derived from Puritan ancestors, whom he accused of "agitating their entire community with signs, and wonders, and dark marvels—poisoning the fountains of education, and constituting part of their religion." Worse, he found "scarcely a superstition of the past three centuries which has not at this very time more or less hold upon individual minds among us."[29] That meant trouble, argued Bernard Whitman in his *Lecture on Popular Superstitions* (1829). If people believed "that witches exist," or that "religious excitements and commotions of the present day are occasioned by the miraculous effusions of the holy spirit," then "trials for heresy, blasphemy, and witchcraft would once more disgrace the annals of our nation."[30] More to the point, Whitman wrote, the "mind that is imbued with a superstitious temperament, is liable to incessant torment, and is prepared to inflict the most atrocious evils on mankind; even murder, suicide, and merciless persecution . . . sanctioned by a superstitious spirit."[31] Or, as the epic poem *The Village* (1816) eulogized:

> when in States neglected virtues faint,
> And catch from vice its all corrupting taint;
> In freeman's hearts when love of country fails,
> And careless negligence of right prevails . . .
> Superstition, with its thousand creeds,
> Frowning on Reason as for Truth she pleads,
> Spreads wide confusion and to rage excites,
> In discord triumphs and in strife delights.[32]

In 1826 the printer David Young rewrote a history of Ransford Rogers, a notorious hoaxster. Rogers convinced a swath of New Jersey citizens to pay him to exorcise faux ghosts. Rogers, Young wrote, with "an intention to extract money from their pockets, endeavored to secure the veil of ignorance upon their minds." He pretended to see buried treasure and arranged the exhibition of ghosts, until at last his victims would "revere Rogers, believing him something more than a man: and such was the influence which he possessed over them, with a despotic power."[33]

To prevent such catastrophes, the state needed to step in. David Reese's *Humbugs of New York* (1838), for example, was dedicated to "the constituted guardians of the public health, public morals, and public peace," and explained the "reign of humbug" as a political crisis, the "serious and important bearing on the public weal which certain impostures in our city are likely to exhibit." Reese also prodded "the more enlightened portion of our population" to watch out for superstition, lest "the prevalence and success of these impostures in the lower walks of life, will neutralize civilization itself."[34] Reese included Mormonism along with phrenology and mesmerism as his "humbugs." Just as "Moses made a law against necromancy, witchcraft, etc.: so that the Israelites would not be tempted to be like the Egyptians," Quitman wrote, so too should Americans ban pretended magical practices. One reader agreed, writing that "the prohibition of palmistry, fortune-telling, and such-like crafty arts, by a special statute of New-York, is an acknowledgement by the legislature that their prevalence endangers the peace of society to a great degree, and that the authority of the magistrate ought to be interposed."[35]

Thus, magic and superstition were not merely folkloric byways or mere cultural curiosities in the early republic; understanding them was essential to the perennial Jeffersonian and Jacksonian dilemmas about the problems of freedom, tyranny, and reason. Witchcraft "belongs to the mind-enslaving and misery-creating family of superstition, and is twin sister to priestcraft," intoned the *Boston Investigator*.[36] Fortune-telling, wrote a critic in 1812, "destroys the tranquility of many . . . fetching the last penny from the purse of indigence." Therefore, "the legislature of New-York has acted wisely in making this a subject of prohibition . . . an example which ought to be imitated by every State in the Union."[37] Some states did; "every juggler and fortune-teller" was classed with prostitutes by Maryland law. Connecticut law categorized as vagrants "all persons using, or pretending to use any subtile craft, juggling . . . or feigning themselves to have knowledge in physiognomy, palmistry, or pretending they can tell destinies, fortunes, or discover where lost or stolen goods may be found."[38]

When organized groups emerged claiming supernatural powers and new revelation, the republican language of magic, fortune-telling, and superstition became instantly attached to these movements. James Smith wrote that Shakers "can see angels and spirits which to others are invisible," and use these pretended supernatural powers to turn white Americans into "voluntary slaves . . . seduced, bewildered, and lost, under strong delusion."[39] In 1810 Smith led a mob that was intent on ransacking an Ohio Shaker village. Shaker "miracles, visions, revelations, superstitions," wrote David Lamson, were the means "by which the elders obtain unlimited sway over the minds of their subjects."[40] Reports about Native American prophets deployed similar language about superstition, whether those came from academic sources (Henry Rowe Schoolcraft's assessment that Pontiac had turned "the mythological and superstitious belief of his auditors to political account"), or from military memoirs (McAfee's assertion that the Red Stick prophets were "dupes of British intrigue and of their own superstition" who made "easy prey to our [US] united forces").[41] The battle with the Red Sticks represents another military foray made against those who claimed they possessed supernatural powers—a literal American war against superstition. These acts were precursors to the Mormon Wars of the nineteenth century and to the vigilante action at Hawn's Mill, Missouri, that claimed the lives of seventeen Mormons in October 1838.[42]

As African Americans developed and embraced a distinctive form of Christianity in the early republic, white theologians and critics branded it as "superstition" with the associated stereotype of tyranny. "Superstitions brought from Africa have not wholly been laid aside," wrote Charles Colcock Jones, and, therefore, African Americans could fall under "the influence of some leader or conjuror or minister, that they dared not to disobey."[43] Regarding the Denmark Vesey conspiracy of 1822, one correspondent claimed that "religion and superstition were used by the more cunning [slaves] to delude the credulous Africans in the plot" to upend the slaveholders' republic. Jack Pritchard, a practitioner of African American conjure, was sentenced to die as part of the Denmark Vesey conspiracy, and the court took the opportunity to explain his particular crime: "You were not satisfied with resorting to natural and ordinary means, but endeavored to enlist on your behalf, all the powers of darkness, and employed for that purpose, the most disgusting mummery and superstition." Such efforts had been intended to sway "the ignorant and credulous." Now, however, "your Altars and your Gods have sunk together in the dust." Pritchard was executed on July 12, 1822.[44]

There were smaller sects, too, that also received opprobrium. David Hudson, in his yellow biography of Jemima Wilkinson, asserted that Wilkinson "was extremely superstitious, and as her followers generally adopted her sentiments and followed her advice in all matters of faith and mystery . . . they became equally so."[45] Nathaniel Wood's New Israelite movement flared briefly in Vermont, then vanished into the antiquarian twilight. Excommunicated by the Congregationalists, Wood founded his own church, which soon became as large as any other denomination in Middletown, Vermont. Wood and his allies operated "by a kind of sorcery," received revelations through divining rods, used the Bible to dig for treasure, and "all the believers became wild fanatics." Wood became convinced that God would send a destroying angel against his enemies on January 14, 1802. The local militia was called out that night to disrupt any Israelite activities for fear of civil insurrection. The town council of Middletown then drummed Wood and the remaining believers out of town—no small feat, since several of Wood's sons held elective office there.[46]

The language that arrayed superstition against republicanism also found a fertile ground in the anti-Catholic campaigns in Jeffersonian America. Enlightenment debates on superstition originated in the Protestant-Catholic conflicts of earlier centuries, and nativists kept the fires burning—sometimes literally—in the early nineteenth century. Lyman Beecher's canonical anti-Catholic text, A Plea for the West, described the battle against Catholics as a choice between "superstition, or evangelical light; of despotism, or liberty."[47]

The 1835 introduction to *Six Months in a Convent*—a text purporting to be a muckraking account of sexual crimes at the Ursuline Convent of Charlestown, Massachusetts—inveighed against the "secret and superstitious community of Catholic Priests and Nuns" which subverted American efforts for "a *Christian* and a *republican* education."[48] The Ursuline convent was burned to the ground by a Protestant mob in 1834. There was much more at work in the rise of American anti-Catholicism than the language of superstition, of course, but it contributed to a popular Protestant perception of Catholics. As Sidney Martin Lipset and Earl Raab wrote, Catholics of the nineteenth century and Jews of the twentieth century became envisioned as a "visible body of ethnic immigrants . . . connected to images of secret, exotic, and conspiratorial institutions."[49] The politics of superstition and its purported *intentional* efforts to fool the credulous did not create anti-Catholicism, but it did feed into it—as it fed into myths of blood libel and secret ceremonies among the Jews in the twentieth century. Shakers, Wilkinsonians, Cochranites, and Mormons were also victims of linguistic politics. It was no accident that anti-Mormons dubbed Smith "Pope Joseph *the First*."[50]

American religious and political thought therefore had classified superstition and magic as notions dangerous to democracy well before Joseph Smith Jr. announced his translation of the Book of Mormon. When he did, of course, the howls went up, decrying that new prophecy, money-digging, and other Mormon activities such as healing, speaking in tongues, and exorcism were all superstition—and therefore a threat to freedom. Eber D. Howe's *Mormonism Unvailed* was the most famous case in point, dubbing Smith "well skilled in legerdemain," which allowed him to dominate "willing dupes" and bend them to his will: "To establish the truth of any pretension . . . required nothing but some little necromancy."[51]

Indeed, the very first printed exposition on the Book of Mormon occurred as part of a more general exegesis on the dangers of superstition. Obadiah Dogberry (the pseudonym of Abner Cole) published a selection from the Book of First Nephi in his *Palmyra (NY) Reflector* on January 2, 1830. Dogberry had an interesting take on the volume: "From a part of the first chapter, now before us, and which we this day publish, we cannot discover anything treasonable, or which will have a tendency to subvert our liberties." Thus, upon hearing of a wondrous new bible and a restored religion, Dogberry *expected* that it would be treasonous or subversive to liberty—and he expected his readers to anticipate the same.

Yet Dogberry's *Reflector* had already been parading examples of the dangers of superstition to his readers in Upstate New York. Dogberry's *Reflector* had only a handful of issues prior to the January 1830 edition, and several of those issues featured a series of articles on a very different false prophet—the "Sabbatai Levi" (Tsevi). Dogberry penned a history of this seventeenth-century Ottoman Jew who proclaimed himself the Messiah and led "deluded and infatuated" followers from across the Mediterranean. Dogberry entitled this series "Imposters," and declared that the Sabbatai Tsevi was a charlatan out for personal power. (Alexander Campbell also referenced Tsevi in his polemic *Delusions*.)[52] Dogberry's series on Tsevi concluded in the same issue that published the first extracts of the Book of Mormon.[53]

Dogberry's infamous "Book of Pukei"—the first printed satire of the Book of Mormon—also connected magic to tyranny and both notions to Smith: the "idle and slothful" people seek a magician to "inform us where the *Nephites* hid their *treasure*." And then "it came to pass, that when the mantle of Walters the magician had fallen on Joseph [Smith], surnamed the prophet . . . the 'idle and slothful' gathered themselves together, in the presence of Joseph, and said unto him, Lo! we will be thy servants forever, do with us, our wives, and our little ones as it may seem good in thine eyes."[54] The critiques of Mormonism as magic and as antidemocratic emerged with the publication of the Book of Mormon itself.

There are numerous other examples of this kind of language in anti-Mormon publications. Notable instances include the way Howe's *Unvailed* introduced the Smith family as "lazy, indolent, and superstitious—having a firm belief in ghosts and witches," and specifically noted Joseph Smith Jr.'s purported skill at "necromancy, juggling [sorcery], the use of the *divining rod*." Howe associated these skills with Smith's ability to gather "a gang of idle, credulous young men" to do work for him. He then compared these qualities to those of Muhammad, who "afterwards became a ruler of Nations."[55] Mormonism, Howe wrote, took advantage of "our worthy fellow citizens [who] have been seduced by the witcheries and mysterious necromancies of Smith and his colleagues."[56] Howe also printed the letters of Ezra Booth, which also made the connection between magic and tyranny; Booth described his experience in the church as a "magic charm of delusion and falsehood . . . to exclude the light of truth and secure me a devoted slave."[57] Mormonism was magic, and magic meant slavery. An 1831 newspaper further declaimed Mormonism as "a lesson" against religions who sought "to regulate and control the public mind." The "infatuation of Mormonism," it assured readers, would not work, for "men's minds in this age will not submit to the control of hypocrisy or superstition or clerical ambition."[58]

Direct political actions against Mormon communities also rang the warning bell of superstition. The citizens of Clay County, Missouri, signed a petition demanding the Mormons vacate the county, for "should this population continue to increase they would soon have all the offices in the county in their hands; and that the lives and property of the other citizens would be insecure, under the administration of men who are so ignorant and superstitious as to believe that they have been the subjects of miraculous and supernatural cures."[59] When John Clark marched his militia to the town of Far West, he accepted Mormon surrender by invoking "that Great Spirit, the Unknown God to rest upon you, and make you sufficiently intelligent to break that chain of superstition, and liberate you from the fetters of fanaticism with which you are now bound—that you no longer worship a man."[60] Mormonism was not the problem; it was merely one facet of the problem of superstition.

Mormonism did not generate the political animus it faced; it stumbled into (and by its success, intensified) an existing predilection against claims of magical and supernatural power by many new sects, often classed as superstition in the new republic. There is no doubt that the Latter-day Saints and their prophet engaged in political activities and made political claims in their opening decades, but the new faith was branded as a source of potential political trouble and tyranny before the Book of Mormon rolled off the press. The idea of superstition—bred in Enlightenment debates and fostered in American political, legal, and military dealings with Shakers, Native American prophets, Wilkinsonians, New Israelites, and others—set the pattern for Mormonism's political reception in America. In that sense, we should reconsider scholarly arguments which suggest that a particular kind of anti-Mormon feeling infected the public mind, or that polygamy was the most significant star in the anti-Mormon constellation, at least in the 1830s.[61]

Moreover, if the charge of necromancy had political as well as religious implications, then historians need to rethink the extent and importance of Smith's magical activities prior to the founding of the church. Smith did participate in these activities, of course, but some scholars may have gone too far in connecting the magical practices of the Smith family to the history of the church Smith founded. If charging someone with being "a firm believer in ghosts and witchcraft" was meant as an accusation of antirepublicanism and not necessarily a valid assessment of fact, we might usefully reassess historiographical analysis that relies on the claims of anti-Mormons as evidence for the extent of Smith's magic. One historian, for example, has taken critics' accusations of Mormon magic and superstition at face value ("in 1829–30, Smith's claims primarily attracted believers in folk magic"), rather than reading these critiques as a cultural response to credulity, miracles, and antirepublicanism. When a minister quipped that John Whitmer's family "believe in witches," he was not identifying these Mormons as practitioners of the Renaissance high occult any more than references to Ann Lee as a "fortune teller" made her a card reader. He was accusing them of superstition—the false belief in the continued presence of witchcraft and miracles, and hence, of being a danger to the republic.[62]

The experience of other sects was bound to Mormonism from the outset. Thomas Campbell, in his 1831 letter denouncing Mormonism, compared Mormons to the Shakers, Wilkinsonians, French Prophets, and other impostors.[63] W. W. Phelps understood the problem: "If you start a church with a prophet in it, every body will be against you, as they were against Ann Lee, Joanna Southcoate, and old Jemima Wilkinson."[64] But the Shakers and Wilkinsonians did not survive to become a worldwide church of millions. Yet, to early American critics, unaware of the Saints' future history, Mormonism was just another entry in a long history of superstitions—a danger to the republic that needed to be removed, like Tenskwatawa's Prophetstown or the Shaker village of Turtle Creek. These ideas and those military actions were the seedbed of Hawn's Mill.

CHAPTER 2

"Many Think This Is a Hoax"

The Newspaper Response to Joseph Smith's
1844 Presidential Campaign

SPENCER W. MCBRIDE

One issue—religious liberty—drove Joseph Smith into the 1844 presidential election. But Smith was hardly a one-issue candidate. He wrapped his call for a federal government empowered to protect the citizenship rights of religious minority groups in a seven-point platform aimed at sweeping political and social reform. Among other things, he advocated for the reestablishment of the national bank, the end of the burgeoning penitentiary system, the territorial expansion of the United States throughout North America, and the abolition of slavery. In some ways, Smith's campaign platform was relevant and innovative; in other ways, it was impractical and naive.[1]

In most presidential elections—and particularly in the political climate of 1844—one might expect a unique platform such as Smith's to capture the attention of the American public. However, this was not the case. While newspapers around the country reported on his candidacy in the months leading up to the controversial Mormon leader's murder in June 1844, few commented on the merits or faults of his political positions. Instead, most of these newspapers focused on Smith as a leader of a rising religious group deemed to be fanatical by mainstream Protestants and on how such an ecclesiastical position might influence the way the American public viewed his candidacy. In some ways, it was a vein of criticism seemingly taken directly out of the anti-Catholic playbook for American politics. Just as the mixture of allegiance to a religious institution unbounded by geographic and national borders was a reason cited by many Americans for opposing the election of Catholics to political office, it was a ready-made argument for the blocking of a Mormon's political ambitions.[2]

In this chapter, I examine the non-Mormon response to Joseph Smith's 1844 presidential campaign in American newspapers. By and large, the non-Mormon press did not take his candidacy seriously. Instead, many newspapers used Smith's campaign as a source of political humor or as a foil to the agenda of their long-standing political or ideological rivals. Yet, underlying the mockery in many instances was a sense that Smith and his political ambitions represented a dangerous combination of church and state. Whether viewed by these commentators as a joke, a threat to democracy, or some combination of the two, the country's newspapers presented Smith as unfit for the presidency and irrelevant to the 1844 election without any serious consideration of his unique campaign platform.

"For the Protection of Injured Innocence"

Smith's prolonged engagement with the federal government commenced in 1839. In November of that year, Smith traveled to Washington, DC, in order to seek redress and reparations for property that the Mormons lost in 1838 when the governor of Missouri, Lilburn W. Boggs, ordered their expulsion from the state under threat of extermination. The Mormons left behind an estimated $2 million worth of improved land for which they either held preemption rights or owned outright by fleeing to western Illinois as destitute refugees. Convinced that they had exhausted all avenues for redress within Missouri, Smith and other leaders of the Church of Jesus Christ of Latter-day Saints focused their attention on the federal government, confident that the merits of their petition would be judged against the principles of the United States Constitution. They were quickly disappointed.[3]

In a December 1839 meeting between Smith and President Martin Van Buren, the eighth president cited electoral concerns in declining to speak in favor of the Mormon petitioning efforts in his annual address to Congress. Even without Van Buren's endorsement, the Mormons submitted a twenty-seven-page memorial to the Senate, which subsequently sent the document to its Committee on the Judiciary. After a three-day hearing, that committee determined that Congress had no jurisdiction in the case and, citing the philosophy of states' rights, insisted that the Mormons must instead appeal to the magnanimity and justice of the State of Missouri. Frustrated, but undeterred, church leaders petitioned Congress at least four more times in the ensuing four years and were denied each time.[4]

Amid this ongoing petitioning process, Smith and his fellow Mormon leaders worked to create a haven for their followers in western Illinois. They founded the city of Nauvoo with a charter that granted powers to city officials designed to better equip them to legally protect residents from religious persecution. They formed a militia that Smith led as lieutenant general. Then, in 1842, Smith was elected mayor. As a result, he became the central figure in the city's religious, military, and political power. Despite these actions—and to a certain extent *because* of them—the Mormons soon found themselves at odds with non-Mormons in the region and feared that violent conflict, similar to what they had experienced in Missouri, would ensue.[5]

As this tension grew in November 1843, Smith wrote a letter to each of the five men expected to be a candidate in the following year's presidential election: Martin Van Buren, Lewis Cass, Henry Clay, Richard M. Johnson, and John C. Calhoun. He asked each man, "What will be your rule of action relative to us as a people, should fortune favor your ascension to the chief magistracy?"[6] Clay, Calhoun, and Cass were the only candidates to respond to Smith's inquiry. Clay was generally sympathetic to the Mormons' plight, but ultimately noncommittal in his response. Calhoun and Cass, on the other hand, made no mistake about where they stood on the question of federal redress for the Mormons. Indeed, Calhoun went so far as to assure Smith that his administration would be free of religious prejudice, but that, according to his views, "the case does not come within the jurisdiction of the Federal Government, which is one of limited and specific powers."[7]

Convinced that the Mormons would receive no help from any man in the pool of presidential contenders, Mormon leaders decided to take matters into their own hands. On January 29, 1844, they nominated Smith as a candidate for president. Smith accepted the nomination, later stating, "I would not have suffered my name to have been used by my friends on any wise as president of the United States or Candidate for that office if I and my friends could have had the privilege of enjoying our religious and civil rights as American citizens." But since he felt that his followers had been denied those rights, Smith declared, "I feel it to be my right and privilege to obtain what influence and power I can lawfully in the United States for the protection of injured innocence." In this same meeting, Smith called on "every man in the city who could speak" to go "throughout the land to electioneer," insisting that "there is oratory enough in the church to carry me into the presidential chair the first slide."[8] Despite this stated trust in the oratorical power of his followers, more than a decade of effective proselytizing had convinced him of the power of adding the printed word to that of the spoken word.[9] Accordingly, Smith enlisted his trusted associate, William W. Phelps, to help him draft a pamphlet that set forth his reasons for seeking the presidency and described his political platform. The campaign would rest on a plan to dispatch church members on political missions armed with a political tract.

Smith recognized that the prospects of electoral success in 1844 were extremely slim. In fact, his campaign coincided with the exploration of several other avenues to obtain redress for past persecutions and to prevent their reoccurrence.[10] Nevertheless, his candidacy energized Mormon communities and more than four hundred men volunteered to canvass the country as electioneering missionaries.[11] This was a clear indication of the populist fervor that Smith relied on to sustain his presidential ambitions. Calhoun, Cass, Clay, Johnson, and Van Buren were each well-established in national politics. Their reputations made their respective candidacies logical and even expected. For these men, the path to the presidency ran through the familiar terrain of the country's established political parties designed to bring their nominees instant support throughout the country.

This was not the case for Smith. He could boast of his experience as the mayor of the burgeoning city of Nauvoo, but even that was atypical in American politics owing to the city's foundation in the community of religious refugees that he led. Smith was running outside the party system and would not benefit from a party's network and mechanisms for mobilizing voters. Church members who followed Smith as a prophet were his electoral base—and his electioneering staff. With their help, he hoped to swell the ranks of his political supporters with other Americans who were dissatisfied with both political parties. Accordingly, Smith crafted a platform that depicted the United States as a country in decline that could only be redeemed by the election of a political outsider whose vision extended beyond entrenched partisan positions and solutions. In this way, Smith's campaign contributed to the establishment of patterns for future populist campaigns in the United States.

"General Smith's Views"

By February 8, 1844, Smith and Phelps had finished drafting the pamphlet that would serve as the centerpiece for Mormon campaigning: *General Smith's Views on the Powers and Policy of the Government of the United States.*[12] Phelps's reading of the pamphlet to a gathering of church members in Nauvoo was met with "the highest degree" of interest, and the church's leadership approved its publication.[13] Smith subsequently ordered the printing of fifteen hundred copies of *General Smith's Views* and the wide distribution of the pamphlet to prominent political leaders and newspapers throughout the country.[14]

As a printed pamphlet, *General Smith's Views* distilled Smith's platform into twelve concise pages. It commenced with a cursory history of the prosperity of the United States under its first seven presidents and the steady decline of the country starting with the inauguration of Van Buren in 1836. "At the age, then, of sixty years," Smith averred in the pamphlet, "our blooming Republic began to decline under the withering touch of Martin Van Buren! Disappointed ambition, thirst for power, pride, corruption, party spirit, faction, patronage; perquisites, fame, tangling alliances; priest-craft and spiritual wickedness in high places, struck hands, and reveled in midnight splendor."[15] Indeed, while Van Buren's refusal to help the Mormons in their petitioning efforts was barely a blip on the eighth president's radar, the act was the focal point for Mormon dissatisfaction with the federal government.[16] Well into the twentieth century, Mormons remembered Van Buren as the epitome of what they viewed as the political malpractice that condoned the confiscation of their lands and the loss of lives in Missouri.[17]

Smith presented a plan to stop what he perceived as the decline of the United States that would restore the country to the glory he believed it had experienced under the leadership of the first seven presidents.[18] He proposed the strengthening of the federal government by granting it the power to put down mobs and to protect the rights and lives of persecuted religious minorities without a formal request from the governors of the states in which the violent persecution was occurring.[19] Yet, in strengthening the federal government, he also wanted to shrink it, calling for a reduction in the size and pay of Congress. "Reduce Congress at least one half," he wrote, before arguing that they be paid "two dollars and their board per diem . . . that is more than a farmer gets, and he lives honestly." Furthermore, Smith advocated for a culture of bipartisanship to pervade in all levels of government, starting with the presidency. "We have had democratic presidents; whig presidents; a pseudo democratic whig president," Smith mused rhetorically, "and now it is time to have *a president of the United States*."[20]

Smith also waded into several contentious public debates. On the issue of territorial expansion, he argued for gradual and organic growth, asserting that "Oregon belongs to this government honorably," that Texas should be accepted into the Union only when that republic "petitions Congress to be adopted among the sons of liberty," and that, "when we have the red man's consent, let the union spread from the east to the west sea."[21] Where the country's criminal justice system was concerned, he assumed a radical position on the controversial rise of penitentiaries, calling on citizens to "petition [their] state legislatures to pardon every convict in their several penitentiaries: blessing them as they go, and saying to them in the name of the Lord, *go thy way and sin no more.*"[22] He advocated for the reestablishment of a national bank "for the accommodation of the people in every state and territory," that "shall never issue any more bills than the amount of capital stock in her vaults and the interest."[23] Smith even devised a solution to the red-hot issue of slavery that was then dividing the country along sectional lines. He urged his countrymen to end slavery by 1850, a feat they would accomplish by Congress purchasing the freedom of every enslaved man, woman, and child from the surplus revenue coming from the sale of public lands and his proposed reduction in congressional salaries.[24]

Smith's platform was certainly relevant. In some matters—the national bank, the gradual expansion of the country's boundaries—he was in line with the positions of the Whigs. But in others—swinging open the doors of penitentiaries and ending slavery by the federal purchase and subsequent emancipation of slaves—his proposed solutions to pressing problems were quite radical for the era, if not impractical and ideologically problematic. The Mormons quite reasonably expected that such a platform would garner national attention while eliciting serious discussion of Smith's ideas and his presidential prospects in the country's newspapers.

"A Western Man with American Principles"

Newspapers had played a central role in American politics long before the American Revolution and that tradition remained alive and well in the 1840s.[25] They were also the preferred medium for many religious organizations trying to simultaneously spread their messages of faith to the public, keep their members apprised of developments within the organization, and interpret news stories in a way that supported their faith claims.[26] The Mormons recognized the effectiveness of newspapers in serving their religious and political goals and established the *Evening and Morning Star* in June 1832, just two years after the church's founding, and several other papers before settling the main body of church members in Nauvoo, Illinois, in 1839.[27]

The two church-owned newspapers in Nauvoo—the *Times and Seasons* and the *Nauvoo Neighbor*—naturally covered *General Smith's Views* and other aspects of Smith's campaign in an extremely positive manner. The editors of these papers rarely acknowledged any conflict between Smith's position at the head of a rapidly growing church and his ambition to hold the highest elected office in the United States. When they did engage in the controversy over the combination of church and state, they simply wrote off their opponents' misgivings to a misguided understanding of the political nature of Christianity. Such a stance was epitomized in a letter to the editor of the

Times and Seasons from "A Friend to the Mormons." This anonymous writer insisted that, in praying that God's "Kingdom come, thy will be done on earth as it is in heaven," Christians were essentially asking God "to destroy the distinction of Church and State on earth; for that distinction is not recognized in heaven."[28]

Yet, while church-owned newspapers read primarily by church members might have roused Mormons to action in support of their prophet's presidential ambitions, these papers were insufficient to reach the millions of non-Mormon voters throughout the rest of the country. Mormon leaders acknowledged this and informed church members of their responsibility to aid in the church's electioneering efforts. In an editorial that appeared in both the *Times and Seasons* and the *Nauvoo Neighbor*, the Mormon apostle John Taylor wrote that "the step we have taken is a bold one, and requires our united efforts, perseverance, and diligence. . . . Mr. Smith is not so generally known personally as are several of the above-named candidates, and although he has been much spoken of as man, he has been a great deal calumniated and misrepresented, and his true character is little known." It was therefore up to church members to "take away this false coloring; and by lecturing, by publishing, and circulating his works, his political views, his honor, integrity, and virtue, to stop the foul mouth of slander, and present him before the public in his own colors, that he may be known, respected, and supported."[29] Mormon leaders clearly cared about the public perception of Smith—at least where their petitioning efforts and his presidential campaign were concerned—and called upon the entire church in the United States to help influence that perception.

But Mormon leaders did not rely on the grassroots efforts of church members alone to try to influence perceptions of Smith in the population centers of the eastern United States. Instead, they put to work their years of publishing experience and founded the *Prophet*, a political newspaper in New York City largely dedicated to Smith's campaign. The prospectus in the paper's first number described the publication in terms typical of sectarian newspapers of that time, as dedicated to "promulgating the Gospel of Our Lord Jesus Christ." It was also designed for the "advocacy and herald of the faith of the Church of Christ of Latter Day Saints," while devoting some of its columns to matters of "Agriculture, Commerce and Manufactures, as well as Foreign and Domestic News of the day." But, based on the paper's content, most important to the editors was its role as "the faithful defender of the Constitution of the United States."[30]

As each new issue of the *Prophet* came off the press, it was clear that, to the editors, defending the Constitution meant promoting Smith and his proposed reforms. The paper celebrated him as "a Western man with American principles," reprinted portions of his political writings, and responded to criticism of Smith's candidacy as it appeared in other newspapers.[31] It also announced political rallies held for Smith in cities throughout the country while declaring the large number of attendees at such meetings as a sign of his growing popularity.[32] Ultimately, the paper found its largest readership in New York City and Boston.[33] Yet, even if it sustained a large dedicated readership, the *Prophet* would always be just one of many publications in the crowded print media market of the eastern United States.

"We Had Almost Said King"

Certainly, Mormon leaders were not so naive as to think that the country's non-Mormon newspapers would respond to Smith's candidacy as positively as their own publications did. But it may have come as a surprise that so few papers were willing to seriously consider the planks of Smith's campaign platform on their own merits. Instead, nearly every newspaper that mentioned Smith's presidential bid mocked the political ambitions of the Mormon leader, or, if they took it seriously, focused almost exclusively on what they perceived to be a dangerous blending of church and state.

The jokes at the expense of Smith and his campaign came quickly. On March 2, *Niles' National Register* relayed reports to its readers of "the encroachments and usurpations of Jo Smith, the despotism of the Nauvoo corporation, and the hostilities of the Mormon legion." Then, a few column inches later, the paper announced Smith as a candidate for president and declared: "Stand out of the way—all small fry."[34] On May 23, the *New York Herald* reported that the Mormons "claim possession of from two hundred thousand to five hundred thousand votes in Nauvoo and throughout the Union, and with that calculate that they can hold the balance of power and make whoever they please President." The *Herald* then mockingly advised "the Mormon delegates—if they can't do the business in the ordinary way of private sale—to hold an auction, and let the Mormon vote go to the highest bidder," before adding that "it seems by this movement that Joe Smith does not expect to be elected President, but he still wants to have a finger in the pie, and see whether something can't be made of it."[35] The *Illinois State Registry* aimed its humor at Smith's non-Mormon running mate, James Arlington Bennett, insinuating that Bennett was friendly with the Mormons primarily in an effort to advance his own career. "We recollect of seeing sometime ago published in the newspapers a letter from Bennett to Smith," the paper's editors quipped, "in which the former asks of the latter to make him Governor of Illinois. We trust that Gen. Bennett will be satisfied with his chance for Vice President!"[36]

Other newspapers that mocked Smith's candidacy weaved into their satirical prose serious critiques of the potentially dangerous combination of religious and political power in a single person. Again, such reasoning invoked much of the same rhetoric employed by those who opposed extending religious freedom—and, by extension, full participation in political processes—to American Catholics. The *People's Organ* of St. Louis reported that "Gen. Joseph Smith, priest, prophet, military leader (we had almost said king) among the Mormons, is out as candidate for President of the United States. There is no joke in the matter—Gen. Jo received seven votes for President on board of a steamboat the other day; shouldn't wonder if he beat [John] Tyler."[37] Indeed, while the *People's Organ* jokingly referred to the concentration of Smith's power in Nauvoo as bordering on that of a king, it reflected very real concerns among several non-Mormons in Illinois and Missouri over the adverse effects of mixing church and state in local and state politics.

The most significant attention that a newspaper paid to Smith's campaign platform came from the *Daily Globe* in Washington, DC, in a caustic editorial titled "A New Advocate for a National Bank." "We have cast our eyes hastily over General Smith's (Mormon Joe) 'Views of the Powers and Policy of the Government of the United States, Nauvoo, 1844,'" the editors wrote, and, after quoting the passage from Smith's pamphlet that favored the reinstitution of a national bank, stated that "the prophet seems to be thoroughly imbued with the whig financial doctrines." In discussing the banking policy that Smith set forth in his pamphlet, they observed that "he sticks to the specie basis, dollar for dollar," and paired the position with Smith's plan for criminal justice reform—that each state "pardon every convict in their several penitentiaries"—in order to bring up the alleged corruption of the officers of the Second Bank of the United States. "We fear that [Smith's] humane recommendation be adopted, the 'specie basis' would soon disappear from Joe's mother bank and branches," the editors declared. "Perhaps, however, we are unnecessarily apprehensive of the small thieves, who fall into the clutches of the law, since the great thieves, who robbed millions from the late whig bank and its satellites, are permitted to roam at large with perfect impunity."[38]

The tone of the editorial in the *Daily Globe* grew even more biting in its concluding paragraphs. "Joseph is unquestionably a great scholar as well as financier," the editors wrote, "Cannot Mr. Clay persuade *the General* to accompany him on his electioneering tour?" Ultimately, the paper's satirical proposal to its readers was "that Joe Smith . . . be made president, and [former

Mississippi Senator and opponent of the national bank] George Poindexter cashier, of the new whig national bank that is not to be; that the mother bank be established at Nauvoo, with branches over all creation."[39] Ironically, as one of the most extensive considerations of the campaign positions set forth in *General Smith's Views*, the *Daily Globe's* editorial was also one of the most mocking of Smith's candidacy.

Just as the *Daily Globe* used Smith's campaign platform as a way to attack Whig financial policies, two Boston newspapers coopted Smith in their own ongoing political endeavors. On May 15, the *Boston Investigator*, a newspaper dedicated to free thought and strongly in favor of the abolition of slavery, complimented Smith on "a plain philosophical discourse, entirely free from cant, and full of the very best advice." The paper briefly listed the main points of *General Smith's Views* before recommending Smith's "opinions on the subject of Abolition" as "worthy of attention. He goes for a liberal and generous policy, and advises Government to use its surplus revenue for the purchase of the freedom of the slaves. He thinks the slaveholders would agree to this, and that no other measure of emancipation is just."[40] Three days later, the *Working Man's Advocate* of New York City reprinted the *Boston Investigator's* piece and added its own commentary. The *Working Man's Advocate* had long prioritized the plight of the poor white laborer in the north over that of the captive black slave in the south, and accordingly argued that "Gen. Smith's plan of taking the surplus revenue to purchase the freedom of the slaves would never do. Before the Working Men of the North can pay taxes to free the Southern slaves, they must *emancipate* themselves from the dominion of land-*Lords*."[41] While these papers did not mock Smith, they certainly did not depict him as a serious contender for the presidency. Rather, they saw in his independent run for the White House an opportunity to reiterate their own long-held positions of antislavery and the rights for working men.

Of course, there were a few exceptions to the prevailing skepticism of Smith's presidential ambitions and general disregard for his political positions in the non-Mormon press. Notable examples among these rare instances include the report of a correspondent published in the *New-York Tribune* as "Life in Nauvoo." In describing Smith's candidacy for president, the correspondent warned the paper's readers that, while "many think this is a hoax—not so with Joe and the Mormons. It is the design of these people to have candidates for electors in every State of the Union; a convention is to be held in Baltimore, probably next month." While he did not state an opinion on Smith's prospects in the presidential race, he did caution readers not to "sneer at [the Mormons], or deem them as of little consequence for good or for evil. They are becoming a potent influence to the people of the State of Illinois."[42]

Whereas the article in the *Tribune* was relatively neutral, positive press for Smith's campaign came in a letter published in a newspaper in Belleville, Illinois, from one of the town's physicians, Dr. William Goforth. Following an interview with Smith in Nauvoo occasioned by the dedication of the Masonic Hall in that city, Goforth wrote the editor of the *Belleville Advocate*. "The name of Joseph Smith, of Nauvoo, is now before the people as a candidate for President of the United States," Goforth wrote. "With this name is proclaimed . . . Jeffersonian Democracy, and free trade and sailors' rights, and the protection of persons and property. The interview on this occasion was satisfactory, & I know not of hearing a sounder policy designed for public inspection and American prosperity."[43] Published on April 18, 1844, the letter was a strong endorsement for Smith and his presidential ambitions. While Mormons certainly read Goforth's endorsement with great satisfaction, this and other such endorsements were outliers. Few non-Mormon newspapers took Smith's candidacy seriously and several were deeply critical of what such a campaign represented.

Still, this general response to Smith's campaign elicits questions of the role of mockery and satire in American politics. Why would the nineteenth-century print media mock some marginal candidates and completely ignore others? What purposes does comedic criticism of office seekers serve? Indeed, it appears that the decision of these different newspapers to satirize Smith, or criticize him in humorous fashion, had deeper ramifications than mere comic relief for a country that was increasingly divided over serious policy issues. In many ways, the mockery of Smith's presidential ambitions served to ward off undecided voters, men without strong allegiances to candidates in either of the two major parties who might seriously consider Smith as a viable candidate. Those who already disliked—or at least distrusted—Smith and the Mormons would almost certainly feel validated by such satirical coverage of the Mormon prophet's candidacy. Those already committed to a Whig or Democratic candidate might simply be amused by it. But those who harbored neither anti-Mormon prejudices nor sustained any partisan allegiance might read such newspaper articles as a warning that publicly supporting Smith would draw similar criticism upon themselves. In essence, mocking and satirical coverage of a political candidate such as Smith could reasonably be interpreted as a strategy designed to get potential supporters to dismiss him before ever seriously considering his various campaign positions.

"When I Get Hold of the Eastern Papers"

The concern expressed by these newspaper editors over the danger presented by Smith adding political ambitions to his role as a religious leader—even if only as the subtext for humorous editorials—was congruent with a long-established American precedent. In fact, the distrust of clergymen serving in political office is as old as the country itself. In 1775 John Adams criticized the inclusion of Reverend John Zubly in the Second Continental Congress, declaring that "mixing the sacred character with that of the statesman . . . is not attended with any good effects."[44] Thus, statesmen such as Adams, who welcomed the preaching of revolutionary politics from the pulpit, were apprehensive of clergymen doubling as politicians. Just as Zubly was not the last clergyman to hold public office, the concern Adams expressed over such a mixture of church and state continued to hover over such instances.[45]

Yet, in the case of non-Mormon newspapers responding to Smith and his presidential campaign, warning cries of a dangerous combination of religious and political power were overpowered by sarcastic prose. This was likely because many Americans viewed Smith as too fanatical and the Mormons as too far removed from mainstream American Christianity for the Mormon leader to be a serious presidential contender. But in Illinois, several non-Mormons saw the threat of Smith combining religious and political authority as clear and present. While there is little compelling evidence that Smith's local critics feared the elevation of the Mormon leader to the presidency, there is ample evidence that they feared his elevation in regional affairs. Indeed, these concerns over Smith's increasing power and influence in local and state politics contributed to his assassination at the hands of a mob on June 27, 1844—just over four months from election day.[46]

Smith and his fellow Mormon leaders viewed their political activity in the 1844 presidential campaign quite differently. "We have as good a right to make a political party to gain power to defend ourselves," Smith declared in a public meeting in Nauvoo on March 7. Just "as the world used the power of government to oppress and persecute us," he explained, "it is right for us to use it for the protection of our rights. We will whip the mob by getting up a candidate for President." He followed this justification with an optimistic assessment of his chances in the campaign: "When I get hold of the Eastern papers, and see how popular I am, I am afraid myself that I shall be elected."[47] When Smith made this claim, he had not yet read the editorial reports of his presidential campaign in eastern newspapers, the first of which were only a few days old on that occasion. It is possible that this was merely political rhetoric or a reference to positive accounts of the Mormons in general and his religious leadership in particular that had previously appeared in some New York newspapers.[48] Or maybe Smith was being sarcastic, fighting satire with satire. In any case, what actually appeared in the eastern newspapers during the weeks and months that followed this statement did not signal any wild popularity for Smith and his positions. The religious-based populism that gave rise to Smith and his presidential campaign contributed to the seeming dismissal of Smith's candidacy in the country's newspapers. He offered solutions to pressing political problems, but to many Americans his status as a charismatic religious leader encapsulated the very reasons they believed that such populism was a danger to the republic.

Yet it would be a mistake to read the mockery of Smith's candidacy as outright dismissal. The print media's response to Smith and his presidential ambitions belied deeper political concerns. Ultimately, they were analyzing a marginal candidate who stood little to no chance of being elected. Indeed, the mockery of Smith's campaign was at times little more than a thin veil designed to cover profound discomfort with the fragile state of democracy in the country and deeply rooted fears that the American political experiment would not survive the challenges coming from Smith and others like him. Satirizing Smith and the Mormons bolstered the efforts of other groups competing for political power in the United States to persuade their fellow Americans of the correctness of their respective paths forward.

CHAPTER 3

Precarious Protestant Democracy

Mormon and Catholic Conceptions of
Democratic Rule in the 1840s

BENJAMIN E. PARK

A month before an anti-Mormon mob killed Joseph Smith on June 27, 1844, a nativist revolt in Philadelphia laid siege to the Irish Catholic population. The riot was incited when leaders of the mob declared that they must defend America from "the bloody hand of the Pope." Two Catholic churches were destroyed, over a dozen people were killed (including one innocent Catholic bystander), and the property damage totaled over $100,000. The beleaguered Catholic community suspended Sunday mass to avoid further attack. Reading about these developments a thousand miles away, the Mormons thought they had found fellow sufferers of America's intolerance. The apostle Willard Richards wrote a letter to Hugh Clark, one of Philadelphia's prominent Catholic aldermen, to express "our sympathies for a people, who are now being mobbed, in the city of brotherly Love (Phila.) as we have been, for many years, in Missouri." Richards claimed they were "the only two [denominations] who have suffered from the cruel hand of Mobocracy." Why were they singled out? According to Richards, it was because their notions of authority and religiosity were "the most obnoxious to the sectarian world of any people." That same month, another Mormon apostle, Parley Pratt, denounced the riots and proclaimed that, while "the Catholics may be the sufferers to-day, [and] the Mormons to-morrow," there was no telling who could be next. Both communities were outcasts from America's Protestant society.[1]

To many Americans in the nineteenth century, Catholics and Mormons represented a direct threat to the nation's democratic order. In return, members of both denominations proclaimed that the nation's Protestant majority had failed to protect their rights as minority groups. Though both sides of this divide agreed that America was a Christian nation, the place of these two sects within the country's political body demonstrated the contested boundaries of the Christian label. Even after disestablishment, Protestantism framed how many understood notions of liberty and democratic participation. Those left on the peripheries struggled to find a footing.

This chapter places Mormonism's political actions during the 1840s within the context of Catholicism's similar struggle, which took place around the same time. It focuses on electoral politics as well as controversial forms of sovereignty, especially Mormonism's Council of Fifty. Identifying and contextualizing alternative modes of political and religious sovereignty outside the Protestant mainstream helps flesh out the tale of the rise of American democracy. Only by better understanding the angst on the peripheries can we get a clearer picture of the eventual dominance of those in the center.[2]

Though ideas concerning the separation between church and state were still contested during the Jacksonian period, there were broad points for agreement. To a majority of American citizens, disestablishment did not imply the separation of religious ideas and democratic action. Far from it, as most believed that political positions were rooted in religious ideals. Massachusetts, the last state to end religious establishment, did not do so until 1833. Along with many other states, it continued to maintain religious oaths for civic office long afterward. Political actors drew from spiritual language and worked in tandem with denominational leaders in order to mobilize secular gains. In return, ministers were eager to buttress their own authority in a democratized society by speaking out on behalf of party platforms. One extreme version of this Protestant coalition, exemplified by the Presbyterian pastor Ezra Stiles Ely, argued that Christians should not be afraid to form "a union of church and state"—as long as it was on the informal level. This would be "a *Christian party in politics*" that would help steer America in the right direction. Due to the majority of Protestant believers, Ely argued, "we are a Christian nation," and "we have the right to demand" that the nation "shall conform to Christian morality." While not all were comfortable with this rhetoric, many believed that disestablishment merely meant that the individual conscience was free to embrace true religion within a market of choice. America society was democratizing, but still within a Christian framework.[3]

Where most Protestants drew the line, however, was with regard to ecclesiastical infringement on personal liberty. Government bodies were not to favor one religious body over another—though the interpretation of "religious body" was often vague and flexible—and ecclesiastical leaders in turn were not to interfere with individual consciences. One New England preacher emphasized that, for democracy to function, there needed to be two forms of religious liberty: "external liberty" which was "the individual claims of the government as a civil right," and "internal liberty," which was "the liberty which the individual claims of the church or ecclesiastical body." This was to be a Christian coalition based on consent. As Nathan Hatch argued, the evangelical impetus during the early republic eroded "respect for authority [and] tradition" and resulted in "the success of common people in shaping the culture after their own priorities rather than the priorities" of their leaders, whether ecclesiastical or political. This fundamental trajectory was "a liberating force" that "subverted centralized authority." Ministers were forced to adapt, for if they wished to retain cultural authority they had to embrace the republican form of persuasion rather than ecclesiastical command. Some merged Protestant belief with republican liberty. One minister went so far as to proclaim that *"Protestantism is the love of Spiritual Liberty."* Especially on the frontier, Protestants had become so dominant that they created, according to one historian, "a religious establishment by proxy" that allowed them to control the political culture without direct clerical involvement. It was a tightrope walk that balanced individual freedom and communal righteousness.[4]

Catholicism tested these boundaries for civic acceptance in the early republic. Not only were Catholics supposedly loyal to a foreign pope, an accusation that drew ire even before the American Revolution, but their predominant conceptions of liberty—in which communal cohesion and institutional authority took precedence over individualist freedom and representative governance—seemed out of step with the dominant model of democratized authority. The historian John McGreevy has noted how the Catholic emphasis on "ordered liberty" posed a particularly salient critique of Protestantism's independent tradition. The persistence of Thomist philosophy, which emphasized the juxtaposition of human depravity and divine sovereignty, laid the foundation for a Catholic revival during the nineteenth century that emphasized the centrality of natural law and hierarchical control. Though many progressive intellectuals both inside and outside of the faith sought to better align Catholic ideas with America's democratic culture, observers mostly viewed such attempts as misbegotten and ill-fated. In response to a growing number of Catholics attempting to accommodate their belief to America's political culture, one Presbyterian minister claimed,

"Romanism is avowedly an *'unchangeable'* system" that was destined for failure. There was no middle ground.[5]

Americans inherited a deep anti-Catholic bias from their British ancestors. The "Popish" threat had always been a watchword in Anglo-American political discourse. Besides traditional denominational rivalry, Catholicism represented a bygone age of superstition ill-equipped for an enlightened modernity. But the young nation's republican discourse added to the list of anti-Catholic complaints. The hierarchical faith was seen as an insult to the world of mental freedom that triumphed in Protestant America. This threat seemed to escalate as thousands of immigrants from Catholic nations flooded America during the 1830s and 1840s and settled in the urban seaport cities as well as on the western frontier. This seemed like a foreign invasion by individuals who did not share democratic values. To avoid divided loyalties, Catholics were forced to denounce their allegiance to the pope if they wished to gain access to civil and political rights. From the Protestant perspective, the Catholic faith demanded a "substitution of authority for conscience," and therefore did not work within a political culture based on individual liberty. Catholics were a unique problem within the American body.[6]

The Catholic reaction to this animus was mixed. Many sought to adopt democratic rhetoric and practices in order to prove their citizenship and patriotism. But others were willing to push back. John Hughes, the bishop of New York, proclaimed that "everybody should know that we have for our mission to convert the world," including all "the inhabitants of the United States" as well as "the Legislatures, the Senate, the Cabinet, the President, and all!" Local congregations, united both in theology as well as their marginalized status, mobilized in order to take advantage of the voting system. They were willing to wield their power if it meant assuring their status. This, in turn, confirmed Protestant fears and heightened animosity. Often, anti-Catholic antagonism led to violence. Dozens of Catholic churches were burned during the 1830s and 1840s, including the famous revolt in Philadelphia in 1844. In response to that outburst of violence, one Philadelphia resident justified the action by claiming it was "dangerous to commit the ballot-box, *the Ark of our Freedom's Covenant*, to foreign hands." Extralegal justice was necessary to preserve the sanctity of democratic governance. This anxiety over Catholic interference eventually led to interdenominational political cooperation among Protestants. Members of different faiths were willing to put aside their differences and unite against the Catholic threat. Part of this mobilization led to the creation of the Know Nothing Party, a nativist group devoted to preserving America's Anglo-American and Protestant heritage against the foreign Catholic invasion. Members of that organization were sworn to "vote only for native born American citizens," and to work toward excluding "all . . . Roman Catholics." Anti-Catholicism had become embedded within America's democratic system.[7]

Though Mormonism was native to America, many critics immediately compared the new faith to the Roman menace. Both groups were hierarchical, both seemed prevalent with the lower class, and both acted as collaborative groups. Some even claimed the Mormons created their own ethnicity, a similar critique found in anti-Catholic rhetoric. Indeed, anti-Catholicism provided a usable model for those who were worried about the rise of Mormonism. As one early anti-Mormon author put it, Mormons were "natural allies" with "Romanism" and its theocratic standard. Nor did the Mormons always shy away from these comparisons. Not only did the association with a global power and ancient faith flatter Joseph Smith and his followers but they also recognized that their sect was related to the similarly beleaguered church. Politically, both churches faced severe problems in Protestant America; theologically, the two faiths rejected the Protestant mantra of individualism and instead hearkened back to a primitive form of priesthood administration and embellished rituals. Joseph Smith once told his followers that the "old Catholic church is worth more than all." The Mormons and Catholics had carved their own niche within America's religious marketplace.[8]

While Joseph Smith and the Mormons experimented with the boundaries of democratic respectability in Ohio and Missouri, their challenges became more direct in Nauvoo, Illinois. They believed the only way to secure power after state governments had failed them was through bloc voting at the discretion of their prophet. As one Nauvoo resident explained to his non-Mormon father: "We give our voats [sic] to the demmecrats [sic]" on some occasions, and the Whigs on others, because due to their "great numbers" they could "gain" the influence they need. The apostle John Taylor was similarly forthright in stating as much in the Mormon newspaper. "It can serve no good purpose that half the citizens should disfranchise the other half," he reasoned, "thus rendering Nauvoo powerless as far as politics is concerned." The Mormons had found their route to political influence: group mobilization through the direction of their priesthood leaders. Just as the Law of Consecration enabled Mormons to pool their resources for financial stability, bloc voting was a mechanism through which they could unite their political power. The 1842 state election proved to be a potent example. Voting in Nauvoo took place in the office of Patriarch Hyrum Smith, where individual votes were carefully and singularly recorded in a ledger. Of the 457 people who cast votes for local, county, and state offices, only eleven did not follow the agreed-upon pattern. Given the split power between Whigs and Democrats in Illinois at the time, Mormonism's ten thousand votes were enough to swing the election. Parties soon admitted that they were now, according to one operative, "depending on the Mormon vote."[9]

Those who observed Mormonism's political operations from the outside were outraged by what they believed to be a corruption of the democratic process. Orchestrating electoral votes through ministerial guidance did not fit the Protestant model of religious liberty. American disestablishment was meant to prevent this form of intersection between ecclesiastical and civic governance. The *Warsaw Signal* editor Thomas Sharp stated that, while the Mormons "have the same rights as other religious bodies," as soon as they "step beyond the proper sphere of [a] religious denomination, and become a political body" they lose the right to appeal to religious liberty. The nearby *Quincy Whig* denounced Mormon voting patterns as a "highhanded attempt to usurp power and to tyrannize over the minds of men." This "clannish principle of voting in a mass, at the dictation of one man" based on "the peculiar religious creed which he promulgates," was "repugnant to the principles of our Republican form of Government." Terms like "clannish" and "tyrannize" were echoes of the anti-Catholic rhetoric taking place at the same time. The Mormons were a menace to the nation's political system, just like the Catholics. Residents in Hancock County of all political stripes joined together to "oppose, as independent freemen, political and military Mormonism." This was a problem that transcended the two-party system.[10]

Bloc voting and ecclesiastical intervention were, to the Protestant mainstream, a tyranny over personal conscience. Democratic sensibilities required the expression of individual will and a detachment from denominational loyalty. To Mormons and Catholics, however, democratic rule had to be checked by the interests of minority groups. At the heart of this conflict were contrasting visions of liberty. Was liberty the chance to freely operate within society, or was it the ability to work within particular communities interwoven together beneath a broad national umbrella? Was religious freedom something to be experienced individually, or collectively? Critics accused Mormons and Catholics of subverting religious freedom and threatening democratic order; Catholics and Mormons countered that they were merely exercising their religious freedom to act as a collective. Their arguments reflected a broader dialogue concerning how America was to govern and balance divided interests. The politician John C. Calhoun argued that the nation was so divided that the government must be structured in such a way as to consider "interests as well as [voting] numbers," so that the voice of the many cannot outstrip the rights of the few. Calhoun's formulation was meant to privilege slaveholders, but in Mormon and Catholic hands the principle also applied to religious practice.[11]

To Mormon authors in the Nauvoo period, true freedom was to be achieved through actualizing their role within a divine order of being. Perhaps the most potent representation of this societal vision came from the apostle Orson Hyde. In a sketch titled "Diagram of the Kingdom of God," Hyde depicted "the eternal Father [who] sits at the head, crowned King of kings and Lord of lords" (see figure 1). Below that one centralized point were ecclesiastical and familial pedigree lines that dictated the order of humanity. "Where-ever the other lines meet," Hyde explained, "there sits a king and a priest unto God, bearing rule, authority, and dominion under the Father." All human society was governed by this priestly network. This image, and its doctrine of consanguineous linkages, highlighted Mormon temple and sacerdotal ideas during the period. But it was also a doctrine of the state—that is, how individuals related to society and how communities were to be governed. The sketch was as much a political theology as it was an ontological one. If much of the mainstream Protestant culture during the period was a

FIGURE 1. Diagram of the Kingdom of God. The Mormon apostle Orson Hyde created this diagram to depict how, from the government to individual families, all human society could be governed by a priestly network. "A Diagram of the Kingdom of God," *Millennial Star* (Liverpool, England), January 15, 1847.

"centrifugal epoch" in which citizens circled away from "centralized authority," as Nathan Hatch described it, Mormonism attempted to reorient those
dispersed pieces back into one coherent whole. To Hyde and his fellow Mormons, liberty could only be experienced within an ordered society.[12]

The fact that Mormons and Catholics fit awkwardly within America's
democratic society—and faced steady opposition as a result—underlines the
Protestant nature of the nation's political culture. Disestablishment opened
the doors for those faiths that embraced a populist and decentralized form of
ecclesiastical control, and benefited those who took advantage of a Christian
libertarian political context, but it proved perilous for those who fell outside acceptable boundaries. For those Protestants who formed what Alexis
de Tocqueville called the "despotic influence of the majority," a democratic
society could only function with shared principles of freedom and consent.
Those who did not fit that model were faced with conflict and, at times,
violence.[13]

Electoral politics were only one form of democratic dissent. Both Mormons
and Catholics also envisioned new, and at times competing, forms of political
sovereignty. America's disestablishment seemed to enshrine secular notions
of democratic governance. When the cacophonous voice of men led to fac-
tionalism and divided interests, some believed the only solution was to turn
to the uniting voice of God. A number of Americans, especially those in marginalized faiths, argued that the only authority strong enough to save them
from oppression was not from the nation's capital, but from divine beings. In
essence, the United States' founding sin was in placing sovereignty on flawed
humanity rather than eternal laws.

In 1844, the same year that the Mormons were losing hope in political
parties and instead nominated Joseph Smith for the presidency, Orestes
Brownson, previously a Unitarian minister and outspoken Transcendentalist in Boston, concluded that the Catholic faith was America's only savior.
This was not the first time he had changed his faith. Originally baptized
a Presbyterian, Brownson later became a Universalist, a skeptic, and then
came to national acclaim as a Transcendentalist. But at every point in his
journey, Brownson feared there was a deeper problem. America, he believed,
lacked spiritual direction, in part because it lacked an authoritative spiritual
director. Without appropriate guidance, American democracy was rudder-
less. The Protestant faith that dominated the nation—and every denomination Brownson flirted with had been part of the Protestant family—had
failed to create the religious brotherhood necessary for universal salvation.
Rather than looking forward to a future of individual triumph and political

salvation, which he believed to be the focus of American culture, it was time they looked to the past for communal stability. "If we cannot have a church unless we go to Rome," he concluded, "let us go to Rome." While not representative of American Catholics during the era, his critiques of democracy reflected a broader anxiety.[14]

This was not just a religious conversion. Brownson's turn to conservatism had a profound political component. "The republican form of government," he wrote, "will prove a total failure, unless the citizens, acting as constituent elements of the government, carry into its administration loyalty to eternal justice." Recent elections, the expansion of slavery, and the continual grinding of the poor proved that "the sovereignty of the people" as "the essence of democracy" was a flawed political philosophy. America's Protestant trajectory had centralized individualism to such a degree that it ignored the importance of social cohesion. Americans must embrace a form of constitutionalism powerful enough "to hinder effectually the majority, when so disposed, from encroaching in its acts or measures on the rights of minorities and individuals." He admitted he had "no faith, as I have often said, in the intelligence of the people." Sovereignty had to be placed somewhere much more stable. For Brownson, that meant turning his spiritual allegiance to Rome; for America, Brownson believed it meant basing their ruling principles upon natural law. The universal reach and doctrinal strength of Catholicism was humanity's only hope. Brownson declared that it was time for the church to "assert the most rigid theological intolerance," which had been central to Catholicism for ages. The democratization project that had bred an anarchic religious marketplace had gone too far.[15]

Writing decades later in the wake of the Civil War's carnage, Brownson believed America had finally learned her lesson. Sacralizing individualism and ignoring the voice of God had only brought chaos. A united faith—what he believed Catholicism offered—was what America lacked in comparison to more established European nations. The United States "has more need of full knowledge of itself," he chided, and that could only be accomplished through divine aid. Pastoral guidance promised "the realization of the true idea of the state." America's "national pride" was in thinking they could base a democracy upon human reason alone. But "it is as bad philosophy as theology," Brownson countered, "to suppose that God created the universe, endowed it with certain laws of development or activity, wound it up, gave it a jog, set it a going, and then left it to go of itself." Revelation was necessary for democracy to function. For "the bulk of mankind a revelation is necessary to give them an adequate knowledge even of the precepts of natural law," he explained elsewhere. Importantly, however, Brownson insisted that this change could only happen through the republican form of persuasion, and he chastised his Catholic colleagues for not embracing America's democratic discourse. American politics needed a course correction, not replacement.[16]

Not all were as committed to retaining some attachment to democratic sensibilities, especially within the Catholic world. Across the Atlantic, there was as much religious animosity toward democratic sovereignty as there was celebration. The reigns of Louis XVIII and Charles X in France were buttressed by an ecclesiastical and theological conservativism that was in response to the French Revolution the previous century. As the nation went through new governing structures, one of the few things that held them together was the support of a Catholic hierarchy and, according to James Kloppenberg, a "resurgent popular religiosity" that made their political culture "increasingly inclined toward more paternalistic—and authoritarian—regimes in church and state alike." The Catholic Church was able to take advantage of a growing skepticism concerning democratic rule. A couple of decades later, the First Vatican Council formalized papal infallibility, an authoritative check against the dangers of unrestrained equalitarianism. While democratic order later became synonymous with liberty and freedom, in the mid-nineteenth century there were enough critics to remind us that it was still a political experiment which was far from being assured success. The origins of sovereignty was still an open question.[17]

But one need not look to Catholicism or Europe to witness attempts to imagine a form of sovereignty in competition with America's democratic majority. Two years after Orestes Brownson lost faith in Protestantism and converted to the Catholic Church, he received word from his brother, Oran, of a similar conversion experience. Oran wrote that just as Orestes became Catholic "because no other church possessed proper authority," he had similarly "changed [his] opinions for the same reasons." To Oran, however, "the proper authority rests among the Mormons." Both Brownson brothers concluded that American Protestantism failed to provide a spiritual anchor in the tempest of modernity. But where Orestes turned to Rome, Oran turned to Nauvoo. Indeed, the religious message that the latter heard from Mormon missionaries struck much the same chord as that which drew the former to Catholicism. And even though Oran's attachment to Joseph Smith proved more fleeting than Orestes's attachment to the pope—he followed his brother's path to Catholic conversion a decade later—this familial navigation reflected a broader cultural symmetry.[18]

The Mormon concept of political power fully blossomed in their Council of Fifty, organized in March 1844. At the council's first meeting, it was agreed that circumstances required them to "establish a Theocracy," wherein impartial decisions could be dictated through divine guidance. Joseph Smith claimed that the earth was "rent from center to circumference, with party strife, political intrigue, and sectional interest" due to the fact that no nation or kingdom acknowledged the role of divine rule. The solution, according to Smith's new council, was to "amend that constitution & make it the voice of Jehovah." They "resolved to draft a constitution which should be perfect, and embrace those principles which the constitution of the United States lacked." This was far from a unique endeavor, as a number of Americans toyed with ideas of constitutional revision during the era. But the Mormon attempt was especially noteworthy in that the new constitution aimed to be based on the laws of God as enunciated through a chosen prophet, and then implemented through a form of theocratic governance. The omnipotent voice of God would finally bring order to the chaotic society of men.[19]

These developments introduced new possibilities for Smith's followers. It allowed them to peel back the layers of disestablishment. One inductee into the council, Albert Carrington, created a scriptural workbook to process the newly organized council. His study wove together passages from Luke, Matthew, and Samuel that spoke of a coming "Kingdom of God." He concluded that "the causes for the blindness of the people" in the political world was due to "the loss of inspiration" from God which led to governments "institut[ing their] own opinions" and "depart[ing] from [the] eternal meaning" of laws. The pure political order was based on "covenants entered into between God and man by revelations." A democratic system that ignored religious authority was one destined for destruction. Both the scriptures and experience pointed to the necessity of theocratic governance. Another member of the council, Orson Hyde, was so disgusted with the disunity of democratic leadership during a mission to Washington, DC, that he described Congress as "a chequer board; the members are players, and are extremely cautious how they move." Because they were intent on pleasing their constituents and political party, rather than focusing on the eternal laws that should dictate human society, they have "become so tangled up" and "the sword must cut them clear." Hyde scoffed when comparing a democratic Congress, where politicians represented only the interests of those who had influence, to the Mormon council, where they were all to work together in establishing God's will. "There is more wisdom and order manifested in one of our councils at Nauvoo, than you would ever see here," he contended. Hyde concluded that, without divine guidance, "a Republican form of Government is as unwieldy in the hands of the people" as a cannon is "in the hands of a school boy." In failing to acknowledge the true origin of rule, the American government had lost its way.[20]

Perhaps the apogee of this line of thinking came with Smith's own position within the council. On April 11, a month into the organization's existence, it was moved "that this honorable assembly receive from this time henceforth and forever, Joseph Smith, as our Prophet, Priest & King, and uphold him in that capacity in which God has anointed him." A convergence of priestly rituals, political angst, and confined triumphalism, the figurative crowning symbolized the extent to which Mormons were willing to push for centralized authority. The vote, of course, was unanimous. Just as Smith ruled over the religious realm with prophetic authority, he was also to rule over the secular world with monarchical power. The vote to grant Smith such religious and authoritative power was a predecessor to Catholics formalizing papal infallibility a couple of decades later. Just as it had been in ancient times, God's chosen spokesperson once again served as the hinge upon which the earthly and heavenly kingdoms would pivot.[21]

Yet Smith, like Orestes Brownson and many of the other American Catholics with goals of assimilation, remained anxious to frame his political developments within modern democratic language. The political culture had shifted so much that even a divine monarchy required republican justification. Smith described the theocratic council's "political title" as "*Jeffersonianism*" and "*Jeffersonian Democracy*," meaning that he believed their governing principles still had some relationship to America's democratic tradition. Yet, to justify this contradictory confluence, Smith revised the definition of democracy in a way that incorporated theocracy, calling it "theodemocracy," a neologism that captured his blended purpose. Individuals still possessed the agency expected in a modern age, but that liberty merely enabled them to follow divine counsel. A "theodemocracy," explained Smith, was when "the people . . . get the voice of God and then acknowledge it, and see it executed." Even the most sacred phrases used to enshrine democracy were revised. Smith explained that the popular American maxim "Vox populi, Vox Dei" should *not* mean the common translation of "the voice of the people *is* the voice of God," but rather "the voice of the people *assenting* to the voice of God." Democracy was such a powerful reality in early America that even its strongest critics drew from its language.[22]

As expected, most of Smith's contemporaries did not find this reasoning persuasive. News of this secret council quickly trickled outside of Nauvoo and garnered heated reactions. George Davis, who edited the *Alton Telegraph and Democratic Review*, in nearby Alton, Illinois, declared that Smith had been "CROWNED KING under God" by a "council of fifty" who had been sworn to "secrecy, *under the penalty of death*." The nature of the council betrayed American ideals. In a letter that was republished in a number of eastern newspapers, Davis explained that this secret council was part of "the Prophet's grand design" to install a theocratic government that would rule the world. Governor Thomas Ford of Illinois later surmised that Smith's desire to "be crowned and anointed king and priest, far above the rest" was the final straw that broke the religion's back. Newspapers as far away as New York reprinted correspondence that accused Smith of corrupting democratic politics through "his triune function of Prophet, Priest and King." This new political body was confirmation that Smith and the Mormons were not willing to work within the boundaries of democratic governance.[23]

The Mormons were such a threat to America's political order that many became convinced that they required an extralegal response. A growing number of dissenters from the Mormon faith and longtime antagonists outside of Nauvoo's borders joined together to extinguish the threat. While Smith, his brother, and several other Latter-day Saint leaders were being held in the county seat of Carthage to be tried for treason, a mob stormed the jail to enact their own verdict. They had hoped that the state's political system could eventually bring an end to the Mormon menace, but the past two years had only brought frustration as Smith used legal maneuverings to remain free and safe. It had come time to act on the will of the people. Ironically, those who eventually killed Smith shared some of his same assumptions concerning democracy's limits: political channels were far too slow, legal controls over religious liberty far too fragile, and political solutions far too corruptible. Democratic governance proved to be both too lenient, allowing dangerous sects to emerge and develop, as well as too encumbered, unable to take the swift justice necessary to protect society. As William Clayton noted, those who killed Smith *"knew that the law could not touch him but powder and ball would."* Threats to democracy at times required vigilante solutions. The hope was that the Mormon threat would abate once their radical leader had perished.[24]

Yet Mormons only became more resolute concerning democracy's failings after Smith's death. The prophet's martyrdom was further evidence that the American nation had lost its way. One apostle did not "believe this government will ever do any thing to protect us. It is a damned wrotten thing—, full of lice, moth eaten, corrupt and there is nothing but meanness about it." In the midst of this turmoil, Brigham Young, Smith's successor, collapsed any boundaries between religious and political authority. The Mormons fully embraced their opposition to America's democratic order. They now recognized that the central point of conflict was a disagreement over the role of religious leadership in civic governance. One member of the Council of Fifty,

William Phelps, accurately posited that "the greatest fears manifested by our enemies is the union of church and state." Whereas Mormons were previously reticent to acknowledge their transgressive state, now they embraced it. "I believe we are actually doing this," Phelps reasoned, "and it is what the Lord designs." Rather than attempting to salvage some form of democratic governance based within the confines of America's boundaries, it was time to admit that an alternate method was required. One apostle, Heber Kimball, "moved that we declare ourselves an independent nation." Another, Orson Pratt, agreed in sentiment, but felt it was unnecessary "inasmuch as the nation has already made us independent." It was time to look outside of America's confines for a fresh start, only this time sanctioned by God's will.[25]

But where would they go? Of all the locations they originally debated, the California region of Mexico seemed most desirable, but for an unsuspected reason. Not only did the Mexican government exert loose control in 1845, which would allow greater autonomy, but the Mormons believed that the current residents in the region might prove to be beneficial neighbors. As Orson Hyde told the Council of Fifty, California seemed an especially optimistic option because "the people of that country are of the Catholic faith." Not only would the Catholics be sympathetic to the Mormons' persecuted past, but they shared similar ideas concerning the sovereignty of God's voice and the dangers of democratic excess. They were colleagues in the quest to

FIGURE 2. Mormons and Catholics Cartoon. In this nineteenth-century editorial cartoon, Thomas Nast depicted Catholics and Mormons as dual threats to American democracy. Library of Congress (www.loc.gov/pictures/item/2010717281/).

THE PROPHET.

SATURDAY MORNING, JUNE 29, 1844.

SUPER HANC PETRAM ÆDIFICABO.

FOR PRESIDENT,

GEN. JOSEPH SMITH,

OF NAUVOO, ILLINOIS.

FOR VICE PRESIDENT,

SIDNEY RIGDON.

OF PENNSYLVANIA.

FIGURE 3. Joseph Smith for President. In several issues of the Mormon-owned newspaper, the *Prophet*, Mormons in New York printed an illustrated endorsement for Joseph Smith's presidential campaign that depicted Smith's candidacy as a divine spark to heal a fractured world. "For President, Gen. Joseph Smith, of Nauvoo, Ill.," *Prophet* (New York), June 2, 1844.

reconstitute the proper relationship between church and state. "Let us go to that country," Hyde reasoned, "where the Catholic feelings and principles prevail." They were anxious to join their ideological kin. This perpetual, if inconsistent, symmetry between the two American outcasts reaffirmed their asymmetry with the nation's Protestant culture. Besides their commitment to ritualism, institutional authority, and demographic diversity, they posed an alternative to America's traditional democratic model. Later, they would be grouped together as "foreign reptiles" and dual threats to America's democratic culture (see figure 2).[26]

It is only fitting, then, that one of the most potent expressions of Mormonism's political theology drew from a scripture that was central to the Catholic tradition. In support of Joseph Smith's presidential candidacy, Mormons in New York printed an advertisement in their newly founded newspaper that announced the Mormon prophet's platform as a divine spark to heal the fractured world (see figure 3). The image depicted the dark clouds of the earth, which represented error and apostasy, being pierced with the divine light of revelatory command. The phrase, "Super Hanc Petram Aedificabo," the Latin text of first half of Matthew 18:16, "Upon this rock I will build my Church," is affixed in the center. The Catholic Church used the passage to emphasize the authority that had been passed down through apostolic and papal leadership, from Peter to current Catholic leaders. In the Mormon telling found in this political advertisement, however, the last part of the phrase, that which translates into "my church," had been excised. It now implied that the "rock" was not limited to ecclesiology, but should also serve as the foundation for political institutions. Just as the Catholic Church believed God's commission to Peter was the repository for religious authority, the Mormons now believed God's commandments to Joseph Smith would be the basis for political order. America's democratic politics had overlooked the spiritual principles of social order.[27]

Seen together, the Catholics and the Mormons presented a competing vision of how democracy functioned and liberty was preserved within a Protestant nation. In the face of a culture that sacralized individual liberty and centralized the personal conscience, these marginalized religious faiths sought social cohesion through religious authority. They believed that American democracy had only brought chaos and confusion. Though their ideas eventually lost out in the long trajectory of American political thought, it is important to explore these alternative models in order to better understand America's eventual results. The American nation was not to be saved through political compromise, but redemption.

CHAPTER 4

"The Woman's Movement Has Discovered a New Enemy—the Mormon Church"

Church Mobilization against the ERA and the NOW's Countermobilization in Utah

NATALIE K. ROSE

"The woman's movement has discovered a new enemy—the Mormon Church—because the church has found a new evil— the Equal Rights Amendment," reported a September 1977 *Los Angeles Times* article. The Church of Latter-day Saints of Jesus Christ's sudden and successful political mobilization against the Equal Rights Amendment (ERA) ratification caught the country by surprise. The journalist Kay Mills, author of the *Los Angeles Times* article, wrote that "nobody cared much" about the church "because feminists had really not counted on the ERA passing in Utah anyway."[1] Thus, when a strong and effective Mormon ERA opposition emerged beyond the Intermountain West, the pro-ERA force was unprepared.

Through an extraordinarily successful mobilization, the "church which rarely ventures into politics so publicly"—as Kay Mills referred to it in 1977— demonstrated it could suddenly and craftily influence the outcome of a national legislative process.[2] Examining how ERA proponents reacted to and interacted with the church during the ERA ratification process elucidates the power of the church's political influence in the last quarter of the twentieth century.[3] Once their feelings of surprise and anger at this opposition subsided, ERA supporters knew they had to rethink their strategies. Ultimately, the church's successful mobilization pushed ERA supporters, specifically the National Organization for Women (NOW), to wholly reconceptualize parts of their own mobilization.

One clear success of the anti-ERA Mormon counterforce was the ability to reach people on the local level. The church assembled remarkable opposition in unratified states by having church members start letter-writing campaigns, knock on doors, start citizens groups not clearly affiliated with the church, and actively participate in both pro- and anti-ERA events.[4] By 1981 the popular feminist consensus confirmed that the church was one of the leading opponents of ERA ratification. Iris Mittgang, the head of the National Woman's Political Caucus, called the church "the single most significant enemy of women's equality in this country." More alarming was the NOW president Eleanor Smeal's dethroning of longtime antifeminist Phyllis Schlafly as the main threat against the ERA. "Phyllis Schlafly is not our key opponent," Smeal explained, "it is the array of the right and their financial backers of which the Mormon Church is a key part."[5]

Taking a page from the Mormons' own religious missionary program and their anti-ERA activism, NOW decided to put ERA supporters on the ground in Utah as ERA missionaries. Starting in the summer of 1981, several ERA activists paid their own way to travel to Utah to serve as missionaries for the Equal Rights Amendment. As an ERA missionary Lena Serge Zezulin, a young attorney, approached strangers, engaged in difficult conversations, had some thoughtful exchanges, and endured slammed doors, screaming, and yelling. Dressed in formal and sensible clothing that espoused a respectful demeanor, Zezulin and her partner looked the part of Latter-day Saint missionaries. When asked by a man about her motivation to work for the amendment, she said: "He wanted to know why we were there, in Utah. I told him that I was there for my grandmothers, my mother, my unborn children. My partner said, 'Before I die, I want to have the rights that you were born with.'" Eventually, the man signed the missionaries' petition for the ERA, to be delivered to President Reagan. Zezulin recalled: "Of all the people that I had spoken to, I felt that I had affected this man the most. It was the best part of the two weeks: the feeling that my understanding of ERA, and my explanation of the relevant issues and of my own commitment, had made a difference."[6]

Thoughtful interactions like this drove the motivation behind the ERA missionary program. The underlying goal was to acknowledge the power of the church's adept political mobilization by copying the church's tactics and to demonstrate that ERA proponents were adept political mobilizers as well. The historian Martha Sonntag Bradley adequately characterized the ERA missionary program as a "witty move but with a deadly serious aim."[7] The president of NOW, Ellen Smeal, explained: "One of the reasons we organized this pilot project of sending ERA missionaries into Utah was to make sure that if women are to be denied equal rights then at least the Mormons will have to think about it."[8] This straightforward and impassioned comment relayed the message that, even though she knew that ratification was an uphill battle, she wanted the main ERA opposition to have a human face connected to those who supported and believed they would benefit from the amendment.

"Many Mormon Women Feel Torn between Equal Rights Proposal and Church"

The proposed Equal Rights Amendment, written by the suffragist Alice Paul in the early 1920s, passed both the Senate and House of Representatives forty-nine years after it was first introduced to Congress and fifty-two years after American women gained suffrage. Opposition from figures like Florence Kelley, a consumer rights and labor reformer, and crises such as the Great Depression and World War II had obstructed the amendment's chances. With the rise of the Second Wave of Feminism and the establishment of NOW, reintroducing and attaining ratification for the ERA became a nonnegotiable priority for many feminists. Getting forward movement toward ratification required picketing and interrupting Senate hearings. In 1971 and 1972, the House and Senate respectively adopted the ERA. Just in 1972 alone, thirty of the necessary thirty-eight states ratified the amendment.[9] With such a rapid and affirming response, ratification appeared to be inevitable.

However, passage of the ERA did not seem inevitable for women who did not identify with feminism. Though unaligned with each other, different pockets of politically conservative, anticommunist, and / or religious women expressed their concern that the feminist movement was encroaching on the government. Moments such as the *Roe v. Wade* decision and the proposed Childcare Act galvanized conservative women to organize on the grassroots level.[10] To many of these women, the ERA threatened a radical restructuring of traditional gender roles. When Phyllis Schlafly, the poised but punchy, virulently anticommunist, conservative activist, announced her opposition to the ERA, under her leadership the anti-ERA movement became nationally streamlined through orchestrated local grassroots organization.[11]

Why did the church's widespread and successful anti-ERA activism catch so many pro-ERA activists and groups by surprise? After the church stopped condoning the practice of polygamy and Utah gained statehood in the 1890s, Mormons were mostly concerned with balancing the pulls of their religious adherence and American identities. Many times, these identities aligned and at other times there was tension as Mormonism moved more into the American mainstream. Aside from episodes like the hearings on the seating of the elected senator Reed Smoot from 1904 to 1907, Mormons appeared to succeed as ideal Americans.[12] By the late sixties and early seventies, the historian Jan Shipps wrote, "the dramatic discrepancy between clean-cut Mormons and scruffy hippies" "completed the transformation of the Mormon image from the quasi-foreign somewhat alien likeness that it had in the nineteenth century to the more 100 percent super-American portrait."[13] It is necessary to note that this image of patriotic Mormons was one of white Mormonism. This variation of Mormonism was not inclusive of black Mormon Americans. The church membership did contend with regular criticism over the church edict that forbade black men to hold priesthood until 1978.[14] This issue did not garner much traction from non-Mormon Americans within the conservative movement who did not identify with, understand, or even respect the needs of the civil rights movement.

The majority of "100 percent super-American" white Mormons voted along with members of the political Right or Conservative Americans after World War II.[15] Though the contours of the American conservative movement had significantly changed between the immediate post–World War II years and throughout the late 1970s and early 1980s, there were still many commonalities across this longer period.[16] As Lisa McGirr asserts in her book about the New Right in Southern California, those who identified with the conservative movement feared "what they perceived to be a decline in religiosity, morality, individual responsibility, and family authority."[17] These fears resonated with a large number of American conservatives including Mormons.

Just as non-Mormon American conservatives were not a monolithic group, neither were Mormons who were affiliated with conservatism. Looking at Ezra Taft Benson and George Romney, two of the most prominent Mormon political figures, side by side reveals a wide discrepancy in the application of conservative actions and values. In the early 1960s, Benson, who served as President Eisenhower's secretary of agriculture, publicly embraced a more extreme conservative worldview in line with the anticommunist John Birch Society. Though he never officially joined the John Birch Society, anticommunism informed his political beliefs, public speaking, and even his reading of the Book of Mormon.[18] As a more moderate Republican who supported civil rights and even the ERA for a time, Romney enjoyed considerable popularity and success as Michigan's governor. During Romney's failed presidential run in which he was considered a sure contender, it was his view on Vietnam, not his Mormonism, that sank his chances.[19] Despite the various iterations of conservatism within Mormonism, both Democratic and

Republican Mormon politicians publicly opposed the ERA. Some of these politicians—such as George Romney and his wife, Lenore—who once publicly supported the amendment, later displayed their vehement opposition.[20]

The Equal Rights Amendment failed to pass the Utah state senate in 1973. However, a 1974 poll published in *Deseret News* revealed that 63.1 percent of church members stated their support for passage of the amendment. These poll results pushed "the LDS general authorities into action," the historian Martha Bradley explains, and after that "everything changed."[21] The Relief Society president Barbara Smith gave a talk in Salt Lake City shortly after the poll results were released. Her speech relied upon many of the regular arguments put forth by ERA opponents; she asserted that the ERA would stop alimony payments for divorced women, lead to a forced draft for women, and take away other protective measures. An unsigned editorial on the Sunday page of the *Church News* a month later kicked up the anti-ERA fervor. Both Republican and Democrat state representatives who supported the amendment prior to the publication of the article now opposed it.[22]

Not all Mormons were against the ERA. Many Mormon women were deeply troubled by the church's stance on the ERA and the subsequent excommunication of the ERA supporter Sonia Johnson. After educating herself about the proposed amendment, Sonia Johnson—a Mormon wife, mother, and academic living in Virginia—felt compelled to support it and eventually started "Mormons for ERA" in 1977. Two years later, she was excommunicated from the church for preaching false doctrine. The church's treatment of Johnson and her subsequent excommunication were viewed as a symptom of the church's hostility toward women and feminism.[23] Laurel Thatcher Ulrich, a Mormon feminist and historian, after reflecting on her reaction to Johnson's excommunication, admitted: "I resented the excommunication because I resented what it taught me about the priesthood. I was astonished to discover that an endowed woman could be tried at the ward level though her husband could not. . . . The vision of that all-male council trying a woman's membership was more revealing than any of the rhetoric on either side." The excommunication was a moment in which she recognized the "immense contradictions within the Church as it struggles to stretch and grow."[24]

Mormon women like Laurel Thatcher Ulrich were at the forefront of key feminist Mormon events and movements throughout the 1970s. In 1971 several women, including Ulrich and the historian Claudia Bushman, edited a special edition of *Dialogue*, an independent journal on Mormon thought first published in 1966. That issue of *Dialogue*—dubbed the Pink Issue—encouraged the women to start their own journal called *Exponent II*, named after the nineteenth-century Mormon women's weekly.[25] Bushman under-scored the significance of Mormon women's writing and talents in the debut issue of *Exponent II*. She wrote: "Exponent II, poised on the dual platforms of Mormonism and Feminism has two aims: to strengthen the Church of Latter-day Saints, and to encourage and develop the talents of Mormon women."[26] Ulrich also offered her own thoughts on Mormon feminism, defining a feminist as "a person who believes in the equality of the sexes, who recognizes discrimination against women and who is willing to work to overcome it." For her, a Mormon feminist subscribes to these ideals and believes they fit in with "the gospel of Jesus Christ [and] with the mission of the Church of Jesus Christ of Latter-day Saints."[27]

But living as a feminist and Mormon was not possible for all women who subscribed to both identities. In an aptly titled 1979 *New York Times* article, "Many Mormon Women Feel Torn between Equal Rights Proposal and Church," the journalist Molly Ivins interviewed Mormon women who opposed the ERA but also women who feared that their pro-ERA activism would cost them their church membership. Others chose to leave the church by falling to inactive church status.[28] The swift and surprising Mormon involvement in anti-ERA activism had effects beyond the church. For ERA supporters, the church materialized as an unwelcome interloper. On the other side, for those who were opposed to the ERA, the strong counterforce built by the church membership was the necessary component to officially kill the amendment's chances.

"They Had Atomic Weapons and We Had Words"

The ratification process for the Equal Rights Amendment dovetailed with several International Women's Year (IWY) state conferences. The 1977 Houston conference and the smaller state conferences were all an outcome of the 1975 United Nations' IWY Conference held in Mexico City. Upwards of eight thousand women, including United Nations delegates and staff, governmental representatives, and some who self-financed their trip, attended the conference. Galvanized by the spirit and agenda set in Mexico City, the National Commission on the Status of Women, led by Representative Bella Abzug, initiated planning for the Houston conference. Ostensibly, the states' IWY meetings served as planning sites to choose delegates and particular issues of importance for each state to bring as their agenda to the national conference in Houston in November 1977.[29]

Despite these intentions, the state IWY meetings transformed into spaces of divisive and often-unproductive confrontations over abortion rights, childcare, financial equality, and the passage of the Equal Rights Amendment. Whereas feminist organizers hoped conservative women would walk away from meetings more enlightened about feminism, conservative women saw these meetings as an opportunity to strengthen support for traditional gender roles, family, and protections for women.[30] IWY organizers assumed that they would educate some women, engage in conversation across ideological lines, and tackle some disagreements between different groups, who presumably shared the larger goal of women's empowerment. Conservative women came prepared to vote against proposals they opposed, take seats on the state's delegations, and have their concerns be heard.

Ultimately, the ERA's biggest proponents grossly underestimated the role that the anti-ERA force, especially under Phyllis Schlafly, would play in the ratification process. For ERA supporters, Schlafly embodied traditional old-fashioned womanhood that did not represent the vast majority of American women. Bound up in this characterization of Schlafly was the assumption that she and her followers were not politically decisive or up for the challenge of defeating an amendment. These assumptions galvanized Schlafly to invest further in ERA opposition and even seek a law degree in the late 1970s.[31] Schlafly, her followers, and the various groups that fought the ERA unequivocally swayed many citizens and politicians to the anti-ERA side.[32]

ERA proponents continually failed to consider the opposition as a substantial threat or to listen to their concerns about the amendment. Spokespeople for the ERA were quoted in news articles and on popular television talk shows spurning criticism directed at the amendment as too outlandish to even acknowledge. One of the ERA opposition's greatest strengths was their ability to conjure up fear about ridiculous (to ERA proponents) outcomes of the ERA, including mandatory unisex bathrooms and the undoing of same-sex schools and children's activities. However, the dismissal of these claims extended to a failure to discuss more grounded fears such as women's financial protection after a divorce, whether women would be drafted, and protective legislation regarding women and work.[33] The lack of pro-ERA engagement with critics and those questioning the ERA propelled events like IWY meetings to evolve into contested spaces.

Mormons emerged as the most capable counter-ERA organizers at the IWY state meetings they attended in mass numbers. With the largest state turnout, the Utah IWY meeting demonstrated that Mormons as political operators were capable of significant influence. Nearly fourteen thousand Mormon women attended the Utah IWY conference when only two thousand were initially expected. The staggering number was the result of widespread recruitment led by church bishops and Relief Society presidents, who called women members to attend the meeting, recruit more women, and vote down all the proposed amendments.[34] Mormon women also overwhelmed attendance at the Montana, Washington State, and Hawaii IWY meetings. The church's anti-ERA action at these conferences garnered national attention. "It was like a war, only they had atomic weapons and we had words," said Maggy Pendleton, an IWY organizer, in a *New York Times* article.[35] In Washington State, IWY leaders were informed the night before their state conference that an additional two thousand women would show up. The organizer of these women Susan Roylance, a Mormon who referred to her group as "the Silent Majority," worried about "the detrimental impact our society is having upon the role of the mother.[36] In response, an ERA supporter said: "This has become Mormon vs. Non-Mormon, and it is most unfortunate because our ability to get together and share ideas has been taken from us."

Mormon anti-ERA action persisted in unratified states such as Nevada, Virginia, and Florida. Though the church leadership continuously denied direct involvement including financial donations to anti-ERA causes, evidence abounded that those in power, from the church presidency to local Relief Society presidents and local bishops, were orchestrating anti-ERA mobilizing. In October 1978, Californian Mormons donated more than $13,000 to anti-ERA candidates in Florida just days before the election. Pro-ERA candidates for state legislature lost these elections. In Nevada, Mormon families took advantage of Family Home Evening, a designated time on Monday evenings when a family spends time together, to canvass against the ERA. Over 90 percent of Mormon Nevadans, which made up one-fifth of the state's voting population, turned up to vote in that state's election. In 1979 the Virginia legislature received anti-ERA mail; Mormons wrote 85 percent of it.[37] After this decisive and covert political mobilization, ERA proponents knew they had to reinvigorate and reconceptualize their ERA ratification strategy.

"A March of 'Feminist Missionaries' in Utah"

With the unexpected disruption of anti-ERA activities at state IWY conferences, the dramatic event of Sonia Johnson's excommunication, and successful anti-ERA mobilization in unratified states, the threat of an unratified amendment loomed large for ERA proponents. NOW's annual three-day conference in 1980 pivoted around strategizing for ratification and how to contend with the Mormon opposition. Covering the conference in the *Los Angeles Times*, the journalist Beverly Beyette wrote that NOW would "stage a nonviolent protest, a march of 'feminist missionaries' on Utah to protest the church's suppression of women."[38]

The missionary program officially began the first week of May in 1981 when several women and a few men set out on the streets of Utah. Instead of the Book of Mormon, the ERA missionaries were armed with the text of the Equal Rights Amendment. Though the missionaries only received forty-eight hours of training, they were effectively schooled in how to engage in meaningful dialogue. These missionaries were directed to "be brief and polite in true missionary demeanor and if faced with opposition, to withdraw."[39] NOW measured support in Utah by having the ERA missionaries ask willing people to sign a petition of support to send to President Reagan and to sign postcards addressed to the church president stating their ERA support. To accomplish this, volunteers were expected to broach the topic of women's income inequality by pointing out facts such as that a Mormon woman made 53 cents for every dollar a man made, six cents below the national average of 59 cents.[40] Missionaries who engaged in substantial conversation then would ask the person to sign the materials. Mormon Utahans were more likely to sign the petition for Reagan than to send a postcard to their church president's office, as many expressed fear of disciplinary action from the church.[41]

The ERA missionary program gained national news coverage during the first weeks of its establishment. Norma Harrison, writing for the *Baltimore Sun*, picked up on the historical roots of women engaging in missionary-like activism: "The precedent for missionary work is a long one for NOW, which claims powerful antecedents in the suffragettes, who sent caravans to the West for one-on-one meetings with women." Harrison also pointed out how these suffragists including Elizabeth Cady Stanton received "the warmest welcome from Mormon women in Utah," some of the first women to exercise the right to vote.[42] NOW's ERA missionary program also fit in with a long trajectory of groups preaching to Mormons. From members of the Reorganized Church of Jesus Christ of Latter-day Saints (RLDS) attempting to convert Mormons to the correct form of their shared religious origins in the nineteenth century to Southern Baptists holding a widespread all-day proselyting effort in the Salt Lake Valley during their 1998 annual meeting held that year in Utah, Mormons were a target for others hoping to change their ways, minds, and religious beliefs.[43] Though NOW was not a religious organization, many of its leaders, members, and volunteers treated the ERA and other feminist measures as akin to sacred work.

Missionaries usually encountered two kinds of reactions from ERA opposition: outright, dramatic rejection and some engagement. A *New York*

Times reporter caught up with a middle-aged married couple named Twiss and Patrick who were ERA missionaries in Midvale, Utah, just a few days after the program began. Patrick Butler, a geologist at the National Aeronautics and Space Administration in Houston, called the ERA work "righteous" work and his wife, Twiss, a mother of five, said there must be "disturbance for forward movement." During their canvassing, they had one woman slam the door in their faces after saying "'I feel I'm as equal as anybody in the whole wide world.'"[44] The young lawyer Lena Serge Zezulin explained that door slams were expected on a daily basis:

> We even got a double door slam. The woman of this particular house observed me and my partner as we canvassed on the other side of her street. She had two kids clinging to her, and a third one visibly along the way. When we rang the doorbell, one of the kids opened the door. She ran up to us, screaming "ERA?!! NO! Never!" Slam!! I tried to insert a few words in between her screams. I finished a sentence as the door closed, hoping to assure her that we would not harm her. She opened the door seconds later, screaming even louder, "Is this harassment?" and slammed it once more.[45]

An even more hostile reaction occurred at that summer's Pioneer Day parade, the day commemorating when Mormons first arrived in the Salt Lake Valley. The incident was described in a *Los Angeles Times* article: "some spectators heckled, threw fruit and spat on ERA missionaries, said Peggy Norman, an Oregon teacher and an ERA missionary. Some people used cigarettes to pop the balloons the ERA missionaries were distributing, she said."[46] The sight of Utahans popping balloons with cigarettes suggests that even inactive or non-Mormons felt that these ERA missionaries were treading on territory where they did not belong.[47]

Aside from slammed doors and quick rebuffs, missionaries did have some productive conversations centered on dispelling falsehoods and clearing up exaggerations. Zezulin reported some of the most common anecdotes she heard from people about the ERA: abortion was mentioned in the text of the amendment, the proposed amendment was forty pages long, it would allow more civil rights for gay men and women, and there would be compulsory coed bathrooms. Zezulin referred to one interaction with a woman that "was especially helpful in revealing our opposition. She greeted us cordially, asked us to sit down, and said: 'I cannot support an amendment that will force me to work!' We asked her to explain. She brought forth a two-inch folder of anti-ERA materials, most of which she did not show us. One of the pamphlets that we saw bore the letterhead of the Freemen Institute (derived from the words 'free men'). It announced, unequivocally, that the ERA will outlaw all social security for homemakers, and that homemakers will have to abandon their families and work."[48] The pervasive misinformation about the ERA was fueled both by larger national forces such as the John Birch Society but also by smaller and regional groups such as the Freemen Institute, a group founded by the Mormon Cleon Skousen that espoused radical right-wing politics.[49] Such interactions with women like this reiterated that many people simply had not read or heard the actual text of the Equal Rights Amendment.

Showing the text of the amendment to willing people was helpful for starting productive dialogue and even changing some minds. Lena Serge Zezulin described influencing a man she called as a "Devout Mormon." The man asked "Is that all?," after reading the amendment. When she thought it was time to move on to the next person, the man surprised her and signed the petition to Reagan. Like many other Mormons he refused to sign the postcard to Kimball, the church president, as he feared "trouble from the church."[50] The ERA missionaries Tom and Cathy Walker also had some hopeful encounters. Upon seeing the actual text, one man said: "This is the whole ball of wax, huh?" He ended up signing the petition to President Reagan but declined to sign the postcard to the church president. At the next house, a woman believed that "the ERA would force women to do 'hard work.'" After talking for some time with the Walkers, the woman signed both the petition and postcard and said: "I hope you get more people, I'll back you every step of the way."[51]

Discussing income inequality between men and women also worked as a rallying point for gaining signatures. The missionaries Twiss and Patrick Butler had success with a woman named Fern Denman who felt compelled to sign the petition for President Reagan urging him to announce his support, as she saw how financial inequality affected her daughter, "who works at a computer company here, makes $5 an hour; men at the plant make between $8 and $9." Pointing to the risk she may have been taking, she admitted: "'My husband's not going to be too happy, but what the heck.'"[52] Though the last comment was likely made in jest, this anecdote points to the evident divisions within families over ERA support in Utah. Fern Denman exemplified the type of ERA supporter who remained mostly invisible in the sea of ERA opposition in Utah.

The ERA missionaries continued to work thirteen at a time for two-week periods as the summer progressed. The coordinator for the ERA missionary program, Becky Fenstermaker, explained that, though many Mormons in the state agreed with the overall wording in the amendment, many just said they "will follow the prophet" (the church president) with his decision not to support the ERA. Despite the overall negative response from Utahans, Fenstermaker insisted that "morale among the missionaries remains high."

NOW extended the ERA missionary program to Southern California. Missionaries in California, shared a similar goal to their peers in Utah: talk to Mormons about the ERA, since many Californian Mormons had given financial support to anti-ERA campaigns in other states. Soon the missionary program extended to unratified states. A whole host of ERA supporters volunteered as missionaries. Graduate and undergraduate students took time off from schools such as Brown University, Smith College, and Harvard University to campaign for the ERA during their spring and winter breaks. Some older professional women quit steady jobs to work to pass the ERA. Retired women traveled from out of state to lead ERA missionary programs.[53]

By March 1982, there were fewer than three months left to reach the deadline for ratification. At a reception to benefit Harvard University students volunteering for NOW, feelings among attendants varied from hopeful to doubtful about the amendment's chances. Betty Friedan, the author of the groundbreaking bestseller *The Feminine Mystique*, who was in attendance, "called the Harvard effort an 'important' part of the ERA effort. 'It's going to take a miracle. but I can't give up hope,' added Friedan."[54]

That miracle never came. On June 29, 1982, the *Chicago Tribune* journalist Joan Beck wrote "Who and What Killed the ERA." It included a detailed list placing responsibility on a number of groups, including insecure males, homemakers, and male chauvinists, as well as specific individuals such as Ronald Reagan, Nancy Reagan, Phyllis Schlafly, Jimmy Carter, and "some religious leaders and Church members who want traditional, patriarchal social and family organization who equate the ERA with divorce, sexual permissiveness, illegitimacy, and abortion." The Church of Jesus Christ of Latter-day Saints was the only specific religion or church that she named. However, Beck also singled out NOW for its failure to "develop a broad enough basis of support among women." She wrote that, while the NOW president Eleanor Smeal "probably worked harder for ERA than any other person," her "zeal . . . alienated many women whose support she needed and helped turn the issue into one that divided instead of united women."[55] Perhaps if NOW and other large pro-ERA organizations had engaged in this missionary activity as soon as the church's anti-ERA stance became evident, the story of the ERA ratification may have ended differently. The earlier implementation of the program would by no means have guaranteed an ERA victory or lessen the church's mobilization, but it could have led to greater clarity about what the ERA would and would not do for women.

Though the church's strategic involvement in anti-ERA activity garnered negative criticism from those inside and outside of the church, it has continued to take sides in contentious culture wars. The battle over the ERA within Mormonism has set a precedent for not only how the church approaches culture wars but also how the church's critics would respond. Employing nearly identical rhetorical and mobilization methods first utilized in the battle over the ERA, the church created and funded robust campaigns against same-sex marriage in many states throughout the 1990s and early 2000s.[56] Mormons made up a majority of volunteers and donations to Yes on 8, a group that aimed to pass Proposition 8, which defined marriage as between a man and women, in California's 2008 election. Those involved in Yes on 8 were advised not to mention their Mormon church membership nor dress like missionaries.[57] Though a Mormon spokesperson did not deny the church's involvement in the Proposition 8 activism, the church's commentary was that they were one of many faith traditions concerned about the sanctity of heterosexual marriage.[58]

Similar patterns seen in the anti-ERA and Proposition 8 organizing have emerged in disagreements over issues specific to the church and its membership. During the 1990s, six church members in the academic world, known as "the September Six," were excommunicated for apostasy after publicly speaking or publishing work about controversial church doctrine including Heavenly Mother. Despite these excommunications, discussions about Heavenly Mother have not disappeared but have continued to emerge in Mormon academic discourse through publication, conferences, and internet social media. In 2014 Kate Kelly, the founder of Ordain Women—a movement to give Mormon women the priesthood—was also excommunicated. Instead of quieting that movement, Kelly's excommunication has reignited it and led to more activism centered around gender parity in the institutional church, doctrine and theology, church services, and in the Mormon home.[59]

Despite the church's rampant success with anti-ERA activism and Proposition 8 and efforts to stop what the church views as apostasy through excommunication, its critics cannot be silenced. The church can exercise its organizational muscle to quash legislative change but it cannot avoid the political and cultural ramifications of such actions. NOW's ERA missionary program was an attempt to show Mormons who the pro-ERA force was, to acknowledge the Mormons' political savviness, to have meaning and respectful exchanges, but also to show the church the pro-ERA force could not be stopped without a fight.

PART II

Power and Sovereignty

Underlying perceptions of Mormon politi-
cal, social, and economic life was the constant concern over the potential,
and occasionally realized, power of the cohesive religious group as well
as its capability to properly exercise sovereignty in the American system
of federalism. Part II demonstrates a contested, contingent, and complex
intersection of Mormons with other Americans in the negotiation of power
and sovereignty in the nineteenth century that lingered into the twentieth. Together, these chapters bring needed nuance to the traditional ideas
of Manifest Destiny and Americanization. Widening the Mormon lens to
engage with larger political and historical contexts of violence, territorial
expansion, and the overall exercise of real power physically, legally, and economically, the authors of the following five chapters illustrate both the fragility and strengthening of majoritarian, national sovereignty over the singular
religious minority.

The violent exercise of power against Indians and Mormons in Illinois,
Amy S. Greenberg reveals, was symptomatic of white manhood and territorial expansion from the Black Hawk War to the expulsion of the Mormons in
1846. Rather than a simplistic look at the Mormon expulsion as one of religious persecution, Greenberg places the Mormon experience in the context
of gender, political culture, and American empire. Noteworthy parallels and

continuities of white male violence against expressions of minority group political authority and potential power set the stage for many of the chapters that follow.

Thomas Richards also engages the context of American empire and imperial interest in the West in his analysis of the contingency of Western geopolitics in the time of Manifest Destiny. Could Mormons be trusted as agents of American empire, as progenitors of US sovereignty, or were they a threatening nonstate power too vast to be accommodated? In providing an answer to this not so simple question, Richards discusses the importance of proximity and presents a nuanced examination of Mormon power in the context of the US–Mexican War.

There is perhaps no more real usurpation of power of American republican governance than the issuance of martial law. On two separate occasions, the Mormon leaders Joseph Smith and Brigham Young proclaimed martial law to protect their people against the threat of violence and the exercise of power of the local and national majorities. In Brent Rogers's chapter, these two Mormon martial law proclamations are analyzed alongside other American instances of martial law and the context of American understandings of arbitrary exercises of power. The Mormon martial law cases were understood to be treasonous, despotic exercises and anathema to civil republicanism at a time that saw a negotiation of power and rights that discounted minority groups and strengthened the majority, even the federal state.

Since the incorporation of Utah as a US territory, Mormons had sought the autonomy of sovereign statehood. The long battle for Utah's statehood has often been summarized with a single word: polygamy. But, as Stephen Smith unveils, what Americans were talking about when talking about polygamy was Mormon sovereignty. For the better part of the second half of the nineteenth century, the US federal government and most Americans deemed as unacceptable the bestowal of sovereignty for Mormons. Smith's use of legal history and congressional records highlights the debates over the transferal of sovereignty. It was a slow forty-year process that saw the federal government's exercise of its own authority over Utah Territory and prevented Mormons from receiving the full measure of autonomy, thus revealing a crucial power dynamic at play with the nation's territorial system.

Matthew Godfrey's chapter takes the fear of Mormon power into the economic, big-business milieu of the early twentieth century. Because of the Mormon interest in the sugar trust and the political machinations surrounding tariffs, the Mormons were still deemed to be a dangerous political power.

The fear of Mormon corporate and political power being exercised through business interests was revealed by muckraking journalists at the time other big-business trusts were being dismantled. In unpacking this history, Godfrey reveals ongoing American fears that the Mormon leadership still controlled the people of the Intermountain West politically and economically, while simultaneously highlighting yet another dimension of Mormon history as being symptomatic of broader American history as opposed to being an anomaly.

CHAPTER 5

"The Way of the Transgressor Is Hard"

The Black Hawk and Mormon Wars in the Construction of Illinois Political Culture, 1832–1846

AMY S. GREENBERG

On March 24, 2004, the Ninety-Third Illinois General Assembly passed HR 0627, tendering an apology to, and seeking the "pardon and forgiveness of the Latter-Day Saints" for "the misguided efforts of our citizens, Chief Executive, and the General Assembly in the expulsion of their Mormon ancestors from the gleaming city of Nauvoo and the State of Illinois" in 1846.[1]

Those who are familiar with the format of apologetic House resolutions will likely surmise that HR 0627's narrative account of the Mormon expulsion from Illinois was brief, direct, and lacking in nuance. House resolutions are, or should be, clear and easily digested. HR 0627 got a number of facts correct about what it described as the "distrust, violence, and inhospitable actions of a dark time in our past." It is true that, in the years after being expelled from Missouri in 1838–39, the Saints developed swamp land in the far west of the state into the thriving economic community of Nauvoo, with a population, in 1844, of between twelve and fifteen thousand people, potentially rivaling that of Chicago. It is also true that the Nauvoo city charter gave the Saints an extraordinary level of home rule, including their own court system and militia, which over time grew to be second in size only to the US Army.[2] Certainly, "the expression of political authority and power" within the Church of Jesus Christ of Latter-day Saints "was seen by many citizens in Illinois" as reason "for caution and concern." Locals saw "the control of local courts by Joseph Smith as autocratic," and block voting by the Saints upset both average Illinois citizens and political control within the Second Party System.[3]

While HR 0627's contention that the Saints were initially expelled from Missouri, and welcomed in Illinois, in part because Joseph Smith was "a strong anti-slavery advocate," is open to debate, and it is worth wondering why the resolution mentions nothing about the explosive effect of news of the new doctrine of polygamy on the Illinois populace starting in 1842, facts prove that the Democratic governor Thomas Ford had Joseph Smith and his brother Hyrum jailed on suspicion of complicity in the destruction of a local anti-Mormon newspaper known as the *Expositor*, and that "a violent mob stormed the Carthage jail on June 27, 1844, causing the deaths of Joseph and Hiram Smith." Nor would an objective observer contest that violence against Mormons increased over the next year and a half, "demonstrated in such acts as the burning of crops, the destruction of homes, and the threaten[ed] extermination of the entire Mormon population." And that, after the Illinois legislature withdrew Nauvoo's charter in 1845, Brigham Young "began sending the community of Latter-Day Saints out of their homeland of Nauvoo, Illinois, across the frozen waters of the Mississippi."[4]

But HR 0627's claim that the exodus of Mormons from Illinois constituted "the largest forced migration in American history," is a good deal harder to justify. Setting aside the international slave trade, and the internal slave trade, the forced relocation of loyalists during the Revolutionary War, and Japanese internment, none of which, admittedly, were quite the same, American history still provides evidence of a forced migration that was very similar: the removal of America's Indians after the passage of the 1830 Indian Removal Act.

Between 1830 and 1837, the Jackson administration drove 46,000 Native Americans from their land east of the Mississippi, including 15,000 Creek Indians and over 15,000 Cherokee Indians. And this forced migration occurred at exactly the same time that Illinois was expelling its own Sac and Fox Indians, immediately before fighting a "war of extermination" against them.[5]

The puzzling amnesia at the heart of the claim that Illinois drove the "largest forced migration in American History" when it expelled its Mormons begins to reveal another, related problem with HR 0627, and that is a narrative that wrongly isolates Mormon expulsion from any larger political context.[6] Because when one steps back, and looks at the remarkably violent history of Illinois in the antebellum era, or widens the lens further, to consider the relationship of violence and politics in the antebellum United States, particularly in the context of Indian removal, or further yet, to consider the relationship between territorial expansion and violent practices of man-hood, the expulsion of Mormons from Illinois looks less like an anomaly than a symptom, with effects that emanated well beyond the boundaries of the United States.

In this chapter, I offer an alternative narrative to that of HR 0627, one that puts Illinois's removal of both Indians and Mormons in the context of gen-der, political culture, and ultimately American empire. I do so by focusing on three Illinois men who experienced both the Black Hawk and Mormon Wars, albeit in very different ways: Thomas Ford, who as governor ordered the Mormon expulsion; John Hardin, the congressional representative and militia general who expelled the Saints; and finally Hosea Stout, who dis-covered his martial manhood by fighting Indians and translated that talent to defending members of the Church of Jesus Christ of Latter-day Saints against anti-Mormon impulses in Nauvoo.

Laurel Thatcher Ulrich, in *A House Full of Females: Plural Marriage and Women's Rights in Early Mormonism, 1835–1870*, offers recent proof of how valuable gender analysis can be to the study of Mormon history. Ulrich pres-ents the early history of the church from the perspective of women empow-ered by their circumstances, revealing how both the Mormon faith, and the challenges of life on the Illinois frontier "pushed against conventional notions of marriage even before the introduction of polygamy. Men called to preach no longer had the ability, or even the obligation, to provide for their families. The overall consequence was a curious reversal of roles."[7] Ulrich argues persuasively that a focus on polygamy and on charismatic male lead-ers has obscured the remarkable authority that Mormon women developed while in Nauvoo. Joseph Smith empowered female leaders, allowed them a formal ecclesiastical organization, and publicly affirmed that "the *keys* of the kingdom are about to be given to them, that they may be able to detect every thing false."[8] Mormon women exercised the gifts of healing, prophecy, and speaking in tongues. When organizing the "Female Relief Society of Nauvoo," they rejected a name for their organization that would connect it to women's relief societies throughout the United States, asserting that, "as daughters of Zion, we should set an example for all the world, rather than confine ourselves to the course which has been heretofore pursued."[9]

But there was a backlash to all that female empowerment. By the time accusations of polygamy and forced plural marriage first began circulating outside the community in 1842, Nauvoo had grown into a thriving settle-ment of ten thousand people. John Cook Bennett's best-selling 1842 exposé, *A History of the Saints: Or, an Exposé of Joe Smith and Mormonism*, brought plural marriage to national attention. Among Bennett's accusations was the claim that the Female Relief Society was a harem established to provide Joseph Smith with sexual partners.[10]

The Female Relief Society gathered more than a thousand names testifying to Joseph Smith's high character, and delivered it to the governor of Illinois, Thomas Carlin. But at the same time, leading advocates in favor of polygamy, including Udney Hay Jacob, argued that the practice was the best check on the growing and dangerous power of women. In *The Peacemaker*, published in 1842, Jacob warned his readers, "Gentlemen, the ladies laugh at your pretended authority."[11] Distressed, in part by the liberality of Illinois's divorce laws, Jacob argued that complex marriage would diminish female authority in marriage, particularly the power of women to leave a divorced husband spouseless. In 1844 Brigham Young dissolved the Female Relief Society, putting women in their place.

Ulrich's analysis of this course of events invites some reflection on the implications of female empowerment, and the challenges of life in Illinois and Missouri on Mormon masculinity. If gender is a mutually constitutive construction, as scholars have demonstrated, then neither the empowerment of Mormon women, nor the backlash against that empowerment, could have taken place in a vacuum.[12] One of the biggest forces in the evolution of masculinity in this period, for Mormons, as for Gentiles, was Indian removal. Protecting women from Indian depredations was a superb route for proving a man's manly virtue, just as performing military service against Indians proved a man's allegiance to both the nation and civilization.[13]

While Mormon men, like Gentile men, could theoretically gain masculine credibility by fighting Indians, this chapter suggests that equating martial virtue and Indian fighting may have hurt Mormon men. This is because ongoing fears of a Mormon-Indian conspiracy throughout the period drove Gentiles to conflate the two groups. The Saints' tenure and expulsion from both Missouri and Illinois were "notably marked by claims that Mormons were combining with Indians to wage war against the government and Protestant white America."[14] Military service against Mormons, like military service against Indians, became a way for Gentile men to prove their martial manhood. Because martial virtue, like patriotism and citizenship, was reserved for white men only in the white imaginary of the 1830s, violence by Indians was read as evidence of their criminality. And because Mormon men were associated with Indians, efforts by Mormon men to fight back against Gentile aggression did not prove their martial virtues. On the contrary, it was seen as evidence of Mormon corruption and disloyalty.[15]

There was no surer route to political prominence on the frontiers of the early American republic than through demonstrated success at Indian fighting. Following in the footsteps of Revolutionary War officers who vanquished Britain's Native American allies, a generation of Democrats in the Old Southwest rode their service under Andrew Jackson in the Creek War directly to office. Colonel Davy Crockett served as a scout for Jackson during the Creek War and was subsequently elected lieutenant in the Tennessee state militia and town commissioner the same year. He won election to the US Congress in 1827. Sam Houston was wounded at the Battle of Horseshoe Bend, and later elected governor of Tennessee. And although James K. Polk was too sickly to fight, he joined the Tennessee state militia during the conflict and proudly wore his militia title of colonel until he was elected president of the United States in 1844.[16]

Although William Henry Harrison, a Whig, parlayed success over Tecumseh's Confederacy in 1813 into a successful presidential bid in 1840, initially at least, Indian killing in the Old Northwest did not translate into political power in the same manner it did in the Southwest. Whether this was because Tecumseh's Confederacy delivered embarrassing defeats to the United States, or because Andrew Jackson's intense personal charisma rubbed off on the many "little hickories" who followed him into battle, is unclear. Certainly, the composition of Illinois settlers, many of whom were drawn from New England, endowed Illinois with a veneer of civilization that was lacking in southwestern states such as Tennessee in the same period. Between statehood in 1818, and 1832, Illinois towns boasted of amenities that illustrated their sophistication, including libraries, schools, and lyceums.[17]

Slavery was illegal (if not unknown) in Illinois, further distinguishing the state, in the eyes of many residents, from the southwestern frontier, where slavery drove settlement. Although a substantial settlement of Sac and Fox Indians in the far west of the state remained well after statehood, when Andrew Jackson was elected president in 1828 on a platform of Indian Removal, most Illinois residents felt that they had resolved their Indian problem via a series of admittedly questionable treaties with the Sac and Fox Indians that had driven those tribes across the Mississippi to Iowa Indian territory. In short, as of 1830 there was little to suggest that Illinois was a frontier where a man's value was based on his ability to vanquish Indian foes.[18]

That is, until the Sac leader Black Hawk and his Kickapoo and Meswakis allies began crossing the Mississippi River into Illinois in 1832 in raiding parties. They stole livestock, destroyed property, and killed and scalped Illinois settlers. They also kidnapped two teenage girls, an event that was reported with outrage across the United States. In response, a frontier militia and organized US troops, deploying out of Jefferson Barracks in Missouri, fought a war of extermination against Black Hawk's warriors, destroying crops, burning houses, and pursuing the band even after they had surrendered. About 450 to 600 of Black Hawk's band, half of the entire population, died in the war that bears his name. Counting both soldiers and settlers, Illinois lost just seventy-seven people. Black Hawk himself survived, won a great deal of sympathy along the Eastern Seaboard, and penned a popular autobiography in 1833 that described his people's mistreatment at the hands of white settlers and the US government.[19]

The Black Hawk War had a profound effect on Illinois political culture. Martial values found new currency in 1830s Illinois, as service in that war became a springboard for office for both Democrats and Whigs. The most famous veteran of the Black Hawk War was Abraham Lincoln, who arrived as a young man in the small town of New Salem, Illinois, a year before the war. He volunteered, and was elected captain of a volunteer militia unit in the conflict. In his three months in uniform, he claimed to have never seen an Indian, which may have been just as well since his unit was woefully unprepared for combat. When the men were mustered into service, thirty of them lacked firearms. After the war, Lincoln successfully drew on his popularity with the militia in order to run for statewide office. In 1858 Lincoln claimed that his election by the militia gave him more pleasure than any subsequent election.[20]

Thomas Ford was another volunteer who found political capital in the Black Hawk War. While service in the militia helped Abraham Lincoln overcome the political liabilities of being relatively unknown and relatively poor, for Ford, military service against the Black Hawk Indians was a highly gendered affair, which allowed him to overcome, in the words of his biographer, "his small and scrawny figure, and homely features, together with his naturally diffident, modest and reserved disposition." That Thomas Ford was (again in the words of his biographer) "totally wanting in self-reliance and virile force" had been a "serious" disadvantage "for the achievement of success and eminence."[21] Like Lincoln, Ford trained as a lawyer, but because he was "destitute of the aggressive vigor necessary for success in worldly affairs, he did not prosper," and could "scarcely defray current household expenses," until a political favor secured him the office of state's attorney for the Fifth Judicial District. The following year, Ford responded to the call for volunteers to fight the Indians, and enlisted. Quickly climbing the political latter after the war, he won election as governor in 1842. There is no question that military service helped a "poor speaker" with what a contemporary termed a "fine squeaking voice" remake himself into a political figure of statewide, manly stature.[22]

John Hardin of Kentucky was another lawyer blessed to be a young man in Illinois in 1832. In many ways Abraham Lincoln's opposite, he was college educated, rich and well-married, with a relatively patrician lineage. Grandson of a Revolutionary War hero, he walked with a military swagger, and cut an "attractive, manly figure." He had a "winning and amiable character," and although "somewhat impulsive" was widely popular among men and women. And he made the most of his advantages. He burned an Indian village to the ground in the Black Hawk War, and became a state representative soon thereafter. In 1840 he was elected brigadier general of the state militia, and in 1843 he was elected as a Whig to the twenty-eighth US Congress, voluntarily retiring after one term to return to Illinois, and ultimately, as will be made clear, military service.[23]

Finally, we have Hosea Stout, a religious seeker born in poverty to Kentucky Quakers. He moved to Illinois at the age of eighteen, with dreams of running a school, but his luck and health were both bad. He drank, likely to excess, had a temper, and failed to discover his calling. At twenty-one, he confessed to his sister, "Misfortune comes upon me at every attempt to make an honest & respectable living. And if I can not make an honest living I am resolved not to live at all."[24] Two months later, Stout volunteered for service against Black Hawk's band, despite worrying about the corrosive effect military service might have on his character. "I was never until now brought sufficiently near the scenes of war to know what effect it would have on me," he later wrote in his autobiography. "Often had I heard the demoralizing effect a soldiers life had upon people. . . . well knowing my own weakness at resisting evil I feared this demoralizing effect of a campaign." He may have had his abusive father in mind when he wrote this; before Hosea's birth, Joseph Stout had been disowned by the Quakers for battling Creek and Cherokee Indians as part of an East Tennessee militia. But Hosea volunteered because he "deeply felt the necessity of rallying to the aid of my country," and once he joined the other soldiers found he "only desired to march to meet the enemy, such is the effect of martial music & warlike speech on the mind of man."[25]

Remarkably enough, Stout discovered military life "suited" him "well"; his health improved, and he "was well able to do all the duties of a soldier." Military service against the Sac and Fox Indians was a revelation. He discovered that "some men were so terrified that they could not be got to stand guard" and that "people were not so purely patriotic as I expected."[26] These were not Stout's problems. After the war ended, there were further revelations. He began conversing with Mormon elders, and "plainly discovered" that his previous religious positions "were wrong & [he] did also verily believe Mormonism to be correct." He met Joseph Smith, and was soon preaching the doctrines of this new faith with an "ease & fluency" that astonished him. In 1838 he was baptized, and joined his fellow Mormons in Missouri just in time to go to battle against hostile Gentile neighbors.[27]

It was natural that Hosea would return to arms in the service of the church; far from the demoralizing effect he feared, military service validated his martial virtues. And in the wake of Indian removal, his faith needed all the protection he could provide it. From the outset, the relationship between Indians and Mormons was complicated. The Book of Mormon claimed that Native Americans were "fallen descendants of ancient Israel in need of redemption." Preaching to Indians was a high priority for the newly founded church, beginning with a proselytizing mission to Indians in present-day Kansas, in 1830. The following year, an Indian Affairs agent warned William Clark, the superintendent of Indian Affairs, about the potential for a Mormon-Indian alliance.[28]

Mormon missionaries first entered Missouri in order to convert Indians living on a reservation, and settled on prairie lands in the north of the state that southern residents derided as being "fit only for Indians and Mormons."[29] While their Indian mission met with limited success, the community flourished, quickly growing in population, much to the dismay of neighbors who accused the Mormons of thievery and assault. They also, according to a local Baptist missionary, "strongly suspected [Mormons] of secretly tampering with the neighboring Indians, to induce them to aid in the event of open hostility." Missourians responded by destroying Mormon crops, burning down Mormon homes, and violently attacking Mormon settlers. In 1833 Mormons were forced from their homes in Jackson County, Missouri.[30]

It did not escape the notice of Gentiles that Missouri's treatment of its Mormon neighbors was similar to neighboring Illinois's treatment of their Sac and Fox Indians the year before. The *New York Commercial Advertiser* made clear that it found Mormon doctrine "ridiculous in the extreme" but knew of "nothing in their character or conduct to . . . draw down upon them the lawless violence of a mob." Clearly "the same spirit of injustice which impelled the borderers to destroy the property and seize upon the possessions of the Sac Indians, has now induced a series of attacks upon the unoffending Mormonites."[31]

Missouri's Mormons resettled in Clay and Caldwell Counties, but as hundreds of church members decamped from church headquarters in Ohio for the supposedly friendlier climes of Missouri in 1837, violence between Mormons and Gentiles escalated dramatically. Brother Stout, in the words of a biographer, was "active" in the "defense of the Saints," and "shared in all the persecutions to which the Saints were exposed in Missouri."[32] But Mormon raids failed to quell reprisals. Both sides turned to the language of extermination. On the Fourth of July, 1838, the Mormon leader Sidney Rigdon announced that if Missourians tried again to drive them from their homes, "it shall be between us and them a war of extermination; for we will follow them until the last drop of their blood is spilled; or else they will have to exterminate us."[33] Amid the violence that eventually broke out, Governor Lilburn Boggs issued an executive order that Mormons be "exterminated or driven from the state."[34] In the winter of 1839, close to ten thousand Mormons crossed into Illinois, and by the summer had established a settlement in Commerce, Illinois, just across the Mississippi River from an Iowa Sac-Fox settlement known as the "half-breed tract."[35]

The Saints established their reserve in land designated for mixed-race descendants of European traders and their Indian partners in an 1824 treaty between the US government and the Sac leader Keokuk.[36] The Saints purchased portions of the half-breed tract from speculators, and hoped to baptize the few remaining Sac and Fox residents. Keokuk himself received the Book of Mormon from Joseph Smith. Black Hawk's son and sons-in-law occasionally made appearances. As in Missouri, conversion among the Indians was limited, but there was a substantial degree of interaction between the two groups. Ulrich's research reveals that Mormon women often enjoyed their encounters with Indians, eating with them occasionally and exchanging complements about their children.[37]

While they rebuilt their community in newly chartered Nauvoo, Illinois, Mormons appealed to the federal government for legal redress for the losses they had incurred in Missouri. Mormons had taken land in Missouri through the federal Pre-emption Act of 1830, and had secured their claims by making improvements to the land. Officials in Washington, DC, encouraged church leaders to get affidavits and bills of damage. Ultimately, more than six hundred Saints petitioned for redress, offering accounts of destruction of property, physical violence, and ultimately forced displacement that were remarkably similar to accounts offered by Black Hawk in his 1833 narrative of the tribal displacement from Illinois.[38]

While only the Mormons spoke of having lost their "rights of citizenship," both groups understood the violence they had sustained as reflecting on the United States itself. After recounting the violence done to him by the "mobers of misoughry," one Saint concluded that recounting further "potickelars" would be "in vain because of the hardness of the harte of this generation."[39] After a similar lament, Black Hawk wondered "how smooth must be the language of the whites, when they can make right look like wrong, and wrong like right." The Indians' standard "of right and wrong," he concluded, "differs widely from the whites."[40] Their appeals, in both cases, failed spectacularly. Both groups emerged from their crises in the 1830s with a clear sense of victimization, and with the understanding that the government could not be trusted.[41]

The Saints needed protection and a militia of their own. Given his brazen performance at the Battle of Crooked River in Missouri, it was natural that when Joseph Smith organized the Nauvoo Legion he would turn to Hosea Stout for leadership. According to contemporary reports, Stout was "a great tall man" skilled at intimidation. Advancing quickly through the ranks, Stout became colonel and then brigadier general of the Saints' military force. He also served on the Nauvoo police force, and as bodyguard for Joseph Smith, who was in constant danger of being kidnapped on charges of murder back in Missouri. Smith made Stout a member of the Council of Fifty, an organization Smith created in March of 1844 in preparation for the Second Coming of Christ. Fighting against the Sac Indians had served Stout well.[42]

This is not to say that things were going well in Illinois. At the same time that public authorities in Missouri justified their Mormon War with judicial testimony that "the leaders of Mormonism and many of their followers are but a gang of murderers, assassins, and robbers," charges of Mormon-Indian conspiracy followed Smith's coreligionists from Missouri to Illinois. The *Boston Christian Watchman* quoted testimony about "mysterious conversation," kidnapping, and "plundering and houseburning" by Mormons, concluding that "Mormon books teach that what land they want is to be got 'by purchase or by blood;' (see 'Doctrine and Covenants,') and also that the Indians are to embrace Mormonism, and to repossess the land. . . . Converts from England are already arriving at their city of Nauvoo."[43]

An exposé published in St. Louis in 1844 by the mayor of a neighboring town in Illinois asserted that Joseph Smith himself had claimed a revelation from God that "the Indians and Latter-Day Saints, under Joe as their king and ruler, were to conquer the Gentiles, and that their subjugation to this authority was to be obtained *by the sword*! . . . It is also a fact, beyond controversy, that the Indian tribes of Sacs and Foxes, Siouxs and Potowattamies, were consulted, and their assent obtained previous to the mock crowning of this unmitigated imposter."[44]

Back in Vermont, an incensed Freemason railed against Mormon claims for damages from Missouri. "We consider all your maneuvering in Missouria was treasonable, and it is evident that you and your clan did consider yourselves a separate nation as much so; as any foreign nation or tribe of Indians would . . . the General government would have no right to grant you any redress, any more than it would any foreign savage tribe of Indians, should they go and fight the Missourians, and were drawn off with the loss of their ponies."[45]

Even sympathetic accounts referred to Indians. The *New York Weekly Herald* led off an account of the declining conditions in Illinois from Rock Island, Illinois, thus: "This place, beautifully situated near the mouth of Rock River, on the banks of the Mississippi, and about 300 miles above St. Louis, is the scene of Black Hawk's career, and that of his forefathers. Here they passed their summers and autumns, in tilling, fishing and hunting; and their winters were whiled away among the buffalo regions in a milder latitude. Their corn-hills and graves are still visible on the banks and bluffs of Rock River, and some remains of their wigwams and huts yet identify their favorite haunts. They were, however, driven out of this lovely spot, and destroyed! Their dwellings were desolated and mostly devoured by the flames of their enemies; but the hills and vallies—the rich bottoms and fertile plains—which, but a few years since, were only trod by the savage and the beast, and rung with the howling of the one and the war-whoop of the other, are now vocal with the voice of civilization and dotted with handsome human dwellings."[46]

Nor was the association limited to Gentiles. When it came to the question of Mormons and violence, Indians were never far in the background. When the apostle Lyman Wight traveled from Illinois to Boston to attend a convention of Mormons in that city, he learned firsthand that intimidation against his faith was not limited to the frontier. Both a female antislavery activist and ruffians in the gallery interrupted the convention. When Wight wrote home that he "thought it best to send some sax & fox Indians to Boston to civilize the city," part of his meaning was clear.[47] Mobbism in Boston demanded a response in kind. But whether Wight imagined Mormons in the role of Sac and Fox Indians, or if he had come to believe, along with other Mormons, that Indians would become the "Battleaxe of the Lord" on their enemies, remains obscure.[48]

Back in Nauvoo, Joseph Smith had had enough of conciliation. "If the mobs come upon you, kill them, I will never restrain you again, but will go and help you," he declared in a council meeting in November of 1843. Brigham Young responded that he "would never put his hand on brother Hosea Stout's shoulder again to hold him back when he was abused."[49] And he did not hold Stout back. In the words of Stout's biographer, he was "a most active and efficient officer in the defense of Nauvoo during all the mobbings and persecutions which culminated in the martyrdom of the Prophet Joseph and others." He had men beaten, and was involved in the murder of at least one anti-Mormon gang leader.[50]

None of this tamed the violence. Gentiles who hoped Smith's murder in 1844 would drive Mormons from the state were dismayed to see increased vitality in Nauvoo, where the Saints were determined to complete a great temple. While the Council of Fifty made a conscious decision to focus on converting Indians, rather than Gentiles, violence between Mormons and Gentiles increased. Stout was at the forefront of the "extralegal defense" of Nauvoo.[51] After the Illinois state legislature repealed the Nauvoo charter and Nauvoo's police force was disbanded, Stout continued to actively protect the city. His unofficial police force severely beat a man for trespassing in the Nauvoo Temple. At the April 1845 general conference of the church, leaders instructed Stout to be ready to "suppress any riot or breach of peace which might happen," and Stout confronted a former Illinois state representative for being "a secret enemy lurking in our midst."[52] The following day, members of a "Whittling society," described as "a gang of twenty or thirty ruffians, with bowie-knives and dirks in their hands whittling sticks" further threatened the former representative. The efforts of Stout and the whittlers caused him to depart the city. Church leaders and the Council of Fifty approved of this type of extralegal protection, even offering a vote of thanks to the "boys" who "whistled the man out of town."[53]

Rumors of Mormon atrocities, including murders by Stout's men, circulated nationally, and were greatly compounded by exposés of Mormon women pressured against their will into polygamous marriages. Martha Brotherton's affidavit that Joseph Smith himself attempted to lead her into a polygamous marriage with Brigham Young was particularly inflammatory, and compelled "readers across the country" to "express their outrage" against the church.[54]

Since classical times, the trope of the endangered female has been employed to stoke outrage among men whose gender identity demands that they protect "helpless" females.[55] In both the Black Hawk War and Mormon Illinois, threats against female chastity justified mob violence in the service of maintaining gender norms. After the circulation of Brotherton's narrative, it became increasingly difficult in Illinois to fight the tide of anti-Mormonism, in part because women's virtue was at stake. Two months after Smith's murder, in August of 1844, Governor Ford turned to Congressman John Hardin, home from his congressional term, to help out with a sticky problem. Ford had to leave the state for two weeks and, given the unsettled state of affairs in Nauvoo, he wondered if Hardin would be willing to step in, if necessary, to contain anti-Mormon violence.[56]

As a US congressman, hero of the Black Hawk War, and militia leader, Hardin was a natural choice. But Ford was also likely to be aware that Hardin's history with Latter-day Saints was complex. As Illinois's leading Whig politician, he had courted the Saints on behalf of the presidential candidate Henry Clay early in the 1844 presidential campaign, before Mormon leaders nominated Joseph Smith as a candidate. And just a few months earlier, he had pledged his support, along with several leading Illinois Democrats in Congress, to a Mormon emigration proposal to Oregon Country, which was jointly controlled by England and the United States.[57] "If any serious difficulties should occur in my absence," Ford specified, "you are hereby authorized to order out such a militia of force of this State as may be sufficient" to "protect all peaceable persona in the enjoyment of their rights under the laws; and suppress all riots and mobs by whomever raised." Recognizing the increasing hysteria in Illinois, he confidentially warned Hardin, "Be careful also that no incendiaries shall have access to your camp for the purpose of infecting the minds of your troops with the spirit of insubordination and mutiny."[58]

When word of a major assault against the sect and countermeasures by Mormons against Gentile neighbors made their way to the governor two months later, Ford turned to Hardin again. Ford, a Democrat, recognized that being seen as protecting Mormons would do nothing for Hardin's reputation in the state, and given that Hardin was Illinois's leading Whig politician, perhaps even a competitor for Ford's job at some point, there was a clear political conflict of interest in Ford ordering a political opponent to damage his and his party's reputation. "The Anti Mormon Party are organizing a great Military Wolf hunt to come off on the 26th and 27th instant," he wrote Hardin. "Their object is to attack the Mormons. I desire to ascertain from you whether you would have any objections to receive order for this service. Some of your friends objected to the last order to you and supposed that I had a design to use you up. . . . God knows that I had no sinister design then or now. I have endeavored my dear sir with all the ingenuity in my power to keep this whole matter free from politics. But I would not wish to force an unwelcome and disagreeable service on you."[59]

Hardin agreed to help Ford. In January 1845, the Illinois House of Representatives withdrew Nauvoo's charter, which ended the Mormon's private militia at exactly the moment when Mormons were most in need of protection. In March the citizens of Nauvoo voted unanimously to incorporate as the town of Nauvoo, and the Mormon elders who made up the town's new board of trustees reinstated the old Nauvoo police force under Hosea Stout. Stout proposed establishing "a picked guard on all the roads leading from Nauvoo to keep our enemies from passing to and from Nauvoo" and in May set to work preparing "in case we should be attacted [attacked] by our enemies."[60] Ford turned to Hardin for a third time. Would Hardin lead troops to Nauvoo, impose the rule of law, even if that meant imposing martial law, and help remove the Mormons from Illinois?[61]

This was no minor request. Ford recognized Hardin's involvement as being potentially politically costly, and Hardin's friends warned him that Ford was attempting to damage his reputation in the state by placing him in the position of protecting the Mormons. Hardin arrived with troops at the end of September, "affirmed that he would take a neutral part in the difficulties and settle them peacefully." Newly published records of the Council of Fifty suggest that Hardin was respectful of Mormon authority, and waited for permission from Stout and other Mormon leaders before investigating reports of stolen property in Nauvoo.[62]

But Hardin's reputation among Gentiles emerged unscathed. My reading of this is that even the most violently anti-Mormon residents of the state trusted Hardin, because they knew about his history in the Black Hawk War. Anti-Mormon forces wanted someone who would "put down the reign of" what one hysterical newspaper report referred to as "this stupendous banditti." They were not disappointed in Hardin's appointment, because they knew he had burned a Sac village to the ground in 1832. "Governor Ford has called out a portion of the militia of the state, and given the command, with discretionary power to settle our difficulties as circumstances may require, to General J. J. Hardin of Jacksonville, formerly member of congress, who is one of the best military officers and most talented and esteemed men of the west," *Niles' National Register* reported. "What measures Gen. Hardin will adopt when he arrives, is of course not known; but we trust there will now be a final settlement and winding up of Mormon troubles in this state."[63]

Hardin led four hundred members of the militia to break up the conflict, and Brigham Young agreed to leave the state in the spring, after completing the temple.[64] That spring, General John Hardin, working in concert with the Saints' police chief Hosea Stout, oversaw the expulsion of the Mormons across state lines. The Mormons praised Stout's "excellent service" in superintending the Mormon "exodus," while the Gentiles of Illinois praised Hardin's "wise and skillful management" of the Mormon displacement. Hardin was credited with putting a stop "to the lawlessness and bloodshed their presence engendered."[65]

Hosea Stout was not a stupid man, and the experience of being persecuted led him to reconsider his participation in the Black Hawk War. At the time, he wrote, he "felt that the interest of my country was above every thing else & I must defend it at the risk of my life and supposed that every one felt the same I did not even suspect that our rulers were full of the political intrigues which I afterwards learned."[66]

Governor Thomas Ford drew a very different lesson from the conflict. Just before his death in 1850, he completed his *History of Illinois*, in which he tried to make sense of antebellum Illinois's remarkable history of vigilante violence, starting with "the horse-thieves and counterfeiters" who "over-ran" the towns of the territory in the years before statehood. "The governor and judges of the territory, seeing the impossibility of executing the laws in the ordinary way, against an organized banditti, who set all law at defiance, winked at and encouraged" vigilante justice. "These regulators in number generally constituted about a captain's company, to which they gave a military organization." They "generally operated at night. When assembled for duty, they marched, armed and equipped as for war, to the residence or lurking-place of a rogue, arrested, tried, and punished him by severe whipping and banishment from the territory." Historians of violence have noted that, in most American communities, vigilante justice is a temporary system that is later replaced by formal institutions of government. Not so in Illinois, where "gangs of rogues" remained, in Ford's account, subject to the necessary punishment of vigilante violence.[67]

"I do not apologize for mobs, all of which I would crush forever, in every part of this free country," Ford wrote. But regardless of the event in question—be it the Black Hawk War; the Mormon War; the 1846 "Regulator War" in which two posses in Southern Illinois, each over one hundred men, set each other's homes on fire, kidnapped, tortured, and killed one another, all in the name of the law; or the infamous 1837 murder of Elijah Lovejoy in Alton, Illinois, by an antiabolitionist mob—he was quite sure who was to blame. Speaking specifically of abolitionists, including Lovejoy, Ford wrote: "No language can be loaded with sufficient severity for the fanatical leaders who, by their violence, by their honest disregard of honest prejudices, drove a peaceful community to a temporary insanity, and to the commission of enormous crimes."[68] And "the same may be said of the Mormons."[69]

Indeed, Ford read, in the history of Illinois, a series of challenges, not to the power of government, but to the power of Illinois men to make their own law through violence. Law and order was undermined by demands for law and order by outsiders who "planted themselves here as firmly as if government was omnipotent, or as if they intended, by way of experiment, to test the power of government to put down the people, on whom alone it rests for support."[70]

In short, Ford blamed Illinois mob violence on its victims; it was the victims who incited a "mobocratic spirit" in the good people of Illinois. "In the year 1840, the people called Mormons came to this state," Ford calmly explained. "Their residence amongst us led to a mobocratic spirit, which resulted in their expulsion."[71] Given Ford's ongoing struggles to prove his masculine virtues, as well as his inability as governor to enforce the rule of law in his own state, it is perhaps understandable that he was willing to blame the victim.[72]

But whatever the problems with his logic, Ford understood clearly that violence begot more violence in Illinois, that success in one battle empowered martial masculinity, and that those who fought the Mormons had themselves been corrupted, in precisely the same way that a young Hosea Stout worried that fighting Indians might corrupt him. "In their long, bitter, and angry contest with the Mormons," Ford wrote, anti-Mormons "had acquired most of the vices of that people, being hurried on by the intensity of bad passions to imitate their crimes, that they might be equal to them in the context. This is one of the inevitable effects of a long-continued faction; and, accordingly, the presence of the Mormons for six years in that part of the country has left moral blotches and propensities to crime, a total dissolution of moral principle among the remaining inhabitants, which one generation passing away will not eradicate, and perhaps will never be effectually cured until they learn by long and dire experience that the way of the transgressor is hard."[73]

Was Hosea Stout right that fighting corrupted a man's character? Was Ford right that the Mormon War left "moral blotches and propensities to crime" and "a total dissolution of moral principle" among the residents of that portion of Illinois? There is certainly an argument to be made that both men were right. Because mere months after Hosea Stout helped lead his people out of Illinois, the United States declared war on Mexico. And nowhere was enthusiasm for war more intense than in Illinois and Missouri. In fact, it was not South Carolina, or Mississippi, or even Texas that sent the most volunteers to Mexico—it was Illinois and Missouri. Illinois's men could not wait to go to Mexico, for glory, if there was to be such. No one expected much of a fight against Mexicans, whom they imagined as not much better than Indians. As one Illinois man wrote to another, Mexico provided "nothing to whip but a parcel of blankeded [sic] half-breeds armed with bows and arrows."[74]

Who should lead the way to Mexico from Illinois? None other than John Hardin. Hardin, colonel of the First Illinois Regiment, was Illinois's very first volunteer. His appointment was a foregone decision after his victory over the Mormons. "You stand very high here with all our Military men and volunteers," one admirer told him.[75] Although in 1845 he was one of Illinois's most avid supporters of Manifest Destiny, once he arrived in Mexico, he lost his appetite for territorial expansion. The problem lay in Mexico's inhabitants, a group that reminded him of a previous military foe. "I have never seen a drunken Mexican," he wrote his law partner back in Illinois. "That is the only good thing I can say about them—they are a miserable race, with a few intelligent men who lord it over the rest. . . . Treachery, deceit & stealing are their particular characteristic—They would make a miserable addition to any portion of the population of the United States."[76] Hardin determined that Mexico was not worth annexing because its native residents were "no better than Indians," and could never be incorporated into the United States. "As for making these Paeons voters & citizens of the United States," he wrote, "it should not be thought of until we are . . . to give all Indians a vote."[77]

US volunteers became notorious in Mexico for their atrocities against Mexican civilians. They burned down towns, desecrated churches, and killed civilians. From the perspective of 1846, it is easy to see that both Ford and Stout were right, and that there was a clear slippage in Illinois, between how Indians, Mormons, and Mexicans were understood and treated, with the result that violent behavior became a habit, a habit that worked to empower a certain martial practice of manhood which promoted the violence that supported it.[78]

Not that Hardin ever participated in extralegal violence in Mexico. He followed the rules of war, and attempted to keep his troops in line, unlike some commanders who turned a blind eye to their men's atrocities. Volunteer vigilantism disturbed him nearly as much as the men of Mexico did.[79]

One possibility Colonel Hardin never mentioned was expelling Mexicans from Mexico, which, while admittedly a ludicrous idea, was an ongoing fantasy among many expansionists, and one grounded in the American experience of Indian removal.[80] Hardin recognized that the presence of Mexicans in Mexico was a settled fact. And because of that, he decided the United States would be better off leaving well enough alone. After Indian removal, and Mormon removal, it is safe to say that he had had quite enough of incompatible populations.

CHAPTER 6

"Like a Swarm of Locusts"

*Perceptions of Mormon Geopolitical Power in
a Non-US West, 1844–1848*

Thomas Richards Jr.

In August 1846, during the first months of the
US–Mexican War, the geopolitical situation in the Mexican territory of Alta
California remained fluid. Although American filibusters had captured the
frontier hamlet of Sonoma on behalf of the United States during the infamous Bear Flag Revolt, and then the US Navy had seized ports along the
California coast, the vastness of the territory meant that the US conquest
remained haphazard and not yet fully assured. In the midst of this uncertainty, Lieutenant Washington Bartlett of the USS *Portsmouth*, which at the
time was anchored in San Francisco Bay, sent a series of off-the-record letters
to Lieutenant Edward Kern. Kern had just assumed command over Sutter's
Fort in the Sacramento Valley, and Bartlett hoped to keep Kern abreast of
the complicated maneuverings of US forces throughout northern California. Yet, in the middle of one of these letters, Bartlett's subject abruptly
changed. Stating that a ship of Mormons had arrived in Yerba Buena (soon
to be renamed San Francisco), Bartlett then took the opportunity to sketch
out the larger implications of this arrival: "There can be little doubt that [the
Mormons] are coming to California like a swarm of Locusts; for my part,
I do not see how such a vast horde of people are to be supported here during
the next year." Bartlett went on to describe the "shrewdness" of the Mormon
leader Sam Brannan, whom he described as playing a "deep game for his
own benefit." Bartlett concluded of the Mormon migrants, "I am certain

they could not have landed, had they arrived before our flag went up. I doubt much whether it pleases [Brannan]—although it does the people."[1]

From these few lines, it is clear that Bartlett believed that the two-hundred-some Mormon seafaring migrants presaged a much larger overland Mormon migration from Nauvoo, Illinois. Tellingly, Bartlett routinely referenced Nauvoo as "Nauvoo," his quotation marks demonstrating that he somehow did not consider the second largest city in Illinois as legitimate. It is also clear that Bartlett doubted Sam Brannan's American patriotism—and, perhaps, the patriotism of other Mormon leaders like Brigham Young—but he still held out hope that the Mormon people as a whole were loyal American citizens who remained pleased at the US flag flying over Yerba Buena. Finally, and most importantly, his comparison of the Mormons to a "swarm of Locusts" and a "vast horde" reveals that he construed the Mormons as a very real geopolitical threat, whose arrival in California would irrevocably ruin the territory's potential prosperity—particularly for recently arrived American immigrants, as well as for the thousands more who would presumably come to the region.

Importantly, Bartlett's fear of the Mormon arrival reflected the fact that he made no presumption about US sovereignty over California. Although he was helping oversee the US conquest, it was not yet militarily assured, and even military victory did not guarantee that the United States would achieve a diplomatic settlement that secured California permanently. Bartlett's attitude was typical of most Americans at the time. While it is likely that a majority of Americans believed in the inevitable demographic triumph of the Anglo-American race over the following decades, the series of political, military, and diplomatic events—beginning with the expansionist James K. Polk's assumption of the Democratic nomination for president in 1844 and culminating with the Treaty of Guadalupe Hidalgo in 1848 that secured the US conquest over half of Mexico's territory—was contingent, contested, and unforeseen. John L. O'Sullivan's supposed prescient discussion of the United States' Manifest Destiny was almost a century off in its forecast, as O'Sullivan claimed that the United States would annex Canada and California "in the fast hastening year of the Lord 1945!"[2] O'Sullivan was typical of Americans at the time, in that no one knew what would happen to the American West.[3]

The Mormon leaders themselves understood the contingency of western geopolitics. Between 1844 and 1847, the Mormons considered moving to Texas, building forts along the Oregon Trail to protect American migrants, allying with Native peoples against the United States (perhaps with the aid of the British), migrating to the California coast, allying with Mexico against the United States, migrating to southern Mexico, migrating to Oregon

Country (which they believed would be controlled by Britain), and allying with the United States against Mexico—the latter they accomplished, resulting in the creation of the Mormon Battalion. While some of these ideas were simply flights of fancy, during their final years in Nauvoo the Mormon leaders devoted considerable attention and resources to others, in particular their 1844 plan to move to Texas and their 1845 plan to ally with Indians. Ultimately, Young and other Mormon leaders chose to migrate to the Salt Lake Valley, but clearly they did not want for other options.[4] These discussions among Mormon leaders involved theology and eschatology, but they also centered on one key on-the-ground assumption: the Mormons possessed very real political, military, and diplomatic power.

Non-Mormons throughout the continent recognized this power, but neither historians of the Mormons nor the larger American West have examined these attitudes seriously, assuming the twin inevitabilities of the US western conquest and the founding of the Mormon Zion in the isolated Great Basin. In this vein, American concerns about Mormon strength can be dismissed as overwrought, unrealistic, or irrelevant; by 1848 the Mormons were ensconced in the Salt Lake Valley, remote but within an expanded United States, so what does it matter if Americans in previous years believed the Mormons would go—or perhaps even seize—some other region on the continent? In essence, this history never came to pass, so the fact that Americans considered it possible can be easily overlooked. Yet examining American attitudes toward Mormon geopolitical power in the mid-1840s provides three important arguments about the place of the Mormons in US and Western history. First, and most simply, in the mid-1840s the Mormons *were* geopolitical players; while many historians of the Mormons have demonstrated that they recognized themselves as such, many other Americans throughout the continent agreed with the Mormon assessment. Indeed, for reasons that were related but not directly linked, both the US policymakers and the Mormons began experiments in expansionism at roughly the same time, and both looked to similar places, most notably Texas, California, and Oregon. Both envisioned substantial western settlement that combined military power with considerable American immigration; in the Mormons' case, this immigration would be augmented by thousands of British Mormons who would join them in the West. Importantly, however, while certain expansionist Americans, particularly those with firsthand knowledge of the Mormons, saw them as competitors in the race to conquer the American West from the outset, the federal policymakers themselves came late to this understanding. Thus, while US and Mormon expansion ran on parallel tracks as early as 1844, it was not until 1846 that these two tracks would fully converge.

Second, while American attitudes toward Mormon geopolitical power were rarely friendly, these attitudes nevertheless differed depending on how far away the Mormons were, and how imminent their presence appeared to be. For Americans in Missouri and Illinois, on the Overland Trail, or living in potential Mormon settlement sites of California and Oregon, Mormon power was something to loathe. For Americans living far from the Mormons, in contrast, Mormon power could be potentially disturbing—but also interesting, and perhaps even beneficial. Indeed, to certain Americans, Mormon migration represented an opportunity for personal, regional, or national gain, particularly because no other coherent and unified force of Anglo-Americans existed on the North American continent.

This latter point leads to a third and final argument: despite more than a decade of hostility and at times outright violence, the Mormons' Americanness remained fluid in the eyes of other Americans. Many Americans, particularly those living in close proximity to the Mormons (or at least potentially so), viewed the Mormons as essentially an anti-American people who were disloyal to the United States and undeserving of the protections of federal and state laws. Yet, for some, principally those living far from the Mormons and/or seeing in Mormon power the potential for personal gain, they remained American. Their whiteness and Anglo-American ethnicity made them trustworthy, whereas various others living in North America—Native peoples, African Americans, Irish immigrants, and Mexicans—were not. These conflicting opinions toward the Mormons' Americanness reflected the fluidity and fragility of Americanness more generally in the Jacksonian era. Certainly, the question of who constituted an American was hardening in these decades; African Americans lost voting rights in many northern states, the Cherokees were expelled from Georgia despite their embrace of American norms, and the Native American Party asserted that Irish Catholics could never assimilate. In all these cases, it was white Americans living near the perceived threat who argued most vociferously for exclusion. Yet in each of these struggles there were also Americans who pushed back against the various attempts to exclude, whether out of moral outrage or personal incentive—or, in many cases, a combination of both, as interests frequently coincided with ideology. Taking a broad viewpoint, the Mormons occupied a similar space as groups like the Cherokees and Irish, in which they existed on a continuum that ran from a feeling of fear and loathing to sympathy and curiosity, and from curiosity and sympathy to friendship and attachment—albeit attachment that was usually self-serving. This continuum was directly correlated to proximity: for Americans living close to the Mormons, they were a group to be dreaded; for those living far from scenes of Mormon

Wars in Illinois and Missouri, the Mormons remained Americans, albeit ambiguously—and, as Americans, they could prove useful. Ultimately, the greater the distance from the Mormons, the more American the Mormons appeared to be.

From the perspective of Americans in the West who were in close proximity to the Mormons or potentially in their migration path, Washington Bartlett's description of the Mormons as a "swarm of Locusts" and a "vast horde" is a good place to start to understand the nature of the Mormon geopolitical threat. The metaphor of a locust swarm was apt in two respects. First, a majority of Americans in the West deplored Mormons just as they deplored locusts. Indeed, locusts embodied a biblical scourge, sent by God as punishment, or perhaps were the work of the devil.[5] More importantly, like locusts, Americans perceived that Mormon strength derived from their unity and their numbers—and, in many ways, they were correct. Although the Church of Jesus Christ of Latter-day Saints was never free from schism, the vast majority of Mormons remained loyal first to Joseph Smith and then to Brigham Young, and the number of adherents to the faith continued to grow. These numbers were impressive: the Mormon population in and around Nauvoo exceeded 10,000, the Nauvoo Legion numbered 3,000 (and was rumored to be almost twice that), and thousands of Mormon converts from the US East and Great Britain would hopefully join this population at some point in the near future.[6] By way of comparison, the *entire* nonnative population in Mexican California numbered 7,000, the population of Oregon's Willamette Valley reached 6,000 in 1846, the Texan Army rarely surpassed 1,000 men during the decade of Texas's independence, and the entire US Army numbered less than 9,000 men in 1844. American newspapers had a penchant for providing these types of demographic figures, meaning that any well-read American would have had concrete knowledge of Mormon strength vis-à-vis populations throughout the rest of the continent.[7]

Moreover, faith and unity of purpose gave the Mormons additional intangible potency that went beyond their already substantial on-the-ground power. While the conflicts in both Missouri and Illinois forced the Mormons from each respective state, in both cases the Mormons had held their own militarily. They were neither defeated nor helpless. Their status stood in contrast to pacifist religious sects like the Shakers, utopian movements like the Owenites, or removed Native Americans in the West. In this respect, the Illinoisan William Richards's solution to the Mormon problem was the exception that proved the rule in regard to perceptions of Mormon geopolitical power. In early 1845, Richards, seemingly a sympathetic and well-intentioned non-Mormon neighbor, wrote Mormon leaders with the suggestion that they petition the federal government for a *"Reserve* to be set apart . . . for the Mormon people."[8] While Richards originally suggested a region in Wisconsin Territory, he believed anywhere would do so long as it lay beyond the borders of any state. Wherever they established this reserve, the Mormons could "erect" a "glorious little commonwealth."[9] Richards believed "24 miles square" would be sufficient for Mormon needs, a rather small amount of land for thousands of people. Richards's inspiration came from the Indian removal in the 1830s, during which the Five Tribes in the US South were forced west to Indian Territory.[10] By suggesting a sort of "Mormon removal," Richards demonstrated that he did not believe the Mormons were a substantial geopolitical threat to US interests. Rather, the Mormons were no more powerful than defeated Indian nations confined to reserves—a geopolitical situation Supreme Court Chief Justice John Marshall famously defined as "domestic dependent nations."[11]

Richards's letter was unique, for no other outside observer believed Mormon power was so insignificant, nor the Mormon threat so easily solved. No other observer equated the Mormons to "dependent" Indian nations. On the contrary, most Americans supposed the Mormons to be quite independent, and believed that wherever the Mormons settled, they could immediately assume control of the region. And, because the Mormons were unclear on their destination until early 1846, and then Mormon leaders deliberately kept their intentions ambiguous in public even after they had agreed on the Salt Lake Valley in private, Americans in the West believed that the Mormon swarm could descend anywhere. This fear was particularly acute for those Americans who either originated from regions that experienced "Mormon troubles," or those who believed the Mormons were coming their way— oftentimes, of course, these people were one and the same. For example, the editor of the *Platte Argus* in Missouri feared for friends who had migrated to Oregon, for the Mormons would arrive and "place the balance of power in their hands." Because the Mormons were "thieves and murderers," the editor pleaded for the local Missouri population to prevent the Mormons from emigrating.[12] The Illinoisan Thomas Sharp, editor of the vehemently anti-Mormon *Warsaw Signal*, warned that if the Mormons were allowed to proceed to California, they would "set up an independent government," and with "hate in their hearts" they would create a "sacerdotal tyranny."[13] The *St. Joseph Gazette* of Missouri believed the Mormon quest for an independent empire would "undoubtedly" be successful, because "they are more united now than ever."[14] In Mexican California, the US consul Thomas Larkin received word from a fellow merchant in Boston that ten thousand Mormons were on their way to the territory, and warned that he should "look out for an avalanche."[15] Larkin's anticipation of the Mormons' imminent arrival is apparent in various letters he wrote during the ensuing months.[16]

Whether the Mormons chose Oregon or coastal California, their arrival would be particularly terrible for the hundreds and thousands of non-Mormon American migrants, for, as one observer put it, there existed "hatred between [the Mormons] and all and every other emigrant from Missouri and Illinois."[17] Indeed, for Americans on the Overland Trail, the idea that thousands of Mormons were out there *somewhere* hovered as an ongoing threat. One writer remembered that rumors floated throughout the wagon trains that the Mormons were traveling five-thousand strong to California, and "they marched with ten brass field-pieces, and that every man of the party was armed with a rifle, a bowie-knife, and a brace of large revolving pistols. It was declared that they were inveterately hostile to the emigrant parties; and when the latter came up to the Mormons, they intended to attack and murder them."[18] After losing his cattle to a stampede of oxen, one migrant equated Mormons with Indians, pondering "whether it was Indians or Mormons, or a section of a herd of buffaloes."[19] For Lilburn Boggs, former Missouri governor and author of the infamous extermination order against Mormons in the late 1830s, this threat was personal. Boggs had originally planned to travel to California, but once he learned that the Mormons were planning to travel to the same destination, he abruptly decided on Oregon instead so as not to cross the Mormons' path.[20] No other emigrants are recorded as altering their route because of the Mormon flight, but the Mormon threat nevertheless remained ever-present at the back of people's minds.[21]

To Americans who supported US conquest of the West, not only would the Mormons immediately swamp the local population—wherever that locality was—but their arrival would act as a check on US expansionist aims. This attitude allowed concerns about Mormon migration to spread beyond western localities to eastern population centers. In early 1846, a correspondent for the *New York Tribune* asked: "Don't you think . . . that these Mormons will make a sorry nucleus on which to build a great, enlightened, and virtuous republic on the shores of the Pacific? Do you suppose, because some of the founders of some of the greatest republics and empires in ancient times were great rascals, such facts are precedents for permitting these Mormons to start an independent community within *our* territory of Oregon?"[22] A story in *Niles' National Register* echoed these sentiments: "Concentrated in any place west of the Rocky Mountains, such a body of men, led by the mystic influence of fanaticism and driven by the sword of a modern Mahomet, leagued probably with a foreign power, would make themselves formidable if not dangerous neighbors."²³

The phrase "leagued probably to a foreign power" likely referenced Great Britain, and the author of this article was not alone in doing so. The Mormons' perceived affinity for Britain was crucial for many who believed the Mormons threatened US expansion, particularly in 1845 and early 1846, when it was still rumored that Mormons would go to an Oregon Country that remained ambiguously shared between the United States and Britain, even as expansionist US newspapers claimed it as *"ours."* Once again, the concern was most immediate in Illinois and Missouri, and newspapers in these regions expressed the belief that the Mormons would undoubtedly seek to place Oregon under the British flag. For example, the *Sangamo Journal* of Illinois stated the case succinctly: "[The Mormons] are said to number 18,000, are bitterly hostile to the Government of the United States, and many of them are Englishmen, and are likely . . . to act in concert with the British and all of their designs."²⁴ The editors of the *Platte Argus* of Missouri felt the implications did not need to be stated, for it was obvious that the Mormons would favor the British Oregon, writing that once the Mormons arrived in Oregon, "it is easy to guess whether the interests of the United States or those of Great Britain would suffer by such a state of things."²⁵ Farther away, Americans did not consider that the Mormons would take such deliberate pro-British actions in Oregon, but at the least their eighteen thousand British converts made a British Oregon more likely.²⁶ As one Kentuckian noted, "[The Mormons] may . . . become British subjects when the vexed Oregon question is settled. I understand many foolish Englishmen left the [?] comforts of home to join the infatuate Mormons three years ago."²⁷ These fears diminished in the aftermath of the Oregon Treaty in the summer of 1846, but they nevertheless demonstrated that some Americans viewed the Mormons as a people who would facilitate further British intervention on the continent.

And yet, for all the sentiment that the Mormon swarm threatened both Americans as a people and the interests of the United States in the West, some observers saw the Mormons in a more ambiguous light—one that was not necessarily favorable, but that did not presume the Mormons were necessarily anti-American either. After all, the vast majority of Mormons *were* Americans; even as religion fundamentally divided Mormon from Gentile in the United States, both peoples shared the same culture, history, and language. Indeed, the Mormons themselves argued for their Americanness in the 1830s in Missouri and in the early 1840s in Illinois as the reason why they deserved federal endorsement and protection from local anti-Mormon forces.[28] This attitude decidedly shifted in the aftermath of Joseph Smith's death, as Mormon leaders blamed the United States for the murder, and even voiced a desire to "wipe [Americans] out of existence."[29] However, vitriol against the United States was only expressed in private. Publicly, the Mormon leaders were careful to maintain a patriotic facade in order to secure American acquiesce for a western migration, pleading that they were a "disfranchised people" who only wanted to find a permanent asylum either inside the United States or beyond its borders.[30] In a letter to state governors asking for their aid or at least opinion, the Mormon leaders expressed a desire to find a home in the West "where the hand of oppression shall not . . . extinguish every patriotic feeling."[31] Publicly, at least, *some* patriotic feeling remained. Thus, Americans having no prior experiences with the Mormons needed to weigh two conflicting versions of Mormon intentions. Either the Mormons remained American patriots as they proclaimed, meaning they still supported US interests on the continent, or the anti-Mormons were correct, and the Mormons were insidious, disloyal fanatics who hoped to undermine US power. Or perhaps the truth was somewhere in the middle. Because of these ambiguities, Americans who were personally unfamiliar with the Mormons could be found on all sides of the issue.

Some Americans bought the Mormons' public expression of US patriotism wholesale. In early 1846, the *Ottawa Free Trader* printed the observations of one traveler passing through Nauvoo, who wrote: "It is expected that [the Mormons] will assemble some 30 or forty thousand strong on the plains of California, and save Uncle Sam the trouble of negotiating for that province."[32] Similar to most who wrote on the Mormons, this writer believed that Mormon numbers gave them the power to seize any region to which they migrated, but he differed in his assumption that a Mormon California would also inevitably be a US California. At the end of his article, it was clear how he came to this belief: "Those who have left Hancock county are as true hearted and patriotic a band of Americans as I ever met, and they scout the idea of carrying any other flag than the 'stars and stripes.' 'They may expel us from the land,' observed one of the rank and file, 'but they cannot drive from our hearts the love of county.'" The *Ottawa Free Trader* described this observer as a "gentleman who is spending a week or two at Nauvoo"; in essence, he was unfamiliar with and unaffected by the years of conflict around Nauvoo, and did not sense the Mormon hostility toward the United States. Ultimately, it seems, this writer believed the patriotic statements of Mormon leaders, and assumed Mormon migration automatically facilitated US expansion.

Other distant (or at least unfamiliar) observers of the Mormons were not as enthusiastic about their US patriotism. The Mormons may have remained American, but it was an ambiguous Americanness, one that other Americans would not necessarily welcome. Thomas Larkin demonstrated this ambiguity best when he predicted that California would soon be under the US flag, and in a letter to the *New York Sun* offered four ways this could happen: "First a fair sale of the Country to the US. . . . Second, by War. . . . Third. By emigration by land. . . . Fourth & last—not the least but the Worst the Mormons. We understand that Narvoo is vacuated and the whole Mormonery is in motion, having found out that C. [California] is the promised land."[33] On the surface, Larkin's was yet another negative portrayal of Mormon migration, yet he still regarded the Mormons as Americans, and thus thousands of Mormons arriving in California would provide for US annexation, albeit in its worst form. Larkin was clearly no Mormon apologist, but neither did he fear that Mormons were trying to secure independence for themselves or that they were working in the interests of Great Britain.

Unlike Larkin, Illinois governor Thomas Ford did believe the Mormons would seek political independence in the West, but he still believed that the Mormons' background as Americans—in particular, *white* Americans—would allow them to assert geopolitical strength far beyond their numbers. When the Mormons sought information from Ford and other state governors on a potential western migration, Ford urged them to go to California, for "it is sparsely inhabited and by none but the Indian or imbecile mexican spaniard." Ford continued, "Why would it not be a pretty operation for your people to go out there, take possession of and conquer a portion of the vacant country and establish an independant government of your own?"[34] Ford disdained the Mormon faith and had little love for the Mormon people, but he clearly believed their Anglo-American background would make the Mormon conquest of California easy. Within US borders, the Mormons were a people apart—a status that Ford, as Illinois governor, understood all too well—but once they moved among Native Americans and "imbecile" Mexicans, Ford believed their superior ethnic background would assert itself. In essence, the farther they traveled from the United States, the more American the Mormons became.

While the anonymous gentleman passing through Nauvoo, Larkin, and Ford made passive predictions about the future of the Mormons on the continent, others actively hoped to employ the Mormons' American background as a potential geopolitical asset. As in Ford's assessment, distance mattered: overlanders or California inhabitants such as Larkin potentially confronting the Mormons directly were immensely concerned with their presence, but

Americans living a distance from the Mormons envisioned them more as a benefit than a danger. No one demonstrated this more than the Texas president Sam Houston. In 1844 Houston negotiated with Mormon emissaries over a potential mass Mormon migration to Texas, and may have been the first non-Mormon living outside of Missouri and Illinois to fully contemplate the potential military might of the Mormons. Houston governed a country in dire straits, with immigration from the United States stalled, an economy in shambles, and a vengeful Mexico refusing to recognize Texan independence.[35] Seemingly knowing little about the Mormon faith, Houston recognized that the Nauvoo Legion would provide a valuable bulwark against Mexican aggression. Assuring the Mormons that their rights would be respected, Houston reportedly "would receive the *Mormon Legion* in Texas as armed emigrants, with open arms."[36] The double emphasis on Mormon military power ("Mormon *Legion*," "*armed* emigrants") revealed that Houston's motivations were hardly an offer of sanctuary to an oppressed religious minority. Houston was echoed by his friend, the Texas land speculator John Walton, who wrote to Joseph Smith: "Had we a man of your energy at the head of affairs, supported by such a force as you could bring into the field, we might crush [Mexico] at a blow."[37] While unstated, it is clear that both Houston and Walton valued the Mormons' background as Americans, for presumably they would augment and integrate with the majority of the Anglo-Texas population, which was also formerly American—their difference of faith notwithstanding. Indeed, Walton believed that if the Mormons came en masse, they would make Texas "no longer a servile dependent on the haughty Briton or fickle Gaul," and the new republic would "stand alone unsupported and unsurpassed in wealth, power, and resources by any nation on the globe."[38] That Walton wanted to counter Britain and France through Mormon migration pointed to an unwritten corollary to his letter: because the Mormons shared American heritage and culture with Anglo-Texans, they could work together toward a common goal. Presumably, whatever reservations Houston and Walton had about Mormonism as a faith or the Mormons as a people took a back seat to the immediate weakness—and potential strength, with Mormon aid—of Texas on the international stage. In this respect, two American peoples could unite around the common cause of making Texas a powerful and prosperous American republic.

Due to both Texas's annexation to the United States and Joseph Smith's murder in the midst of Mormon-Texan negotiations, nothing came of these fledgling connections, but Houston and Walton were not alone in envisioning the Mormons as some sort of American paramilitary force that could further specific geopolitical goals on the continent. For example, Charles Lovell, a merchant from Ipswich, Massachusetts, wrote to Brigham Young to urge him to colonize San Francisco Bay. Lovell noted that the location was the "best, strongest, and safest harbor" on the West Coast, and there the Mormons could supply whaling ships and take advantage of the cheap cattle available in Monterey. Once the Mormons increased in numbers, Lovell believed they would have "entire mastery of the country, and might bid defiance to [their] persecutors."[39] Lovell cared little for the Mormon plight—indeed, he noted in his letter that he believed their faith was "erroneous"—but this faith would presumably not affect his own merchant business. To Lovell, a Mormon colony in San Francisco would facilitate trade between Boston and California, of which he would take obvious advantage. California's economic potential remained relatively untapped for most New England merchants, and presumably the Mormons would provide a reliable trading partner in the territory.[40] And, because they were Americans, Lovell believed that a Mormon would invariably be appointed US consul in California.[41] Ultimately, it served Lovell's personal interest to see the Mormons as Americans; this outweighed any concerns about the Mormons' "erroneous" faith.

Even more ambitious than Lovell in his geopolitical predictions was the infamous Duff Green. Green had made a name for himself as a politician, journalist, entrepreneur, and confidant of various powerful Democratic politicians over the previous two decades, and was an influential clandestine diplomat for President John Tyler first in Britain and then in Texas. In 1847 Green hoped to reap profits from copper mining in St. Domingo, and believed that an American colony on the island would facilitate his business deals. He turned to the Mormons, writing the Mormon leader Charles Dana that the Mormons should colonize St. Domingo and "alter the government to meet their own views." Green praised the climate of the island, noting that "there is no other place in the face of the habitable ground(?) on which the persecuted Mormons would establish with any prospect of becoming an independent and sovereign nation."[42] Looking back, Green's plan may seem outlandish, but he was unquestionably serious at the time, even offering to travel with the Mormons to St. Domingo to "explore the country and make a contract of colonization." Like Houston and Lovell, Green believed the Mormons' American heritage and—stated more explicitly than Houston or Lovell—their Anglo-American racial background would provide for their success in conquering St. Domingo. "When we see what our armies are doing in Mexico we may anticipate what such a body of our people would do in the midst of a people similar in all respects to those of Mexico."[43] The double "our" ("our armies," "our people") demonstrates that, at least to Green, the Mormons were still Americans, and even if they could no longer remain in the United States, their Americanness could prove geopolitically—and therefore economically—useful somewhere else.[44]

Ensconced in his fort in the Sacramento Valley, the Swiss settler John Sutter possibly shared Green's attitude toward the Mormons, although Sutter hoped they would come to California rather than St. Domingo. Sutter would eventually make use of Mormon labor when he hired eighty men from the Mormon Battalion after they were discharged from service, but Sutter's ambitions in regard to the Mormons may at first have been as much geopolitical as economic. Before the US conquest of California, Sutter had essentially created his own private fiefdom in the Sacramento Valley, and his fort and subjugation of local Native peoples had made his power all but unassailable by both the Mexican government and local *Californios*. In 1841 he had threatened the California governor that he would create his own "independent republic," and embraced his brief stint as a brevet colonel in the Mexican Army in 1845 when he tried to help suppress a Californio revolt against Mexico.[45] As US forces conquered California in the summer of 1846, Sutter chafed at his newly subordinate role under the aforementioned Edward Kern, and it was at this point that he first mentioned the Mormons, writing to a confidant that the "Mormons could not get ready this year."[46] By the following summer, Sutter recommended to Sam Brannan that the Mormons should come to the Sacramento Valley, information which Brannan then relayed to the Mormon leaders in Winter Quarters in Nebraska Territory. As Wilford Woodruff put it, "Captain Sutter was vary friendly & wished us to come and Settel near him."[47] Importantly, this message came *before* the arrival of ex–Mormon Battalion soldiers who would prove to be Sutter's best workers. Certainly, the ever-manipulative Brannan may also have been exaggerating Sutter's suggestion, but it seems likely that Sutter was at least contemplating the Mormons as geopolitical allies. Sutter's power and support among American settlers in California had rapidly eroded after he failed to defeat the 1845 Californio rebellion, but a Mormon migration offered a new set of allies—ones that, crucially, did not see eye to eye with Sutter's newly unwelcome American neighbors. Sutter would not have failed to notice that the first Mormons who traveled inland from San Francisco were "armed with rifles and revolvers to defend themselves against hostile Indians."[48] Of course, without concrete evidence, Sutter's plans with the Mormons remain ultimately unprovable, but this instance would neither have been the first nor the last time Sutter possessed grandiose geopolitical ambitions.

Outside of states such as Illinois and Missouri that had been affected by Mormon settlement, predictions of—and plans for—Mormon power in

North America were not ubiquitous. Rather, they were confined to a small set of men who sought US conquest of the continent or at least contemplated the nature of North American geopolitics. Yet the above predictions were remarkable for their geographic diversity. Inhabitants of New England, Washington, DC, California, Texas, and Oregon all thought about where the Mormons would settle, and what would happen when they arrived. It is no surprise, then, that one other person used to thinking geopolitically also considered Mormon power on the continent: President James K. Polk. According to his heavily self-edited diary, Polk did not think about the Mormons for the first year of his presidency, which was quite typical for most Americans living far from the "Mormon troubles." Indeed, the Illinois senator James Semple even warned Polk to prevent Mormon migration in early 1846—notice again another westerner concerned with Mormon geopolitical power—but Polk demurred, claiming he had no authority to prevent emigration based on religion, even if Mormonism was "absurd."[49]

A few months later, however, the United States was at war with Mexico, and potential war with Britain over Oregon Country loomed, making Polk more receptive to concerns about Mormon power on the continent. The person who brought the issue to his attention was Thomas Kane, a Philadelphian with connections to Polk and the Democratic Party, who had struck up an acquaintance with Jesse Little, the new head of the Eastern States Mission that was designed to convert Americans in New England and the Mid-Atlantic states.[50] Whether Kane believed the Mormons were a real threat is debatable, but he clearly understood that playing up Mormon geopolitical power was the best tactic to facilitate Polk's intervention on behalf of the Mormons. At Kane's urging, Little wrote Polk a letter that tactfully but forcefully discussed potential Mormon hostility toward the United States, and even hinted at a foreign alliance: "[The Mormons] . . . are true hearted Americans, true to our country, true to its laws, true to its glorious institutions—and we have a desire to go under the outstretched wings of the American Eagle. We would disdain to receive assistance from a foreign power—although it should be proffered—unless our government shall turn us off in this great crisis and will not help us, but compel us to be foreigners."[51] Polk took the hint, writing in his diary that he needed to "conciliate" the Mormons, and "prevent this singular sect from becoming hostile to the U.S."[52] For two years before this meeting, Mormon expansion and US expansion had proceeded on similar paths, as both Mormon leaders and Polk and his Democratic allies had employed external diplomacy and internal rhetoric to lay the groundwork for their respective geopolitical strategies, but these paths had not yet crossed. Now, with Polk's awakening to the Mormon threat, they did.

Thus, the creation of the famed Mormon Battalion was set in motion, which is a story that has been frequently told and does not need to be related here. However, historians have missed the wider geopolitical significance of the Mormon Battalion. Polk's decision to "conciliate" the Mormons demonstrates that concerns over Mormon geopolitical power had spread to the highest office in the United States.[53] In essence, Polk's agreement with the Mormons proved that Mormon geopolitical strength—or at least its threat—was very real. Indeed, Polk's actions were akin to a military alliance with a foreign power, and not an emigrating body of religious dissenters. Moreover, as we have seen, Polk's attitude toward the Mormons was hardly unique; Sam Houston, Duff Green, Thomas Larkin, and other Americans living throughout the continent also believed Mormon unity and military strength made them formidable geopolitical players. And, once again, the Mormons' American background, cultural affinity, and racial whiteness allowed them to move quickly from potential enemies to actual allies; it is impossible to imagine Polk making a similar decision with various Native peoples, or the *Nuevomexicanos* or *Californios*, some of whom may also have been willing to fight against Mexico if properly courted.

As the Mormon exodus progressed, the US–Mexican War continued, and the Mormon Battalion served faithfully throughout the conflict, public opinion about the Mormons underwent a rapid shift, in which the Mormons transformed from potentially dangerous (or, for a few Americans, advantageous) geopolitical actors to a loyal and sympathetic—albeit misguided—group of American religious dissidents. This transformation was the result of a savvy public relations campaign orchestrated by Thomas Kane and other reformers he had enlisted in the cause. Kane and his allies planted sympathetic columns in various newspapers throughout the country, emphasizing both the current destituteness of Mormon emigrants and their previous unjust treatment at the hands of the United States.[54] Even more importantly from a geopolitical perspective, Brigham Young's choice that Zion would be built in the Great Basin helped alleviate the concerns of most Americans about Mormon aggression on the continent. The Salt Lake Valley was exceedingly remote and seemingly inhospitable, and it remained a question whether the Mormon settlement could even survive on a permanent basis. Moreover, the United States possessed very little knowledge of the Great Basin's Native peoples, ensuring that fears of a Mormon-Indian alliance diminished not only due to distance, but also to ignorance.[55] And, even if the Mormons did remain a distant concern for some Americans, the many triumphs of US forces against Mexico and the unprecedented expansion of the US state gave Americans more confidence, particularly in the West, that the federal government could handle potential Mormon perfidy. Essentially, by moving to the remote Salt Lake Valley at the same time as US conquest enveloped it, the Mormons took the geopolitical question off the table—at least in the immediate future. What would happen in a decade was anyone's guess.

There continued to be exceptions to this portrayal, of course. In the summer of 1847, the *Washington Journal of Commerce* printed a false report that the Mormon Battalion and other Mormon settlers in California had "risen up and rebelled against the American government . . . taken possession of the country . . . and established an independent government of their own."[56] The news quickly reverberated throughout the American press. While some newspaper editors believed the rumor was false, others expressed their concern.[57] In one of the more remarkable responses, the *Morning News* of Connecticut welcomed the Mormon rebellion. According to this paper, the Mormon "vagabonds" were bound to make trouble at some point, and "it is better for them to do it now, than to wait till they strengthen themselves by additions to their numbers, and thus increase their power to do mischief."[58] Another newspaper explained that the report was quite logical, for "the Mormons, prior to the origin of the Mexican war, had designed to establish an empire in California."[59] Yet the use of the past tense was revealing ("had designed"), for it demonstrated that the Mormons were not "establishing an empire" in the present.

When it was determined that it was only a rumor, newspapers quickly printed the story as false, one that had germinated from a person who felt "distrust of, and enmity to the Mormons."[60] Again, the language was telling, for it singled out one person whose anti-Mormon beliefs somehow put him outside the mainstream of American society—never mentioning that this person voiced opinions that would have been mainstream only one year prior, when most Americans felt "enmity" to the Mormons. The paper was implicitly correct, however, for a positive image of the Mormons *had* become mainstream by 1847. Not only were the Mormons no longer a geopolitical threat, but Americans even praised them for their industriousness, order, and ability to flourish in the inhospitable Salt Lake Valley. Even the *United States Magazine and Democratic Review*, hardly a Mormon apologist, deemed the title Deseret "quaint," and described the Mormons as "very regular, well-informed, well-disposed, and hospitable people."[61] So much for the Mormons as a "swarm of locusts"—instead, the Mormons acted as a salve for the excesses of the chaotic late Jacksonian age.

The only observers on the continent (besides Duff Green with his outlandish St. Domingo proposal) who truly believed the Mormons remained geopolitical opportunists were British officials of the Hudson's Bay Company, in particular the governor-in-chief Sir George Simpson.[62] In 1846 the Hudson's Bay Company opened up a fledgling trade with the first few thousand Mormons who had arrived in Salt Lake City. While Simpson at first had little hope for this commerce, by 1847 he was worried that the Mormons would not be able to survive in the inhospitable and isolated Great Basin, and would seek another site for settlement. Because the Mormons had at one point stated publicly that Vancouver Island was the destination of their exodus, and because British Mormons had petitioned Queen Victoria for a place of settlement in 1846, Simpson wrote, "We are not without apprehension they may follow up their original intention." If the Mormons did so, "it would be quite impossible for us, even if assisted by the natives, to dislodge them." Using the same verb as Polk had when creating the Mormon Battalion, Simpson decided to "conciliate" the Mormons by continuing to trade with them, providing for their survival and therefore permanence in the Salt Lake Valley.[63] With Vancouver Island secured for Great Britain via the Oregon Treaty, there was no need for the British to use the Mormons as a bulwark against US expansion—the alliance that so many Americans had feared two years before. Simpson's rather late consideration of Mormon power was typical of British geopolitical ventures in North America during these years, which were almost always behind those of a newly aggressive United States. Indeed, Great Britain's maneuverings in Texas, California, Mexico, and Oregon had gained them little besides the northern half of Oregon Country, and demonstrated that the British were not nearly as concerned with these far-off regions as was the much closer United States. If Simpson or any other British official had considered employing the Mormons toward British ends before the middle of 1846, when Polk's aggressive expansionist measures took full form, perhaps the Mormon exodus and the larger geopolitics of North America would have been different. Of course, perhaps it was once again the Mormons' Americanness (notwithstanding their thousands of British converts) which persuaded British officials that pursuing such an alliance was not worth the effort.

Taking seriously the often-distraught but at times opportunist attitudes toward Mormon geopolitics in the mid-1840s allows us to witness the United States, American identity, and a North American continent in profound flux. Americans did not see Mormons as friends or allies—but, due to the Mormons' American background, many did not yet see the Mormons as enemies either. The United States appeared to be on the verge of spectacular military and diplomatic successes on the continent—but there was an equally likely possibility that US borders would permanently stop at the Rockies. Moreover, American attitudes toward Mormon power validate the Mormon consideration of their own potential geopolitical influence; Joseph Smith and Brigham Young's grandiose plans seem much less unrealistic when one realizes that non-Mormons took these plans just as seriously as the Mormons did. Of course, in the end Mormon geopolitical power in the mid-1840s proved the dog that did not bite due to the Mormon leaders' choice to migrate to the remote Great Basin. There, the Mormons could remain, within US borders but far from American population centers, until Zion's spectacular success made Mormon power an issue that the US federal government could no longer ignore. In the 1850s, the Mormons would reassert their geopolitical power—and so would the United States.[64]

CHAPTER 7

"In the Style of an Independent Sovereign"

Mid-Nineteenth-Century Mormon Martial Law
Proclamations in American Political Culture

BRENT M. ROGERS

Nineteenth-century Americans imbued their republican rhetoric with both fascination and fear of the exercise of power. Born out of resistance to British tyranny, the United States embraced a republican system of self-government to restrain despotism.[1] The framers of the US Constitution inserted into that document guarantees of republican government wherein the military would remain subordinate to civil authority.

Republican ideology instilled in Americans an ardent distrust of arbitrary power.[2] The concept and use of martial law fit into that worldview. Americans frequently referenced the legacy of British tyranny as they conceptualized martial law, or the concentration of power in the hands of a military commander.[3] In the 1850s, for example, the Massachusetts state legislature debated the legality and necessity of martial law. In doing so, one state legislator noted: "It will be recollected that at one period during the revolutionary war, Gen. [Thomas] Gage proclaimed martial law in the city of Boston, and the inhabitants were smarting under the recollection of the violence and wrong committed under this law."[4] Using this revolutionary-era example, Massachusetts lawmakers sought to prevent the abrogation of civil law, individual liberties, and republican politics. Other antebellum Americans also questioned whether local, state, or federal governments could declare martial law and remained wary of its implications for local civil authority. Many used the idea of martial law as a rhetorical device to warn against the excessive expansion of centralized power at a time when suspicion of federal authority grew more intense in American political culture.[5] In the American federal system, civil authority was supreme and, using republican rhetoric, many viewed martial law as a dangerous, dictatorial power—even the antithesis of civil government and constitutional liberties.

Most nineteenth-century Americans believed that military rule ran counter to republican ideology and practice, but republicanism was a protean concept in antebellum American political culture. Americans also mustered republican rhetoric to support martial law when they believed it necessary to preserve the Union and protect American interests in an expanding and increasingly diverse society. For instance, in 1843 Congress retroactively cleared Andrew Jackson from the fine levied on him for his illegal issuance of martial law in New Orleans during the War of 1812 and in so doing declared his actions both heroic and necessary. In the antebellum years, Americans frequently invoked the idea that the "strong arm of the military" was a suitable governing power in times of defense and for the public safety, though typically with the caveat that once the threat was subdued the military would relinquish authority to civil government.[6] In hindsight, Andrew Jackson's proponents could tout his military actions as heroic because his troops ceded their military authority to civil officers after the British threat was defeated. Republican rhetoric was thus contingent when it came to discourse about martial law in antebellum America.

It was not just rhetoric, however, that was contingent. The rights of individuals were also dependent on local, state, and national government to inculcate and protect. Martial law could be constructed as both republican and antirepublican, but in antebellum America, power was often needed to enforce the republicanism and rights (or interests) of the majority. In the negotiation of protection and authority in the antebellum United States, perceived threats to civil and political liberties often informed the environment that contributed to martial law declarations.

Martial law was a subject without true legal status. It was a proclamation, a statement of weakness and necessity. It was the suspension of law, but not a legal creation.[7] Who could proclaim martial law and under what circumstances engendered enduring and elusive debates. It meant something different to different groups of Americans at different times. Whether most Americans deemed martial law to be acceptable was dependent upon varying circumstances. As this chapter will show, Americans generally tolerated declarations of martial law when necessary to safeguard the majority. However, when a minority group, like the Latter-day Saints, made such a proclamation, difficulties ensued.

In the 1840s and 1850s, municipal and territorial authorities declared martial law on many occasions within the United States. Two of those occurrences involved members of the Church of Jesus Christ of Latter-day Saints. Set against the context of contemporaneous debates about martial law, the Mormon cases illuminate antebellum power politics and the perception of Latter-day Saints, and minority groups generally, in the era's American political culture. This was a time in United States history when Americans had begun forcefully occluding certain minority groups from the privileges of republicanism, particularly after the acquisition of Mexican lands in the Treaty of Guadalupe Hidalgo. The duality of rhetoric surrounding martial law elucidates a shifting American mindset, one that simultaneously clung to the revolutionary-era ideology invested in a weak government of popular will while moving toward an increasing acceptance of state power. The tensions among local, state, and federal governments in dealing with martial law declarations reveal the fragility of sovereignty in antebellum America. The Mormon martial law cases thus emphasize the delicate and ongoing negotiation of establishing and exercising power at a critical time in the nation's history.

Prior to the first issuance of martial law for Mormons in June 1844, debates about martial law had emerged in two significant episodes: the so-called Dorr Rebellion in Rhode Island and the congressional debates over refunding Andrew Jackson's fine. As early as the summer of 1841, Thomas Wilson Dorr had become the public face of a movement to revise Rhode Island's 1663 charter, a foundational British document that still governed the state. The charter required that voters own landed property valued at $134 or more, meaning that some 60 percent of adult white males were excluded from the ballot by the early 1840s.[8] Therefore, the colonial charter that remained in force was, according to Dorr and others, inconsistent with a republican form of government. Instead, the charter represented the lingering legacy of a British monarchy that thwarted the popular will. Dorr sought to alter the government to include universal white-male suffrage. He convened a convention to draft a new state constitution and then organized elections independent of the general state election that was to be held in November 1841. As a result, his supporters created a rival state government, called the People's Government, with Dorr as governor. In the legitimate state election, voters selected Samuel Ward King as governor. In late June 1842, Governor King declared martial law in Rhode Island and the state legislature requested that the federal government send troops to help defend against a planned attack by Dorr's followers on the state arsenal in Providence.

Dorr's raid ended unsuccessfully, but the rhetoric about martial law and the nature of sovereign power was significant. The well-known columnist John L. O'Sullivan wrote in favor of Dorr's movement because of his belief that "sovereignty resided in the people" and "resistance to tyranny is a right—nay, a duty—inscribed upon our hearts by Providence."[9] Dorr's proponents expected civil government to represent the people's will, but they believed it had not. When they rebelled, the civil government in turn enacted martial law to restrain Dorr's efforts. Andrew Jackson, the former president who was quite familiar with martial law and was at that time in the throes of his own battle over the questions of use of power in American government, weighed in on the Rhode Island situation. "The people are the sovereign power," Jackson wrote to a confidant in May 1842, "and agreeable to our system they have the right to alter and amend their system of Government when a majority wills it, as a majority have a right to rule."[10] Similarly, then Pennsylvania senator James Buchanan argued that the people "are the source of all power; they are the rightful authors of all constitutions." The people, Buchanan declared further, "are not for ever to be shackled by their own servants."[11] Such understandings of the people as sovereign demonstrated the enduring importance of revolutionary ideology into the antebellum era.[12] In Rhode Island, however, Dorr's opponents viewed the people's will as a threat to tradition and used martial law to restore order. Federal legislators had mixed reactions to events in Rhode Island. Seeing Governor King's martial law declaration as necessary for the public good, one congressman proclaimed that the "State had been put under martial law; and that had saved them . . . from entire desolation."[13] In practice in Rhode Island, the action for and rhetoric of popular sovereignty had failed and strong state authority prevailed.

Alongside the events in Rhode Island, US legislators debated Andrew Jackson's own use of martial law in 1814. In his defense of New Orleans and the southern coast during the War of 1812, Jackson acquired the dubious honor of becoming the first US general to declare martial law. In so doing, Jackson arrested civilians, suspended the issuance of writs of habeas corpus, censored the press, and confiscated and destroyed private property. Though his detractors dubbed him "King Andrew the First," Jackson "believed that declaring martial law at New Orleans had saved the city from capture and possible destruction" and that his decision to subvert civil liberties in fact was imperative to the survival of the Union.[14] The US district court levied a hefty $1,000 fine against the general in 1815 for his actions. In 1842 a national movement began to refund Jackson's money.

The congressional debate over Jackson's fine captured headlines from 1842 to 1844. Americans debated Jackson's use of martial law in conjunction with the Constitution's protection of liberty, revolutionary political ideology, and republican opposition to excessive governmental and military power. As the historian Matthew Warshauer has shown, "the general's detractors lamented fated liberty and warned against the power of a 'military chieftain.'"[15] However, others contended that the martial law declaration and action were both necessary and had saved the country at a perilous time. Senator James Buchanan of Pennsylvania weighed in: "Strictly speaking, we admit he had no Constitutional right to make this declaration; but its absolute necessity for the purpose of defending the place amply justified the act."[16] Buchanan called the act "indispensable to the safety of New Orleans" and argued that such an overriding necessity justified Jackson's use of martial law.[17] Buchanan viewed military power as acceptable and necessary despite the republican belief that such power signified a threat to liberty—and, in fact, Buchanan believed Jackson's actions supported liberty. In this instance, Buchanan believed in the supremacy of martial law, a power that he supported in the later military rule of California.

Senator Benjamin Tappan of Ohio similarly noted that self-preservation is "paramount to all other laws, with States as with individuals."[18] Both Buchanan and Tappan were Democrats, the same political party that Andrew Jackson represented as president of the United States the previous decade. They approved of Jackson's use of military power to subvert civil authority because of the fundamental law of necessity or self-preservation in accordance with Lockean ideas of the same. Buchanan, Tappan, and others could, nearly thirty years removed, laud Jackson's actions with the benefit of hindsight. As one Massachusetts legislator later stated, "whenever a General attempts to declare martial law upon his own responsibility, if he is successful, and protects his country, his country will protect him; and if he does violence and wrong, the laws will punish him. That is the only martial law I want to see in this free country."[19] According to this reasoning, because Jackson's maneuver succeeded, the country could show its gratitude for a heroic preservation of the Union despite any negative precedent that his martial law might have set. In 1844 Congress ultimately decided to return Jackson's fine and in so doing articulated the contingent nature of martial law. In times of necessity, or those deemed necessary after the fact, leaders could suspend civil authority and the protection of liberties that revolutionaries fought for in the 1770s.

Who determined necessity and under what circumstances? This question raised apprehension that the people and their representatives did not possess full sovereignty. At a time in the nation's history when government and military power were being questioned in a republican society—particularly as they related to the possibilities of slavery expansion and the acquisition of new lands in the Southwest and West—the answer had the potential to be explosive. The rhetoric surrounding civil republicanism or popular sovereignty and the legacy of military or governmental authority in practice revealed a deep and elusive contingency.

Several months after Congress voted to refund Jackson's martial law fine, Joseph Smith, the founding Mormon prophet who was simultaneously the mayor and commanding officer of the city's militia, declared martial law in Nauvoo, Illinois. Ongoing tensions between Latter-day Saints and their neighbors hit a fever pitch after June 8, 1844, when Smith and the Nauvoo City Council declared an anti-Mormon newspaper, the *Nauvoo Expositor*, a nuisance and ordered its destruction.[20] On June 10, the Nauvoo city marshal and hundreds of Latter-day Saints carried out Smith's order, an action that non-Mormons viewed as an exercise of absolute power.[21] Joseph Smith's stronghold on local power was about to come under literal fire. Rumors intensified that an anti-Mormon interstate mob was targeting the Mormon city and planning to overthrow its powerful leader. Joseph Smith notified his followers that a mob was coming to destroy "every man and woman who dares believe the doctrines that God hath inspired me to teach to this generation."[22] Claiming to be an obedient follower of all civil laws but fearing that the laws of the country would not protect him or his people, Smith encouraged the ten thousand Nauvoo citizens to preserve the peace, but remain on the defensive against extralegal activities.[23]

To safeguard his followers, on June 18, 1844, Smith put the city of Nauvoo under martial law. He authorized the militia, known as the Nauvoo Legion, to stand ready for defense against mob violence and expressly commanded the legion and the police to forbid that any "persons or property pass in or out of the city without due orders."[24] Smith's declaration of martial law did not occur ex nihilo. He believed that the impending threat was a continuation of violence that the Latter-day Saints had experienced in Missouri where the state's governor had issued an extermination order against Mormons not even six years earlier. In Smith's view, this latest threat was another attempt "to take away our rights and destroy our lives" with apparent impunity.[25] By 1844, however, Smith had assumed greater power to defend his people.

"We are American citizens," Smith said boldly as he demanded the rights that the blood of the revolutionary generation had purchased for him, his followers, and all Americans. Like other proponents of martial law, the Latter-day Saint leader did not want to see American liberty "disgracefully trodden under foot by lawless marauders." Instead, he sought to make a noble effort to preserve the lives of upstanding citizens and to sustain their rights. "Come all ye lovers of liberty," Smith urged, and "break the oppressors rod, loose the iron grasp of mobocracy, and bring to condign punishment all those who trample under foot the glorious Constitution, and the peoples rights."[26] Like Jackson and Dorr, Smith invoked the revolutionary-era idea of the popular will as the center of sovereign power in American politics. Paradoxically, he believed that martial law provided the surest means to secure Mormons' constitutional rights.

Non-Mormons almost universally viewed Smith's martial law proclamation as a manifestation of his dictatorial control over a religious institution, a civil government, and a large military unit.[27] Newspaper editors commented that, instead of protecting the people's rights, Mormon leaders had unnecessarily suspended liberties. Without evidence, they reported that Latter-day Saints had imprisoned nonresidents and non-Mormons or conscripted them into Nauvoo's religious army.[28] Many further claimed that Mormons tortured prisoners and confiscated property. The non-Mormon public believed that martial law in Nauvoo violated civil protections against unreasonable searches and seizures of their property, trial by jury, and the due process of law. It was not enough that Smith "had insulted and trampled on law," a *Warsaw Signal* editorial exclaimed, "he even in a time of profound peace eradicated the Civil law within the city, and in lieu thereof established Military preeminence, which placed the lives and property of all who were in the city, or should visit it, at the disposal of his supreme will."[29] Cries for the Illinois governor, Thomas Ford, to act were loud. Upon hearing of the martial law declaration, the *Warsaw Signal* editorialized: "When the Governor learns that Nauvoo is under Martial Law, if he does not act, there is no need of a Governor."[30]

Governor Ford agreed that Mormon leaders had violated constitutional laws, principally in ordering the destruction of the *Nauvoo Expositor*. Four days after the martial law declaration, on June 22, 1844, Ford wrote to Joseph Smith giving his opinion on the matter. "Your conduct in the destruction of the press was a very gross outrage upon the laws and liberties of the people," the governor opined. Ford proclaimed his high regard for the liberties and rights of free people by boldly stating that he "would shed the last drop of [his] blood" to protect the presses from any illegal violence. Finally, the governor affirmed to Smith, "You have violated the Constitution."[31]

The governor's letter also attacked the joining of various powers that he believed had occurred in Nauvoo. Military authority temporarily replaced civilian government in Nauvoo, but Joseph Smith led both the military and the civilian government. Therein lay the problem of concentrated power and the potential abuse of authority that could result.[32] Joseph Smith and the Latter-day Saints, according to the Illinois governor, were abhorrently using their powers "in a tyrannical manner" by declaring martial law.[33] In the context of heightened tension between the United States and England over western territorial expansion, Ford declared that "even in England" citizens would not tolerate such actions. "No civilized country can tolerate such conduct" especially "in this free country of the United States," Ford explained as he decried the despotism that Smith had exercised over Nauvoo.[34] Much like other debates over the exercise of power in the United States, the Illinois governor perceived this as a battle of republicanism versus authoritarianism with the Mormon leader guilty of striking at the "palladium of liberty."[35] The declaration of martial law proved the singular power of Joseph Smith in the eyes of the governor and other non-Mormons.

Joseph Smith fired back a letter to Ford the same day. In it, he defended his actions as necessary to preserve republicanism. "We truly say that we were obliged to call out the forces to protect our lives, and the constitution guarantees to every man that privilege," Smith asserted as he explained his martial law declaration. He refuted Ford's claims of the union of legislative and military power and reiterated that he had acted only in terms of self-preservation because Nauvoo was under siege and the public safety required it, echoing the rhetoric of necessity surrounding Jackson's martial law declaration. Finally, Smith defended his decision by alluding to the past persecution of Latter-day Saints. He solemnly wrote, "Sir you must not blame us for a burnt child dreads the fire." The Mormons in this analogy were the child burned by a parent government that had made no effort to protect or provide any aid to the minority group. The Mormons had lost confidence in government beyond the municipal level and Smith took the matter into his own hands to protect himself and his people. He declared martial law, in part, to defend "helpless women & children."[36] Smith invoked a common refrain that connected republics and gender: in republics, men protected virtue, a behavior constructed as being passive, feminine, and family centered.[37] Martial law was the only way Joseph Smith could envision preserving both civil rights and family virtue. One could view Smith's martial law declaration simply as an effort to preempt his own loss of power, but his actions and words reveal that he had already lost control.

To diminish Smith's influence, non-Mormons on both sides of the Mississippi River banded together to enact a shift in local power. Ford had Smith arrested and incarcerated in Carthage jail on charges of treason in connection with his issuance of martial law.[38] As Ford later explained, only the governor could declare martial law within the bounds of Illinois. Therefore,

Smith's act was treasonous because it was an "alleged levying of war against the State."[39] In this power struggle, the regional majority ultimately won out over the minority when, on June 27, 1844, a mob invaded the jail and killed Joseph Smith and his brother Hyrum. The informal democratic process of rioting and mob action took over, quickly diminishing the political and even military power of the Mormons. Latter-day Saints were believed to have held too much power and authority because of the overlapping of civil, legal, military, and religious leadership roles of Joseph Smith; only violent "democratic" action against them could rebalance local sovereignty.[40] The regional majority needed to act and did. Their martial behavior was deemed heroic.

A regional newspaper acknowledged that the mobs had acted in rebellion to demolish the "tyrant and his Government," but because they had succeeded in altering the exercise of sovereign authority by removing from power the Mormon leader, they would not be condemned for their actions. Similar to the language of necessity found in the Andrew Jackson refund debates, the *Warsaw Signal* editor Thomas Sharp opined, "Liberty is the price of blood the world over, and whenever it becomes necessary in defence of our civil rights, rebellion itself is justified by the paramount Law of mankind."[41] Non-Mormon opponents believed that Smith was a religious tyrant who had moved to put down mob violence by turning government into a mob. Smith had put the civil law beneath military rule; this was despotism and overextension of power.

In a turn of opinion from earlier martial law declarations, no one lauded Joseph Smith's use of martial law. However, those who took down the monarch earned public praise. They freed the west-central region of Illinois from autocracy and allowed civil republicanism to regain supremacy. In other words, Smith's martial law declaration indicated that free government had failed, but his detractors disagreed. A military dictatorship was not the answer. "When the civil law shall be utterly disregarded and trampled under foot," Thomas Ford later wrote, "the people become wholly unfit for self-government." The Illinois governor, like other non-Mormon citizens, believed that Joseph Smith had abandoned American republicanism and verged on a reign of tyranny by proclaiming martial law. Ford concluded: "The general sentiment in favor of martial law and the disorders calling it forth, are fearful evidences of a falling away from the true principles of liberty."[42]

In his 1854 history of Illinois, Governor Ford starkly contrasted Smith's action in Nauvoo with that of Andrew Jackson. Ford wrote,

> Ever since Gen. Jackson on some great occasions, when the fate of half the country was at stake, *"took the responsibility,"* the country has

swarmed with a tribe of small statesmen who seem to think that the true secret of government is to set it aside and resort to mere force, upon the occurrence of the smallest difficulties. It may be well enough on great occasions to have one great Jackson; but on every small occasion no one can imagine the danger of having a multitude of little Jacksons. Jackson's example is to be admired rather than imitated; and the first may be done easier and safer than the last.[43]

Jackson's case, from the perspective of 1854 as in 1844, was unique and deemed to be necessary. Joseph Smith's martial law declaration, on the other hand, was seen as unnecessary and unjustified by the non-Mormon majority; a people committed to the principles of civil liberty would not permit such an action and resorted to their own form of democratic violence to stop his perceived despotism.[44] The necessity laid with the majority. Just a year after Joseph Smith's death, Governor Ford again feared that violence and martial law in Nauvoo would become ungovernable. Under Ford's authority, the Illinois militia general James J. Hardin was sent to Carthage, the county seat, to restore order and ultimately induce the Latter-day Saints to leave the state in what became a de facto form of martial law. The majority population again agreed with this military action as the Mormon population eventually left Nauvoo under duress and headed west to the Great Basin.[45]

The issue of martial law and the questions surrounding the exercise of power only grew in relevance in the wake of the US–Mexican War and the acquisition of Mexican lands in the West under the terms of the Treaty of Guadalupe Hidalgo. The treaty made the United States a transcontinental nation and brought an immense amount of territory and people under the federal government's jurisdiction and authority. Wartime exigencies enlarged the use of federal military power and the acquisition of the West began a substantial growth in displays of that power. In places such as California, military leaders oversaw the governing of the territory to prevent anarchy and disruption in the transfer of sovereign power. Of the California episode, the then secretary of state James Buchanan stated: "The termination of the war left an existing government, a government de facto, in full operation, and this will continue, with the presumed consent of the people, until Congress shall provide for them a territorial government. The great law of necessity justifies this conclusion." President James K. Polk backed his secretary of state when he gave his annual message to Congress on December 5, 1848. In it, he stated that a military government was necessary to preserve and protect the people, particularly those white Americans living in California, "from the inevitable consequences of a state of anarchy."[46] Again, the concept of necessity justified military rule. James Buchanan expressed his faith that the California military government would "exercise no power inconsistent with the provisions of the Constitution of the United States, which is the supreme law of the land."[47]

Even after territorial governments were formed in the newly acquired western lands, the federal government continued to grapple with the specter of martial law. In Washington Territory, former military commander Isaac Stevens was the federal appointee to the office of governor and soon invoked military rule.[48] In the midst of conflicts with Native peoples in the territory, some of whom received aid from white Americans, Stevens declared a portion of Washington Territory under martial law on April 3, 1856, leading to the suspension of habeas corpus and the arrests of the suspected parties and a federal judge.[49] While Stevens believed his position as governor entitled him to take these actions, public discourse showed that some Americans were less convinced. The editors of the *New York Times* questioned whether a federal officer should subsume civil authority and "be permitted to usurp absolute and despotic power."[50]

The Washington territorial secretary, George Gibbs, wrote to President Franklin Pierce asking him to give his most urgent "attention to this flagrant usurpation of power by Governor Stevens."[51] "The exercise of military power over civil authority," Gibbs stated, marked a dark day in the nation's territorial experiment.[52] National authorities, Gibbs articulated, should not permit such a gross misuse of power.

President Franklin Pierce agreed. After having examined all the evidence, Pierce decided that Stevens's martial law declaration and use of military power was neither justified nor necessary. The president further added to the ongoing conversation about power and liberty when his secretary of state William L. Marcy, writing on his behalf, stated, "It is quite certain that nothing but direful necessity, involving the probably overthrow of the civil government, could be alleged as any sort of excuse for superseding that government temporarily and substituting in its place an arbitrary military rule. The recognition of such an inherent power in any functionary, whatever be his grade or position, would be extremely dangerous to civil and political liberty."[53] The US attorney general Caleb Cushing also weighed in on this declaration of martial law. Since sovereignty over the territories resided with the federal government, the attorney general opined that a proclamation of martial law was not within the legal attributes of a territorial governor, but only vested in the federal executive or legislature.[54] In the end, Stevens was censured by President Pierce but was not removed from office.[55]

Understanding the exigencies of armed conflict with Native peoples, most of the white citizens of the territory applauded Stevens's actions. As the typical settler interpreted the situation, lives and property were in danger and the governor had acted vigorously to save the territory from destruction. In their minds, he was exercising power to protect popular (white, settler) liberties. Federal authorities disagreed, unveiling a continuing and growing tension between the federal and local power in the western territories.

Approximately eighteen months later, the new president, James Buchanan, faced the question of martial law in another western territory. This time it was Utah Territory, though the circumstances were quite different. Just two months into his presidency, Buchanan, a past proponent of using military might in the West, viewed the Latter-day Saint society led by the faith's leader Brigham Young as a threat to civil republicanism. Buchanan quickly decided to send some 2,500 federal troops to install new federal officials and establish proper federal authority in the territory.[56] The president's move demonstrated the federal government's ability to repress a territory and its population. It was the rightful and legal obligation of the federal government to supervise the territories and ensure that a republican form of government was established and maintained within them.[57] A republican form of government, Buchanan asserted in his first public remarks about Utah affairs, had ceased to function in the vast western territory. Referring to Brigham Young—who was not only the president of the Latter-day Saints, but also the governor and superintendent of Indian affairs by virtue of President Millard Fillmore's 1850 appointment—Buchanan noted that "his power has been, therefore, absolute over both church and state" and "there no longer remains any government in Utah but the despotism of Brigham Young."[58] For the president, and in the minds of Americans outside of the Great Basin, the concentration of power in one man evoked a threat to the expansion of liberty in the West.[59]

On September 15, 1857, just over thirteen years after Joseph Smith had declared martial law in Nauvoo, Brigham Young responded to the coming of the federal army with a declaration of martial law, thereby encouraging Utahans to resist the entry of American soldiers into the territory. "We are invaded by a hostile force," Young asserted, "who are evidently assailing us to accomplish our overthrow and destruction."[60] Like the children in John Locke's second treatise, Young argued that the Mormons had matured into political manhood and deserved the rights of self-government. He pleaded for the extension of American citizenship rights to his people and explained that the Latter-day Saints had not experienced those freedoms in their history. The dispatching of the army, which Young considered to be a mob or "an unlawful military despotism," added to what the Mormons recalled as a twenty-five-year history of persecution by state and local governments in Missouri and Illinois. Young insolently declared his right to treat the federal army as a mob "just as though they had been raised and officered in Missouri, and sent here expressly to destroy this people."[61] He further articulated that the ordering of the troops to Utah was illegal (though it was legal; the president or Congress had the constitutional imperative to enforce the guarantee clause and activate the military in time of rebellion)[62] and that it stunk of government corruption and military tyranny.

Eliciting memories of British oppressive uses of military force against the American colonies, Young vented his opinion that the federal army's movement against a local population was contrary to "every constitutional right, every vestige of truth and liberty."[63] The Mormon leader maintained that he and his people were under attack and as a result would resort to "the great first law of self preservation and stand in our own defence" through military action.[64] Young viewed his martial law declaration as utterly necessary, as had Andrew Jackson in New Orleans, Governor Samuel Ward King in Rhode Island, and Joseph Smith in Nauvoo. However, he had apparently not learned from the events in Nauvoo thirteen years earlier and stubbornly attempted to prevent US troops from entering Utah Territory.

Necessity had its limits. As in 1844, Americans did not agree with the Mormons' necessity justification and responded to Young's martial law declaration with cries of despotism. Most, like President Buchanan, already believed that civil republicanism did not exist in Utah. The president and the American public viewed Brigham Young's declaration of martial law as treasonous and in defiance of federal authority. Mormons were perceived as being in rebellion, primarily because of the martial law declaration. Young's statement was called both an absurd proposition and an affirmation of war.[65] Buchanan himself noted that Young's proclamation confirmed the Mormon leader's dictatorial thirst for power and his desire to maintain that power even if it meant engaging in hostilities with the United States.[66] In his second annual message to Congress, Buchanan declared that Young issued his proclamation "in the style of an independent sovereign," thereby equating Young and the Latter-day Saints with monarchy, a subversive imperium in imperio within the American republic that was defying the proper sovereign federal power.[67] The president's desire to extend federal power and limit that of the Mormon leader illuminates the continuing negotiation and fragility of sovereignty in antebellum America. Federal authority was under attack and the government needed to renew its sovereign supremacy in this western territory and over this minority people.

Articles in newspapers expressed fears that the Mormons planned to secede from the United States and establish a nation of their own, a concern especially troubling in a time fraught with fears of southern secession over slavery.[68] Ultimately, while American politicians and pundits questioned Mormons' capability for republican self-government before September 15, 1857, Brigham Young's martial law declaration revealed their incapability. Federal, not local, authority was needed in Utah Territory. "The necessity for adopting these measures," President Buchanan stated, referencing Brigham Young's proclamation and his decision to send military might to Utah, "is now demonstrated."[69] Buchanan justified the perceived necessity for the use of military authority over a civilian population by explaining that it was essential to allow civil republicanism to flourish in the Great Basin. In this instance, against an unpopular minority group, Americans initially applauded the federal government's exercise of military authority to combat the local population's rebellious use of martial law.[70]

With the army en route to Utah, questions emerged as to how the military would help impose a proper civil government in the territory. Would the federal troops declare martial law themselves, in the manner of Andrew Jackson, as imperative to the protection of US interests in the West? A New York Times correspondent thought that a federal declaration of martial law would be an appropriate use of power in the Utah circumstance.[71] The president sent the army to aid a new governor, Alfred Cumming, and other federal civil officers in establishing a republican government and executing federal laws in the territory. The army was, in other words, a posse comitatus at the disposal of civil authority. As Americans had dreamed since the declaration of independence, the military was subordinate to the civil, or at least that was the design and intent for the Utah military expedition.[72]

Still, other opinions emerged about federal authority in the territories. In June 1857, Senator Stephen A. Douglas of Illinois, a major proponent of federal noninterference in the territories, had delivered a speech advocating for the repeal of Utah's organic act and the removal of all local government and civil authority from the territory.[73] Such an action by the federal government would certainly have dangerous consequences, especially given the heated national debate over slavery extension into territorial lands of the West. The logical extension of Douglas's proposal for Utah placed the future of slavery in western territories in peril, especially if a Republican won the presidency given the recently formed Republican Party's platform to prevent slavery in the territories.[74] Writing in April 1858, a New York Times correspondent hoped that Congress would not repeal the organic act in Utah because of the problematic precedent it would set. In this context, the correspondent affirmed that martial law would be contrary to the genius of American political institutions. "The very spirit and letter of the Constitution most certainly forbid the supremacy of the military over the civil authority," the *Times* correspondent stated, "and it will indeed be a sad day in the annals of our Republic when civil jurisdiction fails to accomplish its purpose, and it becomes necessary to declare martial law over so large a number of citizens and over such an extent of our domain."[75]

The raw materials to establish a republican form of government and provide the freedoms and liberties guaranteed by the Constitution were present in Utah Territory despite Young's "presumptuous and unparalleled usurpation of power."[76] James Buchanan agreed. Never intending his military expedition to lead to questions about the repeal of the territory's organic act, Buchanan hailed his Utah action as a success because the proper establishment of a republican civil government was now possible. In his second annual message, the president addressed what had happened in Utah: "The present condition of the Territory of Utah, when contrasted with what it was one year ago, is a subject for congratulation. It was then in a state of open rebellion, and, cost what it might, the character of the Government required that this rebellion should be suppressed and the Mormons compelled to yield obedience to the Constitution and the laws."[77] The results of stationing an army and placing new federal officials in Utah was a cause for celebration for the Buchanan administration. Nevertheless, his decision to enforce civil republicanism via military force had far-reaching ramifications regarding the extent and use of federal power at the literal and figurative crossroads of the West. Questions surrounding the use of federal power in the territories and in the states, particularly as it related to the existence and expansion of slavery, would not go away quietly.

The Latter-day Saints reacted to the vicissitudes of power enforcement as a means of self-preservation, but the minority group was overshadowed by the majority political culture that observed their actions as despotic and a legitimate threat to the expansion of American political liberty in the West. More so than in the writing about other issuances of martial law in the antebellum era, the American public viewed the Latter-day Saint leaders as monstrous and arbitrarily abusing political and military power akin to the British overlords that were ultimately dispatched in the American Revolution. What is more, the Utah military expedition illustrates a growing trend in the federal government's influence in the West. It also reveals the increasing federal tendency to use military power to expand and enforce normative institutions and behaviors to impose on a people and land a certain type of American republicanism and liberty. From the nation's founding, the genius of American political institutions kept the military subordinate to civil authority, but the question of what would happen if civilian authorities at the nation's capital used military might for their political and ideological purposes, particularly in the West, divided many along sectional lines.

For a topic and term that had generated so much discussion and debate in the previous two decades, when the nation found itself at the beginning of the great Civil War, newspaper editors again asked American readers the questions "What is Martial Law?" and "Who has the power to declare it?" They restated their opinion that military rule would lead to the destruction of civil liberties for some as guaranteed in the nation's foundational documents. These articles spoke to the climate of Southern secession and the general panic among slaveholders that the president would concentrate power and use military might—as commander-in-chief—to enforce the liberty of millions of enslaved peoples.[78] The specter of martial force used by the Northern, Republican federal government to prohibit slavery in the West and South had long menaced many white Southerners. But now, as the secession exploded into war, Southern fears of an imbalance toward federal power were confirmed; the president would use any means necessary to reunite the nation and enforce a certain type of American republicanism and liberty.

In 1861, just months after the war began, the Republican president Abraham Lincoln issued the first presidential declaration of martial law, citing the need to protect Florida citizens' lives, liberty, and property against insurrection. Lincoln again imposed martial law and suspended the writ of habeas corpus on September 24, 1862, to protect public safety and suppress rebellion in Kentucky.[79] The president indeed had the power to do so. Congress or the president under the Constitution's article 1, section 8, clause 15, could declare martial law on a national level and use armed force "to execute the Laws of the Union, [and] suppress insurrections and repel Invasions." The Supreme Court case *Luther v. Borden* (1849) provided the precedent and justification for strong presidential action in times of national crisis. Chief Justice Roger Taney's opinion in that case justified the use of broad presidential or federal powers to enforce the Constitution's article 4 guarantee of republican government. In the same case, Supreme Court Justice Joseph Story argued that article 4, section 4 required the federal government to guard against domestic violence.[80] With this 1849 antecedent, it was left to the federal government, namely the president, to enforce the guarantee clause against the secession and rebellion of the Southern states.

Though some viewed Lincoln's presidential martial law declarations as a frightening display of a kingly power, much like detractors of Andrew Jackson had decades earlier, others, including Lincoln himself, saw it as a necessary action to save the Union from its current state of disruption. The Great Emancipator's decision did not occur in a vacuum. The president appears to have understood that the change in power dynamics that had occurred in American political discourse over the previous decades and the circumstances of war justified the use of power and a strong federal government. Lincoln pointed back to Andrew Jackson's use of power, and Congress's 1844 approval of martial law, as precedent for his curbing of liberties during the Civil War.[81] In the end, Lincoln's use of power in the Civil War was deemed necessary to suppress rebellion and extend to more people their freedom, rights, and liberties; it was not done to invoke British-style tyranny.

What are we to take away from this history of martial law, especially as it relates to the Mormons? One answer appears to be the inherent contingency and fragility of power and rights in nineteenth-century discussions of martial law. How Americans viewed the exercise of power through a declaration of martial law depended on circumstances, outcome, and hindsight. Though ostensibly representing a British-style arbitrary abuse of power and corruption, Americans also viewed martial law as republican if exercised by the majority against a minority. If minorities exercised it, as in the Mormon cases, the universal public perception held that martial law was treasonous, a threat to liberty, and despotic. The American public did not believe that this minority group could justifiably use any means necessary to protect their constitutional rights, liberties, and lives. The public and government characterized Mormon martial law as a concentration and abuse of power, playing on American perceptions of religious difference. The discourse surrounding the Mormon examples positioned Smith's and Young's proclamations as utterly threatening to civil republicanism. Even when Mormons believed their actions were necessary for the protection of the rights and liberties of their minority group, their exercise of power was viewed as anathema to American republican governance. Other uses of military rule in the mid-nineteenth century, however, were deemed necessary, both in the moment and upon reflection, and justifiable for the longer-term continuation and extension of American liberty. Although the idea of the imposition of power by an individual in a republican society will always be suspect, when put into action, it can be deemed justifiable by the majority.

This history highlights a trend in the growing use and acceptance of federal power. Although Americans continued to fear the concentration of power in the wrong hands in the style of the British monarchy, these decades revealed an increasingly militarized state that promoted a certain type of civil republicanism and liberty, particularly in the American West and South. This early trend toward greater federal authority proved the inherent difficulties of sharing power in a republican nation of divided sovereignty.

CHAPTER 8

Political Perceptions of Mormon Polygamy and the Struggle for Utah Statehood, 1847–1896

STEPHEN ELIOT SMITH

"It is weirdly true," the literary critic Harold Bloom has observed, that in America "the Mormons are as mainstream as you are, whoever you are, at least in terms of the religion of politics, and the politics of religion."[1] Presumably, this fact is strange only because it has been true for no more than a third of the two-hundred-year history of Mormonism: the idea of the Latter-day Saints as prototypical Americans only began to emerge in the 1940s and 1950s.[2] During the second half of the nineteenth century, things had been quite different. During that time, in the midst of the culture war being waged by the federal government against the Church of Jesus Christ of Latter-day Saints, Mormons were typically characterized as representatives of systems and practices that were quintessentially *un*-American or even *anti*-American.[3]

Because of this history, the 1896 admission of Utah as the forty-fifth state of the Union was a momentous occasion for both the church and the United States.[4] For the church, the admission was the culmination of nearly half a century of persistent efforts for statehood, a cause originally championed by the church president Brigham Young. Since Young had led the first Mormons to settle the Salt Lake Valley, the society of Utah had been closely intertwined with—and often viewed by outsiders as synonymous with—the church and its adherents. For Young and the church, statehood represented political autonomy, something that church leaders especially craved but had not yet experienced. For the better part of the second half of the nineteenth century, the US federal government and most Americans deemed the bestowal of autonomy for Mormons to be unacceptable. Slowly, over a forty-year period, the federal government had exercised its sovereignty over Utah Territory and prevented Mormons from the full measure of autonomy.

No territory of the United States, before or since, had as many applications for statehood rejected or ignored by Congress as Utah had. For a territory to become a state of the Union, it had to meet a variety of criteria, the most important of which was that it have a functioning republican form of government. Even with a proper governing structure, Congress ultimately had the authority to deny statehood to territorial applicants for any number of reasons, thus revealing a crucial power dynamic at play within the nation's territorial system. The federal government dictated the terms of admission and the bestowal of state autonomy. Six constitutional conventions were held in Salt Lake City before Congress passed the 1894 Enabling Act, which set out the conditions for the admission of Utah Territory as a state.[5] Upon admission, the state constitution of Utah was therefore the seventh draft of the document, a record that is unlikely to be surpassed in the nation's future.

At the time of Utah's admission as a state—and indeed, ever since—it has been common to summarize the reasons for the unprecedented delay in a single word: polygamy. To the near unanimous disapproval of members of Congress and American citizens in general, the religious doctrine of plural marriage was openly practiced by Mormons from 1852 to 1890.[6] If one therefore requires a one-word explanation for an apparent forty-year delay in Utah's statehood, "polygamy" is indeed a better answer than any other that could be provided. However, over time, this one-word answer has had a scaffolding of presumptions built upon it, which has led to the formulation of conclusions about the admission of Utah that are both historically and legally dubious.

Of particular note is the popular suggestion that the admission of Utah to the Union was the result of a grand bargain—a quid pro quo in which statehood was given to Utah in exchange for the abandonment of polygamy. The claim is pervasive in both popular and academic writing when the history of Utah or Mormonism is mentioned.[7] While it is true that state prohibition of polygamy was always regarded by Congress—at first implicitly, and in the 1894 Enabling Act itself, explicitly—as one of the *prerequisites* for statehood, this is quite a different matter than suggesting that statehood was traded in exchange for polygamy, or that admission was accomplished pursuant to a quid pro quo. In Utah's case, no simplistic quid pro quo agreement was struck.[8]

For most of the years of the statehood struggle, the church evinced no possibility of abandoning polygamy as a central religious tenet and practice, and many members of Congress correspondingly regarded "Mormon statehood" as a more or less theoretical impossibility. While Mormons in Utah quickly came to regard themselves as full Americans entitled to the same participatory rights in the American republic as were granted to the settlers of California and Oregon with reasonable promptness, debates in Congress reveal that it was common for federal legislators to regard the population of Utah Territory as more akin to what the US Constitution, in its somewhat artless manner, refers to as "Indians not taxed."[9] The Mormons, like the Indians, were neither fully American nor fully foreign: they were living *in* America, but were not living *as* Americans.[10] Due to this political dualism, they could not be granted statehood, but rather—as was the case with the Indians—had to be managed, contained, and, if possible, civilized. Only then could the Mormons be fully absorbed into the American Union.[11]

Convincing the church to abandon polygamy was therefore just one piece of the puzzle. The puzzle itself, as some researchers have long recognized, was the far grander project of Americanizing Utah.[12] In the end, when Utah was admitted as a state, Congress did so not because the church had responded to a proposed bargain; it happened because the Mormon residents of Utah were seen by a majority of the members of Congress to have become more or less American.

Thinking beyond polygamy as an alternative marital model, what it represented is just as important. Polygamy represented cohesiveness among the majority Mormon population, which equated to the potential for long-lasting local power. To many Americans, Mormons were perceived as operating a "kingly government," a theocracy, as opposed to a proper republican form of government.[13] Polygamy buttressed theocracy and therefore represented a fear of the American government that a potentially despotic dictator could and would control the social and political lives of the people in a large geopolitical space within the nation's borders. Autonomy, especially in the form of sovereign statehood, could not be given to the Mormons to protect a barbarous familial system that undergirded their political power. As long as polygamy existed and was a central social institution, Mormons were viewed as unable to exercise proper American sovereignty.

Rather than a quid pro quo, the bestowal of statehood by the federal government in 1896 represented nearly fifty years of territorial management and a steady diminishment of the autocratic threat. This was largely accomplished by minimizing the threat of polygamy. Using antipolygamy moral rhetoric, the US government exercised its sovereignty in Utah to dismantle legal protections and the church's political power. For example, the 1887 Edmunds-Tucker Act strengthened the marriage laws, but more than that, it struck at the power of the church as a political and economic institution.[14] By stationing an army in Salt Lake City and placing non-Mormons in government positions—not to mention the transformative power of the completion of the transcontinental railroad—federal authorities had encouraged a population that diversified business, culture, and politics in Utah. Eventually, the federal government had reduced Mormon political cohesiveness to the point that statehood was finally deemed acceptable. By the 1890s, Mormons no longer sought complete autonomy as they had conceived of it in the 1850s; that had given way to a more ardent desire for acceptability as American citizens.

Because the process was controlled by Congress, the admission of new states to the Union had always been a political act. Although congressional micromanagement of the process for granting statehood reached its apex for Utah's admission, the practice of requiring the satisfaction of preconditions was nothing new.[15] The imposition of prerequisites was especially stringent in cases where the federal government had reason to believe that the residents of the prospective state were somehow less than fully loyal Americans. For instance, after the Civil War, the loyalty and trustworthiness of Southern states were understandably viewed by many Republicans and Northerners with considerable skepticism. As a result, the readmission of the reconstructed Southern states was contingent on a number of strict conditions, including the ratification of the Fourteenth Amendment and other provisions designed to guarantee the equality of the races.[16] The Mormons were suspected of disloyalty of a different kind, and at its core, this is what led to the unprecedented delay in granting Utah statehood.

The Mormons' plans to settle the Great Basin of the Rocky Mountains were formed in 1846 under the leadership of Brigham Young.[17] The first Mormon pioneers arrived in the Salt Lake Valley in July 1847, and by December of that year, the governing body of the church had established Great Salt Lake City as its headquarters and invited Mormon converts from all parts of the world to gather there.[18]

Historians have long debated the philosophical underpinnings of the call to gather. Was it to remove the Mormons from the influence of earthly governments and laws in order to establish a politico-religious independent state and thereby satisfy the scriptural mandate to gather and establish a theocratic Zion?[19] Or did Young and other American Saints retain a desire to remain loyal to their country, with the exodus to the West being motivated simply by a need to find refuge from the religious persecutions and political conflict the church had encountered in multiple states throughout its short history? Although there is evidence for both tendencies, it is clear that, at the very earliest stages, Young had decided that his settlement should be part of the United States: "We anticipate, as soon as circumstances will permit," Young wrote in the December 1847 statement announcing the gathering, "to petition for a territorial government in the Great Basin."[20]

Circumstances did not permit such a petition to be submitted until 1849, and by then Young had decided that the Latter-day Saints should apply for statehood. A constitutional convention was hastily organized and held in Salt Lake City in March 1849, which resulted in the creation of the provisional State of Deseret. The proposed state was vast, encompassing the entire Great Basin, including all of present-day Utah, most of Nevada, and portions of California, Arizona, Idaho, Wyoming, Colorado, New Mexico, and Oregon.[21] The statehood application was discussed, albeit briefly, in Congress. In February 1850, John Wentworth of Illinois introduced into the House of Representatives a petition that opposed the creation of the State of Deseret on the grounds of "the treasonable designs of the Salt Lake Mormons" and that those who submitted the petition for statehood "are in favor of a Kingly Government, are robbers and murderers, and that these men are all in favor of polygamy."[22] Wentworth's statement explicitly tied the problem of autonomy, theocracy, and statehood to the issue of polygamy. The State of Deseret application was denied and proved to be the first in a long string of unsuccessful applications for statehood by the Mormons, but Congress did respond by passing an organic act that created the Territory of Utah from the northern half of the proposed state.[23]

The creation of Utah Territory was but one part of the complex and finely tuned Compromise of 1850, which attempted to balance the competing demands of the country's pro- and antislavery factions.[24] Thus, "Young's vision of a vast Mormon state with Salt Lake City as its capital became a casualty to the political intrigue associated with the issue of slavery."[25] Indeed, the politics of slavery loomed large for Mormon ambitions and rhetoric surrounding polygamy for the next couple of decades.

In addition to the overriding factor of Congress being consumed with resolving slavery-related concerns, the small population of Deseret was a leading reason that federal legislators did not seriously consider statehood in 1849–50. At the time, it was a well-known rule of thumb that a minimum of sixty thousand eligible voters (roughly equivalent to adult men) was required in a region to justify the creation of a new state, and the estimated population of Deseret was well short of this benchmark.[26] However, Young was confident that a shortage of bodies was only a temporary barrier: the church anticipated that, with accelerating Mormon immigration, the total population of Utah Territory would exceed seventy-five thousand by the end of 1850 and would continue to grow as the church's missionary work expanded throughout the world.[27] The establishment of Utah Territory would simply be a way station en route to statehood: the Latter-day Saints would try again.

The second push for statehood gathered steam in March 1856, when a Utah constitutional convention dispatched the church apostles George A. Smith and John Taylor to Washington to present to Congress a petition for statehood and a draft constitution. Brigham Young was confident. In a public sermon, he tipped his hand at Latter-day Saint hopes when he declared that circumstances would "e'er long, give [us] a free and independent State, and justly make [us] a sovereign people"; he had no doubt that such workings were being guided by divine power.[28] Privately, Young mused that statehood might be granted in time for Deseret to cast electoral votes in the 1856 presidential election.[29]

However, Young had greatly misinterpreted the political mood in Washington, if he had considered it at all. Following the church's 1852 public acknowledgment of its doctrine and practice of plural marriage, a popular antipolygamy movement had emerged in the United States, which, within a relatively short period of time, came to dominate Americans' information and opinions about Mormons.[30] This knowledge had a concomitant effect on the political views of Americans, including members of Congress.

Mormon polygamy was debated in the House of Representatives for the first time in 1854.[31] From a religious standpoint, there was no question in the minds of the majority of participants in the debate that the Mormons were, at best, un-Christian. "If these people had a decent religion," Representative John Letcher of Virginia commented, "they would not have polygamy there."[32] As practitioners of a marriage system that was widely regarded as heathen and barbaric, the Mormons were not living as Americans: one representative dramatically recited the history of the downfall of various polygamous societies and concluded that if Congress allowed Mormon polygamy to continue within the United States, it would lead to the same "national decay" that had most recently afflicted the "Ottomans and the Turks."[33] However, the House was unable to come to agreement on whether Congress should attempt to legislatively eliminate what all agreed was an "excrescence on the body-politic."[34]

Near the end of the debate, a lone member of Congress suggested that perhaps the Mormons were true Americans after all. Reciting the Mormon history of persecution and the service of the Mormon Battalion in the

US–Mexican War, Representative William Waters Boyce of South Carolina made an argument that was uncharacteristic for its time.[35] Boyce's remarks must be understood within the context of slavery. During the antebellum era, southerners had occasionally argued in favor of Mormon local self-government, and even the practice of polygamy itself, because of the national conflation made between slavery and polygamy as barbaric institutions. Protecting Mormon local autonomy lent itself to enhanced safeguards for southern local power. What is more, southern legislators' defense of Mormons and polygamy prevented agreement and decisiveness in Congress on how to handle the Mormon question.

As with all political issues of the 1850s, slavery played a central role in the failure to reach consensus. In general, northern-based Republicans adamantly opposed polygamy and supported congressional efforts to suppress it. Southern Democrats and their northern "doughface" sympathizers were ambivalent. While Democrats agreed in principle with the Republican opposition to polygamy as a foreign practice that was at odds with American Christianity, they also realized that if Congress could enact laws to eliminate it, the same federal power to regulate a domestic institution could also be marshaled against slavery.[36]

The most famous indication that Mormon polygamy had become a national political issue came in June 1856 at the Republican National Convention in Philadelphia, where the adopted party platform called for the legislative abolition of both polygamy and slavery, "those twin relics of barbarism."[37] Notably, polygamy was the first of the named twins: the platform referred to "Polygamy and Slavery." This is remarkable considering the central role that slavery played in the politics of late-1850s America and speaks to the degree to which opposition to Mormon political ambitions had grown. Coincidentally, just days after the Republican convention, George A. Smith and John Taylor met with John M. Bernhisel, the delegate of Utah Territory to the House of Representatives, to discuss the pending application for statehood. As reported by Smith, Bernhisel told the apostles that because of the negative feeling toward Mormons among members of Congress, the situation was politically hopeless: "To present our Petition now would be sure defeat, and such a defeat as would keep us out of the Union for years to come."[38] After receiving similar advice from Senator Stephen A. Douglas of Illinois and others in Washington, Smith and Taylor decided that no attempt would be made to present the 1856 petition before Congress.[39]

Meanwhile, anti-Mormonism was well on its way to becoming somewhat of a national crusade. The Utah War of 1857–58 can plausibly be characterized as a failed last-ditch attempt by national Democrats to distract the nation from the issue of slavery and thereby avoid a war between the states.[40] The shiny object that was used by President James Buchanan in his 1857 message to Congress was "the despotism of Brigham Young" in Utah Territory.[41] To Buchanan, the Mormon leader wielded too much power, which had led his people to "insurrection."[42] Congress acquiesced to an "invasion" of Utah to better manage the territory and its people. This action sought to strike at Mormon autonomy and rehabilitate federal sovereignty in the territory. However, the political value for Democrats fizzled when Mormon resistance faded and Young agreed to surrender the governorship of the territory.[43] Not long afterward, Buchanan lost the White House and the country was overcome with a far more serious insurrection and resultant war.

In the 1860s and 1870s, the Utah Mormons were discussed only occasionally in Congress. This is unsurprising: the focus of national attention during these decades was first, national survival, and later, Reconstruction, issues that far exceeded the concerns of fewer than one hundred thousand religious settlers on the frontiers of the country. Nevertheless, Mormon polygamy was odious enough to members of Congress to prompt several vigorous debates and two pieces of legislation during these decades: the 1862 Morrill Act and the 1874 Poland Act.[44] In essence, the two acts were part of the same statutory scheme. The Morrill Act—which sailed through Congress during the Civil War when Southern slavery interests were no longer part of the discussion—criminalized bigamy in the territories, but in practice it was largely ineffectual because it had, as one congressman pointed out, "left the execution of the law against polygamy in the hands of the polygamists themselves."[45] This complaint targeted the lasting problem in Utah: sovereignty. Though a military force was stationed in the territory and non-Mormons ran many of the territorial government posts, Mormons remained largely responsible for administering justice. The Poland Act sought to remedy this oversight by implementing adjustments to the judicial system in which the participation of Mormon judges and jurors in the prosecution of polygamists in Utah would be limited, thereby chipping away at Mormon power.

During the legislative debates that led to these early pieces of legislation, it would not be hyperbolic to say that the Mormons in Utah Territory were vilified.[46] At various points, they were described as being "deluded,"[47] "debased,"[48] "benighted,"[49] and "ignorant fanatics,"[50] words that masked the fear of Americans of a mass mobilization by a despotic dictator. Young was "one of the most wicked" men on earth:[51] a "hoary-headed monster"[52] who "exert[ed] an absolute temporal and spiritual power over his followers."[53] The polygamy practiced by the Mormons was "anti-Christian,"[54] to be sure, but the "cancer"[55] was a marker of the power of the church president. It was that power that Americans highlighted as driving the "barbarous and brutalizing social and political system" in Utah.[56] Congressional representatives continued to comment on the Mormons' exercise of power within the context of polygamy rhetoric. Polygamy was frequently equated with Mormonism itself. Representative Emerson Etheridge of Tennessee took the arguments to their logical conclusion in declaring that American values called for the "extirpation of Mormonism in Utah."[57]

While there was unanimity that Utah would be better off without Mormon polygamy, Congress struggled in these debates to agree on a strategy for its eradication. While many congressmen supported criminal legislation and enforcement procedures of varying severity, after the completion of the transcontinental railroad in 1869, others were content to simply sit back and wait for the inevitable influx of non-Mormons to Americanize Utah.[58] However, with the passage of the Poland Act in 1874, it became clear that a congressional majority was beginning to favor positive action over passive patience.

Although the implementation of the Poland Act did not result in a dramatic increase in the number of polygamy prosecutions in Utah, it did prompt the church and federal officials to agree that George Reynolds, a private secretary to Brigham Young, would be prosecuted in a test case on the constitutionality of the prohibition of polygamy.[59] Ever since the church's official acknowledgment of plural marriage in 1852, Mormon leaders had argued that the practice was protected by the free exercise clause of the First Amendment.[60] But in *Reynolds v. United States*, a unanimous US Supreme Court disagreed. "Laws are made for the government of actions," Chief Justice Morrison Waite declared, "and while they cannot interfere with mere religious belief and opinions, they may with practices."[61] In other words, while the Mormons were free to believe in the religious tenet of plural marriage, it was nonetheless constitutionally permissible for Congress to prohibit its practice. Young had approved of church cooperation in the test case but died in 1877 before the appeal of Reynolds's conviction was heard. As the senior apostle in the church, John Taylor succeeded Young as the head of the church.[62]

Following *Reynolds*, Taylor and other leaders of the church encouraged the Latter-day Saints to participate in what amounted to a campaign of nonviolent civil disobedience whereby polygamist men would willingly submit to criminal sanctions under the Morrill Act.[63] For its part, Congress was all too happy to ensure that such sanctions would be applied. In proposing a bill that would further strengthen antipolygamy enforcement mechanisms, Senator George F. Edmunds of Vermont argued that it was intolerable that Utah continued to be led by polygamists who favored church over state. The Vermont senator again struck at the heart of the issue: theocracy and cohesive political power.

> The government of the Territory of Utah in every one of its practical administrative and political aspects is a government of polygamists. . . . The men who practice that thing are in possession of that government; they are in possession of it in defiance of the states of the United States punishing that thing; they are in possession of it in defiance of all civilized, Christian, modern understanding of what it is right to do. . . . More than that and beyond that, it is not the mere practice of polygamy, bad as it is, but that happens to be an inherent and controlling force in the most intense and anti-republican hierarchy, theocracy, that . . . has ever existed on the face of the earth. The Church of Latter-day Saints . . . controls in every respect every step in the Territorial operations of that community. . . . Is that republican? Can you tolerate in the heart of this continent of republics the building up of a State of that character? That is the question. If you cannot tolerate it, and have the power to dispose of it, are you willing to exercise that power?[64]

Support for Edmunds's bill was strong in Congress. Many legislators felt that there was no question that the eradication of polygamy and what it represented was long overdue. For example, one congressman argued that "polygamy had ceased to be a question susceptible of debate in this country," and that the teachings of civilization, morality, Christianity, and conscience "demand that the crime of polygamy should be wiped out."[65] Although some senators questioned the constitutionality of the bill,[66] and another warned against the dangers of government-sponsored religious persecution,[67] after minimal debate the bill passed relatively easily in both chambers of Congress,[68] and in March 1882, it was signed into law by President Chester A. Arthur.[69]

In an attempt to increase the number of convictions, the Edmunds Act made profound amendments to the Morrill Act.[70] Most significantly, the new act created the misdemeanor of "unlawful cohabitation." As a result, even if the existence of multiple marriages could not be proved,[71] a man could nonetheless be convicted on evidence that he "cohabits with more than one woman."[72] The act also placed severe political restrictions on men found guilty of polygamy or unlawful cohabitation and their wives; such persons were disqualified as voters and became ineligible to hold any public office.[73]

On the ground in Utah, the changes were an overwhelming success for the federal government. The Edmunds Act had led to an overt exercise of authority and an explosion of prosecutions of Mormon polygamists. "The Raid," as it came to be known among Latter-day Saints, led to a swarming of the territory by federal marshals and undercover spies and informants. Bounties were offered for information leading to the arrest of prominent polygamists. Gentiles were encouraged to watch their Mormon neighbors and report any suspicious behavior; children were stopped in the streets by federal marshals and asked about their parents. One researcher has commented on the magnitude and scope of the Raid:

> There are approximately 2,500 criminal cases in the [Utah Territory] court records from 1871 to 1896. . . . More than 95 percent are for sexual crimes, ranging from fornication to bigamy. This level of enforcement far exceeds anything historians have found elsewhere in the country. It is, literally, unique in American legal history, far exceeding, for example, that of seventeenth-century Massachusetts. Almost every sex offense, and many nonsexual prosecutions for crimes like "illegal voting" and "perjury," involved plural marriage in one way or another. The sheer size of the Raid was astonishing, and unprecedented.[74]

Meanwhile, the church had altered its tactics. Just weeks after the passage of the Edmunds Act, the church president John Taylor had subtly suggested to the Saints that, rather than brazenly defying the law, they might find it more beneficial to simply hide polygamous relationships from federal officials. "Now, treat your wives right," Taylor admonished, "but do not subject yourselves to the infamous provisions of the Edmund's act more than you can help."[75] Three years later, in the midst of the Raid, Taylor's advice became more explicit: the Saints were advised in a public speech to avoid the federal authorities and their informants "as much as you possibly can—just as you would wolves, or hyenas, or crocodiles, or snakes," suggesting that "this storm will blow past as others have done."[76] Immediately following the speech, Taylor and nearly all the other senior church leaders "went underground": they disappeared from public view and began leading an itinerant life of "sleeping in hay ricks [and] hiding under floorboards."[77] By 1886 nearly every community in Utah had been raided at least once by federal marshals.[78] During this time, many Saints abandoned Utah and established Mormon colonies throughout the Intermountain West, in northern Mexico, and in the Canadian North-West Territories, in present-day Alberta.[79] Such movement demonstrated a diluting of Mormon authority in action.

Politicians in Washington were delighted by the effectiveness of the Edmunds Act. In 1883, emboldened by the success, President Arthur proposed that Congress dissolve the government of Utah Territory and assume direct federal control over the region.[80] The next year, in his final message to Congress, Arthur repeated the call for the federalization of Utah.[81] Arthur's Republican Party went further: in its 1884 platform, the party called for the prompt and effective suppression of polygamy in Utah "by the military, if need be."[82]

Congress balked at these extreme measures but nevertheless continued to debate several ongoing proposals that had been suggested as a means of strengthening the Edmunds Act. Primary among these was one that would attempt to completely eliminate the church as a source of power and influence in Utah.[83] Thus, when Congress proposed a new measure to combat polygamy in 1887, "it attacked the perceived problem directly. Instead of dismantling Utah's government, Congress dismantled the church."[84] The proposed bill, cosponsored by Senator Edmunds and Representative John Randolph Tucker of Virginia, aimed to eliminate polygamy and Mormon authority by means of disincorporation of the church.

"This bill," explained one congressman, "strikes at the very root of the church. It absolutely repeals the charter which gave it existence."[85] The boldness of the proposal shocked some legislators who were not otherwise opposed to the prosecution of polygamists. Representative Risden T. Bennett of North Carolina and Senator Wilkinson Call of Florida opposed the bill on First Amendment grounds: "If Congress have no power to make a law respecting the establishment of religion," Bennett argued, "have Congress the power to make a law respecting the disestablishment of a religion?"[86] Utah affairs brought to the fore the question of federal authority and religious liberty.

Such arguments, however, were typically met with an answer that sounds particularly startling to twenty-first-century ears—Mormonism was, in fact, not a religion under the Constitution. Senator John T. Morgan of Alabama invoked the American fear of being overrun by foreigners and foreignness when discussing Mormons. In the context of the era's Chinese Exclusion Act, Morgan suggested that Mormonism "would be a very fair religion in China or in any Mohammedan country," but was an undesirable element in the United States.[87]

In a lengthy speech before the House of Representatives, John T. Caine, the delegate from Utah Territory, complained that if suppression of polygamy was the goal, the proposed bill would do nothing to accomplish it beyond what was already being done. "As fast as can be done convictions are now secured and the ease with which they are obtained is of national notoriety," Caine remarked. "It is impossible to expedite convictions without an increase in the number of courts, and this bill does not even hint at such a step."[88]

In his response to Caine, Representative Tucker sniffed that just as "we dissolve the tribal relations of the Indians in order to make the Indian a good citizen; so we shatter the fabric of this church organization in order to make each member of the church a free citizen of the Territory of Utah."[89] In Tucker's rationale, we see one of the clearest articulations of how Congress viewed the Mormon population of Utah Territory: as with Indians, the Saints were not foreigners, but neither were they full American citizens, though they were capable of becoming such. In this light, some measures that otherwise might appear to have been heavy-handed were thought necessary to bring about results that would be for the Mormons' own good. In the end, although a significant number of members of Congress voted against the proposed bill, it nevertheless passed both chambers.[90]

The resultant Edmunds-Tucker Act was a patchwork collection of provisions designed to fully exterminate polygamy and the church as an institution with its attendant political power. Two major changes were directed at solving some persistent evidentiary problems in polygamy trials. First, the act reversed the common-law rule by making a man's legal wife a competent witness in his polygamy or unlawful cohabitation trial.[91] Second, the act established a system of marriage registration in the territories and imposed stiff penalties for noncompliance.[92] Several civil provisions of the act were aimed indiscriminately against Mormons without regard to marital status. The most egregious of these provisions was section 20, which repealed the territorial legislature's 1870 grant of suffrage to women.[93]

However, Congress saw the provisions that struck at the church itself as those that would be most effective in ending polygamy in Utah. Section 17 annulled the 1851 territorial act that incorporated the church and dissolved "any legal existence" the church may have had at the time.[94] The act directed the US attorney general to commence judicial proceedings to enforce the Morrill Act provisions that limited the real property of any church in the territory to $50,000—all church property beyond this limit was to be "forfeited and escheated to the United States . . . and the proceeds thereof applied to the use and benefit of the common schools in the Territory."[95] The remaining $50,000 of church real estate and the personal property of the church was to be judicially transferred to a receiver in accordance with regular corporate windup procedures.[96] Finally, the act dissolved the Perpetual Emigrating Fund Company, which had been established by the church to provide resources and loans to Mormon converts to assist them in immigrating to Utah.[97] Not only was Congress draining the swamp; it was also damming up the inflow.

By July 1887, the federal government had initiated windup proceedings for the church in the Utah Supreme Court.[98] However, apart from this, little practical change resulted from the Edmunds-Tucker Act. As Caine had pointed out to the House, the Utah judicial system had been prosecuting polygamy offenses at full capacity for several years.

The death of John Taylor that very same month fueled speculation that the church would soon capitulate: unlike Taylor, the next senior apostle, Wilford Woodruff, had generally refrained from addressing the issue of polygamy in his sermons and speeches. Upon assuming the leadership of the church, Woodruff learned that the national Democratic Party, which controlled the White House and the House of Representatives, was willing to entertain a petition for Utah statehood. In the coming months, some Utah Mormons even suggested that to gain political advantages, the church-sponsored People's Party should be disbanded and merge with the Democrats, but for the time being Woodruff opposed this step.[99] Still, this spoke to a major change taking place in Utah society. Local politics and parties were being replaced by national affiliations. Anticipating a real chance for statehood, Woodruff instructed the leadership of the church in early 1888 to cease preaching plural marriage to the Latter-day Saints.[100]

On August 1, 1887, Utah voters ratified the sixth draft of the proposed state constitution. Notably, for the first time, the constitution contained a provision that criminalized polygamy.[101] Congress and the media were understandably skeptical of this change in approach, but hearings on Utah's subsequent statehood application were held before the Senate Committee on Territories, and for the first time, the admission of Utah was at least treated by Congress as something that was within the realm of possibility. Woodruff remained privately optimistic throughout 1887 and 1888, but Republican triumphs in the federal election of 1888 dashed any hope of immediate success.[102] In the lame-duck session of Congress that followed the election, an enabling act was passed which provided for the admission into the Union of

North Dakota, South Dakota, Montana, and Washington.[103] Due to the sudden change in political conditions, Utah was simply ignored, and the hearings on statehood were not revived in the new Congress.[104]

In October 1889, six months after Woodruff had been formally installed as the fourth president of the church, the *St. Louis Globe-Democrat* printed a remarkable interview between the eighty-two-year-old Mormon leader and the correspondent Walter B. Stevens. During the interview, Woodruff all but repudiated polygamy: "It was suggested that people would like to hear directly from the head of the church what the attitude is toward the law prohibiting polygamy. Without the slightest hesitation President Woodruff replied, with emphasis: 'We mean to obey it, of course. We have no thought of evading this or any other law of the United States. We are citizens of this government. We recognize its laws as binding upon us. . . . Since the Edmunds-Tucker law we have refused to recommend plural marriages. . . . There must be no more plural marriages.'"[105]

The complete report by Stevens serves as an interesting case study in how perceptions of Mormons by outsiders could change rapidly. It is apparent that Woodruff was not exactly what Stevens had expected when he was dispatched to Salt Lake City to interview the head of the church. Woodruff was, the reporter noted, "a great disappointment to those who have imagined a supposed typical Mormon."[106] After a discussion of plural marriage and the prophetic mantle Woodruff had inherited as president of the church, Stevens commented that "there is not much difference after all between President Woodruff's principle of revelation and that 'still small voice' for which the Christian listens as an answer to his prayers."[107] Stevens closed his article by asking a question that just a few years earlier would have been unlikely: "Is it possible that progressive ideas are at work in the Mormon church?"[108]

Circumstances would soon cause polygamy to again be pressed to the forefront of church affairs and to test how progressive the church would be. In May 1890, the US Supreme Court upheld the constitutionality of the Edmunds-Tucker Act, which had been challenged by the church on First Amendment grounds. The majority of the court held that, just as the Constitution would allow the prohibition of human sacrifice as a religious ritual, so too could it outlaw polygamy "and all other open offenses against the enlightened sentiments of mankind, notwithstanding the pretense of religious conviction by which they may be advocated and practiced."[109] But the constitutionality of antipolygamy laws had already been settled by *Reynolds* more than a decade before, and the majority of the court scarcely seemed to notice that the case posed a new constitutional issue, namely, whether

Congress could under the First Amendment dissolve and seize the assets of a religious body as a sanction for violating such a law. The three dissenting justices of the court argued that it could not, but the majority held that the authority to do so was inherent within the "supreme power of congress over the territories," which was "plenary and general."[110]

The church's defeat in the court, coupled with a 2,400-mile trip in which Woodruff witnessed the dire circumstances that had overcome Mormon communities throughout the Intermountain West, confirmed to him that the church would survive only if it made a clear renunciation of polygamy.[111] There had been no official or unofficial communication between the church and government officials whereby the abandonment of polygamy was proposed as the *quid* in exchange for the *pro* of statehood. Rather, as was recognized at the time, it was simply a choice for the church between "giving up polygamy and giving up everything else."[112]

The opportune moment came in September 1890, when the federal government's Utah Commission issued its annual report, which claimed that the church was still solemnizing polygamous marriages in the territory.[113] In his Manifesto of September 25, 1890, Woodruff asserted that "these charges are false. We are not teaching polygamy or plural marriage, nor permitting any person to enter into its practice."[114] "I now publicly declare," Woodruff concluded, "that my advice to the Latter-day Saints is to refrain from contracting any marriage forbidden by the law of the land."[115] Today, the declaration of the Manifesto is sometimes imagined as a momentous occasion at which the church's opposition to continuing the practice of plural marriage was first devised. But, in fact, the Manifesto is better characterized as an official articulation of a policy that had been unofficially pursued by the church for several years. In this regard, the contemporary press treatment of the Manifesto is revealing; in the days immediately following the announcement, the press outside of Utah largely ignored it.[116] Although in a handful of cases the Manifesto was published verbatim in whole or in part by newspapers in the western states and territories,[117] it passed largely uncommented upon.[118]

The declaration was more broadly noted in non-Utah newspapers two weeks later, when a general conference of the church accepted the Manifesto as "authoritative and binding."[119] But even then, most press observers regarded acceptance of the Manifesto as a formality that simply confirmed the changes that had already taken place in Utah. A *New York Times* editorial published the day after the conference is representative of the general tenor of the reports: "It is not the power of the Government which they have found irresistible, but the greater and more intangible power of American civilization. . . . It was a foregone conclusion that when civilization grew up in Utah the Mormons would be merged into the general mass of American people."[120]

Although statehood was therefore not an immediate *quo* delivered by the government once the Manifesto was adopted, the admission of Utah did at this stage become virtually inevitable. In 1892 the Utah territorial legislature enacted a criminal statute that essentially mirrored the antipolygamy provisions of the Edmunds Act.[121]

Early the following year, with a federal legal infrastructure in place and the development of national party politics in the territory, a committee of the House of Representatives reporting on Utah's application for admission as a state confidently declared that the evidence it had gathered compelled the committee "to believe without doubt or hesitation that the institution of polygamy as taught by the Mormon Church, whether of faith or of practice, is now absolutely stamped out and exterminated."[122] By late 1893, it was politically assured that Congress would soon pass an enabling act for Utah statehood.

In Congress, there were some isolated last throes of opposition. During the House of Representatives debate over what would become the 1894 Enabling Act, Representative Elijah A. Morse of Massachusetts opposed statehood for Utah on the familiar ground of Mormon polygamy. But after decades of vituperative denunciations, most members of Congress had moved on. Polygamy and the potential despotic power structure that it supported was thought to no longer remain in Utah. Another congressman expressed the dissolution of Mormon power in stark terms: "With the Gentiles coming in from every State in the Union, with their common school system that has been adopted and put in operation there, with the political parties divided as they are now in the Territory, it would be impossible for any organization to restore polygamy in that country."[123] The federal government could now bestow sovereign state status. Congress overwhelmingly voted to pass Utah's enabling act and it was signed into law by President Cleveland on July 16, 1894.[124] "This has been a hard struggle for years," Woodruff recorded in his journal upon hearing the news of Cleveland's signature. "It has seemed as though all Earth and Hell had been combined against the Latter-day Saints having a state government. And now we have to give God the glory for our admission into the Union."[125]

For more than forty years, Utah statehood had faced significant opposition in Congress and in American society, which focused on the alternative family model of Mormon polygamy. That marital structure stood as a lasting representative of the threat of cohesive Mormon political power. But the federal government significantly strengthened in the intervening years from 1850 to 1896 and legislated strongly against Mormonism, along with other minority groups (primarily Chinese, Native Americans, and African Americans). Polygamy had been the catalyst and vehicle for the discussion leading to federal action that brought Mormon political power to heel. Following a long struggle in managing Utah away from a solidly autonomous place of and for Mormons, Utah had become diversified enough and Mormon power had dissolved to a point that granting to the people sovereign statehood had become acceptable.

CHAPTER 9

A Snake in the Sugar

Magazines, the Hardwick Committee, and the Utah-Idaho Sugar Company, 1910–1911

MATTHEW C. GODFREY

"The most remarkable partnership in the United States," Judson Welliver, an essayist for *Hampton's Magazine*, declared in 1910, "is that of the Mormon Church and the Sugar Trust, for the domination of the beet sugar business of the country." Using "convincing and authoritative detail," Welliver, in an essay entitled "The Mormon Church and the Sugar Trust," delineated "the facts, never before published, of the business and political alliance of the Sugar Trust and the Mormon Church." In providing this "most startling revelation of the power of Mormonism and of the business intrigue and political inside workings of the Trust," Welliver claimed, he was only doing his duty of presenting Americans with the truth. His article claimed to outline how the Church of Jesus Christ of Latter-day Saints, also known as the Mormon Church, "was a dangerous political power" whose influence had forced senators from Utah, Idaho, Wyoming, Oregon, and Nevada to uphold the sugar tariff. "There is no body of people in America so perfectly organized, so completely controlled politically and in business matters, as the Mormons," Welliver continued. "It is this that has made this hierarchy the power and menace it is."[1] Upon finishing Welliver's essay, readers were left with the impression that Latter-day Saints—through the mechanism of the Utah-Idaho Sugar Company—had used beet sugar to gain complete economic and political dominance over the American West.

Such charges, however fantastic, set off a flurry of articles in national magazines against the Church of Jesus Christ of Latter-day Saints in 1910 and 1911, all exploring what their authors considered to be the outrageous social, political, and economic workings of the church and its leaders.[2] These articles—and especially Welliver's allegations against church leaders, Utah-Idaho Sugar, and the American Sugar Refining Company (also known as the Sugar Trust)—were influential enough to convince the United States House of Representatives to appoint a special committee to investigate the relationship between American Sugar and western beet sugar manufacturers, including Utah-Idaho Sugar. Known as the Hardwick Committee, its investigation showed that many congressmen believed Welliver's allegations, but it also allowed prominent church leaders such as Joseph F. Smith, president of both the church and Utah-Idaho Sugar, and Charles Nibley, presiding bishop of the church and a shareholder in Utah-Idaho, to refute Welliver's charges on a national stage—although some critics did not believe their defense. Ultimately, Welliver's article and the Hardwick investigation showed that the Latter-day Saint church and Utah-Idaho Sugar were caught up in national economic trends that Congress believed were harmful to the United States as a whole.

Welliver's article was part of the muckraking magazine campaign against big business that resulted from the Progressive Movement's push for political and economic reform in the late 1890s and early 1900s. Appalled by the monopolies and capitalistic excesses of the so-called Gilded Age and believing that humankind could elevate itself into higher realms of social responsibility, Progressives called for laws restoring competition in American business and curbing the power of robber barons such as John D. Rockefeller and Andrew Carnegie. These capitalists created corporations such as Rockefeller's Standard Oil Company and Carnegie's US Steel that were in essence both horizontal and vertical trusts—horizontal in that they absorbed all the competition into their business until they held a complete monopoly, and vertical in that they "engaged in a number of different activities, such as purchasing or growing [their] raw materials, fabricating those materials into goods, transporting [their] own products, wholesaling them, or even taking care of retailing them to consumers."[3] Utah's sugar industry was caught up in these trends in industrial America, as it became part of the Sugar Trust—the combination of eastern sugar refiners who dominated the sugar industry—in 1902 when the American Sugar Refining Company bought out half of its stock.[4]

Progressives found a voice for their concerns in muckrakers, journalists writing for popular national magazines at the turn of the twentieth century about social, economic, and political issues in the United States, including the problems created by big business. Most famously, Ida Tarbell penned an exposé of Rockefeller and his Standard Oil Company, which was published as a serial in *McClure's Magazine* beginning in November 1902. Other authors such as Lincoln Steffens, Upton Sinclair, and William Hard took on subjects such as political corruption in St. Louis, Missouri, the meatpacking industry, and the necessity of workmen's compensation. As one historian notes, the muckrakers "exposed unscrupulous practices by banks, brokerage firms, and insurance companies; described corruption in local and state governments; and revealed conditions harmful to working men, women, and children in America's mines and factories."[5]

Although many muckrakers worked hard to ensure that their articles were both well researched and balanced, the fact remained that muckrakers worked for magazines that needed to sell issues in order to make money. Therefore, "muckraking, as it unfolded," according to one scholar, "confusedly suggested, on one side, accurate and penetrating reportage, [and] on the other side irresponsible sensationalism."[6] Some publications, including *McClure's Magazine*, remained interested in high-quality writing and research, but others, including those published by William Randolph Hearst, pushed their authors to emphasize the sensational so as to maximize sales. Regardless of the presence of lurid tales and sensational reporting, muckrakers impacted the passage of Progressive legislation in the United States, including reform measures such as the Pure Food and Drug Act, the Mann Act, and workmen's compensation laws. By educating middle-class readers about corruption in business, the muckrakers led the nation "to unprecedented heights of social awareness, which led to social action."[7]

Catching the tail end of the muckraking influence was the campaign against the Latter-day Saint church that exploded in national magazines in 1910 and 1911. Concerned about a perceived continuation of plural marriage in the church and about the alleged economic and political power of Joseph F. Smith, president of the church, publications such as *Pearson's Magazine*, *Everybody's Magazine*, *McClure's Magazine*, and *Cosmopolitan Magazine* issued a series of articles attacking the church and its leaders with charges of gross social, political, and economic excesses.[8] Many of their accusations, such as those involving polygamy, had been aired in hearings before the United States Congress in 1906 and 1907 on whether Reed Smoot, an apostle in the church, should be seated in the Senate. According to Frank J. Cannon, these hearings had failed "to show the Church's partnership with the 'interests,'" meaning those businesses to which the church was tied.[9] Some articles, including a three-part series by Alfred Henry Lewis in the *Cosmopolitan*, showed no such neglect, comparing Smith and the church to an insidious economic viper intent on taking over the nation by connecting itself with prominent industries in the United States. Lewis hyperbolically insisted that, in terms of money, "the Mormon Church overtowers either the Steel Trust or Standard Oil," and that the goal of church leaders was to "cross the Atlantic, cross the Pacific, and rule the nations of the earth."[10] Although such charges seemed outrageous and, to Latter-day Saints at least, just another episode in their ongoing persecution by the larger United States, the magazine campaign in 1910 and 1911 did not appear to be a concerted anti-Mormon effort. Instead, it had more in common with other assaults in the Progressive Era against perceived corruption in large organizations.[11]

And indeed, to many, the Latter-day Saint church *was* a large organization, in part because of its involvement in business and industry in the Intermountain West. Although the holdings of the church did not approach the fantastic figures imagined by Alfred Lewis, the church had invested in several important industries, including sugar, salt, electricity, coal, and iron. Church leaders justified such investment by arguing that these businesses provided both employment opportunities and cash for its members, thereby allowing them to become more self-sufficient. However, these investments also provided a target for progressive reformers who were convinced that church leaders were fleecing both members and nonmembers to enrich their coffers.[12] Indeed, to outside observers, the church seemed to be part of the excesses that accompanied industrial transformation in the United States in the late nineteenth and early twentieth centuries. The rise of large corporations that dominated American economics and society, the transformation of rural areas in the United States into urban behemoths teeming with pollution, and the growth of industrial labor in these urban areas was disorienting to many Americans. As one historian explained, "of the many changes that have occurred in our history, few if any have made such a deep and lasting difference as the emergence of an industrial civilization and its characteristic institution, the large corporation."[13] As an entity that allegedly controlled its followers' political, economic, and social lives, the Latter-day Saint church seemed to fit this large corporate model which threatened individualism in the United States. That the church whole-heartedly supported an industry—sugar—which thrived on monopoly, large profit, and competitive imbalance only solidified its depiction as a corporate leviathan.

One of the first articles attacking the church as a corporate behemoth appeared in the January 1910 issue of *Hampton's Magazine*. Benjamin B. Hampton, who had made his fortune in advertising, was both proprietor

FIGURE 4.   This editorial cartoon depicting Joseph F. Smith as a king to whom industrial magnates in the United States paid tribute appeared in Alfred Lewis's exposé in the *Cosmopolitan Magazine*. Alfred Henry Lewis, "The Viper's Trail of Gold," *Cosmopolitan Magazine* 50 (May 1911): 831.

and editor of the magazine, and he commissioned a series of articles "on public abuses," including exposés of railroads and smelters. In defending this content, Hampton declared that he and his staff "know a great deal more about the temper of the American people than the politicians do." By publishing such articles, he continued, *Hampton's* could influence Congress to pass reform measures against big business: "Nowadays, we know how to get results."[14]

In 1909 *Hampton's* began publishing a series written by Judson Welliver on the Sugar Trust in the United States. Hampton explained that he chose Welliver to write this series "because of his record for painstaking 'digging' and accuracy and his long training in the highest standards of journalism." Welliver had previously been a journalist in Iowa, working for several newspapers including the *Messenger* (Fort Dodge), the *Journal* (Sioux City), the *Leader* (Des Moines), and the *Tribune* (Sioux City). He then went to Washington, DC, to work for the *Washington Times*, where "his pen [was] unflaggingly at the service of the 'progressives.'" When Theodore Roosevelt became president, he appointed Welliver to investigate and write "a confidential report on the European railway systems," thereby providing Roosevelt with intelligence he needed as he contemplated an expansion of railroads in the United States. Based on that work and his journalistic writings, Hampton believed that Welliver had the ability to untangle "the intricate ramifications of the Sugar Trust" and assigned him to investigate the sugar industry in late 1908.[15]

Hampton's published Welliver's first installment in October 1909. Introducing the series, Welliver outlined his goals to "tell the story of [a] trust founded on the favor of the Government, grown rich and powerful through a constant course of fraud and thievery, drawing rebates from the railroads, bonuses from the Government, defrauding the customs of millions upon millions, keeping one foot on the neck of the cane-sugar grower and another on the raiser of beet sugar, always with one hand at the throat of its competitors and the other in the pocket of the consumer." He proposed to "trace the development of an elaborate system of fraud and theft" and to reveal "how the most trusted officers of the Government have been induced to work for the trust instead of serving the employer to whom they had sworn loyalty." In this way, he would uncover the history of an industry that, after Standard Oil and US Steel, was the largest industrial monopoly in the United States.[16]

The first three installments explained the background behind the formation of the Sugar Trust, which developed largely because of the machinations of Henry O. Havemeyer, head of the American Sugar Refining Company. American Sugar specialized in the manufacture and refining of cane sugar and was the descendant of Havemeyers & Elder, a sugar-refining firm formed in the mid-1850s by Frederick Havemeyer, Henry's father. Capitalizing on opportunities created because of the destruction of the Louisiana sugar industry in the Civil War, Havemeyers & Elder expanded its production under Henry's leadership. Welliver asserted that Henry reached agreements with government agents so that he would not have to pay duties as high as other refiners did. Most of the supply of the raw sugar that American Sugar used in its refining was imported into the United States. A tariff had to be paid on such raw sugar, so any advantage American Sugar could gain on paying the duty gave it an advantage over its competitors. Havemeyer's operation thus prospered while other eastern sugar refiners neared bankruptcy.[17]

Because of the struggles of other refineries, Havemeyer purchased several of them, and on August 16, 1887, merged them to form the Sugar Refineries Company. According to Welliver, the company immediately raised the price of the sugar it sold, creating a backlash from the public. Complaints from the Tammany Hall political machine in New York led to an investigation by the attorney general, and in June 1890, the company was dissolved. Havemeyer, however, had apparently foreseen this outcome and had had his legal counsel examine how to form a new trust under the more permissive laws of New Jersey. On January 1, 1891, the American Sugar Refining Company—which was essentially the Sugar Refineries Company under a different name—formed, with Havemeyer as president.[18]

American Sugar dealt with the refinement of cane sugar, but a burgeoning beet sugar industry existed in the United States as well. Although attempts had been made to establish profitable beet sugar factories since the 1830s, it was only in the 1880s that beet sugar became a moneymaking venture for individuals such as E. F. and Edward Dyer, Claus Spreckels, and the Oxnard brothers. In 1889 Utah got into the beet sugar industry with the establishment of the Utah Sugar Company, a corporation headquartered in Lehi that formed with the financial backing of the Latter-day Saint church and that eventually morphed into the Utah-Idaho Sugar Company. Havemeyer perceived these beet sugar producers as a threat and began focusing on ways to bring them under American Sugar's control.[19]

According to Welliver, one of the key elements in American Sugar's involvement in beet sugar was "the most remarkable partnership in the United States"—that of American Sugar and the Utah-Idaho Sugar Company, which, according to Welliver, "dominat[ed] . . . the beet sugar business of the country." In telling this story in his January 1910 article, Welliver brought to the attention of a national audience "the facts, never before published, of the business and political alliance of the Sugar Trust and the Mormon Church," which, he believed, completely controlled the beet sugar industry. Welliver emphasized that what he was going to explain was "absolutely new" and "the most startling revelation of the power of Mormonism and of the business intrigue and political inside workings of the Trust, that has ever been presented to the public." Clearly, Welliver saw the partnership between American Sugar and Utah-Idaho Sugar as one of the most egregious examples of monopoly and collusion in the United States.[20]

However, after such a spectacular setup, Welliver's exploration of American Sugar and Utah-Idaho Sugar was anticlimactic. Welliver spent most of this article discussing how American Sugar undercut the beet sugar market in 1901 so that it could then purchase beet sugar companies who could not meet their financial obligations. He did show that American Sugar held half of the stock in the factories which made up the Amalgamated Sugar Company, another Utah-based corporation with heavy involvement from the church, but, he stated, he had no positive proof that American Sugar had any stock interest in Utah-Idaho Sugar, although he believed it did. Welliver seemed unaware that Henry O. Havemeyer had purchased a 50 percent interest in the Utah Sugar Company in 1902 (the same year that American Sugar made stock purchases in numerous companies) and that Havemeyer had taken 50 percent of the stock on the formation of the Idaho Sugar Company, the Fremont County Sugar Company, and the Western Idaho Sugar Company in 1903. Therefore, when these four firms merged in 1907 to create the Utah-Idaho Sugar Company, Havemeyer and American Sugar held 50 percent of the shares.[21]

Although apparently unaware of these transactions, Welliver correctly assumed that American Sugar had a large interest in Utah-Idaho Sugar—and he also rightly observed the Latter-day Saint church's tight connection with Utah-Idaho. These connections included the fact that Joseph F. Smith, president of the church, was president of the company and that the board of directors included prominent church leaders such as Anthon H. Lund (a member of the governing First Presidency), Heber J. Grant and John Henry Smith (members of the Quorum of the Twelve Apostles), and Charles W. Nibley (presiding bishop of the church). Because of the close connections between the church and American Sugar, Welliver asserted that Senator Reed Smoot of Utah, who was also one of the church's twelve apostles and who led the fight among Republicans for a continued duty on sugar in 1909, took that position because he was trying to preserve the church's interest in beet sugar. Indeed, the tariff was seen as instrumental to the survival of the beet sugar industry. Although the amount could fluctuate, those importing sugar into the United States typically had to pay around two cents per pound on the product. This duty prevented cane sugar interests from selling sugar at rates that the beet sugar industry could not meet.[22] Therefore, according to Welliver, Havemeyer and Joseph F. Smith directed Smoot to take a strong stand on the sugar tariff because it would aid their financial interests in beet sugar. This was the main point Welliver was trying to make: that the Latter-day Saint church was willing to exert its political influence to keep a tariff on sugar, which ultimately meant that American consumers had to spend more for the product.[23]

Although Welliver's revelations about the church and American Sugar did not seem as stunning as he had promised, they led to a flurry of activity and examination into the Latter-day Saint church's economic interests. Later in 1910, other articles in national magazines provided caricatures of Joseph F. Smith as a greedy robber baron intent on dominating American economics and politics. Richard Barry's article "The Political Menace of the Mormon Church," published in *Pearson's Magazine* in 1910, opened with a paragraph portraying Joseph F. Smith as controlling "six senatorial votes and the electoral votes of three States"—perhaps drawing on Welliver's assertion that in the 1909 vote to retain the sugar tariff, *"Every Republican senator from a state where the Mormon influence is potent in politics—Utah, Idaho, Wyoming, Oregon, Nevada—voted for it."*[24] Barry also depicted Smith as a multimillionaire, and as "one of the guiding forces" in both Washington, DC, and on Wall Street.[25] In November 1910, Barry published another article in *Pearson's* entitled "The *Mormon* Method in Business," which depicted the church as "a commercial organization very well adapted to secure temporal power in the times in which we live." Additionally, Barry claimed that Joseph F. Smith placed tithing revenue that the church received "into the most substantial investments," including the beet sugar industry.[26] A disaffected church member, Frank J. Cannon—son of George Q. Cannon, a former member of the church's governing First Presidency—published a series of articles in *Everybody's Magazine* in 1910 and 1911 that were then published as a book in 1911. Cannon claimed that a connection existed "between the Mormon Church and the great financial 'interests' of the East," and that this connection was "one of the strong determining causes of the perversion of government and denial of political liberty in Utah today." Cannon singled out the church's interest in the sugar industry and the sale of control of sugar factories to the Sugar Trust, declaring that the sale made "a monopoly profit out of the Mormon consumers of sugar." According to Cannon, the church's ties to the Sugar Trust led to Latter-day Saint officials pressuring Cannon, who was in the US Senate in the late 1890s, to support a tariff bill because it benefited the trust.[27]

In 1911 Alfred Henry Lewis's three-part exposé of the church went even further. Lewis insisted that the church owned "huge blocks of stock" in several trusts, including "millions upon millions . . . a golden Pelion on a golden Ossa—in Sugar, Steel, Lead, Copper, Standard Oil, Tobacco." Lewis also claimed that the sugar industry, among others, paid "giant tribute to the Mormon Church." Echoing Welliver's claims, he asserted that Smoot, at the bidding of Joseph F. Smith, "rigg[ed] 'protection' traps to catch Gentile money in favor of the 'protected' trust investments" of the church. Lewis declared that the church would one day have the nation "conclusively" by its economic throat—and its role in the sugar industry would play a large part in that domination.[28]

As overblown as Lewis's assertions were, the claims made in these magazines pushed Congress to take notice of what was going on in the sugar industry—and particularly of the role of American Sugar and the church in beet sugar. Indeed, these articles—and Welliver's in particular—led to a congressional investigation of the American Sugar Refining Company in 1911.[29] On May 9, 1911, the House passed a resolution, authored by Representative Thomas W. Hardwick of Georgia, proposing "that a committee of nine members" investigate the American Sugar Refining Company to discover "whether or not there have been violations of the antitrust act of July 2, 1890," by the corporation. The resolution suggested that the committee also investigate other sugar firms and their relations with American Sugar. In this way, the committee could ascertain whether or not American Sugar or other concerns had restricted competition "among manufacturers or refiners of sugar," increased the price of sugar for the consumer, or decreased the rate that farmers received for their sugar beets and cane.[30] The resolution passed, and on June 12, 1911, the committee—chaired by Hardwick—began taking testimony.[31]

Because of American Sugar's interests in Utah-Idaho Sugar, Utah-Idaho officials became fair game for the committee and Hardwick directed the committee to focus its attention on that corporation. Influenced by the national magazine campaign against the church, and especially Welliver's article, members of the committee tried to discover the extent of Latter-day Saint holdings in beet sugar and the church's influence on the industry. Although the damning claims of the muckraking articles were a large component behind the investigation into Utah-Idaho Sugar, the Hardwick Committee's examination of the company gave leaders such as Joseph F. Smith, Charles W. Nibley, and Thomas R. Cutler an opportunity to respond to the allegations made against them. The church's governing First Presidency had issued a statement in 1911 denouncing muckraking articles as "utterly false and without foundation," but this statement, published in the church's monthly magazine, likely had little circulation outside of the Intermountain West.[32] Now, church officials had a national audience to which they could plead their case.

Cutler, vice president and general manager of Utah-Idaho Sugar, was the first company official to take the stand, doing so on June 23, 1911. Since one of the driving forces behind the establishment of the committee had been accusations that the church, through the Utah-Idaho Sugar Company, was partnering with American Sugar to monopolize the beet sugar industry in the Intermountain West, questions by the committee focused on a couple of key points: how much involvement the Latter-day Saint church had in Utah-Idaho Sugar; the involvement of Henry O. Havemeyer in the management of Utah-Idaho Sugar; and the views of officials of Utah-Idaho Sugar on the tariff.

The committee initially explored the involvement of the church in the corporation. Representative Asher Crosby Hinds set the tone for the questioning of Cutler by immediately asking "why the Mormon Church goes into the sugar business." Cutler stated that the church had become involved in sugar not out of a desire for profits, but because its leaders wished to encourage "anything that affects the welfare of the Mormon people financially," especially if it provided labor. "It is easier to look out for the spiritual welfare of employed people rather than unemployed people?," Representative Hinds asked. "It is their duty, if they can, to help and assist their people financially by providing labor in any way, shape, or form," Cutler answered. He explained further that church leaders "were anxious to provide their people with some labor and some sort of remunerative crop" and believed that beet sugar would fill those needs. The "primary idea" was to "supply the home demand for sugar."[33]

In making these statements, Cutler was only echoing what church leaders had been saying for years. In 1893, for example, Joseph F. Smith had addressed church members and declared that one of the main reasons the church had become involved in the Utah Sugar Company was that its leaders realized that "there was not a single enterprise of a public character [in Utah] that was calculated to give employment to our people." Church leaders thus believed that they had a responsibility to support the beet sugar industry in order to give their followers employment opportunities.[34]

Smith expanded these remarks in his own testimony before the Hardwick Committee. After Representative Hardwick asked him why the church had become involved in the enterprise, Smith explained that it was the policy of the church to help out any "home industry started by our own people" when such businesses could not succeed without the financial help of the organization.[35] According to Charles W. Nibley, "nine out of ten of the interests that the church has helped . . . are just in those extreme cases where people are down and out and they have got to have help."[36]

Because the church had pursued the practice of aiding Latter-day Saint enterprises, Representative Edward H. Madison of Kansas, a committee member, observed that "the Mormon Church constitutes in fact not alone a spiritual organization, but in a sense a business organization." He wondered where the church had obtained money to invest in such businesses. Cutler informed him that it came from the tithing of its members.[37] This raised the question, posed in several national magazine articles, of whether or not an accounting of tithing was made to church members at large, or whether the president of the church refused to disclose it because he merely administered the funds for his own personal benefit.[38] In his testimony, Smith responded that the church maintained regular business records "as correct as any bank" which any member could look at if he or she so desired.[39] Similarly, Cutler explained that a general accounting of funds was presented to church members at the denomination's annual general conference.[40]

Nibley, who, as presiding bishop, was responsible for the church's temporal affairs, elaborated. In 1910 the church had received approximately $1 million in tithes. Of that million, Nibley explained, $378,000 went toward the maintenance of church schools throughout Utah; $250,000 was used to build meetinghouses; $170,000 was used to fund the church's missionary efforts; and over $200,000 was paid out as "sheer charity." Little of the tithing was invested in business because the church did not want to "engage in commercialism and to get into commercial enterprises and make a big lot of money," Nibley declared. Instead, it used its money to help its people. "Anyone of you gentlemen can verify what I say if you take the pains," he concluded.[41] Despite his explanations, others remained convinced that, in the words of *Pearsons* essayist Richard Barry, the church used its tithing in "many shrewd and . . . unscrupulous schemes . . . to acquire property, money, lands, of all sorts."[42]

The Hardwick Committee next examined the accusation that the church, in concert with the American Sugar Refining Company, controlled the western beet sugar industry. Certainly, because of the stockholdings of American Sugar and the church in Utah-Idaho, those two organizations did control that beet sugar company. Smith agreed with Hardwick's contention that "there is no other stockholder, except the American Sugar Refining Co., in the Utah-Idaho Co. with anything like the holdings of the church."[43] However, in the minds of some committee members, the control of the two organizations extended beyond just Utah-Idaho Sugar. Some, accepting Welliver's assertions, believed that Smith used his power as church president to set beet sugar prices and to ensure that western senators voted for tariffs that benefited Utah-Idaho Sugar.[44]

Smith, however, contended that he was no more than a figurehead as president of Utah-Idaho and that he had little real knowledge of how the sugar industry operated. He did not take an active interest in the day-to-day affairs of the corporation, leaving that instead to Cutler. "Are you acquainted with any of the details of the business management of this Utah-Idaho Sugar Co.?," Hardwick queried. "Very little," Smith responded. He could not inform the committee about such things as the daily slicing capacity of Utah-Idaho's factories, the details behind Henry Havemeyer's investment in the Utah Sugar Company, or even how he, himself, had become president of Utah-Idaho Sugar.[45] Although some might claim that Smith was conveniently forgetting his involvement, the minutes of the Utah Sugar Company and the Utah-Idaho Sugar Company indicate that he really did not take a large role in business discussions, deferring instead to Cutler and the other directors.[46]

Utah-Idaho Sugar officials were especially questioned about the relationship between the company, the church, and the American Sugar Refining Company. Nibley testified that he realized that "the general impression" of the public "is that the church has large holdings in the Sugar Trust," mostly because of claims that had been made in magazine articles. However, Nibley stated, the church "has not got a dollar in the American Sugar Refining Co., directly or indirectly."[47] The question of how much control Havemeyer and American Sugar exerted over Utah-Idaho Sugar was a different matter since Havemeyer held half of the company's stock. Despite this situation, Cutler testified, for the most part Havemeyer let Cutler manage the corporation as he wished, and Havemeyer's contact with Smith was minimal. At times, Cutler explained, he asked Havemeyer for his opinions, but he often received advice that was either contradictory or given without any real knowledge of the beet sugar situation in the Intermountain West. Such testimony led Representative Madison to express in frustration "that everybody has conceded that Mr. Havemeyer was a masterful man, and yet nobody ever followed any of his dicta." Madison also wondered whether American Sugar ever sold its sugar in Utah-Idaho's regions, or whether the partnership prevented such competition. Although Cutler admitted that neither he nor Havemeyer were interested in "excessive competition" between the two companies, he explained that American Sugar did send cube sugar into Utah-Idaho's markets. According to Nibley, the two companies had no arrangement as to what prices they would charge for their specific products, and, he believed, the partnership between the two companies "was a benefit not only to the industry in Utah and Idaho but to the people of those States generally."[48]

Another aspect of the beet sugar industry that the Hardwick Committee examined was how essential the tariff was to the health of beet sugar.

Representative George R. Malby, a Republican from New York, first raised the question with Cutler: "What is your judgment as to the necessity for maintaining our present or any tariff on beet sugar?" Cutler bluntly answered, "If you lessen the tariff one iota, we can not . . . pay dividends" to the company's stockholders. Cutler was especially concerned that a reduction in the duty on raw sugar would benefit only the cane sugar refiners, allowing them to sell sugar at a cheaper price that would be prohibitive for the beet sugar industry.[49] The staunch Republicans Charles W. Nibley and Joseph F. Smith were even stronger in their positions. In response to inquiries by the Hardwick Committee, Nibley unequivocally declared that removal of the tariff would ruin the beet sugar industry. Smith, meanwhile, stated that without a tariff "the great industry of beet raising and the manufacture of sugar in Utah and Idaho would, of course, cease." Because cane manufacturers and foreign importers would be able to produce sugar at a lower rate without the tariff, Smith believed that Utah-Idaho Sugar would not be able to compete if Congress reduced the tariff.[50]

Although Smith strongly stated his position, it is questionable whether he had the ability to influence western senators outside of Utah. Welliver had contended that "the Mormon influence [was] potent" in the tariff decisions of politicians in Utah, Idaho, Wyoming, Oregon, and Nevada— a charge echoed by other essayists—but, although Latter-day Saint settlements were in all these states, it is highly doubtful that the church exercised much political influence outside of Utah. Even in Idaho, with its numerous southern Latter-day Saint settlements, members of the church faced opposition from both political parties. According to the historian Claudius O. Johnson, "When [Latter-day Saints] seemed inclined to support Democratic candidates, Republicans railed about the sin of polygamy; when they swung toward the Republican column, the Democrats became concerned about the 'purity of the American home.'"[51] Well into the 1890s, Latter-day Saints were not allowed to vote or hold office in Idaho.[52] The situation improved in the twentieth century, but if the Latter-day Saint leaders could not influence Idaho senators and representatives to allow church members to vote, it is doubtful that they could convince such politicians to support the sugar tariff solely for the sake of the church.[53]

Smith's influence on Utah's senators, especially Reed Smoot—who served as one of the church's governing twelve apostles—was more compelling. All Smith had to do was tell Smoot to work against tariff reduction, the argument went, and Smoot would readily comply. What else could explain why Smoot, who was widely known as a pro-tariff advocate, worked tirelessly in the Senate to preserve the tariff?[54] The reality, however, was that Smoot had embraced the tariff before he became both politically active and a member of the twelve apostles. According to Milton R. Merrill, Smoot's biographer, Smoot had decided in the late 1800s to "abandon the political faith of his ardently Democratic father" and affiliate himself with the Republicans because of that party's "position on the tariff."[55]

After being elected to the United States Senate in 1902, Smoot made several pronouncements about why he supported the tariff. For one thing, he argued, it raised the wages of American workers by enabling producers to make sufficient profits to pay their employees adequately. "I have seen the poverty, the squalor, and suffering" experienced by laborers in other countries, he once observed, "and I have made a vow that no act of mine shall ever place an American workman in the position of having to compete with such conditions."[56] Because, in the words of Merrill, Smoot was "as fully convinced of the validity of protectionism as he was of the theology of Mormonism," the Utah-Idaho Sugar Company had a strong proponent in the Senate to work against Democratic tariff revisions.[57] Indeed, in 1913 Smoot led the Republican fight against a proposed elimination of the duty on sugar. During this battle, Smoot vehemently denied that he supported the tariff because of the influence of Joseph F. Smith or other church leaders. "I represent all the people of Utah," he declared. "I am equally interested in every person in Utah, whether they belong to the church or whether they do not."[58] Likewise, if other western senators voted for a tariff, it was probably because they wanted to protect their own home industries and not because they felt concern for the Utah-Idaho Sugar Company or the Latter-day Saint church. As the historian Thomas Alexander argued, "That [Joseph F. Smith] controlled the votes of senators of six [western] states . . . was fantasy."[59]

In other ways, however, the church wielded indirect influence on behalf of Utah-Idaho Sugar. Although Smith denied before the Hardwick Committee that it was the policy of the church "to encourage sugar growing," he later admitted that, in his duties as an apostle in the 1890s, he had traveled among church members, "trying to get them to subscribe their money" for the building of a Utah Sugar Company factory. However, he refused to concede to Hardwick or other committee members that the church used its influence to persuade farmers to grow beets for Utah-Idaho, claiming instead that the company's business was completely separate from the church.[60]

When the Hardwick Committee concluded its hearings on the American Sugar Refining Company in 1911, it did not take any direct action against Utah-Idaho Sugar. The committee's report condemned the company for its close ties to American Sugar but said little about Latter-day Saint influence in the corporation. The committee also decided to let a case proceeding against American Sugar in a New York federal court penalize that corporation and its interests rather than inflicting a sentence itself. When this case was decided, however, the court only forced American Sugar to admit that it had violated the Sherman Anti-Trust Act in the past.[61]

Utah-Idaho Sugar escaped without punishment, but not unscathed. Because of the investigation, American Sugar began selling off its holdings in beet sugar corporations, eventually divesting itself of its interest in Utah-Idaho Sugar. After this time, American Sugar no longer considered itself an ally with beet sugar and worked against the tariff interests of that industry, ultimately resulting in tariff revisions in 1913 that would eliminate the duty on sugar within three years. The investigation, then, did not have an overt effect on Utah-Idaho Sugar, but it certainly had a deleterious impact on the beet sugar industry as a whole.[62]

However, in many ways the Hardwick Committee hearings helped, rather than hindered, Utah-Idaho Sugar and the Latter-day Saint church because it allowed church officials to refute popular charges. As Reed Smoot wrote in his journal, the testimony of Smith, Cutler, and Nibley caused a "great change in public sentiment towards the Mormon people" regarding the question of business.[63] Whether Smoot was exaggerating was beside the point. The church's First Presidency had issued statements to church members defending the organization against falsehoods in national magazine articles, but the Hardwick Committee hearings enabled church officials to present their explanations to a wider audience.[64]

Despite the defense that Smith, Cutler, and Nibley offered, many were still convinced that the Latter-day Saint church was exerting undue influence in the beet sugar industry. Some Utah citizens, even members of the church, vigorously attacked church leaders because of their sugar interests. Charles G. Patterson, a former bishop in the church who had, according to Smith, become a "'Progressive' of Socialistic tendencies," frequently castigated Utah-Idaho Sugar and its Latter-day Saint leaders for taking advantage of Utah consumers and sugar beet farmers.[65] Patterson firmly believed that Utah-Idaho leaders used ecclesiastical authority to their benefit. "No greater sin can be conceived and perpetrated upon the farmer himself," Patterson observed, "than for his ecclesiastical superiors to conspire to keep him producing the crop." Patterson claimed that bishops and scoutmasters had preached in church meetings that it was necessary for farmers to plant beets solely for Utah-Idaho. "When Presidents of Stakes, bishops, high councilmen and others approach you in the capacity of sugar company hired men," Patterson cautioned church members, "it will help some if you forget everything about them except that they are HIRED by the sugar company to boost for it."[66]

The federal government seemed to agree with Patterson's assessments. Throughout the 1910s and 1920s, several federal agencies charged Utah-Idaho Sugar with unfair business practices. The Department of Justice, for example, investigated Utah-Idaho in 1920 for profiteering in the aftermath of the First World War, only stopping its inquiry when the United States Supreme Court declared the law under which the company was charged to be unconstitutional. In addition, the Federal Trade Commission brought the corporation to trial in the 1920s for unfair business practices because of its attempts to drive competitors out of Utah, Idaho, Nevada, and Oregon. Throughout all these investigations, Latter-day Saint leaders maintained a prominent role in the company. Heber J. Grant, who succeeded Joseph F. Smith as church president, also took Smith's position as president of Utah-Idaho Sugar and held that title throughout the 1920s, becoming more deeply involved in the company's business affairs than Smith had. Nibley, meanwhile, served as general manager of the corporation from 1917 to 1921 and directed the company in its monopolistic policies. Recognizing Nibley's role, several grand juries indicted him in 1920 for profiteering and the Federal Trade Commission targeted him in its case as one of the primary offenders. Although both the Department of Justice and the Federal Trade Commission's investigations were ultimately dismissed because of technicalities, the publicity surrounding them tended to erode whatever good Smith, Cutler, and Nibley had done through their explanations before the Hardwick Committee.[67]

The investigation into the American Sugar Refining Company and Utah-Idaho Sugar in 1910 and 1911 is instructive for several reasons. First, it provides a concrete case of muckraking articles influencing the US Congress to investigate an industry portrayed as monopolistic and injurious to American consumers. Without the flurry of articles in 1910 and 1911—and especially those of Judson Welliver in *Hampton's Magazine*—it is doubtful that Congress would have felt the need to investigate the machinations of American Sugar and its connections to the beet sugar industry. In this instance, the muckrakers shed light on big business in such an alarming way that Congress had to act.

Second, the investigation indicated how connected Utah-Idaho Sugar was to national markets, trends, and companies in the overall sugar industry of the United States. These ties resulted primarily from Henry O. Havemeyer and the American Sugar Refining Company's holdings in Utah-Idaho Sugar and the impact that the tariff had on the corporation. Mormon leaders such as Reed Smoot were instrumental as well, influencing national policies like the sugar tariff in a way that benefited Utah-Idaho's interests.

Third, the investigation showed just how much involvement the Latter-day Saint church and its officials had in the beet sugar industry, highlighting both the financial interest the church had and the influence its leaders held in the business. It also indicated that the involvement of the Latter-day Saint church in beet sugar was of utmost interest to the federal government. A religion that financially supported and invested in beet sugar seemed to be a novel idea to many congressmen, piquing both their curiosity and their sense that combining religion and business may not be in the consumers' best interest. For Latter-day Saints, such ties did not seem that unusual; church leaders often followed the lead of Brigham Young, who, in 1845, "def[ied] any man to draw the line between the spiritual and temporal affairs in the kingdom of God."[68] But to those who were unfamiliar with the church or its doctrines, having religious leaders take an interest in things such as sugar beet cultivation seemed both disconcerting and bizarre.

Such connections alarmed the national populace as well. At the conclusion of the Hardwick investigation, Charles G. Patterson declared that "the history of Standard Oil, or any other monopoly, reveals nothing so hateful, detestable or loathsome as does the history of our Utah sugar monopoly." Indeed, he continued, "when . . . the men . . . sustained [by Latter-day Saints] as leaders and in whom they have reposed confidence bordering on the Divine, deliberately plan to exploit them in a temporal way, it is certainly time to raise the alarm."[69] Likewise, the essayist Bernard DeVoto harangued the church in 1930, claiming that the Latter-day Saints were "a consecrated people whose piety . . . created the Beet-Sugar Trust."[70] As long as church officials continued their association with Utah-Idaho Sugar, individuals such as Welliver, Patterson, DeVoto, and Hardwick would continue to "raise the alarm." Their warnings, they believed, were all in the interest of ridding the nation of a snake in the sugar ready, in the name of economic dominance, to bite anyone it encountered.

PART III

Unity and Nationalism

Mormons have presented the potential to disrupt the political and cultural unity of the American nation. Church leaders possess the religious authority to mobilize the faith's adherents within the American democratic landscape and many of them have, in fact, exercised this political influence. This ability to assemble and affect is not unique to Latter-day Saints, but the faith's centralized ecclesiastical structure and its self-expressed differences from other religious and regional groups have heightened fears that the Church of Jesus Christ of Latter-day Saints and its members could disrupt national unities.

The four chapters in Part III unpack the changing ways that Latter-day Saints have participated in conversations about national unity within the nation's wider context of ever-shifting national needs, emerging alliances, and existing party structures and systems. On the eve of the Civil War, the Mormon quest for statehood threatened a fragile pact that attempted to balance slavery and antislavery factions within existing states and an expanding western frontier. In the twentieth century, American political rhetoric drew a hard line between godly American capitalism and ungodly Russian communism, prompting questions from within and without about the church's place and allegiance. As the culture wars of the late twentieth century reshaped party affiliations and issues, the faith again faced questions about its alignment with mainstream religion and politics.

Matthew Mason, the biographer of the renowned antebellum public intellectual Edward Everett, analyzes a stream of Mormon-themed correspondence between the Boston Brahman and the speaker of the US House of Representatives, John C. Winthrop. Everett opposed admission of a Mormon-dominated state but considered its advancement from territorial status inevitable. Mason contextualizes Everett's position as part of an overall suspicion toward religious zealotry and charismatic religious leaders. Everett looked askance at Latter-day Saints from the point of view of both his Unitarian background and his moderate Whiggery, and as such he represented a larger cultural and political persuasion. But he also wrote within the broader context of the sectional and partisan debates leading to the Compromise of 1850. In that setting, he worried about what he saw as the church's history of stirring up strife everywhere they lived, something best not incorporated in territorial—and eventually state—form in an already overly fractious Union.

Rachel St. John places the Latter-day Saint political experience within a broader landscape of shifting political identities and allegiances in the middle decades of the nineteenth century. After being granted territorial status, Utahans proclaimed their devotion to the US Constitution, served as government officials, and facilitated overland travel and settlement in the West. Yet this was also the period in which the church came closest to political independence, developing separate and semiautonomous economic, political, and military institutions in the Great Basin. This history of divided loyalties and ambivalence about the United States has often made the Mormon experience seem like an aberration. But it was not. Nineteenth-century North America was filled with people who, like the Saints, were in the process of puzzling out the relationship between their political allegiances, identities, and ideals. Rather than a simple choice between loyalty or treason to the United States, nineteenth-century North America offered a range of alternate national identifications. Some of these lined up with existing governments—American, Mexican, Cherokee, British—but others presumed the possibility that new political configurations were possible—Confederate, Texan, Métis, Mormon.

Twentieth-century Latter-day Saints navigated a different political and cultural landscape as J. B. Haws explains in his analysis of midcentury media coverage. National magazines presented a picture of the church at the middle of the twentieth century that was decidedly tamer than its nineteenth-century iteration, and journalists repeatedly depicted that change as worthy of commendation, even celebration. Beneath the change, Haws found an apparent abandonment of church political aspirations. In an era marked by consensus thinking, journalists happily depicted Latter-day

Saints as joining the ranks of America's mainstream denominations. Not only do these portrayals offer a telling backdrop against which journalists painted the Mormon past; they also established the terms by which the Saints could—and even should—negotiate public respectability and national unity moving forward.

As the twentieth-century unfolded, perhaps no Latter-day Saint claimed more of the national spotlight than Ezra Taft Benson, a Mormon apostle and the secretary of agriculture in the Eisenhower administration. Patrick Q. Mason argues that during four decades from the 1950s through the 1980s, Benson was the subject of national media interest and scrutiny, most intensively during his eight-year tenure in Eisenhower's cabinet, but still frequently in the years thereafter, culminating in his elevation to the presidency of the Church of Jesus Christ of Latter-day Saints in 1985. Due to both his outspokenness and prominence internally and externally, Benson became a principal filter for how the church publicly engaged with "the historic conflicts of our time," including anticommunism, civil rights, church and state, the women's movement, international and domestic conflict, and the rise of conservatism. Exceptional in many ways, Benson was not truly representative of all Latter-day Saints or their faith. Yet he came to represent them, both in his official capacity as a senior ecclesiastical leader and as a public figure whose religion rarely escaped mention when he appeared in the media. In the national gaze, Benson stood as a symbol of the church and its members and how they were situated in modern American religion, culture, and politics.

CHAPTER 10

"Rather Than Recognize This Wretched Imposture"

Edward Everett, Rational Religion, and the Territory of Utah/Deseret

MATTHEW MASON

In December 1849, Edward Everett, who had recently retired as president of Harvard College after a distinguished scholarly and political career, was perturbed at the idea of Mormons getting their own territory or state under the name of Deseret. Mormon leaders had petitioned Congress for admission as a state, with territorial status as a "plan B." The direct route to statehood seemed to have momentum in Congress until late December 1849, when members raised questions about the Latter-day Saints' true loyalties. The other complications (chief among them the legality of slavery) involving territories in this era of Congress prolonged this discussion. But given that one major purpose of the period of territorial tutelage before statehood was to ascertain and strengthen territorial populations' loyalty to the United States, this question of allegiance was central to the issue of a territory or state for Mormons. American statesmen in this period deemed not only statehood, but also territorial status, as privileges to be merited rather than as rights.[1] While the Mormons' fate hung in the balance, Everett wrote to his friend—and speaker of the House—John C. Winthrop to register his protest. One key source of Everett's consternation with the proposed name was his overall suspicion toward religious zealotry and charismatic religious leaders. He looked at them askance from the point of view of both his Unitarian background and his moderate Whiggery. Like other religious and reforming Whigs, he had long sought to police the boundaries between reform and fanaticism. But that police work took on an increased urgency in the larger context of the sectional and partisan debates of the late 1840s. Everett's exchange with Winthrop and others thus illuminates not only a formative moment in Utah and Mormon history, but also a crucial moment for the Whig persuasion.

On December 1, 1849, when Everett wrote to Winthrop, he was fifty-five years old and in semiretirement from public affairs. He had been the first American to earn a PhD (from Göttingen University in 1817), a classics professor at Harvard, a Unitarian minister in Boston, the editor of the *North American Review*, a five-term representative to Congress, the governor of Massachusetts, US minister to Great Britain, and president of Harvard. Through it all, he had sought with varying degrees of success to balance his deep commitment to the American Union with his equally deep investment in the Whig ethic of Improvement that embraced not only internal improvements but also a wide array of moral and social reforms (including a moderate brand of antislavery). After happily resigning from the Harvard presidency in January 1849, he held no particular post either private or public, but continued to be an influential voice within the Whig Party.[2]

Everett's letter to Winthrop captured the full range of his objections to statehood under a name derived from Mormon revelations. The relevant passage reads, in full:

> I see among the projects for the [new] session [of Congress], that the new Mormon settlement of "Deseret" is to be admitted as a State. I greatly doubt the Constitutionality of incorporating a fanatical horde under a purely hierarchical government into the Union.—I do not consider Mormonism to be republicanism.—It is, on the contrary, the worst species of despotism viz. spiritual despotism. If they must come in, I hope it will not be by the name of "Deseret," if as I suppose that word is a part of the Mormon jargon. If it is a native Indian word, I have no objection to it; but I cannot bear the thoughts of going to Jo. Smith's Revelations for the name of one of the States of the Union. There are a plenty of well sounding Indian words, & any thing could be submitted to rather than recognize this wretched imposture.—But I cannot but hope that Congress will take some pains to inform themselves who & what these People are, before they are admitted to the Union. They have been driven out of Missouri & out of Illinois;—and in both cases have been, I doubt not, much wronged. But if they are a set of people calculated to incur, to this extent, the ill-will of their

neighbors, is it wise by admitting them into the Union to run the risk of a civil war in their defence?[3]

Ten days later, Winthrop, who was in the middle of a serious fight to keep his position as speaker of the House of Representatives, pronounced Everett's "suggestions about the State of Deseret" to be "judicious." In 1852 Everett confided in his son-in-law: "I believe it was owing to me, that their pretended Egyptian name 'Deseret' did not get into the Statute book," the territory being named Utah instead.[4] Everett's manifest pride in influencing this result was an adjunct to the larger concerns about the state and prospects of both the Union and true reform that made up the text and subtexts of his letter to Winthrop.

Everett's constitutional concerns about accommodating the Mormons stemmed in large part from his lifelong sense of the sacredness of the Union. That constitutional federation of states, held together by the consent of the governed, represented the high point of the long story of human liberty. Because this vision of the Union rested so firmly on consent rather than force, this brand of nationalism was an especially vigorous example of what Benedict Anderson has famously termed an "imagined community." Nationalists such as Everett were constantly trying to convince their fellow Americans to commit their whole hearts to the nation. But as with every imagined community, there was the possibility of exclusion as well as inclusion; even as Everett and his fellow laborers worked to expand the boundaries of this affective Union, they in no way abandoned the idea of boundaries.[5] The stakes involved with this balancing act were all the higher in the late 1840s and early 1850s because the uncertainty of liberal nationhood had gone on its most recent display with the failure of the revolutions of 1848 in Europe.

Admission into such a Union at such a time should not be granted lightly, so if Everett fully had his way Congress would not admit the Mormons under any name. "Is there not a great constitutional objection," he asked his friend, the influential senator Daniel Webster, in early 1850, "to the admission into the Union of a Mormon state?" To reward them with territorial status and thus put them on the road to statehood would constitute "granting the highest privilege, in the power of Congress to bestow, upon a band of fanatics and adventurers."[6] As his letter to Winthrop suggested, to admit a people of such dubious ability to satisfy the Constitution's requirement that Congress guarantee a republican form of government for all future states and territories would be playing entirely too fast and loose with the cornerstone document of the sacred Union.

That Union was also in an extremely fragile state when Everett wrote these missives to his policymaker friends in Washington. The Wilmot Proviso, which would have banned slavery from any territory seized from Mexico by war, had roiled the nation since 1846. The donnybrook it set off led to a full-scale conflict in and beyond Congress over a range of issues related to slavery's place and future in the nation. Calls had already gone out, for instance, from southern state legislatures for a secession convention in Nashville that would meet in June 1850.[7] Gathering as much information as he could from his semiprivate position, Everett expressed his deep-seated anxiety that all this partisan and sectional strife would destroy the American experiment in self-government. Especially when the stormy Congress met, starting in December 1849, Everett felt a relentless wave of fear for the beloved Union. "I have never known the political horizon so dark as at the present day," he moaned in one diary entry. That was saying something for someone who had been in public life since the 1810s.[8]

In this fraught setting, Everett was convinced that incorporating yet another discordant element was the very last thing the fractious Union needed. The Mormons, he reminded Webster, "have made trouble wherever they have set themselves down." But to grant them territorial government, he wrote to Winthrop in a later epistle, would constitute a promise "to protect them" against any persecutors.[9] Thus, his dire talk of the near certainty of civil war upon Mormon territorial admission in the closing lines of the above excerpt from his first letter to Winthrop.

The charged political atmosphere of 1849–50 also contributed to people like Winthrop's amenability to Everett's project of substituting a more rational name for "Deseret." Sectional moderates of all stripes fretted that this sectional crisis was elevating extremists in both north and south, just as all past crises had done. Winthrop's failure to win reelection as speaker of the House—and indeed the weeks-long failure of any candidate to secure the speakership in the first session of the Thirty-First Congress beginning in December 1849—was a personally as well as politically alarming example of the effects of polarization. Many apprehensive observers wondered aloud whether this paralysis was rendering the United States a failed state. "In the present condition of parties," Winthrop groused to Everett on December 11, "it will not surprise me, if" the projected Deseret Territory "comes in just as it is, in spite of any efforts which may be made by reasonable, conservative men." He would certainly try to implement Everett's suggestions for alternative names, but "I am writing in my seat, with too much hubbub about me to be quite responsible for the character or contents of my letter," let alone to guarantee the outcome of this or any other motion in that Congress.[10]

Most of Winthrop's peers seem to have been entirely indifferent to the issue of the territory's name. Members of the Thirty-First Congress did not single out Deseret for any particular debate, considering it only in the context of larger debates about the constitutionality of admitting states vs. territories, the boundaries of Texas, and the future of slavery in New Mexico, Deseret, and California; they certainly showed none of this special interest in the issue of Deseret's name. Beginning in July 1850, congressmen started to refer to the names Utah and Deseret interchangeably, but the debates in which those names appeared were not about the proper name for the territory. By September it had quietly become simply "Utah" in the debates. This would seem to support Everett's interpretation that he, a well-connected person who cared about the name issue more than almost anyone else, had secured that outcome via Winthrop.[11] But at any rate, Winthrop's and Everett's private writings made it clear why, in their minds, this seeming side issue related directly to these other headline issues. The seemingly low-stakes question of the name of the future Utah Territory took on increased importance for them because it was one barometer of whether conservative men had completely lost power to zealots.

The perception of Mormons as religious zealots was another vital part of this discussion among these Massachusetts Whig elites. At first blush, this seems counterintuitive within the landscape of antebellum religion and politics. Throughout its life, the Whig Party had sought to advance a moral reform agenda at all levels of American politics. There was no cause within the capacious orbit of the Benevolent Empire to which at least some Whigs did not publicly attach themselves. The Whig base also identified more openly with Protestant faith than did the Democratic base, and believed that that faith should have full expression in politics. The likes of Everett and Winthrop wholeheartedly embraced and advocated all these aspects of Whig political culture. The Democratic Party, on the other hand, housed a coalition of citizens who were deeply suspicious of do-gooders and those who embraced the Benevolent Empire but sought to keep divisive moral issues from politics.[12] Given all this, Democrats would seem more likely than the likes of Winthrop and Everett to spearhead objections to including "the Revelation of Jo. Smith in the fundamental law of this hopeful new state," as Everett put it to Webster.[13]

But, for Everett as for so many other nineteenth-century Americans, the distinctive nature of Mormonism forced him to ponder just what constituted religion.[14] Throughout the late 1840s into the early 1850s, Everett was experiencing a mild case of faith crisis with religion as practiced in Massachusetts.

He regularly attended both Congregational and Unitarian services, but at least a solid plurality—if not outright majority—of his Sunday diary entries between 1847 and 1852 bemoaned how both of his state's dominant denominations needed serious reinvigoration, usually by means of a better liturgy. "Some new Dispensation is sorely needed," he concluded in 1847 after attending a Congregationalist service that he found neither solemn nor interesting. In 1850, after yet another worship service at which he found "the audience thin—cold—dull," his exasperation found a fascinating form. "Oh, that I were an enthusiast, a fanatic, a Mormon, a fifth monarchist.— Anything fervid & glowing."[15] Of course, the inveterately rational Everett could never be any such thing. But diary outbursts of this sort show just how much the proper form religion should take was on his mind.

Mormonism failed that test. It was, instead of an actual religion, just so much "wretched farrago of" Joseph Smith's creation and outright "nonsense." "The Mormon delusion" affronted his sense of reason. From what he had read, he believed Mormons to be "a mixture of rogues & dupes, the latter greatly predominating." This was ultimately why "to admit their gibberish into the statute book is going too far."[16] The prospect of just such an admission was alarming enough to him that he went public with his chagrin that more of his fellow Americans were not alarmed. In late February 1850, Everett hastily wrote an article on the Deseret issue and sent it to the leading Washington newspaper, the *National Intelligencer*. "It is high time some one spoke out on the subject," he told the editors in his cover letter. But "I do not wish to be known as the author," he added, "for that would imply a personal controversy with some mormon prophet, in which victory would be as discreditable as defeat."[17]

In this article, published as "The State of Deseret," Everett granted that "other subjects of a more urgent nature" had kept the Mormons' "application to be admitted into the Federal Union" from garnering "a greater degree of public attention." The first question germane to this issue, Everett insisted, is "Who and what are Mormons? The answer is, they are a sect of fanatics" who have been "deluded" by "the abominable fraud" and "pure fiction" of "Joe Smith" that was the Book of Mormon. In both Missouri and Illinois, this group composed of "simple fanatics" and "adventurers of every kind" had "incurred the ill-will and odium of their neighbors." But in spite of persecution, and "to the disgrace of the age[,] this wretched imposture flourished." Now settled in "the region of the Great Salt Lake," they had established a "pretended *theocratic* government," and "revelations are as regularly announced to them as the orders of the day by a commanding general in time of war." But now, "Congress is asked to make to this sect, not of Christians but of Mormons, of believers not in Jesus Christ but of [sic] Joe Smith," the gift an "act of admission, on terms of equal membership, to this Union of States!" To this screed he added his (anonymous) weight as a classical scholar to deny that "Deseret" had any origins in ancient Egyptian as claimed. "The entire Book of Mormon being a forgery out of whole cloth, it is of course idle to discuss the meaning of any thing contained in it." But Everett still protested "against the incorporation of any of this jargon into the statute-book of the United States." "We may smile at the egregious absurdity" of Mormons' numerous "delusions, and yet not think it prudent to assist" this numerous horde "to plant themselves" in such a strategic location on the continent and within the Union.[18] It added up to Everett's public effort to maintain the borders of both religion and the Union.

Everett was not the only reforming, improving Whig to work such a patrol. John Quincy Adams, for instance, was the poster boy for the Whig ethic of Improvement, but detested fanaticism masquerading as reform.[19] The utter impracticability of the American Colonization Society's scheme to transport masses of freed African American slaves to Africa struck him as especially offensive on this score. "There are so many considerations of difficulty and of delicacy mingling with" the subject of slavery, Adams recorded in his diary, "that I would gladly keep aloof from it altogether." But he worried that the ACS, "which, like all fanatical associations, is intolerant, will push and intrigue and worry till I shall be obliged to take a stand and appear publicly among their opponents." And it was not just the political inconvenience of their fanaticism that troubled Adams. "Their project of expurgating the United States from the free people of color at the public expense, by colonizing them in Africa, is, so far as it is sincere and honest, upon a par with John Cleves Symmes's project of going to the North Pole, and travelling within the nutshell of the earth." Symmes, who had served in the US Army from 1802 to 1816, first announced his "hollow Earth theory" in 1818 by distributing a circular "to every learned institution and . . . to numerous distinguished individuals, throughout the United States." Symmes lectured in western cities of the United States beginning in 1820, and in 1822 and 1823 petitioned Congress to support an expedition to one or both of the earth's poles.[20] The ACS seemed like a mainstream reform organization to most observers, receiving far less abuse and ridicule than Symmes did. Taking in both northerners and southerners, it attracted many Americans who thought of it as a valid potential solution to the problem of slavery.[21] So Adams was showing a high level of vigilance by trying to keep the ACS out of the true reform club. Although he offered these thoughts only in his journal—and in private conversations with ACS boosters—Adams was prepared to openly denounce the ACS if that became necessary. Adams piled ridicule on both the ACS and Symmes for the same essential reason that Everett had raised such a fuss about the Deseret issue. They were both card-carrying reformers who wanted to keep that club pure and its reputation safe from the crazies.

Everett thus had good reason to celebrate his alleged influence on changing the territory's name, and likely was also glad that Utah came in as a territory rather than a state. These were minor, symbolic victories to be sure, especially when compared to the larger, Union-saving victory that was the Compromise of 1850 in the minds of Unionists like him. But symbolism mattered, in part because it was connected to those larger issues. The purity of the Union had been saved from incorporating the jargon of pseudoreligionists.

CHAPTER 11

Ambiguous Allegiances and Divided Sovereignty

*Mormons and Other Uncertain Americans
in Nineteenth-Century North America*

RACHEL ST. JOHN

From erstwhile rebels to ardent patriots, Mormons have had an uneven relationship with the US government throughout the history of the Church of Jesus Christ of Latter-day Saints. This varied history has led to questions about Mormons' political identities and allegiances as both contemporaries and historians have sought to locate Mormons somewhere between citizens and foreigners. At no time was the relationship between Mormons and the United States more ambivalent than in the middle of the nineteenth century. At that time, Mormons proclaimed their devotion to the US Constitution, served as government officials, and facilitated overland travel and settlement in the West. And yet this was also the period in which Mormons faced the greatest persecution at the hands of Americans and came closest to political independence, developing separate and semiautonomous economic, political, and military institutions and relocating to the Great Basin. In Utah, the Mormons pursued their plans for establishing God's kingdom on earth—a kingdom that most Americans saw as a threat to US sovereignty. In this context, Mormon settlement, political authority, economic development, and relations with the Great Basin's Native populations all threatened to disrupt US claims to the region. Add to this anti-Mormon prejudice and the Mormons' continued suspicion of government officials and non-Mormons, and it is no wonder that a military conflict erupted between the US federal government and the Mormons in 1857.

This history of divided loyalties and ambivalence about the United States has often made the Mormon experience seem like an aberration. But it was not. Nineteenth-century North America was filled with people who, like the Mormons, were in the process of puzzling out the relationship between their political allegiances, identities, and ideals. From Aaron Burr to Stephen F. Austin to Jefferson Davis, many nineteenth-century Americans found fault with the direction the US government was taking, questioned whether they would remain within the evolving United States, and at times sought to form their own nations to better suit their political, economic, and cultural needs.

The histories of these uncertain Americans remind us of the tenuousness of state power and national identity in the United States' first century. The Church of Jesus Christ of Latter-day Saints emerged in and alongside the adolescent United States and its experience similarly sheds light on the struggles over sovereignty and allegiance in the nineteenth century. In this young nation-state, neither national identity nor the authority of the federal government were clearly established. A product of that lack of definition and sovereignty, the Mormon experience helps us better understand the range of those contests and the attenuated and uneven development of federal power and American national identity in nineteenth-century North America.

National loyalties were particularly tenuous on the frontiers of the new nation and among westward-moving Americans and recent immigrants, with whom the Mormons would be counted. In the United States' first decades, settlers in present-day Tennessee and Kentucky considered seceding from the new confederation, either to establish independent republics or to join with the Spanish Empire.[1] Spain, and then Mexico, continued to be a draw for frontier settlers, including the likes of Daniel Boone and Moses and Stephen Austin, who relocated to Missouri and Texas, respectively.[2] The formation of the Republic of Texas in 1836 was a product of the persistent consideration of alternative republics and made other such ventures seem more viable. As Thomas Richards argues in his dissertation, "The Texas Moment: Breakaway Republics and Contested Sovereignty in North America, 1836–1846," the example of Texas provided encouragement to Cherokees in Indian Territory, American Patriots on the Canadian border, American emigrants in California and Oregon, and Mormons in Illinois, all of whom were interested in forming their own independent "breakaway republics."[3]

It was in this context, in the early 1840s, that the leaders of the Church of Jesus Christ of Latter-day Saints first began to develop institutions that flirted with autonomous government. Following years of persecution in New York, Ohio, and Missouri, Mormons began to gather on the banks of the Mississippi River where they founded the city of Nauvoo in 1839.

By that time, four things were clear: (1) the church's membership was growing; (2) their leaders, particularly Joseph Smith, had grown more ambitious in their pursuit of religious reformation and political and economic power; (3) they faced real enemies; and (4) they could not count on established government authorities to help them. As a result, the Mormons undertook to carve out a space of political, economic, and legal autonomy in Nauvoo and to raise a military force to defend it.

Enacted by the Illinois legislature in December 1840, the Nauvoo city charter practically made Nauvoo a semisovereign city-state within Illinois. The charter granted the city council the "power and authority to make, ordain, establish, and execute, all such ordinances, not repugnant to the Constitution of the United States, or of this State."[4] It also gave the municipal courts unprecedented authority to grant writs of habeas corpus.[5] In addition, the charter empowered the city council to establish a "body of independent militarymen, to be called the 'Nauvoo Legion.'"[6] Under the leadership of Smith, who commanded the force as lieutenant general (a rank last held in the United States by George Washington) and made military training compulsory, the Nauvoo Legion grew rapidly. With four thousand members, this Mormon army equaled half the size of the entire regular US Army.[7] With the protection of the Nauvoo city charter and the Nauvoo Legion, the Mormons were able for a time to build a thriving city in Nauvoo. By 1844 the city and its environs were home to upwards of fifteen thousand residents and rivaled Chicago as the largest city in Illinois.[8]

The size and unity of the Mormon population gave the church growing political power in Illinois, but also provoked resentment and suspicion among its neighbors. Continued tensions with surrounding populations and lack of support from government officials left the Mormons vulnerable and increasingly ambivalent about their prospects within the United States. By 1844 the church had undertaken a series of ambitious, new projects that marked the extension of the church administration into what were clearly governmental affairs and revealed the tension between the Mormons' pursuit of security and power and their loyalty to the United States. As they simultaneously launched a campaign to elect Joseph Smith as president of the United States and surveyed western sites in anticipation of the need to leave the country, the Mormons demonstrated their ability to straddle the line between serving and subverting the goals of the US government.

Responsibility for both Smith's campaign and the selection of a western settlement site fell to a new, secret governing body, the Council of Fifty or the Council of the Kingdom of God. Established in March 1844, the council's broad mission was the establishment of a Kingdom of God over which Smith would rule as king.[9] Historians have long acknowledged that the Council of Fifty operated as a "shadow government" the purview of which extended well beyond church affairs.[10] However, with the Joseph Smith Papers Project's publication of the entirety of the minutes of the Council of Fifty for the period between 1844 and 1846, it is now clearer than ever before that Smith and other Latter-day Saint leaders intended the formation of this council as "the beginning of the literal kingdom of God on earth."[11] The creation of the council reflected a broader sense among Mormons that religion and government should not be separated.[12] Assembling the Council of Fifty was a critical step toward forming what Joseph Smith called a "theodemocracy."[13]

What Mormons' attempt to merge church and state would mean for the United States was not clear. Although it is certain that few Americans would have supported the transformation of the United States into a Mormon theodemocracy, there is no reason to believe that Mormons, like Smith, who were both loyal to the US Constitution and devoted to the creation of a Kingdom of God, did not genuinely believe this was a good and achievable goal, even if it required a selective embrace of the nation's founding principles. As one member of the Council of Fifty, George Miller, recalled in 1855 (eight years after he had broken with the church), the council agreed to run Joseph Smith and Sidney Rigdon for president and vice president respectively, and, "in case they were elected we would at once establish dominion in the United States, and in view of a failure we would send a minister to the then Republic of Texas to . . . get them to acknowledge us as a nation. . . . And if successful in this matter we would have dominion in spite of the United States."[14] With the Council of Fifty, the church took a clear, if concealed, step in the direction of crafting a theocratic government. Whether it would be hostile to the United States, was, from the Mormons' perspective, for the American voters to decide.

How many people believed the Kingdom of God could truly compete with the United States in anything but a millennial sense is impossible to know. What did seem possible in the short run was the establishment of a separate Mormon state outside the United States. It was to this goal that the Council of Fifty devoted much of its energies.

Like most mid-nineteenth-century Americans striving for independence and opportunity, the council looked to the West. Located in the borderlands between empires and nations where no Euro-American polity had secured its sovereignty, places like Texas, Oregon, and Alta California seemed to offer promising sites for Mormon settlement. It is no coincidence that each of these locations had been or would be selected as sites for possible alternative republics by other actors in the nineteenth century. Even before the success of the Texas Republic, Americans and Mexicans—not to mention the Native peoples who in fact maintained independent polities—had considered a series of alternative national configurations in the Texas borderlands. Oregon and Alta California also saw a series of possible nation-building movements emerge as Californios, Americans, and Hudson's Bay fur traders toyed with independence.[15]

Although an independent theocracy was the Mormons' goal, they saw no need to entirely disentangle their own interests in the West from those of the United States. There is no doubt that Smith's primary fealty was to the church. But, in running for president in 1844, he clearly believed and sought to convince others that Mormon and US national interests were one and the same. Both, he believed, would be well served by extending American authority in the West. As such, the annexation of Texas was a central part of his campaign platform.[16] He also presented a memorial to President John Tyler in March 1844 asking for authority to raise "100,000 men to extend protection to persons wishing to settle Oregon and other portions of the territory of the United States, and extend protection to the people in Texas."[17] That these soldiers would also serve as scouts and military support for any future Mormon emigration seems self-evident. Even Orson Hyde, the Mormon representative in Washington, DC, acknowledged that this force, although authorized by the federal government, would not be part of the US Army. When congressmen in Washington rejected the plan on the grounds that the British would see this force as a violation of the joint occupation of Oregon, Hyde insisted that "these volunteers are not to be considered any part or portion of the army of the United States, neither acting under the direction or authority of the United States."[18] It is little wonder that the president did not grant authority for this venture. But what is more interesting is how Hyde's, perhaps ill-advised, recognition of the separation between a Mormon army and the US Army revealed the extent to which the two did in fact exist as separate bodies, the former not necessarily subordinate to the latter.

At the same time that Smith and other Mormon leaders publicly tried to couch their interest in the West within the broader framework of US expansion, they also secretly began to develop plans to relocate the church outside US boundaries so as to establish an independent theocratic nation. In February 1844, Smith instructed the twelve apostles to dispatch a delegation to "investigate the Locations of California & Oregon & find a good Location where we can remove after the Temple is completed.—& build a city in a day—and have a governme[n]t of our own—in a hea[l]thy climate—."[19] Around the same time, Lyman Wight, one of the twelve apostles, proposed relocating to Texas where he suggested the Mormons would be welcomed by southerners and Indians alike.[20] Throughout the spring of 1844, the Council of Fifty weighed the possibility of moving to Texas, Oregon, or California. As the minutes recorded on March 11, 1844 reveal: "All seemed to agree to look to some place where we can go and establish a Theocracy either in Texas or Oregon or somewhere in California &c."[21] Writing from Washington, DC, in April, Orson Hyde deferred to Smith's "superior wisdom" to "determine whether to go to Oregon, to Texas, or to remain within these United States," but he warned that "the sooner the move is made the better, . . . If the saints possess the Kingdom, I think they will have to take it, and the sooner it is done, the more easily it is accomplished."[22]

For Joseph Smith, the move would not come soon enough. On June 27, 1844, an armed mob attacked the jail in Carthage, Illinois, where he was being held on charges related to the destruction of the *Nauvoo Expositor* which had published articles critical of him. They shot Joseph, his brother, Hyrum, and two companions multiple times. Joseph and Hyrum died within minutes.[23]

Following the murder of Joseph Smith, the church experienced a crisis of leadership. In the struggle to determine Smith's successor, the church fractured. While some Mormons pledged their loyalty to Smith's younger brother and remained in the East and others followed a recent convert named James Strang who set up a colony on Beaver Island in Lake Michigan, the majority of the church recognized the authority of the Quorum of the Twelve Apostles and its president, Brigham Young.[24] Under Young's leadership, the church began to relocate to the West. Rather than settling in Texas, Oregon, or California, the Mormons eventually settled in the Great Basin. Located on the far northern frontier of the Mexican Republic, inhabited only by Indians, and surrounded by mountain ranges, the Great Basin seemed to offer the isolation and autonomy that the Mormons sought. The first party of settlers arrived in the Salt Lake Valley in the summer of 1847.

Yet, even as the Mormons began their exodus to the West seeking isolation from their fellow Americans and government officials who seemed at best indifferent to their persecution and at worst hostile to their interests, the United States launched an invasion of Mexico which threw the future of the Great Basin into question. In the Mormons' response to these changing conditions, we yet again see evidence of their ambivalent relationship to the United States. A little over a month after the United States declared war on Mexico, on June 1, 1846, the Mormon's new agent in Washington, DC, Jesse C. Little, wrote to President James K. Polk rehearsing the Mormons' plight and asking for government assistance in support of their westward migration. He informed Polk that there were as many as fifty-five thousand Mormons (an exaggerated number) from Nauvoo, the British Isles, and the

Sandwich Islands who were poised to move to California. Referring to his own patriotism and family ties to the American Revolution, he insisted that these people, presumably even the forty thousand emigrants who he claimed were coming from Great Britain, were "true hearted Americans, true to our country, true to its laws, true to its glorious institutions—and we desire to go under the outstretched wings of the American Eagle."[25] However, alongside these proclamations of patriotic loyalty, Little issued a threat: "We would disdain to receive assistance from a foreign power—although it should be proffered—unless our government shall turn us off in this great crisis and will not help us, but compel us to be foreigners." "Means for the gathering of poor we must obtain," he continued, warning that "if I cannot get it in the land of my Fathers I will cross the trackless ocean where I will find some friends to help."[26]

Considering that Polk was particularly worried that the British might try to claim California, Little's warning that the Mormons might look for assistance across the Atlantic, paired with his claim that forty thousand British Mormons were en route to California, was cause for concern. By the following day, Polk and his cabinet had authorized Colonel Stephen J. Kearney to enlist Mormon volunteers in the US Army "with a view to conciliate them, attach them to our country, & prevent them from taking part against us."[27] Polk also clarified that Kearney should be sure that the Mormon volunteers numbered only five hundred and never made up more than one-fourth of the whole force once it reached California.[28] He clearly did not trust them. Whether this effort succeeded in increasing the Mormons' emotional attachment to the United States is hard to tell, but we do know that the Mormons did not form an alliance with the British and ultimately remained within the United States.

The formation of a Mormon Battalion, made up of five hundred Mormon men enlisted at a refugee camp in Iowa, also benefited the church. The enlistees' pay and clothing allowances provided critical material assistance at a moment when the Mormons desperately needed funds to support their migration to the West. For the five hundred volunteers, the costs of their travel were covered by the federal government. During their journey to New Mexico and on to California, the Mormon Battalion saw little action, but learned a great deal about the western part of North America which the church intended to make the new base for the Kingdom of God.[29]

In 1848 two of its members were present for an event that would profoundly influence the trajectory of both Mormon and US history—the discovery of gold in California. For although the two Mormon Battalion veterans—who were working for John Sutter when they witnessed James

Marshall's discovery of gold in the South Fork of the American River—could not have known it then, this discovery would unleash a flood of gold-seekers across the Great Basin and cement the West Coast's ties to the United States, dooming Mormon hopes for isolation and independence, as well as their hopes for settling in California.[30]

The extension of US authority over the Far West, followed immediately by the California Gold Rush, foreclosed many of the alternative nations that had seemed possible only a short time before. Not only did the US conquest subsume the short-lived Bear Flag Revolt, but the arrival of US troops and the influx of emigrants fundamentally changed the demographic and political conditions in which Californios and Americans alike had imagined they might form new governments and in which John Sutter had presided over a private fiefdom in the Sacramento Valley.[31]

However, although many westerners' hopes of independent nationhood faded, circumstances on the ground continued to challenge federal sovereignty across the West. Even as white settlers, with the support of the federal government, sought to eradicate Native power, Indians remained the dominant force over most of the interior West. White settlements and army encampments represented pockets of American authority. But, even within these, lack of military authority, conflicts over the dispensation of justice, challenges to government officials, disputes over slavery and sectional politics, and dissatisfaction with the incompetence and corruption of political appointees were widespread.[32] The struggle between Mormons and the federal government that unfolded over the 1850s and culminated in 1857 in the Utah War, then, was distinctive, but not aberrant. It was symptomatic of the broader problem of a government stretched too far over people with ambiguous loyalties.

Moreover, this conflict unfolded in the context of an evolving federal system in which the exact balance of power between federal, state, and local interests remained unresolved. In the years immediately preceding the Civil War, Americans were preoccupied with a range of questions about how power should be shared between local, state, and federal governments, and between different officials and populations at each level of government. These questions, in the form of nullification, states' rights, and popular sovereignty, framed the sectional debates over slavery. But while we are used to thinking of these questions in terms of the sectional struggle, they were equally significant in the federal government's efforts to manage the West. As Brent M. Rogers has argued, mid-nineteenth-century Americans understood the dispute between the governance of Utah within the context of popular sovereignty.[33] Although the United States' acquisition of the Great

Basin and the effects of the Gold Rush meant that the Mormons remained within US territory, they did not predetermine the balance of sovereignty between the US federal government and local Mormon settlers. Unable to escape the United States completely, the Mormons would continue to have an ambivalent relationship with it until the end of the nineteenth century.

In Utah, the church leadership quickly organized the State of Deseret and applied for admission to the Union as a sovereign and independent state. This move signaled the Mormons' willingness to remain under the umbrella of US authority, but, at a moment in which most Americans believed that state sovereignty rivaled that of the federal government, was also an attempt to establish self-rule.[34] A committee of Mormons wrote a state constitution, based on the US and Iowa constitutions. Brigham Young was the only candidate for governor. The Mormons claimed extensive territory for their proposed state, including not just present-day Utah, but most of Arizona and Nevada and parts of Colorado, Wyoming, Idaho, New Mexico, Oregon, and California, including, importantly, seaports on the Southern California coast.[35] They hoped that this vast territory, with the church president at its head, would form the base of the Kingdom of God in North America.

In making this aggressive move to claim statehood, Mormons acted similarly to other westerners. Settlers in Oregon, California, and Texas had formed provisional governments.[36] In the wake of the US–Mexican War and the discovery of gold, Californians, impatient to secure statehood and frustrated with military governance, preemptively formed a state constitutional convention and sought admission to the Union, skipping the territorial stage and ignoring Congress's prerogative to put them off.[37]

However, while Congress, albeit after prolonged debate and a near sectional crisis, admitted California as the thirty-first state, it refused to accept Deseret. Not only did the proposed state lack the requisite population of sixty thousand (in 1850 the total non-Indian population was only twelve thousand), but Congress was unenthusiastic about creating such a large state, let alone putting it in the hands of a Mormon theocratic government. Instead, in 1850 they created the Territory of Utah, rejecting both the Mormons' suggested Book of Mormon name and significantly reducing the territory's size.[38]

Although this was not what the Mormons had wanted, there were immediate signs that the federal oversight suggested by territorial status would not significantly limit self-rule. Clearly recognizing who held power in the Great Basin, President Millard Fillmore appointed Brigham Young as both territorial governor and Indian superintendent in Utah. It was under his authority and through networks of church power that most territorial functions were carried out.

To the extent that these functions were administered by Mormons who had been appointed as government officials and that they served the interests of the US state in establishing white settlements, displacing Indians, and supporting overland travel and communication, they were state-building projects. But they also served Mormon interests and were carried out by people who saw their primary loyalty not to the US government, but to the church. In that sense, they served both the United States and a distinctly Mormon state-building project. In the subsequent decade, anti-Mormon prejudice and suspicion would lead many federal officials and non-Mormons to question whether Mormon policies were intended to undermine US authority in the Great Basin.

The Mormons adopted distinctive laws and practices that set the territory apart from the rest of the United States and made many non-Mormons nervous. Breaking with the procedures for surveying and distributing land that the US Congress had established over the previous six and half decades dating back to the Land Ordinance of 1785, the church hierarchy, drawing on earlier plans developed in the Mormons' eastern settlements, established a plan for the division of land and distributed lots. The result was a communal system of land ownership (as well as water distribution) that scandalized many non-Mormon observers. They also developed a distinct legal system. In 1854, rejecting the standard practices of relying on legal precedents and English common law, the Legislative Assembly passed laws stipulating that only laws and court decisions originating in the territory could be brought to bear in court hearings.[39]

The few non-Mormon federal officials who were sent to Utah discovered that the Mormons did not welcome their involvement in their affairs or in state functions over which the church had already cemented its control. Government surveyors fell under particular suspicion because of the Mormons' fears that they would divide and make available for sale land that Mormon settlers had already claimed.[40] When Judge Lemuel G. Brandebury arrived in Utah in the summer of 1851 to swear in Brigham Young as territorial governor, he learned that the (Mormon) attorney general had already done so months earlier.[41] Federal appointees reported that Brigham Young had announced that "the United States judges might remain in the Territory and draw their salaries, but they should never try a cause if he could prevent it."[42] Within months of their arrival in Utah in 1851, four prominent, non-Mormon, federal officials—Brandebury, Judge Perry Brocchus, the territorial secretary Broughton D. Harris, and the Indian affairs subagent Henry R. Day—abandoned their posts to return to Washington where they denounced the Mormons and Brigham Young for subverting federal authority.[43]

To the extent that these disputes over law and authority broke down along religious lines, they were unique. However, the instability of the legal system was in keeping with much of the West. Vigilante justice was not unusual in the nineteenth-century United States, especially in the West where the government presence was thin on the ground. This was particularly true in California where lynch mobs defied state-sanctioned judicial proceedings and violently took law enforcement into their own hands.[44]

Disputes also arose between Mormons and non-Mormons over the administration of Indian affairs. Millard Fillmore initially appointed Brigham Young as superintendent of Indian affairs, and Mormons—for religious as well as economic and security reasons—diligently undertook to negotiate with the Native inhabitants of the Great Basin. Their efforts quickly brought them into conflict with military officials and other Americans who perceived that the Mormons were attempting to cultivate alliances with the Indians and to turn them against other Americans. Over time, and particularly in the context of violent encounters between Native peoples and the US Army, this came to be a major critique of Mormon rule.[45]

Yet, in this sense too, Mormons were not unique. Throughout the West, local people and federal officials came into conflict over the proper treatment of Indians. Interestingly, in contrast to Utah where officers cast aspersions on the Mormons for cultivating too friendly relationships with Indians, it was usually federal troops who complained that locals were too violent and uncontrolled in their encounters with Indians. California Indians, finding little to no security in state-sponsored reservations, faced genocidal attacks and enslavement.[46] In New Mexico, Indians and Hispanos persisted in raiding Native communities for slaves, despite federal attempts to discourage the practice.[47] In both Colorado and Arizona, notorious massacres resulted in part because of local people's refusal to recognize military officials' designation of peaceful Indians.[48]

In the face of mounting condemnations from federal officials, Mormons insisted that it was they who knew best how to govern themselves and the region in which they had settled. They complained that too many of the federal appointees were corrupt and misused their power. This was a common grievance across the West. Staffed largely by political appointees who lacked sufficient oversight, territorial governments were rife with corruption.[49] Moreover, the Mormons insisted that, in the face of the officials' departures, they had no choice but to take on their governmental functions themselves. "No people exists who are more friendly to the government of the United States, than the people of this Territory. The constitution they revere, the laws they seek to honor," Brigham Young insisted in a letter to President

Millard Fillmore. "But the non-execution of those laws in times past for our protection, and the abuse of power in the hands of those intrusted [sic] therewith. . . . It is for this we have cause for complaint."[50]

Armed with these justifications, Young remained the dominant authority in Utah Territory. Although the term of his appointment as governor ended in 1856, President Franklin Pierce was unable to replace him. Pierce's selection, Colonel Edward Steptoe, who had spent time in Utah, reported that Utah was a "religious oligarchy" and decided that he did not want to be the one to challenge Young's authority. In the absence of a replacement, Young continued as de facto governor.[51]

Part of what made the possibility that the Mormons might secede and establish an independent theocracy in the Great Basin so threatening was that the United States' control of its much-lauded, vast, continental nation was so tenuous and rested so precariously on the federal government's ability to retain the loyalty and subservience of the polities with which it shared sovereignty. Much of the territory the United States claimed remained in effect under the authority of Indians. From New Mexico to California and from Utah and across the Plains, the war to make US sovereignty real raged on in local conflicts and negotiations between Native peoples and white American settlers. The US government had implicitly outsourced much of its Indian fighting to private individuals—miners in the Sierra foothills, Texas Rangers, and Mormons. However, the state's dependence on these local settlers also left it vulnerable. Nineteenth-century Americans needed only to look to Mexico to see how terribly awry a nation's dependence on frontier settlers could go. Empresarios like Stephen Austin and John Sutter had proved to be fickle in their national loyalties. Given the ongoing tensions between Mormons and the United States, no US official could expect that if given the opportunity, Brigham Young might not prove to be equally inclined to abandon his loyalty to the United States.

And, of course, the United States also faced other challenges to its sovereignty in the 1850s. Indeed, the central preoccupation of the period was not whether the federal government could hold the West (which to be fair was in doubt), but whether it could retain control of the South. Talk of secession and division had emerged periodically since the thirteen colonies had first joined together in revolution, but by the 1850s the possibility of the secession of one or more of the southern slaveholding states was becoming increasingly likely. Across the South, pro-secession "fire-eaters" gave speeches, wrote pamphlets, and held conventions dedicated to the premise that the southern states must secede from the Union to protect slavery and the southern way of life.[52] As we know, seven of these states eventually did secede in the winter and spring of 1860–61. By that time, some Americans expected that the secession of the southern states would cause a domino effect in which California, Oregon, Washington, and New Mexico, as well as Utah, would also leave the United States and establish independent polities in the West.[53]

It was in this context that the US federal government and the Mormons remained locked in a relationship of mutual dependency and distrust. The crux of the problem, from the government perspective, was that it needed the Mormons, both to perform state functions and because losing them might mean losing Utah, but most Americans, including most federal officials, were also suspicious of the Mormons' loyalties and hostile to their religious beliefs and practices. The Mormons, for their part, had little faith in the federal government or most Americans, but they hoped that in Utah they could achieve enough autonomy and security to prepare for the ascendance of the Kingdom of God, a millennial vision that, for believers, hovered tantalizingly within reach.

The Mormons' desire for autonomy and the mutual distrust between Mormons and many of the non-Mormon travelers, traders, settlers, and officials with whom they came in contact led to a series of clashes throughout the 1850s. Most of these conflicts were characterized by no more than heated rhetoric and mutual recriminations, but, for about a year between the springs of 1857 and 1858, they came dangerously close to provoking an outright war when President James Buchanan appointed new territorial officials and ordered a force of 2,500 soldiers to escort them to Utah. The events surrounding what became known as the Utah Expedition or Utah War (although it never crossed over into outright warfare) brought into relief both the federal government's and the Mormons' dissatisfaction with how sovereignty was shared in Utah Territory.

The crisis began with Buchanan's decision in the spring of 1857 to appoint new territorial officials for Utah. The distribution of political appointments was a regular part of an incoming administration's responsibilities, but when Buchanan and his cabinet began to look into the situation in Utah, they discovered a territory under the control of a governor whose term had expired and a throng of angry government appointees, many of whom had abandoned their posts. It is not clear what exactly provoked Buchanan, just weeks after taking office, to begin making plans to dispatch a large military force to confront the Mormons. He was most likely influenced both by the general climate of anti-Mormonism in American culture and the steady stream of complaints that non-Mormons had sent back from Utah Territory over the preceding years.[54]

However, if Buchanan was aware that there was broad political appeal in anti-Mormonism, the issues that were most prominent in the reports he considered as he made his decision to send troops, and that he would consistently reference in justifying his actions, were not questions of morality, but of sovereignty. Buchanan's interest in Utah may have begun with his need to make appointments, but he had quickly come to believe that much more was at stake. "The civil government of Utah Territory," the troops' orders explained, "are in a state of substantial rebellion against the laws and authority of the United States."[55] "As Chief Executive Magistrate," Buchanan would later insist, "I was bound to restore the supremacy of the Constitution and laws within [Utah's] limits."[56] Buchanan intended the Utah Expedition as an unequivocal assertion of federal authority over the distant territory and its overly independent inhabitants.

The Mormons, however, rejected these charges. As long as a successor had not taken office, Brigham Young maintained, he remained the legal governor of Utah Territory.[57] Denouncing the army expedition as unlawful, he issued a proclamation to the people of Utah: "We are invaded by a hostile force, who are evidently assailing us to accomplish our overthrow and destruction."[58] Young did not acknowledge the government's argument about federal supremacy, insisting instead that the government was motivated by religious prejudice and unfair accusations. Evoking their constitutional rights as American citizens, he called on the Mormons to rally to their self-defense, declared martial law, and limited transcontinental travel through the region.[59]

With neither Young nor Buchanan seemingly willing to back down, the Utah War could have ended in disaster. As it was, the territory was thrown into turmoil for a year as the Mormons prepared to defend against an armed invasion or, if necessary, abandon their homes in a scorched-earth operation. In this context of heightened fear and animosity, some non-Mormons became caught in the cross fire. Most notoriously, in September 1857, members of the Nauvoo Legion in southern Utah enlisted Paiute Indians in an attack on a party of overland migrants en route to California. In what became known as the Mountain Meadows Massacre, they murdered 140 men, women, and children in cold blood, allowing only seventeen children, who they believed would be too young to remember, to live.[60]

However, aside from this tragic event and a few other isolated incidents of violence, the so-called Utah War never produced combat. Nor did the expedition do much to solidify federal authority. Although Buchanan had set out to make a show of force, the Utah War also underscored the limitations of the federal government's power in the West. The expedition required

2,500 men stationed at Fort Leavenworth to be diverted from the crisis in "Bleeding Kansas" to travel more than one thousand miles to Utah. As they moved across the Plains, they suffered from attenuated supply chains and poor communication. They were also vulnerable to Indian attacks, for their path to Utah led through what was, although claimed by the United States, still clearly Indian country. Exacting a toll for the army's passage, Cheyenne raiding parties drove off hundreds of cattle that were intended to feed the soldiers. The army was forced to augment its forces and divert some troops to pursue Indians. As they approached Utah, Mormon guerillas also attacked the army's supply trains, burning supply wagons and driving off oxen and cattle. Given its late start and slow progress, the expedition failed to make it to Utah before winter weather settled in on the Plains. Not only was the expedition forced to wait out the winter at Fort Bridger, but hundreds of horses and stock animals perished in the cold before it arrived there.[61]

Meanwhile, as the soldiers waited out the winter, a series of envoys from the federal government traveled to Utah where they met with Brigham Young and successfully negotiated a resolution to the conflict. The Mormons agreed to accept a new, non-Mormon governor, Alfred Cumming, and to allow the army to enter Utah.[62] No Mormon officials were charged with treason. Brigham Young remained as president of the church and also continued to influence the judicial system and to exert enormous power through his authority over the church members and his personal control of church property.[63]

Sovereignty in Utah continued to be shared, although not without contention, by the church and the federal government. Buchanan had achieved a nominal victory in installing Cumming as governor and establishing a military outpost in Utah, but the cost was significant. Not only did he fail to distract the nation from its more pressing preoccupation with slavery, but he also spent between $14 and $40 million dollars for what was ultimately achieved through negotiations. He also diverted a significant portion of the US Army to Utah, where it would remain the United States' largest garrison when the Civil War began three years later.[64] Rather than a symbol of federal strength in the West, this outpost, like the expedition that led to its creation, signaled how thinly stretched and dependent on local support US sovereignty was.

The conflicts over who should govern Utah laid bare the unresolved issues concerning the relationship between the Mormons and the United States, but also shed light on a broader struggle over the balance between local and national interests and the development of state power in North America during the nineteenth century. In discussing Utah, historians often focus on polygamy, which can make the conflict over Mormonism seem like a moralistic sideshow to the dramas of slavery and states' rights, federalism versus centralism, and local versus imperial rule that dominated the period. However, while denunciations of the Mormons' practice of plural marriage reflected genuine concerns about social order, the overarching issue was sovereignty, and whether the way in which the Mormon population and the federal government shared it was equitable and sustainable. By focusing on questions of divided sovereignty and uncertain loyalties, we can see the struggles between Mormons and the federal government as an important chapter in the history of the evolution of state power in North America.

CHAPTER 12

Mormons at Midcentury

"Crushed Politically, Curtailed Economically," but Winning
"Universal Respect for Their Devotion and Achievements"

J. B. HAWS

This chapter is driven by two questions—and politics is a subtext for both: What was it about the American national mood in the middle of the twentieth century that made things feel so welcoming for Latter-day Saints? And what was it about Latter-day Saints in the middle of the twentieth century that made Americans seem so welcoming? In other words, this is a story about the fifties.

"The fifties." There is something potent just in that phrase, in the evocation of mental images of that middle decade of the twentieth century. Even Americans who were born and raised a half century later still seem to have some psychic connection to the fifties. It says something that in 2017 the *New York Times* columnist David Brooks felt that he had to "[note] that the 1950s aren't coming back," even though Brooks himself said he was "very much in the 1950s Christian theologian tradition."[1] What is it that makes so many long for that era?

The power of artistic and nostalgic portrayals of that decade certainly accounts for some of that pull. Everything seemed possible in the fifties—or at least in the fifties world that subsequent movies have created. Think *Hoosiers* here: tiny Hickory High—161 students strong—could take down dominant South Bend High School. Optimism and progress were the currency of the day. And even Americans who might not pay attention to the intricacies of American historiographical shifts would likely agree that it makes sense that the 1950s saw a turn toward "consensus history," an "interpretive framework" that had as its focus, as one student of that history put it, "what had united Americans rather than what had divided them."[2] The idea of consensus just seems to fit the 1950s.

There may be special reasons for Latter-day Saints to feel nostalgia for that time, too. What some commentators have called the "long fifties"—the period from the end of World War II to the end of John F. Kennedy's presidency—also corresponds with a time that a past director of the Church of Jesus Christ of Latter-day Saints' Public Affairs Department called "the golden era of Mormonism." It was an era when Latter-day Saints may have felt, more so than at any other time before or since, that they were in step with the wider American culture.[3]

The journalist Kenneth Woodward, an astute observer of American religion for fifty years, recently published a book that was part memoir and part twentieth-century history of religion in America. He made a well-reasoned defense of the 1950s against those who would argue for its conformity and blandness and unthinkingness. He is persuasive on a number of points—civil rights, the arts, public intellectualism.[4] But his description of trends in American religion during the post–World War II years reinforces the idea of a strong impulse toward consensus and unity.

At the heart of this chapter is an argument for one such signal of this desire for American religious consensus: the press's treatment of Mormonism at midcentury. What should not be overlooked in this treatment is an implicit, underlying message that matters of politics trumped matters of theology.

The two quotes in the subtitle of this chapter come from national magazine stories published in 1947—and anyone with an eye for Mormon history will understand why American journalists were writing about Mormons in 1947.[5] That year marked the centennial of the Latter-day Saints' epic trek west to their new Great Basin home. Oxen, bonnets, and covered wagons loom large in the American imagination about the conquest of the West, and magazine editors nationwide were not going to miss a chance to put those iconic images on their pages. But the resultant stories have much more to say than that. Perhaps more than anything, these articles offer a glimpse into the American public's view of Latter-day Saint religious life at a key pivot point in the history of the Church of Jesus Christ of Latter-day Saints.

In 1947 (or in the two years on either side of that centennial), *Time* and *Newsweek* had cover stories on the Mormons, and *Life* magazine, the *Nation*, the *Christian Century*, the *New York Times*, the *Los Angeles Times*, the *Christian Science*

Monitor, and the *Chicago Tribune* all weighed in. There emerges a common picture in these articles of a version of Mormonism in the mid-twentieth century that was decidedly tamer than its nineteenth-century iteration, and journalists, again and again, depicted that change as worthy of commendation, and even celebration, especially in connection with political aspirations—or more accurately, with the abandoning of those aspirations. That is, by 1947 a decrease in fear about Mormon theocratic ambitions seemed to open space for an increase in favorable feelings for Mormons. These 1947 portraits can thus offer a benchmark of American attitudes toward Latter-day Saints at a time when mainstream American society prized consensus and unity, and when journalists were likewise happy to depict Latter-day Saints as joining the ranks of America's religious denominations. As historian Peter Novick has written of the World War II era, "Circumstances of national mobilization are inherently inhospitable to dissent"—and Mormons mobilized with the rest of the nation.[6] In subtle ways, these journalists' stories have hints of prescription mingled in their descriptions of Mormonism. Not only do these portrayals offer a telling backdrop against which journalists painted the Mormon past; they also set out the terms by which Latter-day Saints could (and even *should*) negotiate respectability moving forward in American society.

I want to trace three broad impulses that are repeatedly evident in this coverage which reflect and reinforce the religious and political spirit of the times: the importance of a unified and collective American religiosity—and hence the intentional diminishing of Mormon theological distinctiveness; the religious turn toward positive thinking—and hence the focus on Mormon healthy-mindedness; and the robust celebration of democracy as the superior counterpoint to communism or totalitarianism—hence the emphasis on the church's lack of political control, even (perhaps especially) in the political leanings of church members.

The impulse toward a shared American religious unity sets the stage, and the looming threat of both communism and nuclear warfare must be the contextual backdrop for any discussion about American politics and religion in the mid-twentieth century. Here is one chronological signpost to orient our discussion: US president Harry Truman announced the foreign policy doctrine that would come to bear his name—the policy of American defense support for nations under threat of Soviet expansion—in March 1947, only four months before the Mormon pioneer centennial. It seems almost impossible to overstate just how thoroughly the Cold War "shaped everything," as the historian William Chafe put it, "defining issues according to moralistic assumptions," with "the battle in the world [being] between good and evil, believers and nonbelievers"; the fact that "godless" was often the modifier that preceded American conversations about "communism" highlights the religious implications in this geopolitical posturing.[7] Religiosity became one of the markers of differentiation, of what it meant to be an American.[8] Five years after the pioneer centennial, Dwight Eisenhower, US president-elect in December 1952, would say: "Our form of government has no sense unless it is founded in a deeply-felt religious faith, and I don't care what it is."[9]

World War II had made its mark on the contours of America's religious landscape, too. The historian Mark Noll called the war "a harbinger of ecumenical activity as it drew together in common tasks, often for the first time, representatives of most of the nation's denominations."[10] Signs of that ecumenism abounded: the National Association of Evangelicals formed in 1942; the World Council of Churches in 1948; the National Council of Churches in 1950 (growing out of the union of several groups with the older Federal Council of Churches). And as Edwin Gaustad and Leigh Schmidt point out, only months after atomic bombs decimated Hiroshima and Nagasaki, a representative of the Federal Council of Churches called for unity above all else, in the face of these new threats to the very survival of the human race. "The fate of the world," this representative, Richard Fagley, wrote, "therefore, in a literal sense depends upon the ability of the moral and religious forces . . . to call men effectively to repentance, worship, and service."[11]

The mood of postwar America was thus one of unity but also of a remarkable renewal of religiosity—or as Kenneth Woodward put it, "The Fifties . . . were exceptional for yet another important reason . . . : [America] was awash in a culture of belief."[12] Statistical evidence puts an exclamation point to Woodward's observation. The social scientists Robert Putnam and David Campbell note that "weekly church attendance [among young adults in their twenties] skyrocketed from 31 percent in February 1950 to an all-time record for young adults of 51 percent in April 1957, an astonishing rate of change in seven years, implying millions of new churchgoers every year."[13] Church membership numbers skyrocketed, too: "By 1960," the historians Paul Harvey and Philip Goff write, "65 percent of Americans were members of a church or synagogue, the highest level in the country's history. Just as amazing is the fact that 96 percent of the population claimed adherence to a specific group, which indicates a level of public expectation that individuals have a religious affiliation, even if they only rarely or never attended services." Simply put, "the Cold War . . . set in motion a more traditional revival of religion across the land."[14]

But there was a uniquely political cast to this revival. Putnam and Campbell have labeled the 1950s the "high tide of civic religion," this moment when "religion and Americanism were brought together to an unusual degree," to use Sidney Ahlstrom's phrase.[15] Religion became part of the American bulwark, part of a unified front against a common enemy. Perhaps nothing better captures that civic religion temperament better than President Eisenhower's encouragement of church attendance as a patriotic act. Later observers agree, again and again, that "religion and democracy were as wed in the minds of citizens as atheism and communism." The evangelist Billy Graham, who emerged on the national scene after a 1949 revival, would say: "If you would be a true patriot, then become a Christian. If you would be a loyal American, then become a loyal Christian."[16] What "seemed to be the message," Kenneth Woodward has written, is that "to be American was to believe in God."[17]

One effect of this sense of shared civic religion, of the preeminence of this common denominator of a belief in God, was that it created space—perhaps unexpectedly—for more religious pluralism. Kevin Schultz has argued that the postwar pivot in the American religious landscape was the turn from a Protestant (especially mainline Protestant) America to a "tri-faith America," where Americans saw their nation as one of Protestants and Catholics and Jews.[18] And this came to signal all that was best about American freedoms. Colleen McDannell noted that Americans sought to distance themselves from Nazism's insistence on racial and ethnic homogeneity: "After all, it was Hitler, not democratic Americans, who could not tolerate difference."[19]

This tolerance of diversity only extended so far; Americans of color were not immediately imagined in this tri-faith national portrait. This point complicates straightforward narratives about American religious consensus, and so we must not move past it too quickly. African American pastors and parishioners lived the reality of midcentury segregation in their religious lives as much as they did in other aspects of their day-to-day lives—but they lived that religious reality somewhat differently, too. In the case of church life, racial separation involved an important element of agency. That is, segregated churches reflected prejudice as well as preference and prerogative: preference and prerogative on the part of black church leaders to maintain independence and dignity in the face of inveterate prejudice on the part of white American religionists, such that African American ministers and church boards most often operated in parallel denominations with their white counterparts.[20]

Black Metropolis, an important sociological snapshot published in 1945, included a report on "The Churches of Bronzeville" (Chicago's South Side). The researchers noted that only "ten per cent of the churches" (which numbered around five hundred in that part of the city) "and less than ten per cent of the churchgoers in Bronzeville are affillitiated with white denominations," denominations where "in state and national organizations . . . Negroes wield very little influence." Black members of these denominations found again and again that "individual white congregations in these sects do not welcome Negro members. . . . On the whole, Bronzeville sticks to the 'Race Churches.'" The majority of churchgoers were "affiliated with one of the two Negro National Baptist Conventions," whose "congregations and ministers have virtually no face-to-face relationships with any of their white coreligionists." Sadly, one area in which there had been recent interaction between black and white coreligionists was in matters of real estate—*Black Metropolis* researchers noted that when "Negroes purchased the white churches and synagogues in the Black Belt area as the white population moved out," the transactions "often embittered Negroes against their white brethren, whom they accused of unloading church property on them at exorbitant rates during the Fat Years."[21]

Kevin Schultz asserts that tri-faith accommodations eventually even "helped soften the ground for the civil rights movement of the 1960s."[22] Still, it is not difficult to see why, in the words of the theologian Michael Battle, "African American spiritual leaders . . . were deeply troubled by how white social gospelers conveniently left out the problem of racism."[23] Historians have noted this same turn, this same impatience with the social gospel, in Martin Luther King Jr.'s thinking.[24] Emblematic of the race-based blind spot in much of American religious thinking was the criticism that came to King from a group of self-described sympathetic white ministers in Birmingham, Alabama, who chided King for moving too fast and too boldly, criticism that prompted his unforgettable response from his jail cell in Birmingham.[25]

That blind spot is also easily detectable in retrospect in Thomas O'Dea's landmark book *The Mormons* (published in 1957). O'Dea delved deeply into many of the doctrines and practices of the Church of Jesus Christ of Latterday Saints, but the church's policy of prohibiting the priesthood ordination and full temple participation of its black members was not even mentioned in O'Dea's treatment, as if the issue was so unremarkable as to not even register on the general public's radar in the 1950s.[26]

The tide of midcentury religious consensus, of a broad civic religion, thus did not lift the black church into national participation and acceptance in the way that it did other groups, including, as Patrick Allitt has pointed out well in contrast, American Mormons, who in many ways gained access to "first-class citizenship" in what was essentially *white* America, despite their previously suspect religious leanings.[27] What Americans in the 1940s *did* imagine about the national portrait of faith was something along the lines of one powerful visual: the image of four chaplains—two Protestants, one Catholic, one Jew—interlocking their arms in prayer as their ship, the SS *Dorchester*, sank—and all this after they had given away their life jackets because of a shortage of the life preservers.[28] This meant that the trajectory of religious attitudes in the country was in the direction of accepting diversity, albeit along the lines of shared Judeo-Christian values ("a term invented in this period"), values which seemed more crucial than denominational intricacies. This was the era of adding "under God" to the pledge of allegiance (1954), of officially adopting "In God We Trust" on all currency (1956).[29] One sociologist of suburban life in the 1950s noted that the people he observed were "Protestants, Catholics, and Jews who believe in an increasingly similar God, share an increasingly similar Judeo-Christian ethic, and worship in an increasingly similar way."[30]

Of course, painting with broad brushstrokes can obscure the finer details, and many religious groups often resisted the impulse toward ecumenism, if such meant abandoning the religious convictions that gave a group its raison d'être.[31] Fundamentalist Christians, for example, were reluctant participants in ecumenical projects. Catholics and Jews who moved to the suburbs demonstrated their belief that "persistent communalism," creating and preserving social connections primarily with like-minded coreligionists, "was a good thing." Religious boundaries were not obliterated; on the contrary, Kevin Schultz contends that this type of communalism "gained widespread acceptance in Tri-Faith America."[32] The key, though, was that America was no longer only a Protestant nation. The national war effort had galvanized the nation's citizens to see themselves as more alike than different. Catholics and Jews and Protestants were "Americans all."[33]

This current certainly drew Mormonism into that newly conceived religious mainstream, too. The fact that this shift in the public's perception of Latter-day Saints was well underway in the postwar years comes into sharper focus as we move from generalities about American religion in the "long fifties" to the particularities of Mormon-themed stories in the pioneer centennial year. The spirit in the magazine and newspaper articles about Mormonism in 1947 was one of celebration more than wariness—and even more than grudging acceptance. *Newsweek* noted that the "modern pseudo-pioneers in their automobiles" decorated with plywood "oxen" and wagon tops "were in a sense a symbol of how far the Mormons and Utah had come in 100 years. . . . Even the 'Gentiles'—as all non-Mormons are called by church members—feel that the Latter-day Saints have done a Samson's task in building not only a great church, but a great state."[34]

Mormonism as a religion was distinct and different, of course, but those differences seemed to fade into the accepted denominational diversity of

American religion. Latter-day Saints did not want to be identified as Protestants, but when census forms or polling organizations classed Mormons as a "species of Protestants, albeit a unique and identifiable one," this spoke to the way that Mormons, at the hands of a number of American arbiters of cultural acceptance, seemed to be undergoing a process of denominational normalization.[35] The *Christian Science Monitor* suggested that "whatever difficulty others may find in accepting the teachings of the Church of Latter Day Saints, the Mormon people have won universal respect for their devotion and achievements."[36] The religious differences—even aberrations—of Latter-day Saints came across as historical anomalies that had given way to modern sensibilities. This was even true—and surprisingly so—with the perennially problematic question of polygamy. *Newsweek* treated it only in passing, almost indifferently, by reasoning that "the polygamy issue skyrocketed out of all proportion to its actual existence. It played little part in the Utah trek, for the Mormons under Brigham Young, Smith's successor, were still only looking for a home." Later, "the Saints clung to it [polygamy] as much through stubbornness as belief."[37]

This was telling. These articles from the 1940s are as revealing today in what they promote about Mormon beliefs as much as in what they downplay—or do not even mention. There was little to no discussion of central Mormon doctrines and practices like the nature of the Trinity, the Book of Mormon, and temple ordinances. Instead, when the *Los Angeles Times* had to summarize the message that the Church of Jesus Christ of Latter-day Saints's three thousand missionaries were "spreading . . . all over the world," that message was characterized as "the gospel of brotherly love (and hard work)."[38] By the middle of the twentieth century, with polygamy long behind the Mormons, what now seemed most representative of Latter-day Saint faith was the way it transmitted values that were at the core of the American story. Not to be missed was the fact that the *Los Angeles Times* noted that many in this cadre of Mormon missionaries were war veterans, another nod to that sentiment of "Americans all."[39]

In one of the best-illustrated articles of that centennial year, the magazine *School Arts* did portray Latter-day Saints as unique in one important aspect, with these opening lines: "Craftwork and Art come naturally to the young descendants of a creative pioneer people who conquered a desert and transformed it into a place of beauty and usefulness." While such an assertion might amuse (or dishearten) modern readers who are not so gifted in "craftwork," it nevertheless seems significant that the verdict of the author was that "this younger generation has inherited much of the spirit of its pioneer ancestors, ancestors who were for the most part master craftsmen and artisans in every field."[40] This act of conquering a desert, of making it something beautiful and useful, resonated well with the notes being sounded by a number of the best-known religious writers of the era. Protestant minister Norman Vincent Peale's book *The Power of Positive Thinking* (1952), became a phenomenal bestseller—and it came on the heels of Catholic bishop Fulton J. Sheen's *Peace of Soul* (1949) and Rabbi Joshua Loth Liebman's *Peace of Mind* (1946). Billy Graham's *Peace with God* would come out in 1953. "The national effort to adjust to post-war conditions as well as persistent uncertainty internationally (communism, the atomic bomb)"—all of this, Mark Noll observes, "fostered a climate in which religion was enlisted in the search for psychological repose."[41] The sociologist Will Herberg published a highly influential book in 1955, *Protestant—Catholic—Jew*. Readers saw in Herberg's treatise a critique of the blandness that tri-faith America was generating—a "sterility" in theological (especially mainline Protestant theological) thought, to use Paul Harvey and Philip Goff's characterization.[42] But in 2013 Matthew Hedstrom pushed back against Herberg's complaints by pointing out the importance of a "middle brow" religious book culture—around books like the bestsellers mentioned earlier—in these same postwar years. Hedstrom saw the *interfaith* popularity of works like those of Rabbi Liebman, or the Catholic monk Thomas Merton, as evidence that there was broad religious interest in "pragmatic concerns for everyday utility of spirituality while indicating very little interest in official theology or creeds"—and, in that, "Herberg's fears about the lack (if not decline) of orthodoxy seem at least partially realized." But in Hedstrom's analysis: "Rather than an evisceration of faith, what Herberg called the 'inner disintegration and enfeeblement of historic religions,' the emerging spirituality fostered by mass-marketed books marked the culmination of decades of liberal religious efforts to craft forms of spirituality adequate to meet the challenges of modern life."[43] And the contemporary reporting on Mormonism offered examples of precisely that kind of utility in the Mormon system. From the *Los Angeles Times* reporter again: "'If most of us were brought up like the Saints,' a non-Mormon psychiatrist in one of Salt Lake's Army hospitals told me, 'there'd be little future in psychoanalysis.'"[44]

If a reader who knew nothing about Mormonism had his or her first introduction to the faith through these articles at midcentury, the one Mormon tenet he or she would certainly encounter is the commitment to individual agency and industry, and the connected impulse to provide for the poor and needy through giving them opportunities for work and dignity as well. The Mormon Welfare Plan became a stock feature in the 1947 stories about the pioneer centennial, a ubiquitous marker of Latter-day Saint respectability that catalyzed the reputational transformation that the historian Thomas Alexander detected in his book *Mormonism in Transition*. By 1930, Alexander observed, the Mormons' "health code, the Word of Wisdom, and increased genealogical activity in many ways replaced political solidarity and polygamous marriage as the distinctive features of Mormon society."[45] In line with that observation, Jan Shipps's landmark "Satyr-to-Saint" study of a century's worth of media portrayals positions the mid-1930s as a public perception pivot point. By Jan Shipps's inventive rating system, it was in the mid-1930s that the overall tone of Latter-day Saint–related stories crossed from the negative to the positive side of the scale.[46] It is not insignificant, of course, that the Latter-day Saint leadership introduced the churchwide Security Plan (later Welfare Plan) in 1936. The plan drew wide acclaim almost immediately, so much so that critics complained that the press often exaggerated Mormon successes—yet those criticisms largely went unnoticed. Some saw the enthusiasm for the Latter-day Saint approach as a politically motivated "anti–New Dealer's sweetest dream," but the only lasting impression was that the Mormons' "took care of their own."[47]

By 1947 that was the watchword on Latter-day Saints. Their industriousness and efficiency offered something unparalleled, as the *Los Angeles Times* reported it: "Confirmed capitalists as they [Mormons] now are"—an important note in this era of deep anxiety about communism—"they still cherish as seriously as ever the ideal of self-sufficiency—both as individuals and as a group. To achieve it, the Mormon Church now runs the largest single mutual benefit association in the world. 'It is unnecessary for any Latter-day Saint to ask for government relief,' you are told flatly by J. Reuben Clark, Jr., who helped establish the Church Welfare Plan."[48] A strong undercurrent of concern about the appropriateness of government welfare still permeated American politics. In early 1950, Indiana senator Homer Capehart's exasperated question to his colleagues articulated that very thing: "How much more are we going to have to take? Fuchs and Acheson and Hiss and hydrogen bombs threatening outside and New Dealism eating away at the vitals of the nation! In the name of Heaven, is this the best America can do?"[49] For readers who were sympathetic to the threat of persistent "New Dealism," Latter-day Saints seemed to offer a better way.

The effect of this self-sufficiency and hard work contributed to healthymindedness and optimism; Mormons even "seem less gloomy than most about the atom bomb," the *Los Angeles Times* suggested.[50] This was a picture of a church that was both prosperous and generous—and using its resources in respectable ways. Gone was much of its nineteenth-century zeal for a theocratic kingdom. And that is a point which deserves to be underlined.

When "Utah was admitted to the Union," *Time* summarized, "the old enmity between Mormon and Gentile disappeared, and the modern history of the church began." That modern history included the growth of Salt Lake City, "one of the cleanest and friendliest cities in the U.S., and one of the healthiest"—a city that was "as peculiarly American as Mormonism itself." This sense of Americanness had to be due, in part, to Mormons' "[winning] their war with wastes and sagebrush, sun-parched alkali flats and barren mountains." *Time* predicted visitors would notice the "glowing look" of Salt Lake City's residents, and then stand in "awe" at the "spectacular manifestations of Mormon diligence and industry."[51]

Mormonism's theological past was treated as quaint, if anything. Joseph Smith was described as "handsome, tall, wavy-haired, [with] long eyelashes and a faint but unmistakable resemblance to Comic Danny Kaye." That comparison to one of America's best-loved actors is intriguing; did it somehow have the effect of making Joseph Smith seem less alien? More performer than prophet? In any case, instead of portraying him as deceptive or demonic, *Time* in 1947 painted Mormonism's founder as a dreamer. Joseph Smith "had a fecund imagination and an instinctive sense of drama and command," and this meant that "life with the prophet was always exciting," since "at times he received divine revelation almost monthly."[52]

But Mormonism in 1947 was unquestionably tamer. The "last revelation" had been in 1890, the magazine told readers, and the current prophet was "quiet" and "earnest" and "impressive," and "most Mormons—and non-Mormons—agreed that he had done very well" in his role as the church's president. His face was on the cover of *Time*—appropriately, too, since he seemed to be the face of midcentury Mormonism: "polite, lively, [and] deeply religious."[53]

Almost as if to reassure readers, in case there were any who still worried about the fires of fanaticism smoldering among Utah's peculiar people, the 1947 *Time* article began by noting that "a divine revelation in 1947 would amaze no man more than Mormonism's tall, white-bearded, 77-year-old President George Albert Smith"—and then ended with three telling observations: "Mormon voters have a mind of their own"; "the new generation of Mormons shows a tendency to drift into unorthodoxy," such that "the number of backsliding 'jack-Mormons' is increasing"; and "Mormonism is changing with the rest of the world."[54]

These same themes played out in a number of stories published around the country that year. True, *Newsweek* noted, "Utah's senators, two congressmen, and Gov. Herbert B. Maw are all Mormons—but the church itself can no longer dictate the votes of its citizens." The proof for *Newsweek* of that voter independence was the strong support for Franklin D. Roosevelt among Mormons generally, even as the church's presidency supported Alf Landon (in the 1936 election) and others. There were no fears of a voting bloc here: "Today," the *Los Angeles Times* affirmed, "the Mormons are generally to be found in the conservative camp in both the Republican and Democratic party."[55]

The importance of this perceived change in Mormondom cannot be missed, especially since a much different perception of Mormon political posturing would still have been well within the long memories of some readers. After all, the protracted US Senate hearings that wrestled over the appropriateness of seating senator-elect (and Latter-day Saint apostle) Reed Smoot had finally concluded only forty years earlier; Smoot's election itself had sparked petition drives that counted their signatures in the millions, all opposing Smoot's eventual seating.[56] The furor over Reed Smoot's potential political subservience to a prophet-leader reflected a long history of American mistrust of Mormons' mingling of politics and religion.

It was bloc voting by Latter-day Saints in Illinois—and, in particular, bloc voting that showed no regard for party loyalty—that then-governor Thomas Ford said had "arrayed against [the Mormons] in deadly hostility all aspirants for office who were not sure of their support." The newspaper editor Thomas Sharp—a man who stood trial as one of the coconspirators in the deadly attacks on Joseph and Hyrum Smith—eventually called for that kind of hostility against what he saw as a "politico-military Church" whose members could "sway the destinies of the whole county, and probably the state" through their collective voting power.[57]

The situation became even more pronounced when the Latter-day Saints migrated to the Great Basin, when ecclesiastical officers and government officials were one and the same in Utah's early territorial period. To Latter-day Saints, such an arrangement made perfect sense, given their commitment to building a heavenly kingdom on earth.[58] As federal opposition both to this theocratic system and to Mormon polygamy intensified, Latter-day Saints saw political unity as key to their right of self-determination and self-preservation. Thomas Alexander, in noting the growing pains that came as the church discontinued polygamy in the 1890s, wrote that "few things caused the LDS Church as much difficulty during the nineteenth-century as single party politics"—yet the irony is that it took strong church hierarchical pressure to induce some church members to join the Republican Party in order to have two viable parties in Utah that did not simply cleave along Mormon/non-Mormon lines.[59]

That, then, is what was so remarkable in the *Los Angeles Times'* observation in 1947 about the Mormon presence in *both* Democratic and Republican camps: the success—essentially in a generation—of Latter-day Saint efforts to foster a new political reality in Utah. The fact that this reality had become, by the middle of the twentieth century, a facet of Mormonism's public portrait is made even more noteworthy by contrast.[60] In the thick of nineteenth-century congressional sanctions against Mormon plural marriage, only six decades before the pioneer centennial, a Massachusetts newspaper had suggested that "not polygamy but the power of the Priesthood is the real danger. . . . The essential principle of Mormonism is not polygamy at all but the ambition of an ecclesiastical hierarchy to wield sovereignty: to rule the souls and lives of its subjects with absolute authority, unrestrained by any civil power."[61]

Subtle overtones of this sentiment persisted in 1947, almost as reminders that the gravest of Mormon transgressions in the past had been the desire for the hierarchy to wield "absolute authority," to claim "civil power." *Newsweek* called the Mormons "formerly a persecuted minority because of their religious *and political* beliefs"; Fawn Brodie, herself a disaffected Mormon and celebrated biographer of Joseph Smith, wrote in the *New York Times Magazine* that "the frontier rose against [Joseph Smith]" because "he flouted certain basic American traditions—by secretly practicing polygamy *and openly mixing in politics.*"[62]

But now, the *Nation* trumpeted, the "ecclesiastical situation" in Utah was such that "the rank and file resent the leaders' interference in political affairs and vote the other way." This meant, happily, that "one might assume, then, that the Mormon church dominates the politics of the state; and so it does, but in a curiously reverse fashion. . . . The secret of success in Utah politics consists of arousing the active opposition of the Mormon hierarchy," since "the saints refused to accept the hierarchy's political dictation." Roosevelt's success—and the success of Democratic candidates in general—made, for the *Nation*, "exhibit A" of that voter independence.[63]

In 1947 the story of the Latter-day Saints was largely the story of the church that Thomas O'Dea would write about ten years later. It was the archetypal American success story. Mormons wrote the book on taming the wilderness. They had abandoned, *Time* told its readers in 1947, their "once militant" ways and adopted a benign wholesomeness befitting the nation's religious denominations.[64] One caveat to note here—though this might be stating the obvious—is that while 1947 was a big press year for Mormons, the fact that a dozen or so national-level articles constituted a big press year speaks to Mormonism's minority status and relative obscurity. Mormonism's regional limitations, too, in the Intermountain West was a prominent message in many of these stories. So benign did the church seem at midcentury, in fact, that some of O'Dea's contemporaries would wonder if Mormons were on the path to obsolescence, now that the tough sledding of pioneer settlement was behind them. Already in 1947 that tone had permeated media coverage. Fawn Brodie wrote for the *New York Times Magazine* that "the church has receded from a position of complete domination over the political, economic, and moral aspects of Mormon life"—and that "the truly faithful Mormon is getting rarer."[65] Importantly, too, the story of the Mormon pioneers at one hundred was also mostly a Utah story—a story of an extremely well-run state that fit comfortably in twentieth-century America.

Newsweek perhaps summed up Mormonism's place in American society most succinctly: "Crushed politically, curtailed economically, the Mormons have learned to exist in a modified Zion of live and let live." From a twenty-first century vantage point, and given the turns that would come in the 1970s and 1980s, there is irony in *Newsweek*'s July 1947 assessment that the Mormon concessions which facilitated Utah's statehood symbolized the fact that "the Church had been broken as a political force."[66] But from a mid-twentieth century perspective, for many Americans, there must have been considerable relief.

Yet the reality is that we are twenty-first century readers of these articles from the past, so it is almost impossible *not* to peek ahead, so to speak, not to let our minds fast-forward to the ebbs and flows in the public's perception of Latter-day Saints in the 1970s and 1980s, or surrounding the 2008 and 2012 presidential campaigns. We find irony, yes—but illumination, too. Given that favorable press coverage focused on Mormons at midcentury so often worked to emphasize Mormon detachment from politics, it makes sense that Mormon prominence in the 1970s campaign against the Equal Rights Amendment, for example, or in two recent presidential campaigns, would evoke different responses from a journalistic corps that still worried about mixing religion and politics, still worried about theocratic coercion. Even the increased attention to heterodox Mormon theology that bubbled up to the surface of the national consciousness in the 1980s cannot be separated too starkly from political concerns, since that rise in evangelical Christian anti-Mormonism coincided with the rise of the Religious Right. Christians who worried about preserving the United States as a Christian nation became increasingly concerned about the growth—in numbers and legitimacy—of Latter-day Saints, a religious group that many Christian commentators saw as either confused or counterfeits, or something of both.[67]

Ethan Yorgason and Chiung Hwang Chen have reminded us that analyses of positive public attention of Mormons can "obscure as much as they illuminate," and that pedestals can be restrictive. Yorgason and Chen's "model minority" reading of press coverage of Mormons—a reading in the vein of scholarship on the treatment of Asian Americans—is worth considering here. Emphasis on Mormon exceptionalism, they suggest, could be read as an attempt to *keep* Mormons marginalized, distinct.[68] By another token, exuberant press celebration of Mormon respectability could also be motivated by a desire to *encourage* Mormon respectability—to tame Mormonism of its exoticness and reward it for all-Americanness.

All of this raises more questions than we have space to consider here, but this at least leaves us thinking about the challenge of trying to measure, to gauge, the forces that shape public perception—and the lasting meaning or impact of those forces on various "eye of the beholder" audiences. It brings to mind the sociologist Armand Mauss's explorations of "optimum tension" on the assimilation-retrenchment spectrum, as a religion navigates its place in a host society, or Terryl Givens's comment to filmmaker Helen Whitney, in 2007, that Latter-day Saints want to be "mainstream enough" to get "a fair hearing."[69]

With talk of Danny Kaye in the 1940s on the one hand, and talk of *The God Makers* in the 1980s on the other, one might be left to wonder if there are only two options for the Mormon image—that Latter-day Saints are either quaint or else somehow disquieting, either cute or cultish. From the perspective of those who are interested in getting beyond stereotypes or superficiality, however, that is what makes recent developments—post-2008 or 2012 developments—in the public's attention and conversation about Mormonism so intriguing. That is also what makes checking in on the Mormon image at various points in American history a revealing exercise, in that the comparative potential such snapshots offer can generate the important questions this present volume is considering about the push-pull dialogue which is shaping the meaning of the word "Mormon" in America.

CHAPTER 13

The Historic Conflicts of Our Time

Ezra Taft Benson and Twentieth-Century Media
Representations of Latter-day Saints

PATRICK Q. MASON

In October 1953, only nine months after Ezra
Taft Benson commenced work as secretary of agriculture in the Dwight D.
Eisenhower administration, Wallace F. Bennett, the Republican senator from
Utah, told the Salt Lake Rotary Club: "There is no other man in America
today, not even President Eisenhower himself, in whom the historic conflicts
of our time are symbolized as they are in our own Ezra Taft Benson." Pointing to the significance of the man who not only sat in the cabinet but also
served as one of the twelve apostles of the Church of Jesus Christ of Latter-
day Saints, Senator Bennett opined: "I feel that it is not too much to say that
as the decisions go in which [Benson] is the central figure, so may go the
trend of America in our time."[1]

Even allowing for Bennett's rhetorical hyperbole with a hometown crowd,
it is true that Ezra Taft Benson was a central figure in postwar American
politics who represented the confluence—and sometimes conflict—between
the various stripes of Mormon and American conservatism. Hardly laboring
in obscurity as subsequent secretaries of agriculture typically have, Benson
appeared on the cover of national news magazines such as *Time*, *Newsweek*,
and *U.S. News and World Report*.[2] He was one of only two cabinet officials
to serve the entire eight years of the Eisenhower administration, and was
constantly in the spotlight as one of the most active and controversial figures
of the administration and the national Republican Party. Fierce critiques and

frequent calls for his resignation were matched by an equal outpouring of accolades and genuine respect.[3]

Benson lived most of his adult life in the public spotlight. He was ordained an apostle within the Church of Jesus Christ of Latter-day Saints in 1943, was tapped for a cabinet position in 1952, then rose through the ranks of church leadership until becoming church president and prophet in 1985, serving nine years until his death in 1994. During those decades of public service and ecclesiastical leadership, Benson was the subject of national media interest and scrutiny. Especially in the 1950s and 1960s, he was one of a small handful of Latter-day Saints of sufficient public stature to receive consistent media attention. Much of that scrutiny focused purely on his political activities, but a significant share of national (and international) reporting also commented on his Mormon heritage, deep faith, and apostleship. Ezra Taft Benson was therefore one of the primary lenses through which the media, and by extension the American public, perceived and came to understand the church and its people in the second half of the twentieth century.

Exceptional in many ways, Ezra Taft Benson was not actually representative of all Latter-day Saints. Nevertheless, he came to represent them, both in his official capacity as a senior ecclesiastical leader and as a public figure whose faith often received mention when he appeared in the media. A strongly opinionated leader, Benson took clear and often controversially conservative positions on many of "the historic conflicts of our time," including anticommunism, the proper role of government, civil rights, church and state, the women's movement, international and domestic conflicts, and the culture wars. Due to his prominence both internally and externally, Benson thus become a prism through which the American public and the media perceived Latter-day Saints and their religion. However problematic and incomplete this media representation through a single figure was, in the national gaze Benson served as a symbol of Mormonism and how it was situated in modern American religion, culture, and politics. His particular brand of archconservatism was divisive even within the ranks of the mostly conservative church leadership, but Benson's visibility and outspokenness had helped cement the perceived and often real alliance of Latter-day Saints with American political, social, and religious conservatives since the 1960s.

In this chapter, I trace American public representations of Mormonism by looking both through and at Ezra Taft Benson as a media filter. The corpus of sources under consideration here does not consist of all the extensive national press coverage of Benson, but rather those treatments that either commented on or interpreted modern Mormonism through the lens of Benson's life and career. Two phases of media commentary emerge. The first, corresponding with Benson's cabinet service in the 1950s, was largely irenic, even laudatory. Benson clearly emerged in multiple media accounts during the decade as the world's most famous Latter-day Saint. Indeed, in many accounts it appeared his was the *only* name that reporters could summon when pointing to a contemporary Mormon of any prominence and general respectability. In an era that Jan Shipps has identified as the apex of a positive Latter-day Saint public image in America, Benson was the apogee of the correspondence between Mormon values and mid-twentieth-century American values: patriotism, faith, work ethic, and traditional family roles.[4] On the latter score, the entire Benson family played a public role as paragons of Mormon—and American—family life.

Media commentary about the Church of Jesus Christ of Latter-day Saints noticeably shifted in the 1960s, entering a more critical phase with darker tones that lasted through the end of the century. At least three broader contextual factors contributed to the religion's declining fortunes in the media, even as the church was experiencing an internal golden age of sorts in terms of growth and vitality. First, most church leaders, including Ezra Taft Benson, embraced the conservative side of the emergent culture wars, putting them crossways with the generally liberal media establishment that came to sympathize with the civil rights, women's, youth, and gay rights movements.[5] Second, following the high-water mark of American public religiosity during the Eisenhower years, the American public's confidence in religion and religious institutions began to wane in the 1960s, a trend that continued (and indeed advanced) throughout the last third of the century and into the new millennium. In other words, the warm glow surrounding public religion in the 1950s proved to be unsustainable, and the church thus suffered from the same general reputational decline as virtually all other American churches in the late twentieth century.[6] Third, the second half of the twentieth century witnessed the systematic dismantling of the historic connections between religion (specifically Protestant Christianity) and the state, particularly a complex of laws and customs that scholars have aptly named the "moral establishment." Led by the Supreme Court, a changing national legal and political context redefined the role of religion in American public life and enforced a stricter separation between church and state.[7] Those who spoke out against such trends, including Benson and other Latter-day Saint leaders, found themselves increasingly at odds with the general thrust of American law, politics, and culture.

In short, both Mormonism and America were on the move in the late twentieth century, but the trajectories of the Church of Jesus Christ of Latter-day Saints and the nation's cultural and media elites progressively diverged. As an increasingly senior and perpetually outspoken ecclesiastical leader within the church after his departure from the cabinet, Ezra Taft Benson was frequently highlighted in the media as a representation of darker forces that were ascendant within late twentieth-century Mormonism: archconservatism, authoritarianism, fundamentalism, and hostility toward civil rights and women's equality. The evolution of Benson's image in the national media thus serves as a signifier for broader trends whereby the Latter-day Saint image transitioned from normal and respectable in the 1950s to peculiar and even dangerous in the 1960s and subsequent decades.

"In No Sense a Freak or Fanatic"

The period immediately following World War II was an era of unprecedented growth and respectability for the Church of Jesus Christ of Latter-day Saints. In the 1950s, the church thrived under the leadership of David O. McKay, a genial, dignified, forward-looking leader who both exuded and exemplified the comfortable fit of Mormonism in American public life. Postwar American prosperity was also good for the church. An increasingly prosperous middle class raised tithing levels and stabilized church finances so as to fund an ambitious (and sometimes too aggressive) building program. New meetinghouses dotting the landscape, combined with a major emphasis on missionary work that resulted in a substantial surge of new converts, raised the profile of Mormons and Mormonism in locales across North America and Western Europe. The Mormon Tabernacle Choir won a Grammy Award in 1959. And one of the church's apostles, Ezra Taft Benson, sat in the cabinet and even led the nation's political leaders in prayer.[8]

Prior to his nomination to the cabinet, Benson was well known in agricultural regions due to his earlier work as executive secretary of the National Council of Farmer Cooperatives, which represented about 4,600 groups across the country. That, plus his role as a "world religious leader" by virtue of his ordination as one of the church's twelve apostles in 1943, earned him notice in local newspapers when he presided over regional church conferences in places such as Florida and South Dakota, far beyond the Mormon corridor.[9]

Newspapers across the United States and even abroad took note when Benson emerged as the nominee to head the Department of Agriculture in the new Eisenhower administration. The wire report, widely published on front pages nationwide, blandly listed both Benson's professional background as a local, state, and national agricultural administrator as well as his current position in hierarchy of the church.[10] Subsequent stories elaborated in much greater detail about Benson's Mormon pioneer heritage and his years of active commitment to the church, including a yearlong mission to Europe in 1946 to rebuild churches and provide humanitarian aid in the wake of the Second World War. In addition to outlining his agricultural experience and philosophy, the *Saturday Evening Post* rehearsed Benson's ecclesiastical career in detail. The *Post*'s account stretched back to Benson's baptism at age eight and the series of priesthood ordinations common to faithful Latter-day Saint boys and men, then spent several more columns outlining Latter-day Saint theology and history.[11] *Time* magazine's April 13, 1953, cover story profiled Benson as a man who "spoke with the voice of God" while serving as a missionary in England and for whom "prayer is the basic fuel."[12] A Cincinnati columnist went so far as to argue that Benson's religious affiliation should be considered as one of his chief qualifications for the job. "One thing is certain," the columnist asserted. "Mr. Benson is a Mormon and of all groups in the United States the Mormon people have demonstrated more sense and sound economics in dealing with the problems of agriculture and the great depression than any other."[13] Benson's status as one of the church's senior ecclesiastical leaders, mentioned early on only as a point of interest, now took on historical import, as papers noted that "he is the first clergyman in the cabinet for more than a century."[14]

This fact should not go unappreciated. From 1953 to 1961, a Latter-day Saint apostle, the rough equivalent to a Roman Catholic cardinal, was seventh in the line of succession to the US presidency.[15] Given his junior status in the Quorum of the Twelve Apostles and the tradition of selecting the next president of the church according to seniority within the quorum, Apostle Benson was actually closer to occupying the White House than the Latter-day Saint presidency during the 1950s. Both in terms of Mormon history and the history of church and state in America, it is remarkable that an apostle's nomination to a senior position in the executive branch did not generate substantial controversy, let alone legal or constitutional challenges. Benson's nomination came less than a half century after the Reed Smoot hearings, in which that Latter-day Saint apostle's election to the US Senate prompted years of national outrage and extensive congressional scrutiny.[16] More broadly, the relative silence regarding the religious component of Benson's nomination and then tenure as secretary of agriculture, even from liberal political opponents, speaks volumes about the nature of public faith and civil religion in the Eisenhower era. Cultural and demographic shifts in addition to jurisprudential development at the Supreme Court on First Amendment issues meant that the 1950s represented the last possible moment when church and state were sufficiently aligned in America that a senior clergyman could serve in the cabinet.[17] Though many fervently religious people have held senior political offices, including the presidency, since the 1950s, none have simultaneously held the kind of ecclesiastical and executive office that Benson did.

Benson's prominence helped ensure that Mormonism benefited from this era of good feelings regarding religion in public life. He took the occasion of his nomination to affirm his belief, widely held by other Latter-day Saints and drawn from Joseph Smith's revelations, that "the Constitution of this land, embodying as it does eternal principles, was established by men whom a kind Providence raised up for that purpose."[18] This religiously infused patriotism, honed over the course of decades as a key element of the Latter-day Saints' quest for respectability, was a key factor in transitioning Mormonism from a national pariah to the national mainstream.[19] Benson personified this shift, in part because, throughout the 1950s, he was often the lone example of an actual contemporary Latter-day Saint who newspapers across America could name.[20]

Indeed, Benson both contributed to and represented the normalization that Latter-day Saints had achieved in the 1950s. A review of Thomas F. O'Dea's landmark book, *The Mormons* (1957), published in the *Holland (MI) Evening Sentinel*, gave apt expression to this normalization. The reviewer, Arnold Mulder, stated that until recently he "had the conventional conception of the Mormons that perhaps most Americans have. I thought of them as more or less freakish, made up mostly of fanatics and lacking in common sense." This began to change when he gained "a real live Mormon as a good friend." His friend "was as sensible, as well balanced mentally and culturally, as any young man I have ever known. . . . He was a normal, healthy-minded, highly-intelligent young man not to be distinguished from the general run of young Americans." Mulder supposed that O'Dea's new book was based on similar interactions with actual Latter-day Saints, and thus became less an exposé of a mysterious, menacing cult than a sober-minded, analytical examination of "an interesting phase of American life." Ezra Taft Benson was a prime example of the church's midcentury integration. As Mulder noted, it was well known that Benson was a "practicing clergyman in the Mormon Church. But he [was] in no sense a freak or a fanatic. He [had] the respect even of most of those who oppose[d] him for purely political reasons." This brief book review demonstrated the impact of personal associations with Latter-day Saints scattering across the country in the postwar period, a new genre of academic scholarship on Mormonism aiming for objectivity rather than polemics, and the national prominence of Ezra Taft Benson as an Latter-day Saint signifier to produce an irenic view that "Mormons, too, are people," woven seamlessly into the fabric of postwar American life.[21]

The entire Benson family came to represent Mormon normality by way of exemplifying the ideals of postwar American domestic life. *Time* gave its readers a peek into the Benson household, which showed the family praying, reading scriptures, doing chores, dancing around the jukebox, and together deciding curfews and how much television the kids could watch.[22] Newspapers around the country reported about a party of "the Cabinet wives" hosted by Flora Benson in May 1954. Mamie Eisenhower, Pat Nixon, and the wives of other senior officials in the Eisenhower cabinet attended the lunchtime gathering. The absence of alcohol was notable, as was the family talent show featuring the Benson children. Flora Beth danced, Barbara sang with the Brigham Young University Madrigal Group which was on tour in the area, and Reed gave a reading from Henry Wadsworth Longfellow. One reporter suggested that it seemed to be a scene right out of Louisa May Alcott's *Little Women*. Taking the occasion to comment more broadly on Benson family life, the press approvingly observed that "the Bensons, who are devout Mormons, have their own family cooperative. They have no servants, and running the big household is a truly collective enterprise. Together the family plans the week's meals and shopping."[23] A half century earlier, authors across the country had complained that Mormons were intent to "destroy the unity and happiness of families and communities," and were, in short, "home wreckers."[24] Now, in the 1950s, *Leave It to Beaver* could have been set in the Benson home—though with troublemaking Eddie Haskell nowhere to be found.

The correspondence of American and Latter-day Saint values spanned from the domestic sphere to the arena of international relations. Though he wore his faith on his sleeve wherever he traveled, perhaps the most significant instance of Benson carrying the flag of American—and indeed global—Christianity came at the end of an official visit to the Soviet Union as secretary of agriculture in 1959. Escorted by a pack of reporters, on his way to the airport Benson attended a service at Moscow's Central Baptist Church. In their column published in *U.S. News and World Report*, Grant Salisbury and Warren Leffler wrote: "It turned out to be one of the most moving experiences in the lifetime of many of us. One newsman, a former marine, ranked it with the sight of the American flag rising over the old American compound in Tientsin, China, at the end of World War II." Benson addressed the crowded church through a translator. The cabinet secretary extended the greetings of "millions and millions of church people in America and around the world," then launched into a sermon. "Our

Heavenly Father is not far away," he preached. "I know that God lives. He is our Father. Jesus Christ, the Redeemer of the World, watches over this earth. He will direct all things. Be unafraid, keep His commandments, love one another, pray for peace and all will be well." As Benson spoke of Jesus Christ's resurrection and the certainty of the afterlife, reporters wrote that "muffled sobs could be heard in the small church. These people, after all, were sacrificing their chances of participating in the gains of the Communist society of Russia. Though worshiping God no longer is forbidden in the Soviet Union, those who do so usually find themselves cut off from advancement." Secretary-Apostle Benson concluded: "I leave you my witness as a church servant for many years that the truth will endure. Time is always on our side. God bless you and keep you all the days of your life, I pray in the name of Jesus Christ." The congregation waved handkerchiefs and tearfully sang the hymn "God Be with You Till We Meet Again" as Benson and his party left the church.[25]

The symbolic value of the Moscow episode was substantial. Here was the national media reporting in the warmest terms about a Latter-day Saint apostle serving as an envoy of both American democracy and global Christianity in the heart of godless Soviet Russia. If religion was understood to be one of America's primary weapons in the civilizational struggle of the Cold War, here was a Mormon wielding it fearlessly behind enemy lines. That it may be inappropriate for an executive officer of the United States to preach a Christian sermon while on official business apparently occurred to no one. It was a high point for Christianity as America's unofficial religion, and successfully positioned the church as one of the family of Christian denominations promoting and participating in the religion of national life.

"Moving Backward"

Benson's eight years in the cabinet corresponded roughly with the first decade of David O. McKay's presidency of the Church of Jesus Christ of Latter-day Saints, and marked what most scholars have agreed was the apex of Latter-day Saint assimilation into American culture and religion. In the most important study of twentieth-century Mormonism, the sociologist Armand Mauss persuasively argued that "by the 1960s the Mormon movement had become so successful in living down the nineteenth century, and in dealing with the predicament of disrepute, that it had entered a new stage in its history." A core group of conservative senior Latter-day Saint leaders intuited that if the pendulum swung too far toward assimilation, Mormonism's distinctive identity would be threatened, perhaps even lost. They therefore orchestrated a series of reforms that led to a period characterized by what Mauss dubbed "retrenchment," or "a renewed emphasis on Mormon distinctiveness."[26] In short, the internal character of the church began to change in the 1960s. It increasingly stood in contrast to the new American liberal order characterized politically by the Kennedy and Johnson administrations and socially and culturally by the civil rights, youth, women's, and gay rights movements—all of which were at least initially opposed by the senior Latter-day Saint leadership.

The religious studies scholar Jan Shipps has contended that the national media's positive portrayals of Latter-day Saints continued well beyond the 1950s. As she wrote: "It was the dramatic discrepancy between clean-cut Mormons and scruffy hippies that completed the transformation of the Mormon image from the quasi-foreign, somewhat alien likeness that it had in the nineteenth century to the more than 100 percent super-American portrait of the late sixties and early seventies." Furthermore, "the contrast with the radical Left made the image of the Saints even more appealing than it had been in the fifties, making this a time when at least middle America's perceptions of the Saints would be overwhelming positive."[27] The historian J. B. Haws has helpfully complicated this narrative by demonstrating that, by 1965, the church's policy of denying priesthood ordination and temple participation to blacks had started to erode what had been an overwhelmingly positive national media image during the previous decade and a half. By the time George Romney ran for president in 1968—becoming the second contemporary Latter-day Saint, along with Benson, to be a household name in America—the positive postwar Mormon image already showed signs of being somewhat precarious.[28]

Just as the media had held up Ezra Taft Benson as the paragon of Mormon normality in the 1950s, he emerged as a troubling sign of Mormon deviance from the liberalizing political and social order in the 1960s. To be clear, Americans did not suddenly shift from conservative to liberal, leaving Latter-day Saints out in the cold. In 1969 Richard Nixon famously appealed to the "silent majority" of (especially white) citizens nationwide who remained skeptical of or alienated by the new American liberalism. The postwar church thrived in the Intermountain West and burgeoning white suburbs of Southern California, Phoenix, Washington, DC, and elsewhere, finding comfort and common cause with those who would build the conservative movement from the grassroots.[29] Indeed, Latter-day Saints became important allies in the emergence of the Religious Right, even if they and their new political bedfellows still engaged in sometimes severe theological battles.[30]

Ezra Taft Benson became a problem for the Mormon image beginning in the 1960s not because he inhabited this emergent conservative stream of American life, but rather because he publicly leapt outside its main channels. In a move that has still not been adequately documented or explained by scholars, Benson lurched dramatically and rather suddenly from the center-right position he had held as cabinet secretary to the far right occupied by the John Birch Society and other archconservative organizations. Although Benson never formally joined the John Birch Society, he frequently spoke out on its behalf, asserting on multiple occasions that he was convinced the society "was the most effective non-church organization in our fight against creeping socialism and godless communism."[31] Throughout the 1960s, Benson cited liberally from John Birch Society materials and authors in his apostolic addresses in the church's semiannual general conferences. His outspokenness and advocacy earned him the opprobrium of even many of his fellow conservatives in church leadership who thought he had become too political and diverged too far from the mainstream.[32]

Much of the nation agreed. The media reported that at least some Latter-day Saints were embarrassed by Benson's statements and worried that he would inexorably link the church to the John Birch Society in the public eye.[33] Newspapers across the nation took note when Benson publicly declined to deny the claims of the Birch Society founder Robert Welch that Dwight D. Eisenhower was "a dedicated, conscious agent of the Communist conspiracy."[34] The nationally syndicated columnist Drew Pearson frequently assaulted Benson's embrace of the Birch Society and archconservatism. Pearson claimed that the church of the mid-1960s was "moving backward," with Benson as the chief culprit among a cadre of senior leaders who had become "fearful of philosophical brushes with the outside world." The columnist contrasted this defensive approach with the more expansive and ecumenical spirit that David O. McKay had embodied before his health declined. In particular, Pearson excoriated "the right-wing propaganda which Benson has droned out with the deadly monotony of an Indian tom-tom."[35] Many newspapers covered the feud between Benson and the Democratic congressman Ralph Harding of Idaho, a faithful Latter-day Saint who openly denounced the apostle on the floor of the House for his propagation of Birch Society ideologies.[36] Benson's identification with the Far Right gained further notoriety when newspapers publicized that a group of John Birch supporters was recruiting him to run for the presidency in 1968 as a third-party candidate, with the segregationist Strom Thurmond of South Carolina as his running mate.[37]

In one respect, the various reports demonstrating that Benson was at odds with his fellow church members and leaders revealed that the church of the 1960s encompassed an array of diverse voices and perspectives all vying for prominence, just as one would expect in any large organization. Previously seen as embodying the entire tradition, now Benson was joined by others on the stage who represented Latter-day Saints in the public eye. For instance, newspapers pointed to Benson as an archetypical conservative foil in contrast with moderate to liberal voices such as George Romney and the founders of *Dialogue: A Journal of Mormon Thought*.[38]

But Benson had something that Ralph Harding, George Romney, and the *Dialogue* founders did not: a position as an increasingly senior apostle within the church hierarchy. Just as Benson had personified a normalized Mormonism in the 1950s, he now represented a Latter-day Saint leadership at odds with the modernizing trends of other religious groups in the 1960s. Even the generally conservative *Wall Street Journal* observed that Benson's brand of Mormonism seemed out of step with contemporary religious trends: "While the leadership of larger denominations—Catholic, Methodist, Presbyterian, Lutheran—has moved toward liberal positions on such social questions as racial discrimination and Government poverty-fighting, the Mormon high command of which Mr. Benson is a member remains deeply conservative. In great part this is due to certain doctrinal teachings unique to Mormonism. But it is also due to the energetic efforts of Mr. Benson, whose flirtation with the John Birch Society has produced deep divisions within the church and has roiled Mountain-State politics." While pointing out that there remained liberal Democrats within the church, the *Wall Street Journal* reported that the "aggressive conservatism" of Apostle Benson seemed to have the upper hand dictating not only the church's theology but also the political and social views of its members.[39] Subsequent episodes—such as Benson's attendance at the 1971 convention of the Citizens Councils of America alongside the nation's most famous segregationists—only reinforced the notion that Benson remained firm in his far-right politics and seemed to be taking the church with him.[40]

As the American culture wars heated up in the 1970s and 1980s, the church largely solidified its conservative identity. There were multiple factors that contributed to the alignment of Latter-day Saints and conservatives, largely revolving around social issues including civil rights, feminism, and gay rights. Benson made it clear that as the gap between the Right and the Left grew, Latter-day Saints had a choice to make, and it was not between two equally legitimate options. Asked in a public interview whether "a good Mormon could be a liberal Democrat," Benson stated: "I think it would be very hard if he was living the gospel and understood it."[41] As declining health incapacitated the church president Spencer W. Kimball, church members and Mormon watchers nationwide began to fear the implications of Ezra Taft Benson becoming the church's next prophet and president. The *Los Angeles Times* referred to him as "a fervent anti-Communist and anti-feminist who holds ultra-conservative views."[42] The *Chicago Tribune* cited the authors Robert Gottlieb and Peter Wiley who claimed that a Benson presidency would be "far more authoritarian and politically conservative . . . heighten existing political and doctrinal tensions within the hierarchy and membership at large and further alienate women members unhappy with their subservient roles in the church."[43] The *Baltimore Sun* quoted critics who called Benson "the Jerry Falwell of Mormonism," thus likening him to one of the fundamentalist architects of the Religious Right.[44] When Benson did assume the church presidency, the *Nashville Tennessean* referred to his reputation for "fundamentalism" as "a dogmatic churchman, rabid anti-communist and right-wing true believer."[45] Once hailed in the press as proof that Latter-day Saints were neither freaks nor fanatics, now Benson became the face of Mormon authoritarianism, archconservatism, subservience of women, dogmatism, and fundamentalism.

Just as the legacy of Ezra Taft Benson is complex, so too were the national perceptions of the Church of Jesus Christ of Latter-day Saints and its members in the second half of the twentieth century. Americans never viewed the religion only through the lens of Ezra Taft Benson, but he was a primary filter for the national media in the 1950s and remained a familiar face representing Latter-day Saints until his death in 1994. While the church and its members benefited from the positive press associated with Benson during his cabinet years, their reputation conversely suffered when Benson's politics and public statements began to diverge so sharply from national norms.

Beginning in the 1960s and accelerating in the 1980s, when Ronald Reagan took over the White House and Ezra Taft Benson assumed the presidency of the Church of Jesus Christ of Latter-day Saints, Mormonism and American conservatism came to reinforce one another. Latter-day Saints had become a reliable Republican voting bloc, and GOP leaders returned the favor by treating Mormonism like a respectable religion.[46] As the nation entered into its "age of fracture," Latter-day Saints as a whole did not even try to straddle the widening divide.[47] Pushed from within by Benson and other like-minded leaders who were fearful of cultural change and pulled from without by the prospect of political influence and social respectability, most American Latter-day Saints came to believe that their religion was, in the words of a Los Angeles television news broadcaster who had recently converted to the faith, "essentially conservative."[48] The view from the outside corresponded with this self-assessment. In a national survey conducted by the Pew Research Forum in 2011, in which respondents were asked to describe Mormonism in only one word, "conservative" was one of the most popular responses.[49]

The alliance of Mormonism and conservatism did not happen by accident. By virtue of his national prominence and ecclesiastical office, Ezra Taft Benson had one of the largest and loudest megaphones in the church. His voice was among the few that the media heard and then broadcast to a national audience. Given the relative paucity of nationally famous Latter-day Saints who could counterbalance Benson's archconservatism, the media reinforced Benson's own narrative that his style and brand of Mormonism was determinative for the whole, though dissenters might snipe at the margins. External representations of the religion thus reinforced internal moves toward retrenchment and consolidation, closing off space for differing perspectives to appear as anything but alternative—and fringe—voices. Benson taught that "the prophet will not necessarily be popular with the world or the worldly."[50] Perhaps. But the world and the worldly will pick up on the prophets' and apostles' voices, transmit them over the wire and the airwaves and the internet to readers and listeners, rendering their particular representations of the religion normative, even exclusive. The national media may have no interest in refereeing between competing claims within a given church, but they nevertheless play a role as gatekeepers for which perspectives define the religion's character and identity to interested onlookers around the nation and world.

NOTES

Preface

1. For examples of examinations of the ambiguous state of Mormons in American political culture at different moments in United States history, see J. Spencer Fluhman, *"A Peculiar People": Anti-Mormonism and the Making of Religion in Nineteenth-Century America* (Chapel Hill: University of North Carolina Press, 2012); Kathleen Flake, *The Politics of American Religious Identity: The Seating of Senator Reed Smoot, Mormon Apostle* (Chapel Hill: University of North Carolina Press, 2004); and Sarah Barringer Gordon, *The Mormon Question: Polygamy and Constitutional Conflict in Nineteenth-Century America* (Chapel Hill: University of North Carolina Press, 2002).

2. John Adams to John Taylor, December 17, 1814, Washburn Collection, Massachusetts Historical Society, Boston.

Introduction

1. R. Laurence Moore, *Religious Outsiders and the Making of Americans* (New York: Oxford University Press, 1986), 27, 32.

2. David E. Campbell, John C. Green, and J. Quin Monson, *Seeking the Promised Land: Mormons and American Politics* (New York: Cambridge University Press, 2014), chaps. 2–3. See also "Mormons: Certain in Their Beliefs, Uncertain in Their Place in Society," Pew Research Center, Religion and Public Life, January 12, 2012, http://www.pewforum.org/2012/01/12/mormons-in-america-executive-summary/; and Aleksandra Sandstrom and Becka Alper, "6 Facts about U.S. Mormons," Pew Research Center, Fact Tank, September 30, 2016, http://www.pewresearch.org/fact-tank/2016/09/30/6-facts-about-u-s-mormons/.

3. Daniel Walker Howe, "Emergent Mormonism in Context," in *The Oxford Handbook of Mormonism*, ed. Terryl L. Givens and Philip L. Barlow (New York: Oxford University Press, 2015), 36.

4. Leonard J. Arrington, *Great Basin Kingdom: An Economic History of the Latter-day Saints, 1830–1900* (Cambridge, MA: Harvard University Press, 1959), vii.

5. Philip L. Barlow, "Chosen Land, Chosen People: Religious and American Exceptionalism among the Mormons," in *Mormonism and American Politics*, ed. Randall Balmer and Jana Riess (New York: Columbia University Press, 2015), 102–14; Moore, *Religious Outsiders*, xv, 45.

6. Moore, *Religious Outsiders*, 25–47; Terryl L. Givens, *The Viper on the Hearth: Mormons, Myths, and the Construction of Heresy* (New York: Oxford University Press, 1997); Sarah Barringer Gordon, *The Mormon Question: Polygamy and Constitutional Conflict in Nineteenth-Century America* (Chapel Hill: University of North Carolina

Press, 2002); Patrick Mason, *The Mormon Menace: Violence and Anti-Mormonism in the Postbellum South* (New York: Oxford University Press, 2011); J. Spencer Fluhman, *"A Peculiar People": Anti-Mormonism and the Making of Religion in Nineteenth-Century America* (2012; repr., Chapel Hill: University of North Carolina Press, 2014); Christine Talbot, *A Foreign Kingdom: Mormons and Polygamy in American Political Culture, 1852–1890* (Urbana: University of Illinois Press, 2013), 1, 2.

7. Armaund L. Mauss, *The Angel and the Beehive: The Mormon Struggle with Assimilation* (Urbana: University of Illinois Press, 1994), ix.

8. Mauss, *Angel and the Beehive*, ix–x, 4–5, 22, 60; Richard N. Ostling and Joan K. Ostling, *Mormon America: The Power and the Promise* (New York: Harper Collins, 1999), 91; Harold Bloom, *The American Religion: The Emergence of the Post-Christian Nation* (New York: Simon and Schuster, 1992), 80. For histories that employ the model, see Gustive O. Larson, *The "Americanization" of Utah for Statehood* (San Marino, CA: Huntington Library, 1971); Edward Leo Lyman, *Political Deliverance: The Mormon Quest for Statehood* (Urbana: University of Illinois Press, 1986); Edwin Brown Firmage and Richard Collin Mangrum, *Zion in the Courts: A Legal History of the Church of Jesus Christ of Latter-Day Saints, 1830–1900* (Urbana: University of Illinois Press, 1988); Marvin S. Hill, *Quest for Refuge: The Mormon Flight from American Pluralism* (Salt Lake City, UT: Signature Books, 1989); Ken Verdoia and Richard A. Firmage, *Utah: The Struggle for Statehood* (Salt Lake City: University of Utah Press, 1996); Claudia Lauper Bushman and Richard Lyman Bushman, *Building the Kingdom: A History of Mormons in America* (New York: Oxford University Press, 1999); Kathleen Flake, *The Politics of American Religious Identity: The Seating of Senator Reed Smoot, Mormon Apostle* (Chapel Hill: University of North Carolina Press, 2004); and Terryl L. Givens, *The Latter-day Saint Experience in America* (Westport, CT: Greenwood Press, 2004). For a mildly sensational version of the theory, see Stephen Mansfield, *The Mormonizing of America: How the Mormon Religion Became a Dominant Force in Politics, Entertainment, and Pop Culture* (Brentwood, TN: Worthy, 2012).

9. An excellent study of the church in this period is Thomas G. Alexander's *Mormonism in Transition: A History of the Latter-day Saints, 1890–1930* (Urbana: University of Illinois Press, 1996).

10. Flake, *Politics of American Religious Identity*, 1, 2; David E. Campbell, John C. Green, and J. Quin Monson, *Seeking the Promised Land: Mormons and American Politics* (New York: Cambridge University Press, 2014), 5; Mauss, *Angel and the Beehive*, 16; Jan Shipps, *Mormonism: The Story of a New Religious Tradition* (Urbana: University of Illinois Press, 1985), 111; Terryl L. Givens, *People of Paradox: A History of Mormon Culture* (New York: Oxford University Press, 2007).

11. Nearly thirty years ago, the Columbia University historian Richard Bushman characterized the field as being marked by "a division between the works of believers and nonbelievers," and by 2001 the most comprehensive analysis of Mormon history writing had accomplished little beyond criticizing nineteenth-century authors and illuminating the relationship of twentieth-century writers to church-owned institutions. As recently as 2007, the religious studies scholar and noted Mormon-watcher Jan Shipps concluded that the field remains bifurcated. Richard L. Bushman, *Joseph Smith and the Beginnings of Mormonism* (Urbana: University of Illinois Press, 1984), 189; Ronald W. Walker, David J. Whittaker, and James B. Allen, *Mormon History*

(Urbana: University of Illinois Press, 2001); Jan Shipps, "Richard Lyman Bushman, the Story of Joseph Smith and Mormonism, and the New Mormon History," *Journal of American History* 94, no. 2 (September 2007): 498–516; Richard Lyman Bushman, "What's New in Mormon History: A Response to Jan Shipps," *Journal of American History* 94, no. 2 (September 2007): 517–21.

12. On Joseph Smith, see Richard Lyman Bushman, *Joseph Smith: Rough Stone Rolling; A Cultural Biography of Mormonism's Founder* (New York: Alfred A. Knopf, 2005); and *The Joseph Smith Papers* (Salt Lake City, UT: Church Historian's Press, 2008–present), josephsmithpapers.org.

13. Stephen C. LeSueur, *The 1838 Mormon War in Missouri* (Columbia: University of Missouri Press, 1987); Alexander L. Baugh, *A Call to Arms: The 1838 Mormon Defense of Northern Missouri* (Provo, UT: Joseph Fielding Smith Institute for Latter-day Saint History and BYU Studies, 2000); and Leland H. Gentry and Todd M. Compton, *Fire and Sword: A History of the Latter-day Saints in Northern Missouri, 1836–1839* (Salt Lake City, UT: Greg Kofford Books, 2011); Andrea G. Radke-Moss, "Silent Memories of Missouri: Mormon Women and Men and Sexual Assault in Group Memory and Religious Identity," in *Mormon Women's History: Beyond Biography*, ed. Rachel Cope, Amy Easton Flake, Keith A. Erekson, and Lisa Olsen Tait (Madison, NJ: Fairleigh Dickinson University Press, 2017), 49–81.

14. See Gordon, *Mormon Question*; and Talbot, *Foreign Kingdom*.

15. For introductions of Mormonism and American politics, see Balmer and Riess, *Mormonism and American Politics*; J. B. Haws, *The Mormon Image in the American Mind: Fifty Years of Public Perception* (New York: Oxford University Press, 2013); and Luke Perry and Christopher Cronin, *Mormons in American Politics: From Persecution to Power* (Santa Barbara, CA: Praeger, 2012).

Chapter 1. "Some Little Necromancy"

1. Benjamin West, *Scriptural Cautions* (Hartford, CT: Webster, 1783), 5; affidavit of Sarah Bean, in *Portraiture of Shakerism*, by Mary M. Dyer (n.p., 1822), 35.

2. William Haskett, *Shakerism Unmasked* (Pittsfield, MA: B. H. Walldey, 1828), 131.

3. Ezra Stiles, *Literary Diary*, 3 vols. (New York: Scribner, 1901), 2:510–11.

4. David Lamson, *Two Years' Experience among the Shakers* (West Boylston, MA, 1848), 30, 28.

5. John Murray, *Bath-Kol* (Boston, MA: Coverly, 1783), 83.

6. "The Book of Pukei," *Rochester (NY) Gem*, May 15, 1930, in *New Witness for Christ in America*, ed. Francis W. Kirkham, 2 vols. (Independence, MO: Zion's, 1951), 2:46–49.

7. "Blasphemy," *Rochester (NY) Daily Advertiser*, April 2, 1830, in Kirkham, *New Witness*, 2:40; *Palmyra (NY) Freeman*, reprinted in *Rochester (NY) Advertiser and Telegraph*, August 31, 1829.

8. Origen Bachelor, *Mormonism Exposed,* quoted in in Kirkham, *New Witness*, 2:159, 161.

9. Kenneth H. Winn, *Exiles in a Land of Liberty: Mormons in America, 1830–1846* (Chapel Hill: University of North Carolina Press, 1990), 144.

10. E. D. Howe, *Mormonism Unvailed* (Painesville, OH, 1834), 12.

11. Robert Breckinridge McAfee, *History of the Late War in the Western Country* (n.p., 1816), 497.

12. Ephraim Stinchfield, *Cochranism Delineated* (Boston, MA: Hews and Goss, 1819), 8, 3.

13. Alan Taylor, "The Early Republic's Supernatural Economy: Treasure Seeking in the American Northeast, 1780–1830," *American Quarterly* 38, no. 1 (Spring 1986): 6–34, quote on 22; D. Michael Quinn, *Early Mormonism and the Magic World View* (Salt Lake City, UT: Signature, 1998), xxii.

14. Stephen C. Harper, "'Dictated by Christ': Joseph Smith and the Politics of Revelation," *Journal of the Early Republic* 26, no. 2 (Summer 2006): 275.

15. Adam Jortner, *Blood from the Sky: Miracles and Politics in the Early Republic* (Charlottesville: University of Virginia Press, 2017), 68.

16. See Jortner, *Blood from the Sky*, 107–8.

17. Leander W. Cogswell, *History of the Town of Henniker, Merrimack County, New Hampshire* (Concord, NH: Republican Press, 1880), 90–91; Robert F. W. Meader, "Another Lost Utopia," *Shaker Quarterly* 4, no. 1 (Fall 1964): 123–24.

18. Andrew Jackson to Tennessee Troops, April 2, 1814, *The Papers of Andrew Jackson*, ed. Harold D. Moser, David R. Hoth, Sharon Macpherson, John H. Reinbold, 10 vols. (Knoxville, TN: University of Tennessee Press, 1991), 3:57.

19. Stuart Clark, *Thinking with Demons: The Idea of Witchcraft in Early Modern Europe* (New York: Oxford University Press, 1997), 474–75.

20. Clark, *Thinking with Demons*, 477.

21. John Spencer, *A Discourse Concerning Prodigies* (Cambridge: John Field, 1663), vi.

22. Francis Hutchinson, *Historical Essay Concerning Witchcraft* (London: R. Knaplock, 1718), 181–82.

23. John Hale, *A Modest Enquiry into the Nature of Witchcraft* (1702; repr., Boston, MA: Kneeland and Adams, 1756), 148.

24. Robert Calef, *More Wonders of the Invisible World*, in *Narratives of New England Witchcraft Cases*, ed. George Lincoln Burr (Mineola, NY: Dover, 2002), 301.

25. For a full treatment of these demonologies, see Jortner, *Blood from the Sky*, chap. 3.

26. William Bentley, "History of Salem," in *Collections of the Massachusetts Historical Society*, 1st ser., 10 vols. (1799; repr., New York, 1968), 6:268–70.

27. *Debate Proposed in the Temple Patrick Society: Whether Witches Had Supernatural Power* (Philadelphia: Young, 1788), 3, 10, 12.

28. Joseph Lathrop, *Illustrations and Reflections on the Story of Saul's Consulting the Witch of Endor* (Springfield, MA: Henry Brewer, 1806), 14; Frederick Quitman, *A Treatise on Magic* (Albany, NY: Balance Press, 1810), 27.

29. John Greenleaf Whittier, *The Supernaturalism of New England* (1847; repr., Baltimore: Clearfield, 1997), 1–3.

30. Bernard Whitman, *Lecture on Popular Superstitions* (Boston, MA: Bowles and Dearborn, 1829), 63.

31. James Thacher, *An Essay on Demonology, Ghosts, and Apparitions* (Boston, MA: Carter and Hendee, 1831), 1.

32. Enoch Lincoln, *The Village* (Portland, ME: Edward Little, 1816), 50–52.

33. David Young, *The Wonderful History of the Morristown Ghost: Thoroughly and Carefully Revised* (Newark, NJ: Benjamin Olds, 1826), 72, 21, 31.

34. David Reese, *Humbugs of New-York* (New York: John Taylor, 1838), 22–23, 266.

35. "Quitman on the Popular Prevalence of Magical Notions," *Medical Repository of Original Essays and Intelligence* (August–October 1810): 183–84.

36. *Boston (MA) Investigator*, September 1, 1841.

37. Aaron C. Willey, "Observations on Magical Practices," *Medical Repository of Original Essays and Intelligence* (February–April 1812): 377–82.

38. "An Act Relating to Vagrants in the City of Baltimore" (1804), in *Laws of the State of Maryland*, ed. Virgil Maxcy, 3 vols. (Baltimore: Nicklin, 1811), 3:211; *Public Laws of the State of Connecticut*, 2 vols. (Hartford, CT, 1808), 1:689; *Laws of the State of New-York*, 2 vols. (Albany, 1813), 1:114.

39. James Smith, *Remarkable Occurrences Lately Discovered Among the People Called Shakers* (Paris, KY: Lye, 1810), 5, 17.

40. Lamson, *Two Years' Experience*, 28, 30.

41. Henry Rowe Schoolcraft, *Algic Researches* (1839; repr., Mineola, NY: Dover, 1999), 116; *Richmond (VA) Enquirer*, April 13, 1814, quoting the *Milledgeville (GA) Journal*, March 20, 1814.

42. Alexander L. Baugh, "Jacob Hawn and the Hawn's Mill Massacre: Missouri Millwright and Oregon Pioneer," *Mormon Historical Studies* 11, no.1 (Spring 2010): 1–25.

43. Charles Colcock Jones, *The Religious Instruction of the Negroes* (Savannah, GA: T. Purse 1842), 127–28.

44. *Designs against Charleston: The Trial Record of the Denmark Vesey Conspiracy of 1822*, ed. Edward A. Pearson (Chapel Hill: University of North Carolina Press, 1999), 280. Yvonne P. Chireau, in *Black Magic: Religion and the African-American Conjuring Tradition* (Berkeley: University of California Press, 2003), 67, notes that all evidence of Pritchard's conjure comes from secondary sources. Therefore, we should consider the possibility that this sentence was against an apparent "necromancer," and perhaps not against a true practitioner of magic.

45. David Hudson, *Memoir of Jemima Wilkinson* (1821; repr., New York: AMS, 1972), 141–42.

46. Barnes Frisbie, *History of Middletown, Vermont* (Rutland, VT: Tuttle, 1867), 45–64. Frisbie's history is borne out by what little primary source evidence is available. See Robert Parks, *History of Wells, Vermont* (Rutland, VT: Tuttle, 1869), 80–81, for Nancy Glass's oral history. Historians and contemporaries have rushed to connect these sects to Mormonism rather than view all of them as distinct entries in a broader style of religion (and its vitriolic backlash). Frisbie's account of the New Israelites included a letter claiming that "their movement gave origin to the Mormons, the vilest scheme of villany and corruption that has ever cursed the country" (Laban Clark to Frisbie, January 30, 1867, in Frisbie, *History of Middletown*, 57). David Hudson's biographer invented a story of Wilkinson's failure to walk on water—a story that was later (falsely) associated with Joseph Smith Jr. (Stanley J. Thayne, "Walking on Water: Nineteenth-Century Prophets and a Legend of Religious Imposture," *Journal of Mormon History* 36, no. 2 [Spring 2010]: 170–71).

47. Lyman Beecher, *A Plea for the West* (Cincinnati, OH: Truman and Smith, 1835), 12.

48. *Six Months in a Convent*, reprinted in *Veil of Fear: Nineteenth-Century Convent Tales by Rebecca Reed and Maria Monk*, ed. Nancy Lusignan Schultz (West Lafayette, IN: NotaBell Books, 1999), 7.

49. Sidney Martin Lipset and Earl Raab, *The Politics of Unreason: Right-Wing Extremism in America, 1790–1970* (New York: Harper and Row, 1970), 49.

50. Howe, *Mormonism Unvailed*, 145, emphasis in the original.

51. Howe, *Mormonism Unvailed*, 43.

52. Alexander Campbell, *Delusions: An Analysis of the Book of Mormon* (Boston, MA: Benjamin Greene, 1832), 85.

53. *Palmyra (NY) Reflector*, January 22, 1830, and December 22, 1829.

54. Kirkham, *New Witness*, 2:51–53.

55. Howe, *Mormonism Unvailed*, 11–12.

56. Howe, *Mormonism Unvailed*, 94.

57. Howe, *Mormonism Unvailed*, 176.

58. *New York Morning Courier and New York Enquirer*, September 1, 1831. For a sample of further examples, see A. Campbell, *Delusions*, 85, 90, 94; *New York Spectator*, November 22, 1838; *Rochester (NY) Gem*, May 15, 1830; *Ohio Star*, reprinted in *Painesville (OH) Telegraph*, August 25, 1831.

59. Quoted in Howe, *Mormonism Unvailed*, 140. See also *Missouri Intelligencer and Boon's Lick Advertiser*, August 10, 1833, reprinted in *Among the Mormons*, ed. William Mulder and A. Russell Mortensen (New York: Knopf, 1958; repr., Salt Lake City, UT: Western Epics, 1994), 76–80.

60. Joseph Smith Jr., *History of the Church of Jesus Christ of Latter-day Saints,* 7 vols., ed. B.H. Roberts (Salt Lake City: Deseret, 1971), 3:203–4.

61. The assertion of a distinctive anti-Mormonism is often a result of abstracting Mormon claims (and anti-Mormon responses) from previous condemnations of earlier sects and supernatural claims. See, for example, Terryl L. Givens, *By the Hand of Mormon: The American Scripture That Launched a New World Religion* (New York: Oxford University Press, 2002), chap. 6; and Richard Lyman Bushman, *Joseph Smith: Rough Stone Rolling; A Cultural Biography of Mormonism's Founder* (New York: Vintage Books, 2007), 88–94. These authors often mention the presence of pre-Mormon sects, but they miss the ways in which debates over earlier sects established the patterns of anti-Mormonism as they emerged in the early republic. J. Spencer Fluhman, *"A Peculiar People": Anti-Mormonism and the Making of Religion in Nineteenth-Century America* (Chapel Hill: University of North Carolina Press, 2012), for example, notes the roles of both magic and politics in early anti-Mormonism, but does not connect the two. As Fluhman's primary point is not the origins of anti-Mormonism but its effects on American religious language, I do not see his work as in opposition to my own. See Fluhman, *"Peculiar People,"* 43–48.

62. Quinn, *Early Mormonism*, 236, 239, xxii. See also Marvin S. Hill, *Quest for Refuge: The Mormon Flight from American Pluralism* (Salt Lake City, UT: Signature, 1989); and Harper, *"'Dictated by Christ,'"* 275. A similar misreading of anti-Mormon critics, I contend, affects the analysis of such venerable volumes as John Brooke's *Refiner's Fire* and Fawn Brodie's *No Man Knows My History*.

63. Thomas Campbell to Sidney Rigdon, February 4, 1831, reprinted in *Mormonism: Embracing the Origin, Rise, and Progress of the Sect*, by James H. Hunt (St. Louis, MO: Usick and Davies, 1844), 110.

64. "Letter No. 6," Kirtland (OH) *Messenger and Advocate*, April 1835. On anti-Mormonism and its relationship to other "antis," see Fluhman, *"Peculiar People,"* 19.

Chapter 2. "Many Think This Is a Hoax"

1. For general overviews of Smith's presidential campaign, see Fawn Brodie, *No Man Knows My History: The Life of Joseph Smith*, 2nd ed. (New York: Alfred A. Knopf, 1971), 362–66; Richard Lyman Bushman, *Joseph Smith: Rough Stone Rolling; A Cultural Biography of Mormonism's Founder* (New York: Alfred A. Knopf, 2005), 512–17; Richard Lyman Bushman, "Joseph Smith's Presidential Ambitions," in *Mormonism and American Politics*, ed. Randall Balmer and Jana Riess (New York: Columbia University Press, 2016), 3–13; John Bicknell, *America 1844: Religious Fervor, Westward Expansion, and the Presidential Election That Transformed the Nation* (Chicago: Chicago Review Press, 2015), 29–49; and Robert S. Wicks and Fred R. Foister, *Junius and Joseph: Presidential Politics and the Assassination of the First Mormon Prophet* (Logan: Utah State University Press, 2005), 81–92.

2. On the nature and role of anti-Catholicism in American politics, see Maura Jane Farrelly, *Papist Patriots: The Making of an American Catholic Identity* (New York: Oxford University Press, 2012); and Sydney E. Ahlstrom, *A Religious History of the American People*, 2nd ed. (New Haven, CT: Yale University Press, 2004), 555–68.

3. Joseph Smith to Hyrum Smith and High Council, December 5, 1839, in *The Joseph Smith Papers: Documents*, vol. 7, *September 1839–January 1841*, ed. Matthew C. Godfrey, Spencer W. McBride, Alex D. Smith, and Christopher James Blythe (Salt Lake City, UT: Church Historian's Press, 2018), 66–73 (hereafter cited as *JSP: Documents*).

4. Memorial to the United States Senate and House of Representatives, ca. October 1839 and January 27, 1840, and Appendix 1: Report of the Senate Committee on the Judiciary, March 4, 1840, in *JSP: Documents*, 7:138–74, 539–43; Bushman, *Joseph Smith*, 394–98, 513–14.

5. Bushman, *Joseph Smith*, 403–16.

6. Joseph Smith to Henry Clay, Lewis Cass, John C. Calhoun, Richard Mentor Johnson, and Martin Van Buren, November 4, 1843, Joseph Smith Collection, Church History Library, Church of Jesus Christ of Latter-day Saints, Salt Lake City, Utah (hereafter cited as Joseph Smith Collection, CHL).

7. John C. Calhoun to Joseph Smith, December 2, 1843, Joseph Smith Collection, CHL.

8. Joseph Smith, journal entry, January 29, 1844, in *The Joseph Smith Papers: Journals*, vol. 3, *May 1843—June 1844*, ed. Andrew H. Hedges, Alex D. Smith, and Brent M. Rogers (Salt Lake City, UT: Church Historian's Press, 2015), 3:170 (hereafter cited as *JSP: Journals*); Wilford Woodruff, journal entry, February 8, 1844, in *Wilford Woodruff's Journal, 1833–1898: Typescript*, ed. Scott G. Kenney, 9 vols. (Midvale, UT: Signature Books, 1983), 2:349.

9. On the significant role of print culture in early Mormon proselytizing, see Terryl L. Givens and Matthew J. Grow, *Parley P. Pratt: The Apostle Paul of Mormonism* (New York: Oxford University Press, 2011), 5–7.

10. See Spencer W. McBride, "The Council of Fifty and Joseph Smith's Presidential Ambitions," in *The Council of Fifty: What the Records Reveal about Mormon History*, ed. Matthew J. Grow and R. Eric Smith (Provo, UT: Religious Studies Center, Brigham Young University), 21–30.

11. On the electioneering missionaries and their canvassing efforts throughout the United States, see Derek Ralph Sainsbury, "The Cadre for the Kingdom: The Electioneer Missionaries of Joseph Smith's 1844 Presidential Campaign" (PhD diss., University of Utah, 2016).

12. Joseph Smith, *General Smith's Views of the Powers and Policy of the Government of the United States* (Nauvoo, IL: John Taylor, 1844).

13. Wilford Woodruff, journal entry, February 8, 1844, in Kenney, *Wilford Woodruff's Journal*, 2:349.

14. Bushman, *Joseph Smith*, 512–17.

15. Smith, *General Smith's Views*, 7.

16. In the corpus of the surviving papers of Martin Van Buren, only two indicate that Smith met with the eighth president, both of them letters introducing Smith. See Elizabeth Howard West, *Calendar of the Papers of Martin Van Buren* (Washington, DC: Government Printing Office, 1910), 382; letter of introduction from James Adams, November 9, 1839, in *JSP: Documents*, 7:53–55; and letter of introduction from Sidney Rigdon, November 9, 1839, in *JSP: Documents*, 7:57–59.

17. Spencer W. McBride, "When Joseph Smith Met Martin Van Buren: Mormonism and the Politics of Religious Liberty in Nineteenth-Century America," *Church History: Studies in Christianity and Culture* 85, no. 1 (March 2016): 158.

18. In *General Smith's Views*, Smith wrote that "General Jackson's administration may be denominated the acme of American glory, liberty, and prosperity." See Smith, *General Smith's Views*, 7.

19. Smith, *General Smith's Views*, 10.

20. Smith, *General Smith's Views*, 8–9, 11.

21. Smith, *General Smith's Views*, 10. On the differing political and martial approaches to westward expansion during this era, see Amy S. Greenberg, *Manifest Manhood and the Antebellum American Empire* (New York: Cambridge University Press, 2005).

22. Smith, *General Smith's Views*, 9. On the antebellum debate over the rise of the American penitentiary system and the debate over reform in the criminal justice system, see Edward L. Ayers, *Vengeance and Justice: Crime and Punishment in the Nineteenth-Century American South* (New York: Oxford University Press, 1984), 34–72.

23. Smith, *General Smith's Views*, 9–10. On the debate over the reestablishment of the national bank in the late 1830s and early 1840s and its projected impact on the American economy, see Daniel Walker Howe, *What Hath God Wrought: The Transformation of America, 1815–1848* (New York: Oxford University Press, 2007), 588–95; and Jessica M. Lepler, *The Many Panics of 1837: People, Politics, and the Creation of a Transatlantic Financial Crisis* (New York: Cambridge University Press, 2013), 210–18.

24. Smith, *General Smith's Views*, 9.

25. Jeffrey L. Pasley, *"The Tyranny of Printers": Newspaper Politics in the Early American Republic* (Charlottesville: University of Virginia Press, 2001.

26. John Hayward, *Religious Creeds and Statistics of Every Christian Denomination* (Boston, MA: John Hayward, 1836), 118–52.

27. Peter Crawley, *A Descriptive Bibliography of the Mormon Church*, 2 vols. (Provo, UT: Religious Studies Center, Brigham Young University, 1997), 1:17–23, 32–33.

28. "A Friend to the Mormons," *Times and Seasons* (Nauvoo, IL), March 15, 1844.

29. "For President, Gen. Joseph Smith," *Times and Seasons*, March 1, 1844.

30. "Prospectus," *Prophet* (New York), May 18, 1844. On the publishing history of the *Prophet*, see Crawley, *Descriptive Biography of the Mormon Church*, 254–56.

31. The phrase, "A Western man with American principles," appeared as a subtitle to an article declaring Smith's candidacy. See "For President, Gen. Smith of Nauvoo, Illinois," *Prophet*, May 25, 1844. For an example of the paper reprinting portions of Smith's political writings, see "An Appeal to the Freemen of the State of Vermont," *Prophet*, May 25, 1844. For an example of the paper printing a response to criticism of Smith's campaign, see "The Globe," *Prophet*, May 18, 1844.

32. For examples, see "Jeffersonians Attend!!" and "Jeffersonian Convention," *Prophet*, June 8, 1844.

33. See Crawley, *Descriptive Bibliography of the Mormon Church*, 255–56.

34. "Illinois: The Mormons," and "A New Candidate in the Field," *Niles' National Register*, March 2, 1844.

35. "Mormon Movements," *New York Herald*, May 23, 1844.

36. *Illinois Weekly State Journal*, March 14, 1844. A letter from Bennett to Smith in which the former expressed interest in moving to Illinois and running for governor was reprinted in newspapers throughout the country in late 1843 and early 1844. See "For the Times and Seasons," *Times and Seasons*, November 1, 1843. Ultimately, the Smiths removed Bennett from the ticket because they mistakenly thought that he was born in Ireland. See *JSP: Journals*, 3:190n839, 294n1355.

37. "New Candidate," *People's Organ* (St. Louis, MO), March 6 1844.

38. "A New Advocate for a National Bank," *Daily Globe* (Washington, DC), March 14, 1844.

39. "A New Advocate for a National Bank," *Daily Globe*, March 14, 1844.

40. "General Smith's Views of the Powers and Policy of the United States," *Boston Investigator*, May 15, 1844.

41. *Working Man's Advocate* (New York), May 18, 1844.

42. "Life in Nauvoo," *New-York Tribune*, May 28, 1844.

43. William Gano Goforth, Letter to the Editor of the *Belleville Advocate*, in *Belleville (IL) Advocate*, April 18, 1844.

44. John Adams to Abigail Adams, September 17, 1775, Adams Family Papers, Massachusetts Historical Society.

45. Spencer W. McBride, *Pulpit and Nation: Clergymen and the Politics of Revolutionary America* (Charlottesville: University of Virginia Press, 2016), 95.

46. On the general consensus among scholars that, inasmuch as politics factored into the motives of Smith's assassins, they were local and state politics, see Bushman, *Joseph Smith*, 522–23, 540–41; and Dallin H. Oaks and Marvin S. Hill, *Carthage Conspiracy: The Trial of the Accused Assassins of Joseph Smith* (Urbana: University of

Illinois Press, 1975), 11–20. The most prominent example of scholars arguing that presidential politics were behind a national conspiracy to elect Henry Clay by eliminating Smith from the presidential campaign, see Wicks and Foister, *Junius and Joseph*. For a detailed critique of the theory of Wicks and Foister, see Michael W. Homer, "A National Conspiracy?," *Dialogue* 39, no. 2 (Summer 2006): 165–67.

47. Wilford Woodruff, journal entry, March 7, 1844, in Kenney, *Wilford Woodruff's Journal*, 2:358.

48. Several positive accounts of Smith and the Mormons had appeared in eastern newspapers, including the *New York Herald*. In 1841 Smith lauded the *New York Herald's* editor, James Gordon Bennett, for his balanced reporting on the Mormons. See entry for December 18, 1841, in Nauvoo City Council Minute Book, CHL.

Chapter 3. Precarious Protestant Democracy

1. Willard Richards to Hugh Clark, May 24, 1844, copy in Willard Richards Papers, Church History Library, Church of Jesus Christ of Latter-day Saints, Salt Lake City, Utah (hereafter cited as CHL). "Jeffersonian Meeting," *Prophet* (New York), June 15, 1844. The apostle Orson Hyde would similarly express sympathy for the Catholics, saying they "are persecuted and oppressed similar to what we are" a year later. Council of Fifty, Minutes, March 18, 1845, in *The Joseph Smith Papers: Administrative Records; Council of Fifty, Minutes, March 1844–January 1846*, ed. Matthew J. Grow, Ronald K. Esplin, Mark Ashurst-McGee, Gerrit J. Dirkmaat, and Jeffrey D. Mahas (Salt Lake City, UT: Church Historian's Press, 2016), 329–30 (hereafter cited as *JSP: Council of Fifty, Minutes*). For the Philadelphia Nativist Riots, see David Montgomery, "The Shuttle and the Cross: Weavers and Artisans in the Kensington Riots of 1844," *Journal of Social History* 5, no. 4 (Summer 1972): 411–46.

2. For an overview of the relationship between Mormons and Catholics in the nineteenth century, see Mark W. Cannon, "The Crusades against the Masons, Catholics, and Mormons: Separate Waves of a Common Current," *BYU Studies* 3, no. 2 (Winter 1961): 23–40; and Matthew J. Grow, "The Whore of Babylon and the Abomination of Abominations: Nineteenth-Century Catholic and Mormon Mutual Perceptions and Religious Identity," *Church History* 73, no. 1 (March 2004): 139–67. My theoretic modeling of convergences between Mormon and Catholic notions of authority draws from Matthew B. Bowman, "Toward a Catholic History of Mormonism," *Journal of Mormon History* 41, no. 1 (January 2015): 198–216.

3. Ezra Stiles Ely, *The Duty of Christian Freeman to Elect Christian Rulers* (Philadelphia, PA: William F. Geddes, 1828), 6–11. For the formation of Christian politics based on individual liberty, I have relied upon Philip Hamburger, *Separation of Church and State* (Cambridge, MA: Harvard University Press, 2002), esp. 193–251. For the role of ministers in taking advantage of a democratized culture, see Jonathan D. Sassi, *A Republic of Righteousness: The Public Christianity of the Post-Revolutionary New England Clergy* (New York: Oxford University Press, 2001); Amanda Porterfield, *Conceived in Doubt: Religion and Politics in the New American Nation* (Chicago: University of Chicago Press, 2012); and Spencer W. McBride, *Pulpit and Nation: Clergymen and the Politics of Revolutionary America* (Charlottesville: University of Virginia Press, 2017).

4. S. K. Lathrop, *The Nature and Extent of Religious Liberty* (Boston, MA: I. R. Butts, 1838), 3; Nathan O. Hatch, *The Democratization of American Christianity* (New Haven, CT: Yale University Press, 1989), 6, 9, 11, 15; Leonard Bacon, *The Christian Alliance* (New York: S. W. Benedict, 1845), 19; David Sehat, *The Myth of American Religious Freedom* (New York: Oxford University Press, 2011), 69; Sarah Barringer Gordon, "The First Disestablishment: Limits on Church Power and Property before the Civil War," *University of Pennsylvania Law Review* 162 (2014): 334. See also Steven K. Green, *The Second Disestablishment: Church and State in Nineteenth-Century America* (New York: Oxford University Press, 2010). For a countering view that argues for a more inclusive religious culture during the period, see Chris Beneke, *Beyond Toleration: The Religious Origins of American Pluralism* (New York: Oxford University Press, 2016).

5. John McGreevy, *Catholicism and American Freedom: A History* (New York: W. W. Norton, 2004), 36–37; H. A. Boardman, *Lecture Delivered in the Walnut Street Presbyterian Church* (Philadelphia, PA: Hooker and Agnew, 1841), iv–v. See also Jon Butler, "Historiographical Heresy: Catholicism as a Model for American Religious History," in *Belief in History: Innovative Approaches to European and American Religion*, ed. Thomas Kselman (South Bend, IN: University of Notre Dame Press, 1991), 287–88; Jay Dolan, *Catholic Revivalism and the American Experience* (South Bend, IN: University of Notre Dame Press, 1978); and Ann Taves, *The Household of Faith: Roman Catholic Devotions in Mid-Nineteenth Century America* (South Bend, IN: University of Notre Dame Press, 1986). Catholicism is notably absent in Hatch's *Democratization of American Christianity*, as his focus on "the rise of full-fledged populist clergy" restricted their inclusion (12).

6. Samuel Seabury, *The Supremacy and Obligation of Conscience: Considered with Reference to the Opposite Errors of Romanism and Protestantism* (New York: Billin and Brother, 1860), 21. Philip Hamburger argues that it is in response to the Catholic threat that "Protestants would eventually elevate separation of church and state as an American ideal." Hamburger, *Separation of Church and State*, 202.

7. John Hughes, quoted in Hamburger, *Separation of Church and State*, 209; John Hancock Lee, *The Origin and Progress of the American Party in Politics: Embracing a Complete History of the Philadelphia Riots in 1844* (Philadelphia, PA: Elliott and Gihon, 1855), 248; James P. Hambleton, *A Biographical Sketch of Henry A. Wise, with a History of the Political Campaign in Virginia in 1855* (Richmond, VA: J. W. Randolph, 1856), 51–52.

8. J. B. Turner, *Mormonism in All Ages, or the Rise, Progress and Cause of Mormonism* (New York: Platt and Peters, 1842), 8; Joseph Smith, sermon, June 16, 1844, in *The Words of Joseph Smith: The Contemporary Accounts of the Nauvoo Discourses of the Prophet Joseph*, ed. Andrew F. Ehat and Lyndon W. Cook (Provo, UT: Religious Studies Center, Brigham Young University, 1980), 382. For the ethnic descriptions of early Mormonism, see W. Paul Reeve, *Religion of a Different Color: Race and the Mormon Struggle for Whiteness* (New York: Oxford University Press, 2015), esp. 14–51.

9. Stephen Longstroth to Thomas Longstroth, July 8, 1845, CHL; "For the Neighbor," *Nauvoo (IL) Neighbor*, August 2, 1843; Illinois, Hancock County, Nauvoo Precinct Election Returns, August 1, 1842, CHL; John Hardin to John Stuart, December 28, 1842, CHL. For Mormon voting patterns during these early years, see Robert B. Flanders, *Nauvoo: Kingdom on the Mississippi* (Urbana: University of Illinois Press,

1965), 220–21; and George W. Gayler, "The Mormons in Illinois Politics, 1839–1844," *Journal of the Illinois State Historical Society* 49 (1956): 50–51.

10. "The Mormons," *Warsaw (IL) Signal*, May 19, 1841; "Joseph Smith," *Quincy (IL) Whig*, January 22, 1842. See also "Mormons," *Peoria (IL) Register and Northwestern Gazetteer*, January 21, 1842; George W. Gayler, "A Social, Economic, and Political Study of the Mormons in Western Illinois, 1839–1846" (PhD diss., Indiana University, 1955), 161–62; Gayler, "Mormons in Illinois Politics," 50; and Flanders, *Nauvoo*, 221–22.

11. John C. Calhoun, "A Disquisition on Government," in *The Works of John C. Calhoun*, ed. Richard K. Crallé, 6 vols. (New York: D. Appleton, 1854–57), 1:28–29. For competing conceptions of "liberty" and "order" from an earlier period, see Michael Jan Rozbicki, *Culture and Liberty in the Age of the American Revolution* (Charlottesville: University of Virginia Press, 2011); and Eric Slauter, "Rights," in *The Oxford Handbook of the American Revolution*, ed. Edward G. Gray and Jane Kamensky (New York: Oxford University Press, 2012), 447–64.

12. Orson Hyde, "Diagram of the Kingdom of God," *Millennial Star*, January 15, 1847; Hatch, *Democratization of American Christianity*, 15. See also Jonathan A. Stapley, "Adoptive Sealing Ritual in Mormonism," *Journal of Mormon History* 37, no. 3 (Summer 2011): 53–118; Samuel M. Brown, *In Heaven as It Is on Earth: Joseph Smith and the Early Mormon Conquest of Death* (New York: Oxford University Press, 2012), 203–47; and Kathleen Flake, "The Development of Early Latter-day Saint Marriage Rites, 1831–1853," *Journal of Mormon History* 41, no. 1 (January 2015): 77–102.

13. Alexis de Tocqueville, *Democracy in America: Part the Second; The Social Influence of Democracy* (New York: J. and H. G. Langley, 1840), 114.

14. "Bishop Hopkins on Novelties," *Brownson's Quarterly Review* (Boston, MA), April 1844. For Brownson's conversion, see Patrick W. Carey, *Orestes A. Brownson: American Religious Weathervane* (Grand Rapids, MI: Wm B. Eerdmans, 2004), 134–53.

15. "The Church," *Brownson's Quarterly Review*, January 1844; "Popular Government," *Democratic Review* (Boston, MA), May 1843; "Civil and Religious Toleration," *Brownson's Quarterly Review*, July 1849.

16. Orestes Brownson, *The American Republic: Its Constitution, Tendencies and Destiny* (1866; repr., Wilmington, DE: ISI Books, 2003), 1, 3, 82, 173; Brownson, "Our Lady of Lourdes" (1875), in *Orestes A. Brownson: Selected Writings*, ed. Patrick W. Carey (New York: Paulist Press, 1991), 272.

17. James Kloppenberg, *Toward Democracy: The Struggle for Self-Rule in European and American Thought* (New York: Oxford University Press, 2016), 588–98, quote on 597. For the First Vatican Council, see August Hasler, *How the Pope Became Infallible: Pious IX and the Politics of Persuasion* (New York: Doubleday, 1981).

18. Oran Brownson's letter and background are found in Matthew J. Grow, "'I Consider the Proper Authority Rests among the Mormons': Oran Brownson to Orestes Brownson on Oran's Conversion to Mormonism," *Mormon Historical Studies* 4, no. 2 (Fall 2003): 191–98, quote on 195.

19. Council of Fifty, Minutes, March 11, 1844, in *JSP: Council of Fifty, Minutes*, 40; "The Globe," *Times and Seasons* (Nauvoo, IL), April 15, 1844; Joseph Smith, journal entry, March 10, 1844, in *The Joseph Smith Papers: Journals*, vol. 3, *May 1843–June 1844*, ed. Andrew H. Hedges, Alex D. Smith, and Brent M. Rogers (Salt Lake City, UT:

Church Historian's Press, 2015), 201; Council of Fifty, Minutes, March 19, 1844, in *JSP: Council of Fifty, Minutes*, 54.

20. Albert Carrington, "Kingdom of God," notebook, March 4, 1845, CHL; Orson Hyde to John E. Page, May 6, 1844, CHL.

21. Council of Fifty, Minutes, April 11, 1844, in *JSP: Council of Fifty, Minutes*, 95–96.

22. Council of Fifty, Minutes, April 11, 1844, in *JSP: Council of Fifty, Minutes*, 90, 92–93, 95–96. Patrick Mason has ably demonstrated how many Mormons saw theocracy and democracy not only as complementary but also as inseparable. Patrick Q. Mason, "God and the People: Theodemocracy in Nineteenth-Century Mormonism," *Journal of Church and State* 53, no. 3 (Summer 2011): 350, 357–58. For Mormonism's sacramental and covenantal notion of voting habits and prophetic authority, see Kathleen Flake's "Ordering Antinomy: An Analysis of Early Mormonism's Priestly Offices, Councils and Kinship," *Religion and American Culture* 26, no. 2 (Summer 2016): 147, 152, 166–67.

23. George T. Davis, "An Authentic Account of the Massacre of Joseph Smith," in *Cultures in Conflict: A Documentary History of the Mormon War in Illinois*, ed. John E. Hallwas and Roger D. Launius (Logan: Utah State University Press, 1995), 105; "From Nauvoo," *New Hampshire Statesman and State Journal*, October 11, 1844; Thomas Ford, *A History of Illinois, from Its Commencement as a State in 1818 to 1847* (Chicago: S. C. Griggs, 1854), 321–22; "Mormon Politicians," *New-York Daily Tribune*, May 28, 1844.

24. William Clayton, "Events of June 1844," in *JSP: Council of Fifty, Minutes*, 193.

25. Council of Fifty, Minutes, March 18, 1845, 336; Council of Fifty, Minutes, March 4, 1845, 285; and Council of Fifty, Minutes, May 10, 1845, 454; all in *JSP: Council of Fifty, Minutes*.

26. Council of Fifty, Minutes, March 18, 1845, in *JSP: Council of Fifty, Minutes*, 329–30.

27. "For President, Gen. Joseph Smith, of Nauvoo, Ill.," *Prophet* (New York), June 2, 1844.

Chapter 4. "The Woman's Movement Has Discovered a New Enemy—the Mormon Church"

1. Kay Mills, "Feminists Fighting Mormon Stand on ERA," *Los Angeles Times*, September 17, 1977.

2. Mills, "Feminists Fighting Mormon Stand on ERA."

3. Given that much of the anti-ERA force was attributed to the church in the late 1970s and 1980s, it is curious that scholarship on the Mormon involvement remained slim until the mid-2000s. When the church was so effective in influencing their membership to campaign for anti–same-sex measures in the early 2000s, such as Proposition 8 in California, more scholarly attention turned to the Mormon political activism in the late twentieth century. Work by scholars like Martha Sonntag Bradley and J. B. Haws has placed the church's leadership and membership at the center of the fight against the ratification of the ERA. See Martha Sonntag Bradley, *Pedestals and Podiums: Utah Women, Religious Authority and Equal Rights*

(Salt Lake City, UT: Signature Books, 2005); J. B. Haws, "The Politics of Family Values, 1972–1981," in *The Mormon Image in the American Mind* (New York: Oxford University Press, 2013), 74–98.

Marjorie J. Spruill and Neil Young include Mormons as integral members of the religious right in their explorations of late twentieth-century politics, gender, and religion. See Marjorie J. Spruill, *Divided We Stand: The Battle over Women's Rights and Family Values That Polarized American Politics* (New York: Bloomsbury USA, 2017); and Neil J. Young, *We Gather Together: The Religious Right and the Problem of Interfaith Politics* (New York: Oxford University Press, 2015).

4. See Bradley, "Anti-ERA Activism in Key States," in *Pedestals and Podiums*, 281–329.

5. Judy Foreman, "It's Do or Die for the ERA—Mormon Power Is the Key," *Boston Globe*, June 30, 1981.

6. Lena Serge Zezulin, "An ERA Missionary in Utah," *Feminist Studies* 8, no. 2 (Summer 1981): 461.

7. Bradley, *Pedestals and Podiums*, 394.

8. Muriel Dobbin, "ERA Crusaders Seek Utah Converts," *Baltimore Sun*, May 5, 1981.

9. For a history of the ERA, see Bradley, "A Brief History of the Equal Rights Amendment," in *Pedestals and Podiums*, 29–49.

10. Kristin Luker, *Abortion and the Politics of Motherhood* (Berkeley: University of California Press, 1984), 126–56; Spruill, *Divided We Stand*, 71–74.

11. Spruill, *Divided We Stand*, 79–80.

12. In 1903, Mormon apostle Reed Smoot was elected to the Senate. Instead of beginning his term, the Senate held a three-year-long hearing in which it was to be determined if his religion would deter him from serving as a senator. During the span of the hearing, it was revealed that several plural marriages had occurred after the announcement of the Manifesto in 1890. This revelation once again brought fears of Mormon otherness to the forefront of mainstream America. To combat the rampant anti-Mormonism, the present church president Joseph Fielding Smith issued the Second Manifesto in 1904, which would excommunicate anyone who continued to practice polygamy. See Kathleen Flake, *The Politics of American Religious Identity: The Seating of Senator Reed Smoot, Mormon Apostle* (Chapel Hill: University of North Carolina Press, 2004), 91–92.

13. Jan Shipps, "Surveying the Mormon Image since 1960," in *Sojourner in the Promised Land: Forty Years among the Mormons* (Urbana: University of Illinois Press, 2000), 100.

14. Scholarship on the priesthood ban for black men has expanded since 2014. With this scholarship, a debate about the origins of the ban has emerged. For more, see "Race and the Priesthood," accessed November 3, 2018, www.lds.org/topics/race-and-the-priesthood?lang=eng; and Max Perry Mueller, "History Lessons: Race and the LDS Church," *Journal of Mormon History* 41, no. 1 (January 2015): 139–55.

15. For more on how the majority of the Utah church members' voting patterns and politics changed, see Jan Shipps, "Ezra Taft Benson and the Conservative Turn of 'Those Amazing Mormons,'" in *Mormonism and American Politics*, ed. Randall Balmer and Jana Riess (New York: Columbia University Press, 2015), 73–84.

16. For purposes of delineating the origins and rise of the American conservative movement as it is historically understood through the post–World War II era, I rely upon periodization set forth by Lisa McGirr and Michelle Nickerson. Both cite the conservative movement as a loosely self-defined movement coming to fruition in the early 1960s with overtures in the 1950s. While different conservative movements and groups had varying motivations, goals, mobilization methods, and structures, they shared commonalities such as anticommunism, antistatism, and fears of internationalism, and the need to uphold traditionalism, the nuclear family, gender roles, religious freedom, and capitalism. See Lisa McGirr, *Suburban Warriors: The Origins of the New American Right* (Princeton, NJ: Princeton University Press, 2001), 5–11; and Michelle M. Nickerson, *Mothers of Conservatism: Women and the Postwar Right* (Princeton, NJ: Princeton University Press, 2012), xiv–xviii.

17. McGirr, *Suburban Warriors*, 10.

18. Patrick Q. Mason, "Ezra Taft Benson and (Book of) Mormon Conservatism," in *Out of Obscurity: Mormonism since 1945*, ed. Patrick Q. Mason and John G. Turner (New York: Oxford University Press, 2016), 65, 70.

19. Haws, "Politics of Family Values," 12–14.

20. "Mrs. Romney Talks of Women's Roles," *Milwaukee (WI) Journal*, April 17, 1975; "Romney: ERA Home for 'Moral Perverts,'" *Associated Press*, December 17, 1979.

21. Bradley, *Pedestals and Podiums*, 97.

22. Suzanne Dean, "Mormon Opposition Chills Prospects for ERA in Utah," *Washington Post*, February 18, 1975.

23. Bradley, *Pedestals and Podiums*, 108–9.

24. Laurel Thatcher Ulrich, "The Pink Dialogue and Beyond," *Dialogue* 14, no. 4 (1981): 36.

25. Anne Kirchheimer, "Living: Feminism and the Mormon Church," *Boston Globe*, December 12, 1979; Carrel Hilton Sheldon, "Launching Exponent II," *Exponent II* 22, no. 4 (September 1999), accessed February 13, 2017, http://www.expo nentii.org/history.

26. Claudia L. Bushman, "Exponent II is Born," *Exponent II* 1, no. 1 (July 1974): 2, quoted in *Mormon Feminism: Essential Writings*, ed. Joanna Brooks, Rachel Hunt Steenblik, and Hannah Wheelwright (New York: Oxford University Press, 2016), 3.

27. Ulrich, "Pink Dialogue," 30.

28. Molly Ivins, "Many Mormon Women Feel Torn between Equal Rights Proposal and Church," *New York Times*, November 26, 1979.

29. For more information on the International Woman's Year conference in Mexico City and the corresponding conferences in the United States, see Spruill, "The Gathering Storm," 114–39, and "Armageddon State by State," 140–65; both in *Divided We Stand*.

30. Spruill, *Divided We Stand*, 144.

31. Spruill, *Divided We Stand*, 76.

32. Jane J. Mansbridge, *Why We Lost the ERA* (Chicago: University of Chicago Press, 1986), 164.

33. Bradley, *Pedestals and Podiums*, 79–82.

34. Neil J. Young, "'The ERA Is a Moral Issue': The Mormon Church, LDS Women, and the Defeat of the Equal Rights Amendment," *American Quarterly* 59, no. 3 (September 2007): 623.

35. John M. Crewdson, "Mormon Turnout Overwhelms Women's Conference in Utah," *New York Times*, July 25, 1977.

36. "Hot Issues Split Women's Conference," *Walla Walla (WA) Union-Bulletin*, July 10, 1977.

37. Bradley, *Pedestals and Podiums*, 474.

38. Beverly Beyette, "NOW Pledges to Stump for ERA," *Los Angeles Times*, October 7, 1980.

39. Norma Harrison, "Equal Rights Amendment: NOW Will Take Case to Mormons," *Los Angeles Times,* May 7, 1981.

40. "An Appeal to the Members of the LDS Church," National Organization for Women ERA Missionary Project, M243.8 A646L 1981, Church of Jesus Christ of Latter-day Saints History Library, Salt Lake City, Utah. Research notes courtesy of Keith Erekson.

41. Andrea Goettinger, "Mormons to Be Asked to Back ERA Campaign," *Los Angeles Times*, October 2, 1981.

42. Harrison, "Equal Rights Amendment."

43. For more on RLDS missionizing in Utah, see Don Bradley and Brian C. Hals, "LDS Joseph vs. RLDS Joseph: The Battle to Control the Public Memory of Joseph Smith," in *The Persistence of Polygamy*, 3 vols., ed. Newell G. Bringhurst and Craig L. Foster (Independence, MO: John Whitmer Books, 2003), 2:202–43. For more on the Southern Baptist Convention in Salt Lake City, see Jan Shipps, "Media Coverage of the Southern Baptist Conference in Salt Lake City," in *Sojourner in the Promised Land*, 143–54.

44. George Rain, "Equal Rights 'Missionaries' in Mormon Country," *New York Times*, May 15, 1981.

45. Zezulin, "ERA Missionary in Utah," 458–59.

46. "'I Will Follow the Prophet': Utah 'Missionaries' Crusade in Utah," *Los Angeles Times*, September 4, 1981.

47. Adherent Mormons are expected to follow the church's dietary code, the Words of Wisdom, which does not allow the smoking of tobacco. Thus, any Utahans smoking publicly were likely to be inactive Mormons or not a part of the church membership.

48. Zezulin, "ERA Missionary in Utah," 459.

49. Bradley, *Pedestals and Podiums*, 118.

50. Zezulin, "ERA Missionary in Utah," 460–61.

51. Joe Contreras, "Selling ERA to Mormons," *Newsweek*, July 13, 1981.

52. Rain, "Equal Rights 'Missionaries' in Mormon Country."

53. Deborah Churchman, "NOW Recruits Volunteers to Work for ERA Passage," *Christian Science Monitor*, December 24, 1981; Georgia Dullea, "Women Give Up Careers to Crusade for Equality," *New York Times*, November 8, 1981.

54. "Harvard Students to Serve as 'Missionaries' during ERA Ratification Campaign in Illinois," *Harvard Crimson*, March 17, 1982.

55. Joan Beck, "Who and What Killed the ERA?," *Chicago Tribune*, June 29, 1982.

56. For more on Mormon-led involvement in campaigns against same-sex marriage, including the Proposition 8 campaign, see Neil J. Young, "Mormons and

Same-Sex Marriage: From ERA to Prop 8," in Mason and Turner, *Out of Obscurity: Mormonism since 1945*, 144–69.

57. Joanna Brooks, "When Mormons Mobilize: Anti-Gay Marriage Prop. 8 Effort 'Outed'?," *Religion Dispatches*, February 2, 2010.

58. Young, "Mormons and Same-Sex Marriage," 162–63.

59. Joanna Brooks, "Mormon Feminism: An Introduction," in Brooks, Steenblik, and Wheelwright, *Mormon Feminism*, 19–20.

Chapter 5. "The Way of the Transgressor Is Hard"

1. 93rd Illinois General Assembly, HR 0627, 2004, http://www.ilga.gov/legisla tion/fulltext.asp?DocName=&SessionId=3&GA=93&DocTypeId=HR&DocNum= 0627&GAID=3&LegID=8066&SpecSess=&Session=.

2. Act to Incorporate the City of Nauvoo, December 16, 1840, in *The Joseph Smith Papers: Documents*, vol. 7, *September 1839–January 1841*, ed. Matthew C. Godfrey, Spencer W. McBride, Alex D. Smith, and Christopher James Blythe (Salt Lake City, UT: Church Historian's Press, 2018), 472–88 (hereafter cited as *JSP: Documents*).

3. The population of Nauvoo has been contested. For the higher figure, see Richard Lyman Bushman, *Joseph Smith: Rough Stone Rolling; A Cultural Biography of Mormonism's Founder* (New York: Vintage Books, 2007), 385; for the lower figure, see the introduction to *Cultures in Conflict: A Documentary History of the Mormon War in Illinois*, ed. John E. Hallwas and Roger D. Launius (Logan: Utah State University Press, 1995), 1.

4. 93rd Illinois General Assembly, HR 0627. Richard Bushman argues in favor of Joseph Smith's antislavery beliefs, but there is no evidence that those beliefs played a role in the Illinois Mormon expulsion. Bushman, *Joseph Smith*, 516–17.

5. PBS, "People and Events: Indian Removal, 1814–1858," accessed March 1, 2017, http://www.pbs.org/wgbh/aia/part4/4p2959.html.

6. The isolation of Mormon expulsion from any larger political context is a hallmark of Mormon-authored accounts, according to the religious scholar Jan Shipps. Jan Shipps, "The Mormon Past: Revealed or Revisited?," *Sunstone* 6 (November– December 1981). 57. The problem is compounded by America's striking historical amnesia when it comes to American Indians. See, for example, the essays in *Partial Recall: Photographs of Native North Americans*, ed. Lucy Lippard (New York: New Press, 1992).

7. Laurel Thatcher Ulrich, *A House Full of Females: Plural Marriage and Women's Rights in Early Mormonism, 1835–1870* (New York: Alfred A. Knopf, 2017), 32.

8. Quoted in Ulrich, *House Full of Females*, 68.

9. Ulrich, *House Full of Females*, 64.

10. John Cook Bennett, *A History of the Saints: Or, an Exposé of Joe Smith and Mormonism* (Boston, MA: Leland and Whiting, 1842); Ulrich, *House Full of Females*, 81.

11. Quoted in Ulrich, *House Full of Females*, 103.

12. On the mutually constitutive nature of gender, see Bruce Dorsey, *Reforming Men and Women: Gender in the Antebellum City* (Ithaca, NY: Cornell University Press, 2002), 3–6.

13. On the role of gender in Indian warfare in the early American republic, see Laurel Clark Shire, *The Threshold of Manifest Destiny: Gender and National Expansion in Florida* (Philadelphia: University of Pennsylvania Press, 2016).

14. Brent M. Rogers, *Unpopular Sovereignty: Mormons and the Federal Management of Early Utah Territory* (Lincoln: University of Nebraska Press, 2017), 101–4, quote on 103.

15. Amy S. Greenberg, *Manifest Manhood and the Antebellum American Empire* (New York: Cambridge University Press, 2005), 1–17.

16. Amy S. Greenberg, *A Wicked War: Polk, Clay, Lincoln, and the 1846 U.S. Invasion of Mexico* (New York: Vintage Books, 2013), 26–27. On Polk being called Colonel, see James K. Polk, *Correspondence of James K. Polk*, ed. Herbert Weaver and Wayne Cutler et al., 13 vols. (Knoxville: University of Tennessee Press, 1969–2017).

17. "Correspondence of the Phoenix," *Vermont Phoenix*, July 1, 1847; Ellen Hardin Walworth, "To the Christian Herald," January 25, 1905, manuscript, Walworth Family Archive, Saratoga Springs History Museum, 1; Ellen Hardin Walworth, "Mrs. Ellen Hardin Walworth," *American Monthly Magazine* (July 1893), 42–49.

18. Eric Foner, *The Fiery Trial: Abraham Lincoln and American Slavery* (New York: W. W. Norton, 2010), 6–8, 45–51; Patrick J. Jung, *The Black Hawk War of 1832* (Norman: University of Oklahoma Press, 2007), 20–22, 50–53.

19. On the Black Hawk War, see Black Hawk, *Life of Ma-ka-tai-me-she-kia-kiak or Black Hawk* (Boston, MA: Russell, Odiorne and Metcalf, 1834); John W. Hall, *Uncommon Defense: Indian Allies in the Black Hawk War* (Cambridge, MA: Harvard University Press, 2009); Jung, *Black Hawk War of 1832*.

20. Abraham Lincoln to Jesse W. Fell, December 20, 1859, in *The Collected Works of Abraham Lincoln*, ed. Roy P. Balser et al., 9 vols. (New Brunswick, NJ: Rutgers University Press, 1953–55), 3:512; Greenberg, *Wicked War*, 48–49.

21. J. F. Snyder, "Governor Ford and His Family," *Journal of the Illinois State Historical Society (1908–1984)* 3, no. 2 (1910): 45–51, quote on 45, http://www.jstor.org/stable/40193411.

22. Snyder, "Governor Ford and His Family," 48.

23. Albert J. Beveridge, *Abraham Lincoln: 1809–1858*, 4 vols. (Boston: Houghton Mifflin, 1828) 1:180; Gustave Koerner, *Memoirs of Gustave Koerner, 1809–1896*, ed. Thomas J. McCormack, 2 vols. (Cedar Rapids, IA: Torch Press, 1909), 1:499.

24. Quoted in Hosea Stout, "Autobiography of Hosea Stout, 1810 to 1835," ed. Reed A. Stout, *Utah Historical Quarterly* 30, no. 3 (July 1962): 251.

25. Stout, "Autobiography of Hosea Stout," 254; Stephen Prince, *Hosea Stout: Lawman, Legislator, Mormon Defender* (Boulder, CO: Utah State University Press, 2016), 7.

26. Stout, "Autobiography of Hosea Stout," 255.

27. Stout, "Autobiography of Hosea Stout," 257.

28. Jeffery O. Johnson and W. Paul Reeve, "Mormonism and Native Americans," in *Mormonism: A Historical Encyclopedia*, ed. W. Paul Reeve and Ardis E. Parshall (Santa Barbara, CA: ABC-Clio, 2010), 305–12; Rogers, *Unpopular Sovereignty*, 101–2.

29. Prince, *Hosea Stout*, 55.

30. Isaac McCoy, Statement, November, 28, 1833, quoted in Rogers, *Unpopular Sovereignty*, 103; Prince, *Hosea Stout*, 55–69.

31. "Civil War in Missouri," *New York Commercial Advertiser*, November 29, 1833.

32. Andrew Jenson, *Latter-day Saint Biographical Encyclopedia* (Salt Lake City, UT: Arrow Press, 1920), 3:530.

33. Stephen C. LaSeur, *The 1838 Mormon War in Missouri* (Columbia, MO: University of Missouri Press, 1990), 37–43.

34. *Document Containing the Correspondence, Orders, etc. in Relation to the Disturbances with the Mormons; and the Evidence Given before the Hon. Austin A. King* (Fayette, MO: Office of the Boon's Lick Democrat, 1841), 61.

35. Ulrich, *House Full of Females*, 30–31.

36. Ulrich, *House Full of Females*, 36.

37. Ulrich, *House Full of Females*, 37.

38. Spencer W. McBride, "When Joseph Smith Met Martin Van Buren: Mormonism and the Politics of Religious Liberty in Nineteenth-Century America," *Church History* 85, no. 1 (March 2016): 158; Clark Johnson, ed., *Mormon Redress Petitions: Documents of the 1833–1838 Missouri Conflict* (Salt Lake City, UT: Bookcraft, 1992); Memorial to the United States Senate and House of Representatives, circa October 1839–January 27, 1840, in *JSP: Documents*, 7:195–60.

39. Johnson, *Mormon Redress Petitions*, 144–45.

40. Black Hawk, *Life of Ma-ka-tai-me-she-kia-kiak or Black Hawk*, 109, 87.

41. Ulrich, *House Full of Females*, 54.

42. Hawkins Taylor, quoted in *Cultures In Conflict: A Documentary History of the Mormon War in Illinois*, ed. John E. Hall was and Roger D. Launius (Logan: Utah State University Press, 1995), 54; Jenson, *Latter-day Saint Biographical Encyclopedia*, 3:531; Prince, *Hosea Stout*, 92–112; *The Joseph Smith Papers: Administrative Records; Council of Fifty, Minutes, March 1844–January 1846*, ed. Matthew J. Grow, Ronald K. Esplin, Mark Ashurst-McGee, Gerrit J. Dirkmaat, and Jeffrey D. Mahas (Salt Lake City, UT: Church Historian's Press, 2016), xx (hereafter cited as *JSP: Council of Fifty, Minutes*).

43. Quoted in the *Christian Watchman* (Boston, MA), May 14, 1841.

44. George T. M. Davis, *An Authentic Account of the Massacre of Joseph Smith* (St. Louis, MO: Chambers and Knapp, 1844), 5–9.

45. Typed transcript letter "to the Editor of the Warsaw Signal, Hancock County, Illinois," February 15, 1844, 3, Thomas C. Sharp and Allied Anti-Mormon Papers, Western Americana Collection, Beinecke Rare Book and Manuscript Library, Yale University.

46. "Rock Island, Illinois," *New York Weekly Herald*, June 15, 1844; see also "Correspondence of the Journal of Commerce," *New York Journal of Commerce*, March 27, 1840.

47. Quoted in Ulrich, *House Full of Females*, 119.

48. Rogers, *Unpopular Sovereignty*, 103.

49. Prince, *Hosea Stout*, 92.

50. Jenson, *Latter-day Saint Biographical Encyclopedia*, 3:531.

51. *JSP: Council of Fifty, Minutes*, 393nn636, 637; see also *The Joseph Smith Papers: Journals*, vol. 3, *May 1843–June 1844*, ed. Andrew H. Hedges, Alex D. Smith, and Brent M. Rogers (Salt Lake City, UT: Church Historian's Press, 2015), 147–48, 293n1345.

52. Juanita Brooks, ed., *On the Mormon Frontier: The Diary of Hosea Stout, 1844–1861*, 2 vols. (1964; repr., Salt Lake City: University of Utah Press and the Utah State Historical Society, 1982), 1:32–34.

53. Hawkins Taylor, quoted in Hallwas and Launius, *Cultures in Conflict*, 54; *JSP: Council of Fifty, Minutes*, 393n637. On the origins of the Whistling society, see *JSP: Council of Fifty, Minutes*, 318–19n424.

54. Hallwas and Launius, *Cultures in Conflict*, 121–25.

55. Cynthia Enloe, *Bananas, Beaches, and Bases: Making Feminist Sense of International Politics*, 2nd ed. (Berkeley: University of California Press, 2014), 1–36; Laura Sjoberg, *Gendering Global Conflict: Towards a Feminist Theory of War* (New York: Columbia University Press, 2013), 248–79.

56. Anson G. Henry to John J. Hardin, January 18, 1844, Hardin Family Papers, Chicago History Museum (hereafter cited as Hardin Family Papers).

57. Letter from Orson Hyde to Joseph Smith, April 25, 1844, 2, Joseph Smith Papers, accessed March 10, 2017, http://www.josephsmithpapers.org/paper-summary/letter-from-orson-hyde-25-april-1844/2. On Smith's entry into the presidential race, see Spencer McBride's chapter in this volume.

58. Thomas Ford to John J. Hardin, August 5, 1844, Hardin Family Papers.

59. Thomas Ford to John J. Hardin, September 18, 1844, Hardin Family Papers.

60. *JSP: Council of Fifty, Minutes*, 356–57n534, 426n727, 448nn795–96; Hallwas and Launius, *Cultures in Conflict*, 267–70.

61. See H. E. Dennison to John J. Hardin, September 23, 1845, Hardin Family Papers; Brigham Young, *The Journal of Brigham Young* (Provo, UT: Council Press, 1980), 100.

62. *JSP: Council of Fifty, Minutes*, 479, 483–85.

63. "Mormon War," October 18, 1845, *Niles' National Register (1837–1849)*, 19, 109, http://ezaccess.libraries.psu.edu/login?url=http://search.proquest.com/docview/136909890?accountid=13158.

64. Brigham Young to John J. Hardin, W. B. Warren, S. A. Douglas, and J. A. McDougall, October 1, 1845, Hardin Family Papers; Ulrich, *House Full of Females*, 124–25.

65. Ellen Hardin Walworth, "Charter Member, Application for Membership #5," December 1890, Manuscript Collection, Daughters of the American Revolution Library, Centennial Hall, Washington, DC; Jenson, *Latter-day Saint Biographical Encyclopedia*, 3:532. See also Frederick Gerhard, *Illinois as It Is* (Chicago: Keen and Lee, 1857), 118–19. The displacement of the Mormons of Illinois was hardly fair, but Susan Sessions Rugh, who has looked closely at the Mormon War in rural Illinois communities, has concluded that, even in small communities where Mormons and Gentiles interacted regularly, Gentiles embraced expulsion. A non-Mormon, Jary White, was active in the September 1846 Mormon War, despite being married to a Mormon himself. Susan Sessions Rugh, "Conflict in the Countryside: The Mormon Settlement at Macedonia, Illinois," *BYU Studies Quarterly* 32, no. 1 (1992): 156. See also her book-length treatment by the same title, *Conflict in the Countryside*.

66. Stout, "Autobiography of Hosea Stout," 254.

67. Thomas Ford, *History of Illinois, from Its Commencement as a State in 1814 to 1847, Containing a Full Account of the Black Hawk War, the Rise, Progress, and Fall of Mormonism, the Alton and Lovejoy Riots, and Other Important and Interesting Events* (Chicago: S. C. Griggs, 1854), 232–34. On vigilante violence, see Roger D. McGrath, *Gunfighters, Highwaymen, and Vigilantes: Violence on the Frontier* (Berkeley: University of California Press, 1984).

68. Ford, *History of Illinois*, 238–39.

69. Ford, *History of Illinois*, 251.

70. Ford, *History of Illinois*, 251.

71. Ford, *History of Illinois*, 232.

72. Strangely enough, both of Governor Ford's sons would die at the hands of vigilante mobs in Kansas in the 1870s, an irony that Ford was fortunately never privy to. J. F. Snyder, "Governor Ford and His Family," *Journal of the Illinois State Historical Society (1908–1984)* 3, no. 2 (1910): 50–51, http://www.jstor.org/stable/40193411.

73. Ford, *History of Illinois*, 431.

74. E. H. Merryman to John J. Hardin, Springfield, May 22, 1846, Hardin Family Papers, 16.

75. Geo. Davis to John J. Hardin, Alton, May 30, 1846, Hardin Family Papers, 16.

76. John J. Hardin to Smith, Parras, MX, December 10, 1846, Hardin Family Papers, 17:3.

77. John J. Hardin to "Dear Henry" (Capt. John Henry), Parras, MX, December 16, 1846, Hardin Family Papers, 17:3.

78. On atrocities in Mexico, see Greenberg, *Wicked War*; and Paul Foos, *A Short, Offhand, Killing Affair: Soldiers and Social Conflict during the Mexican-American War* (Chapel Hill: University of North Carolina Press, 2002), 113–37.

79. Greenberg, *Wicked War*, 135–39, 153–59.

80. See Greenberg, *Manifest Manhood*, 125–28.

Chapter 6. "Like a Swarm of Locusts"

1. Washington Allon Bartlett to Edward Kern, August 6, 1846, in *The Fort Sutter Papers, with Critical and Historical Commentaries*, ed. Seymour Dunbar (New York 21), Manuscript 26, 1–2. According to Brannan himself, his group of Mormons were stunned to see the US flag flying over Yerba Buena, for they "had looked forward to a peaceful condition of things under Mexican rule." Sam Brannan, "Accounts of the Mormons in California, c. 1878," mss HM 4089–4090, Huntington Library, San Marino, California.

2. John L. O'Sullivan, "Annexation," *United States Magazine and Democratic Review* (New York) 17 (1845): 10.

3. Over the past decade, historians have begun to dismantle the Manifest Destiny narrative that portrays inevitable US conquest of the West, although the paradigm remains in most syntheses of the era. For a recent historiographical summary of these findings, see Andrew C. Isenberg and Thomas Richards Jr., "Alternative Wests: Rethinking Manifest Destiny," *Pacific Historical Review* 86, no. 1 (February 2017): 4–17. See also Thomas Richards, Jr., *Breakaway Americas: The Unmanifest Future of the Jacksonian United States* (Baltimore: Johns Hopkins University Press, 2020).

4. Historians have discussed some of these options extensively, but the recent publication of the Council of Fifty minutes has revealed that Mormon geopolitical calculi were even more remarkable than previously thought, and require a new historical account. See *The Joseph Smith Papers: Administrative Records; Council of Fifty, Minutes, March 1844–January 1846*, ed. Matthew J. Grow, Ronald K. Esplin, Mark Ashurst-McGee, Gerrit J. Dirkmaat, and Jeffrey D. Mahas (Salt Lake City, UT: Church Historian's Press, 2016) (hereafter cited as *JSP: Council of Fifty, Minutes*). Examples of specific discussions within this volume include, for Texas, 142–46; for Oregon, 53, 181, 267; for a Native alliance, 253–60, 462–71; for California, 328; for southern Mexico, 271. For discussion of a Mormon-Mexican alliance against the United

States, see "A Concise View of the Policy of the Latter Day Saints in Reference to Their Emigration to California" (1846), Brigham Young Office Files, Church History Library, Church of Jesus Christ of Latter-day Saints, Salt Lake City, Utah (hereafter cited as CHL). Other relevant works include Klaus Hansen, *Quest for Empire: The Political Kingdom of God and the Council of Fifty in Mormon History* (Lansing: Michigan State University Press, 1967); Marvin S. Hill, *Quest for Refuge: The Mormon Flight from American Pluralism* (Salt Lake City, UT: Signature Books, 1989); D. Michael Quinn, *The Mormon Hierarchy: Origins of Power* (Salt Lake City, UT: Signature Books, 1994); Michael Scott Van Wagenen, *The Texas Republic and the Mormon Kingdom of God* (College Station: Texas A&M University Press, 2002); and Thomas Richards Jr., "The Texas Moment: Breakaway Republics and Contested Sovereignty in North America, 1836–1846" (PhD diss., Temple University, 2016), 273–339.

5. Jeffrey A. Lockwood, *Locust: The Devastating Rise and Mysterious Disappearance of the Insect That Shaped the American Frontier* (New York: Basic Books, 2004), 31–43. For a summary of the various roots of anti-Mormonism during this time period, see Terryl L. Givens, *The Viper on the Hearth: Mormons, Myths, and the Construction of Heresy* (New York: Oxford University Press, 1997), 40–59.

6. On Nauvoo, see Benjamin E. Park, *Kingdom of Nauvoo: The Rise and Fall of a Religious Empire on the American Frontier* (New York: Liveright, 2020); Robert Bruce Flanders, *Nauvoo: Kingdom on the Mississippi* (Urbana: University of Illinois Press, 1965). See also the chapters in *Kingdom on the Mississippi Revisited*, ed. Roger D. Launius and John E. Hallwas (Urbana: University of Illinois Press, 1996); the editors give a valuable bibliographic essay of all works on Nauvoo, 251–67.

7. For estimates of the Mormons, see, for example, *Public Ledger* (Philadelphia), August 1, 1846; "The Mormons," *Jeffersonian Republican* (Stroudsburg, PA), quoting the *Sangamo (IL) Journal*, February 5, 1846; "Late from the Mormon Camp," *Sangamo Journal*, July 23, 1846; "From Nauvoo," *Ottawa (IL) Free Trader*, March 20, 1846; "Late from the Mormon Camp," *Daily National Intelligencer* (Washington, DC), July 22, 1846; "Deserted Temple in the West – A Lesson," *Newark (NJ) Daily Advertiser*, August 9, 1847. Estimates of other populations are ubiquitous. Examples from the year 1845 include California—"Oregon, Texas, and England," *Public Ledger* (Philadelphia), May 21, 1845; Texas army—*Baltimore Sun*, July 30, 1845; Oregon—*Milwaukee Daily Sentinel*, November 5, 1845.

8. William Richards to George Miller, January 14, 1845, in *JSP: Council of Fifty, Minutes*, 234.

9. *JSP: Council of Fifty, Minutes*, 235.

10. *JSP: Council of Fifty, Minutes*, 217.

11. Cherokee Nation v. Georgia, 30 US, 5 Pet. 1 1 (1831).

12. "Shall They Go?," *Boon's Lick Times* (Fayette, MO), quoting the *Platte Argus* (Platte City, MO), November 15, 1845.

13. "California – The Mormons," *Warsaw (IL) Signal*, November 19, 1845.

14. *St. Joseph (MO) Gazette*, November 21, 1845.

15. John H. Everett to Thomas Larkin, December 12, 1845, in *The Larkin Papers*, ed. George P. Hammond, 10 vols. (Berkeley: University of California Press, 1953), 4:121.

16. Thomas Larkin to F. M. Dimond, March 1, 1846, in *Larkin Papers*, 4:216; Larkin to James Buchanan, March 6, 1846, in *Larkin Papers*, 4:232; Larkin to *New*

York Sun, April 1846, in *Larkin Papers*, 4:355–56. This rumor seems to have circulated among many California residents; see Henry Dalton to Abel Stearns, February 18, 1846, Abel Stearns Papers, Huntington Library, San Marino, California.

17. Neil Howison to George Abernethy, December 21, 1846, MSS 929, George Abernethy Papers, Oregon Historical Society, Portland.

18. Edwin Bryant, *What I Saw in California: Being the Journal of a Tour, by the Emigrant Route and South Pass of the Rocky Mountains, across the Continent of North America* . . . (New York: D. Appleton and Co., 1848), 15, also 26.

19. John Cox Memoir, MSS 722, Oregon Historical Society, Portland.

20. Months into the journey, Boggs changed his mind again, and eventually did settle in California. Kristin Johnson, *Unfortunate Emigrants: Narratives of the Donner Party* (Logan: Utah State University Press, 1996), 121.

21. Richard E. Bennett, *We'll Find the Place: The Mormon Exodus, 1846–1848* (Norman: University of Oklahoma Press, 2009), 176–77; Lilburn Boggs to Hubert Howe Bancroft, n.d., California Miscellany, C-E 65:21, Bancroft Library, Berkeley, California.

22. *Milwaukee Daily Sentinel*, quoting the *New York Tribune*, January 19, 1846; emphasis in the original.

23. "The Mormons," *Niles' National Register*, January 3, 1846.

24. "The Mormons," *Jeffersonian Republican* (Stroudsburg, PA), quoting the *Sangamo (IL) Journal*, February 5, 1846.

25. "Shall They Go?," *Boon's Lick Times* (Fayette, MO), quoting the *Platte Argus* (Platte City, MO), November 15, 1845.

26. This estimate comes from Bryan J. Grant, "The Church in the British Isles," in *Encyclopedia of Mormonism*, vol. 1, ed. Daniel H. Ludlow (New York: Macmillan, 1992), http://eom.byu.edu/index.php/British_Isles,_the_Church_in.

27. George Carvill to Eliza Boyle, December 29, 1845, MS 6223, Brigham Young Church History Project Collection, 1977–1981, CHL.

28. Brent M. Rogers, "'To the Honest and Patriotic Sons of Liberty': Mormon Appeals for Redress and Social Justice," *Journal of Mormon History* 39, no. 1 (Winter 2013): 36–67.

29. Brigham Young, March 18, 1845, in *JSP: Council of Fifty, Minutes*, 341; for similar anti-American statements, see 299, 328, 331, 336, and 351.

30. LDS Church to US state governors, 1845, in *JSP: Council of Fifty, Minutes*, 313.

31. LDS Church to US state governors, 1845, in *JSP: Council of Fifty, Minutes*, 316.

32. "From Nauvoo," *Ottawa (IL) Free Trader*, March 20, 1846.

33. Larkin to Messrs M. Y. Beach & Sons, April 1846, in *Larkin Papers*, 4:355. Larkin's consistent misspellings were likely a strategy, for he rarely misspelled words in his personal letters. Larkin was trying to portray himself as an unlettered—and therefore typical—American settler of California, and thus an accurate and unbiased portrayer of California events. In this letter, he did not sign his own name, but wrote as "Paisano."

34. Thomas Ford to Brigham Young, April 8, 1845, in *JSP: Council of Fifty, Minutes*, 429.

35. For the travails of independent Texas, see Andrew J. Torget, *Seeds of Empire: Cotton, Slavery, and the Transformation of the Texas Borderlands, 1800–1850* (Chapel Hill: University of North Carolina Press, 2015), chap. 6.

36. James Arlington Bennet to Willard Richards, June 4, 1845, MS 1490, Willard Richards Journals and Papers, 1821–1854, CHL. No direct letter from Houston exists. While Bennet's grandiose personal ambitions to head the Nauvoo Legion may have caused him to exaggerate Houston's enthusiasm, Houston's interest is consistent with both his recognition of Texan weakness and his savvy geopolitical maneuvering between Great Britain and the United States. For a detailed examination of the Mormon-Texas negotiations, see correspondence and minutes in *JSP: Council of Fifty, Minutes*, 140–45; and Van Wagenen, *Texas Republic and the Mormon Kingdom of God*.

37. John H. Walton to Joseph Smith, June 3, 1844, in Journal History, CHL.

38. John H. Walton to Joseph Smith, June 3, 1844, in Journal History, CHL.

39. Charles Lovell to Brigham Young, October 20, 1845, CR 1234-1, Brigham Young Office Files, CHL.

40. New England merchants had been trading with California for decades, and some had reaped profits to such an extent that they had settled in the territory. Nevertheless, in comparison with the whole of New England trade, California remained a backwater. On these New England merchants in California, see Doyce Nunis, "California's Trojan Horse," in *Contested Eden: California before the Gold Rush*, ed. Ramón Gutiérrez and Richard J. Orsi (Berkeley: University of California Press, 1998), 306–10.

41. Another New England merchant, Samuel Hastings, also sought to take advantage of a Mormon colony in San Francisco, although he was less explicit in how he envisioned Mormon settlement would work. See Samuel Hastings to Brigham Young, December 29, 1845, CR 1234–1, Brigham Young Office Files, CHL; Hastings to Thomas Larkin, November 9, 1845, in *Larkin Papers*, 4:91; and Hastings to Larkin, January 22, 1846, in *Larkin Papers*, 4:177.

42. Duff Green to Charles Dana, November 2, 1847, CR 1234-1, Brigham Young Office Files, CHL.

43. Duff Green to Charles Dana, November 2, 1847, CR 1234-1, Brigham Young Office Files, CHL.

44. On Green, see W. Stephen Belko, *The Invincible Duff Green, Whig of the West* (Columbia: University of Missouri Press, 2006). See 431–32 for Green's relationship with the Mormons.

45. For Sutter's threat of an "independent republique," see John Sutter to Jacob Leese, November 8, 1841, C-B 10, Mariano Vallejo Papers, Bancroft Library; for Sutter's scheming overall, see Albert L. Hurtado, *John Sutter: A Life on the North American Frontier* (Norman: University of Oklahoma Press, 2006), 16–203.

46. John Sutter to William Leidesdorff, September 1, 1846, MSS C-B 631, John Augustus Sutter Correspondence and Papers, Bancroft Library.

47. Wilford Woodruff, journal entry, July 1, 1847, in *Wilford Woodruff's Journal, 1833–1898: Typescript*, ed. Scott G. Kenney, 9 vols. (Midvale, UT: Signature Books, 1983), 2:222; George Smith to John Smith, July 5, 1847, MS 1326, John Smith Papers, CHL.

48. Sam Brannan, "Accounts of the Mormons in California, c. 1878," mss HM 4089–4090, Huntington Library.

49. James K. Polk, *The Diary of James K. Polk: During His Presidency, 1845–1849*, ed. Milo Milton Quaife, 4 vols. (Chicago: A. C. McClurg, 1910), 1:205–6.

50. On Thomas Kane, see Matthew J. Grow, *"Liberty to the Downtrodden": Thomas L. Kane, Romantic Reformer* (New Haven, CT: Yale University Press, 2009).

51. Jesse Little to James Polk, June 1, 1846, in *Army of Israel: Mormon Battalion Narratives*, ed. David Bigler and Will Bagley (Logan: Utah State University Press, 2000), 34.

52. Polk, *Diary*, 1:443–50.

53. On the creation of the Mormon Battalion, see Gerrit John Dirkmaat, "Enemies Foreign and Domestic: US Relations with Mormons in the US Empire in North America, 1844–1854" (PhD diss., University of Colorado, 2011), 103–48; and Bigler and Bagley, *Army of Israel*, 31–49.

54. Grow, *"Liberty to the Downtrodden,"* 71–83.

55. On the United States' ignorance of Utah's natives, see Brent M. Rogers, *Unpopular Sovereignty: Mormons and the Federal Management of Early Utah Territory* (Lincoln: University of Nebraska Press, 2017), 99.

56. "Washington, July 23, 1847," *Farmer's Cabinet* (Amherst, NH), quoting the *New York Journal of Commerce*, July 29, 1847.

57. *Republican Farmer* (Bridgeport, CT), July 27, 1847.

58. *Morning News* (New London, CT), July 29, 1847.

59. "California," *New Hampshire Sentinel* (Keene), July 29, 1847.

60. *Baltimore Sun*, July 29, 1847.

61. "New Mormon State – Deseret," *United States Magazine and Democratic Review* 25, no. 137 (November 1849): 472–75.

62. For a more detailed analysis, see Richard Bennett, "The Lion and the Emperor: The Mormons, the Hudson's Bay Company, and Vancouver Island, 1846–1858," *British Columbia Studies* 128 (Winter 2000/2001): 45–46.

63. Sir George Smith to the Governor, the Deputy Governor, and the Honourable Hudson's Bay Company, June 24, 1848, as quoted in Bennett, "Lion and the Emperor," 45–46.

64. As Brent Rogers noted, in the 1850s Mormon Deseret was undoubtedly the strongest polity in the American West. See Rogers, *Unpopular Sovereignty*, 10.

Chapter 7. "In the Style of an Independent Sovereign"

1. Charles Royster, *A Revolutionary People at War: The Continental Army and American Character, 1775–1783* (Chapel Hill: University of North Carolina Press, 1979), 5–12.

2. Joyce Appleby, "Republicanism in the History and Historiography of the United States," *American Quarterly* 37, no. 4 (Autumn 1985): 461.

3. In a special message to Congress in 1822, James Monroe stated that the military must always remain subordinate to civil authority in a republic. According to Monroe, King George's violation of this principle was one of the key grievances outlined in the Declaration of Independence. James Monroe, "Special Message to the House of Representatives Containing the Views of the President of the United States on the Subject of Internal Improvements," May 4, 1822, online at the *American Presidency Project*, directed by Gerhard Peters and John T. Woolley, http://www.presidency.ucsb.edu/ws/?pid=66323; see also Matthew Warshauer, *Andrew Jackson*

and the Politics of Martial Law: Nationalism, Civil Liberties, and Partisanship (Knoxville: University of Tennessee Press, 2006), 7.

4. *Official Report of the Debates and Proceedings in the State Convention, Assembled May 4th, 1853, to Revise and Amend the Constitution of the Commonwealth of Massachusetts*, 3 vols. (Boston, MA: White and Potter, Printers to the Convention, 1853), 3:429.

5. Suspicion of federal authority in antebellum America often surrounded the issue of slavery's expansion to new territories in the West. In 1846, during the US–Mexican War, the Pennsylvania Democrat David Wilmot proposed an amendment to an appropriations bill to limit the growth of slavery in any annexed territory resulting from an American victory in the war. The amendment, called the Wilmot Proviso, drew the ire of southerners who then declared that any federal efforts to limit the expansion of slavery would end in the secession of southern states from the Union. As sectional concerns grew over the prospect of congressional prohibition of slavery in new territorial acquisitions, the specter of southern secession was prominently raised. For more on suspicion of federal authority, particularly as it related to slavery extension, see Michael A. Morrison, *Slavery and the American West: The Eclipse of Manifest Destiny and the Coming of the Civil War* (Chapel Hill: University of North Carolina Press, 1997); and Michael F. Holt, *The Fate of Their Country: Politicians, Slavery Extension, and the Coming of the Civil War* (New York: Hill and Wang, 2004).

6. "Martial Law," *Daily National Intelligencer* (Washington, DC), May 2, 1861.

7. Caleb Cushing to William L. Marcy, February 3, 1857, in *Official Opinions of the Attorneys General of the United States*, 43 vols. (Washington, DC: R. Farnham, 1858), 8:371, 374.

8. Erik J. Chaput, *The People's Martyr: Thomas Wilson Dorr and His 1842 Rhode Island Rebellion* (Lawrence: University of Kansas Press, 2013), 3.

9. John L. O'Sullivan, "The Rhode Island Question," *United States Magazine and Democratic Review* (July 1842): 71–81.

10. Andrew Jackson to Francis P. Blair, May 23, 1842, in *Correspondence of Andrew Jackson*, ed. John Spencer Bassett, 6 vols. (Washington, DC: Carnegie Institution, 1933), 6:153.

11. *The Works of James Buchanan*, ed. John Bassett Moore, 12 vols. (Philadelphia: J.B. Lippincott Company, 1908), 3:146.

12. Chaput, *People's Martyr*, 6.

13. "Twenty-Eighth Congress. First Session," *Daily National Intelligencer*, March 9, 1844.

14. In the presidential contest of 1824, Andrew Jackson recognized that some believed him to be "a most dangerous and terrible man . . . and that I can break, & trample under foot the constitution of the country." In-text quote and footnote quote from Warshauer, *Andrew Jackson and the Politics of Martial Law*, 2, 5–6.

15. Warshauer, *Andrew Jackson and the Politics of Martial Law*, 238.

16. Senator James Buchanan of Pennsylvania on General Jackson's Fine, in *Appendix to the Congressional Globe*, Senate, May 12, 1842, 27th Cong., 2nd Sess., 363.

17. Senator James Buchanan of Pennsylvania on General Jackson's Fine, in *Appendix to the Congressional Globe*, Senate, May 12, 1842, 27th Cong., 2nd Sess., 363.

18. Warshauer, *Andrew Jackson and the Politics of Martial Law*, 118–19.

19. *Official Report of the Debates and Proceedings in the State Convention, Massachusetts, 1853,* 3:435.

20. *Nauvoo (IL) Expositor,* June 7, 1844.

21. For more on the destruction of the *Nauvoo Expositor,* see Richard Lyman Bushman, *Joseph Smith: Rough Stone Rolling; A Cultural Biography of Mormonism's Founder* (New York: Vintage Books, 2007), 539–42; and Dallin H. Oaks and Marvin S. Hill, *Carthage Conspiracy: The Trial of the Accused Assassins of Joseph Smith* (Urbana: University of Illinois Press, 1979), 14–58.

22. Joseph Smith, Discourse, June 18, 1844, in Joseph Smith, History, 1838–1856, vol. F-1, p. 118, Church History Library, Church of Jesus Christ of Latter-day Saints, Salt Lake City, Utah (hereafter cited as CHL).

23. Joseph Smith, Mayor's Proclamation to John P. Greene, June 17, 1844, Joseph Smith Collection, CHL.

24. Joseph Smith, Martial Law Proclamation, June 18, 1844, Joseph Smith Collection, CHL; Order to Hosea Stout, General Orders, June 17, 1844, MS 3430, folders 20, 22–23, Nauvoo Legion Records, CHL; Jonathan Dunham to Nelson Higgins, June 17, 1844, Orders to the Nauvoo Legion Second Cohort, MS 3430, folder 11, CHL; MS 3430, folder 10, Nauvoo Legion, History, CHL. For more on the interstate nature of the conflict, see Brent M. Rogers, "'Armed Men Are Coming from the State of Missouri': Federalism, Interstate Affairs, and Joseph Smith's Final Attempt to Secure Federal Intervention in Nauvoo," *Journal of the Illinois State Historical Society* 109, no. 2 (Summer 2016): 148–79.

25. Joseph Smith, Discourse, June 18, 1844, in Joseph Smith, History, 1838–1856, vol. F-1, p. 118, CHL.

26. Joseph Smith, Discourse, June 18, 1844, in Joseph Smith, History, 1838–1856, vol. F-1, pp. 118–19, CHL.

27. Untitled, *Warsaw (IL) Signal,* June 19, 1844; "From Nauvoo," *Ottawa (IL) Free Trader,* June 28, 1844; "Communications," *Warsaw (IL) Signal,* July 31, 1844; "The Mormon Difficulties," *Quincy (IL) Whig,* July 24, 1844; "The Mormons," *Alton (IL) Telegraph and Democratic Review,* June 22, 1844.

28. "Postscript, Mormon Difficulties in Illinois," *Warsaw (IL) Signal,* July 24, 1844.

29. "The Act and the Apology," *Warsaw (IL) Signal,* July 10, 1844; Thomas Ford to Joseph Smith, June 22, 1844, Joseph Smith Collection, CHL.

30. Untitled, *Warsaw (IL) Signal,* June 19, 1844.

31. Thomas Ford to Joseph Smith, June 22, 1844, Joseph Smith Collection, CHL. Other regional newspapers also reported on Smith's declaration of martial law and Ford's response that it violated the Constitution; see "The Mormon Difficulty," *Quincy (IL) Whig,* June 26, 1844.

32. Thomas Ford, *A History of Illinois* (Chicago: S. C. Griggs, 1854), 332–33.

33. Thomas Ford to Joseph Smith, June 22, 1844, Joseph Smith Collection, CHL.

34. Thomas Ford to Joseph Smith, June 22, 1844, Joseph Smith Collection, CHL.

35. "The Act and the Apology," *Warsaw (IL) Signal,* July 10, 1844.

36. Joseph Smith to Thomas Ford, June 22, 1844, Joseph Smith Collection, CHL.

37. Ruth H. Bloch, "The Gendered Meanings of Virtue in Revolutionary America," *Signs,* 13, no. 1 (Autumn 1987): 37–58.

38. Joseph Smith, journal entry, June 25, 1844, in *The Joseph Smith Papers: Journals,* vol. 3, *May 1843—June 1844,* ed. Andrew H. Hedges, Alex D. Smith, and Brent M.

Rogers (Salt Lake City, UT: Church Historian's Press, 2015), 307; John Fullmer to George A. Smith, November 27, 1854, Historian's Office, Joseph Smith History Documents, ca. 1839–60, CHL.

39. Ford, *History of Illinois*, 337.

40. See Ford, *History of Illinois*, 322–24, 355–58; see also David Sehat, *The Myth of American Religious Freedom* (New York: Oxford University Press, 2011), 1–10.

41. "Communications," *Warsaw (IL) Signal*, July 31, 1844.

42. Ford, *History of Illinois*, 429.

43. Ford, *History of Illinois*, 429.

44. Ford, *History of Illinois*, 435.

45. *The Joseph Smith Papers: Administrative Records; Council of Fifty, Minutes, March 1844–January 1846*, ed. Matthew J. Grow, Ronald K. Esplin, Mark Ashurst-McGee, Gerrit J. Dirkmaat, and Jeffrey D. Mahas (Salt Lake City, UT: Church Historian's Press, 2016, 479; Robert Bruce Flanders, *Nauvoo: Kingdom on the Mississippi* (Urbana: University of Illinois Press, 1975), 328–29.

46. Buchanan quote from Gary Lawson and Guy Seidman, *The Constitution of Empire: Territorial Expansion and American Legal History* (New Haven, CT: Yale University Press, 2004), 183; James K. Polk, Special Message to the House of Representatives of the United States, December 22, 1846, online at the *American Presidency Project*, directed by Gerhard Peters and John T. Woolley, http://www.presidency.ucsb.edu/ws/?pid=67945.

47. James Buchanan to William Voorhies, October 7, 1848, excerpt reprinted in Lawson and Seidman, *Constitution of Empire*, 183.

48. Kent D. Richards, "Isaac I. Stevens and Federal Military Power in Washington Territory," *Pacific Northwest Quarterly* 63, no. 3 (July 1972): 81–86.

49. Untitled, *New York Times*, July 5, 1856; "The Troubles in Washington Territory," *New York Times*, August 7, 1856.

50. "The Recent Trouble in Washington Territory," *New York Times*, October 3, 1856.

51. George Gibbs to Franklin Pierce, May 6, 1856, in US Senate, "Message from the President of the United States," S. Ex. Doc. No. 98, 34th Cong., 1st Sess., 2.

52. Enclosure in George Gibbs to Franklin Pierce, May 6, 1856, in US Senate, "Message from the President of the United States," S. Ex. Doc. No. 98, 34th Cong., 1st Sess., 3.

53. William L. Marcy (secretary of state) to Isaac I. Stevens, September 12, 1856, in US Senate, "Message from the President of the United States," S. Ex. Doc. No. 41, 34th Cong., 3d sess., 56.

54. Caleb Cushing to William L. Marcy, February 3, 1857, in *Official Opinions of the Attorneys General of the United States*, 43 vols. (Washington, DC: R. Farnham, 1858), 8:374.

55. "Interesting from Washington," *New York Times*, August 18, 1856.

56. James Buchanan, *First Annual Message from the President of the United States to the Two Houses of Congress at the Commencement of the First Session of the Thirty-Fifth Congress* (Washington, DC: Cornelius Wendell, 1857).

57. The Constitution authorized the acquisition of new territory and permitted the development and addition of new states out of these lands, if the people in

those geopolitical entities operated a republican form of government. US Const., art. 4, secs. 3, 4. see also Robert F. Berkhofer Jr., "The Northwest Ordinance and the Principle of Territorial Evolution," in *The American Territorial System*, ed. John Porter Bloom (Athens: Ohio University Press, 1973), 45; and Peter S. Onuf, *Statehood and Union: A History of the Northwest Ordinance* (Bloomington: Indiana University Press, 1987), xiii.

58. Buchanan, *First Annual Message*.

59. "Interesting from the Plains," *New York Times*, November 19, 1857.

60. Brigham Young, Proclamation, by the Governor, September 15, 1857, Utah State Historical Society, Salt Lake City, Utah (hereafter cited as USHS).

61. "Late and Important from Utah," *New York Times*, January 14, 1858.

62. US Const., art. 1, sec. 8, and art. 4, sec. 4. For more on other federal laws that justified James Buchanan's decision to send the army to Utah, see Brent M. Rogers, "A 'Distinction between Mormons and Americans': Mormon Indian Missionaries, Federal Indian Policy, and the Utah War," *Utah Historical Quarterly* 82, no. 4 (Fall 2014): 251–71.

63. "Late and Important from Utah," *New York Times*, January 14, 1858.

64. Young, Proclamation, September 15, 1857, USHS.

65. "Letter from Captain Marcy," *New York Times*, November 19, 1857. Within the headline of "Martial Law Proclaimed in Utah—The Mormon Forces Called Out," "Departure of Mormons from California," *New York Times*, December 29, 1857. "From the Utah Expedition," *New York Times*, December 11, 1857; "The Utah Expedition," *New York Times*, March 4, 1858.

66. Buchanan, *First Annual Message*.

67. James Buchanan, *Second Annual Message to Congress on the State of the Union*, December 6, 1858, online at the *American Presidency Project*, directed by Gerhard Peters and John T. Woolley, http://www.presidency.ucsb.edu/ws/?pid=29499.

68. "The War Department and the Utah Expedition," *New York Times*, December 10, 1857; US Congress, *Report of the Secretary of War in Message from the President of the United States, 35th Cong., 1st Sess., 1857, Ex. Doc. No. 2* (Washington, DC: Cornelius Wendell, Printer, 1857), 7–8.

69. Buchanan, *Second Annual Message*.

70. "News of the Day," *New York Times*, November 18, 1857.

71. "From the Utah Expedition," *New York Times*, December 11, 1857.

72. Buchanan, *First Annual Message*.

73. Douglas argued that the Latter-day Saints operated a nonrepublican form of government based on their peculiar institution of plural marriage and allegedly subversive alliances with American Indian tribes. Congress, Douglas believed, had the right to repeal the territory's organic act, remove it as a geopolitical entity, and assert federal sovereignty over that jurisdiction. The Illinois senator and chairperson of the Senate Committee on Territories further asserted that the federal government could repeal the organic act because the Mormons disavowed their allegiance to the United States and they were "alien enemies and outlaws, unfit to exercise the right of self-government." Douglas emphasized that Mormons were incapable of exercising popular sovereignty in the territory and that they only sought statehood to "protect them in their treason and crime, debauchery and infamy." Furthermore, he argued

that to shelter them in their "treasonable" and "bestial" practices by allowing them to govern themselves would be a disgrace to humanity and civilization and potentially fatal to American interests in the West. "Kansas—The Mormons—Slavery: Speech of Senator Douglas: Delivered at Springfield, Ill, 12 June 1857," *New York Times*, June 23, 1857. For more on Douglas and his Utah popular sovereignty rhetoric, see Brent M. Rogers, *Unpopular Sovereignty: Mormons and the Federal Management of Early Utah Territory* (Lincoln: University of Nebraska Press, 2017), 164–77.

74. The 1856 Republican platform coupled polygamy with slavery as the "twin relics of barbarism" and further stated that it was the "right and the imperative duty of Congress to prohibit in the Territories" those twin relics as unnatural excesses in American culture, excesses that were buoyed up by the opposing Democrat Party. Kirk H. Porter and Donald Bruce Johnson, eds., *National Party Platforms* (Urbana: University of Illinois Press, 1966), 27.

75. "From the Utah Army," *New York Times*, April 7, 1858.

76. "From the Utah Army," *New York Times*, April 7, 1858.

77. Buchanan, *Second Annual Message*.

78. "Is a Citizen Soldiery Dangerous to Liberty?," *New York Times*, September 16, 1858; "What Is Martial Law," *Ripley (OH) Bee*, April 25, 1861; "What Is Martial Law?," *Daily Morning News* (Savannah, GA), May 1, 1861.

79. Abraham Lincoln, "Proclamation 84—Declaring Martial Law, and Suspending the Writ of Habeas Corpus in the Islands of Key West," May 10, 1861, online at the *American Presidency Project*, directed by Gerhard Peters and John T. Woolley, http://www.presidency.ucsb.edu/ws/?pid=70134; Abraham Lincoln, "Proclamation 113—Declaring Martial Law and a Further Suspension of the Writ of Habeas Corpus in Kentucky," July 5, 1864, online at the *American Presidency Project*, directed by Gerhard Peters and John T. Woolley, http://www.presidency.ucsb.edu/ws/?pid=69993; and James A. Dueholm, "Lincoln's Suspension of the Writ of Habeas Corpus: An Historical and Constitutional Analysis," *Journal of the Abraham Lincoln Association* 29, no. 2 (Summer 2008): 47–66.

80. Chaput, *People's Martyr*, 91–92.

81. Warshauer, *Andrew Jackson and the Politics of Martial Law*, 15.

Chapter 8. Political Perceptions of Mormon Polygamy and the Struggle for Utah Statehood, 1847–1896

1. Harold Bloom, *The American Religion: The Emergence of the Post-Christian Nation* (New York: Simon and Schuster, 1992), 85.

2. Ethan Yorgason, "The Shifting Role of the Latter-day Saints as the Quintessential American Region," in *Faith in America: Changes, Challenges, New Directions*, ed. Charles H. Lippy, 3 vols. (Westport, CT: Praeger, 2006), 1:151.

3. Christine Talbot, *A Foreign Kingdom: Mormons and Polygamy in American Political Culture, 1852–1890* (Urbana: University of Illinois Press, 2013), 53.

4. The admission of Utah formally occurred on January 4, 1896, pursuant to a presidential proclamation. Grover Cleveland, "A Proclamation," January 4, 1896, 29 Stat. 876 (1896), reprinted in James D. Richardson, comp., *A Compilation of the Messages and Papers of the Presidents* (New York: Bureau of National Literature, 1897), 6120–21.

5. Conventions were held in 1849, 1856, 1862, 1872, 1882, and 1887. For a summary of the constitutions that were drafted in each, see Jean Bickmore White, *The Utah State Constitution* (New York: Oxford University Press, 2011), 4–10. For the enabling act, see An Act to enable the People of Utah to form a Constitution and State Government, and to be admitted into the Union on an equal footing with the original States [1894 Enabling Act], 28 Stat. 107 (1894).

6. The practice of polygamy, not publicly acknowledged prior to 1852, may have begun in the church as early as 1831 under the leadership of the church founder Joseph Smith, and was authorized by a revelation from God that was canonized by the church. *The Doctrine and Covenants of the Church of Jesus Christ of Latter-day Saints* (Salt Lake City, UT: Church of Jesus Christ of Latter-day Saints, 2013), sec. 132. After the Manifesto of 1890, which officially ended church sanctioning of polygamy, occasional plural marriages continued to be contracted. By 1904 contracting new polygamous marriages had become strictly forbidden by the church, but some Mormon men continued to cohabit with their plural wives well into the twentieth century. For a discussion, see B. Carmon Hardy, *Solemn Covenant: The Mormon Polygamous Passage* (Urbana: University of Illinois Press, 1992). For the most recent statements of the church on its polygamous past, see "Plural Marriage in the Church of Jesus Christ of Latter-day Saints," www.churchofjesuschrist.org/study/manual/gospel-topics-essays/plural-marriage-and-families-in-early-utah; "Plural Marriage in Kirtland and Nauvoo," www.churchofjesuschrist.org/topics/plural-marriage-in-kirtland-and-nauvoo; "Plural Marriage and Families in Early Utah," www.churchofjesuschrist.org/topics/plural-marriage-and-families-in-early-utah; and "The Manifesto and the End of Plural Marriage," www.churchofjesuschrist.org/topics/the-manifesto-and-the-end-of-plural-marriage.

7. This tendency is far too common to provide anything close to a comprehensive survey, but the following examples are representative of the range of sources and the common tenor of the claim. "The Mormons came under intense political and legal pressure to abandon polygamy. They did so in 1890 after one of Young's successors, Wilford Woodruff, received divine prompting to suspend it. As a quid pro quo, Utah was granted statehood." Patrick Allitt, *Religion in America since 1945: A History* (New York: Columbia University Press, 2003), 60. Several sources claim that Mormons exchanged polygamy for statehood. See, for example, Margaret Denike, "The Racialization of White Man's Polygamy," *Hypatia* 25, no. 4 (2010): 855; Dennis C. Mueller, *Reason, Religion, and Democracy* (Cambridge: Cambridge University Press, 2009), 276; Steven Surman, "Disenfranchised Mormons Speak Out," *Gay & Lesbian Review Worldwide* (October/November 2009): 27; Peggy Fletcher Stack, "A Seat at the Table," *Salt Lake Tribune*, April 3, 2004; Peg McEntee, "Polygamy Shouldn't Bar Utah Couple from Adoption, High Court Told," Associated Press, June 12, 1989; and Nancy Bentley, "Marriage as Treason: Polygamy, Nation, and the Novel," in *The Future of American Studies*, ed. Donald E. Pease and Robyn Wiegman (Durham, NC: Duke University Press, 2002), 363.

8. 1894 Enabling Act, sec. 3. "And said Convention shall provide by ordinance irrevocable without the consent of the United States and the people of said State— First. That perfect toleration of religious sentiment shall be secured, and that no inhabitant of said State shall ever be molested in person or property on account of his or her mode of religious worship; *Provided*, That polygamous or plural marriages are

forever prohibited." W. Paul Reeve, "The Mormon Church in Utah," in *The Oxford Handbook of Mormonism*, ed. Terryl L. Givens and Philip L. Barlow (New York: Oxford University Press, 2015), 47.

9. California was granted statehood in 1850; Oregon in 1859. US Const., art. 1, sec. 2, cl. 3.

10. To a large extent, church leaders encouraged this tendency. The Bible quotes Jesus as telling his disciples that "ye are not of the world" (John 15:19), and the church taught its members to be "in the world but not of the world." See, e.g., Brigham Young, "Remarks Delivered in the New Tabernacle, Salt Lake City, May 6, 1870," *Journal of Discourses* 14 (1872): 15–22; Moses Thatcher, "Remarks Delivered at the General Conference, Friday Afternoon, April 4th, 1884," *Journal of Discourses* 25 (1884): 114–15; and F. D. Richards, "Discourse Delivered at the Annual Conference, Held in the Tabernacle, Logan, Cache County, Saturday and Sunday, April 4th and 5th, 1885," *Journal of Discourses* 26 (1886): 164–65.

11. Talbot, *Foreign Kingdom*, 52.

12. There have been three book-length studies that have described the process of Americanization underlying the Utah statehood project: Gustive O. Larson, *The "Americanization" of Utah for Statehood* (San Marino, CA: Huntington Library, 1971); Edward Leo Lyman, *Political Deliverance: The Mormon Quest for Utah Statehood* (Urbana: University of Illinois Press, 1986); and Ken Verdoia and Richard A. Firmage, *Utah: The Struggle for Statehood* (Salt Lake City: University of Utah Press, 1996).

13. For a discussion, see Talbot, *Foreign Kingdom*, 105–28.

14. An act to amend an act entitled "An act to amend section fifty-three hundred and fifty-two of the Revised Statutes of the United States, in reference to bigamy, and for other purposes," approved March twenty-second, eighteen hundred and eighty-two [Edmunds-Tucker Act], 24 Stat. 635 (1887).

15. For a complete discussion, see Eric Biber, "The Price of Admission: Causes, Effects, and Patterns of Conditions Imposed on States Entering the Union," *American Journal of Legal History* 46 (2004): 119–208.

16. Biber, "Price of Admission," 143–44.

17. Before selecting the Great Basin region, Young had considered leading the Saints to Oregon, Mexican California, the Republic of Texas, or Vancouver Island. John G. Turner, *Brigham Young: Pioneer Prophet* (Cambridge, MA: Belknap Press of Harvard University Press, 2012), 121.

18. For a history of these early stages of the Mormon exodus, see Richard E. Bennett, *We'll Find the Place: The Mormon Exodus, 1846–1848* (Norman: University of Oklahoma Press, 2009). Brigham Young, "General Epistle from the Council of the Twelve Apostles to the Church of Jesus Christ of Latter-day Saints Abroad Dispersed throughout the Earth" (December 23, 1847), *Latter-day Saints' Millennial Star* 10, no. 6 (March 15, 1848): 81.

19. The command from God to the Latter-day Saints to establish Zion is a consistent theme found throughout the revelations of Joseph Smith in the *Doctrine and Covenants*. For a discussion of Zion in Mormon doctrine, see A. Don Sorensen, "Zion," in *Encyclopedia of Mormonism*, ed. Daniel H. Ludlow, 4 vols. (New York: Macmillan, 1992), 4:1624.

20. Young, "General Epistle," 84. In 1847 the Great Basin was part of the Upper California region of Mexico. At the time Young wrote, the Mormons had provided

about five hundred volunteers to the US Army for the campaign against Mexico, and it was evident that the United States would be victorious in the war. In February 1848, six months after the first Mormons arrived in the Great Basin, Mexico and the United States agreed to the Treaty of Guadalupe Hidalgo, which transferred all of Upper California to the United States. For a discussion of the treaty, see *The Treaty of Guadalupe Hidalgo, 1848: Papers of the Sesquicentennial Symposium*, ed. John Porter Bloom (Las Cruces, NM: Yucca Tree Press, 1999). Elsewhere in the announcement of the gathering, Young exhibited the competing tendency by declaring that "the kingdom which we are establishing is not of this world, but is the kingdom of the Great God." "General Epistle," 87.

21. Richard H. Jackson, "Mormon Wests: The Creation and Evolution of an American Region," in *Western Places, American Myths: How We Think about the West*, ed. Gary J. Hausladen (Reno: University of Nevada Press, 2003), 142–43.

22. Cong. Globe, 31st Cong., 1st Sess. 413 (1850) (Rep. John Wentworth of Illinois).

23. An Act to Establish a Territorial Government for Utah [Utah Organic Act], 9 Stat. 453 (1850). At the time of its creation, Utah Territory consisted of all of present-day Utah, a large portion of Nevada, and smaller parts of Wyoming and Colorado.

24. The main provisions of the enacted compromise were: (1) California was admitted to the Union as a free state; (2) the extensive slave trade in the District of Columbia was abolished, but slavery was still permitted therein; (3) a new Fugitive Slave Act was enacted, which required residents of both slave and free states to assist in the return of runaway slaves to their owners; (4) the territories of New Mexico and Utah were created, with the decision on the slavery status of the territories being deferred until grants of statehood; and (5) Texas surrendered a substantial portion of its territory to the federal government in exchange for Washington's assumption of $10 million of the carryover debts of the Republic of Texas. 9 Stat. 446a, 452, 453, 462, 467a. For a complete discussion, see Holman Hamilton, *Prologue to Conflict: The Crisis and Compromise of 1850*, rev. ed. (Lexington: University Press of Kentucky, 2005).

25. Jackson, "Mormon Wests," 142–43.

26. Edward Leo Lyman, "Larger Than Texas: Proposals to Combine California and Mormon Deseret as One State," *California History* 80, no. 1 (2001): 26–27.

27. Lyman, "Larger Than Texas," 27.

28. Brigham Young, "Discourse," *Deseret News*, March 26, 1856.

29. Brigham Young to Thomas L. Kane, April 14, 1856, Brigham Young Collection, Church History Library, Church of Jesus Christ of Latter-day Saints, Salt Lake City, Utah (hereafter cited as Brigham Young Collection, CHL).

30. For discussions of this popular movement, see Terryl L. Givens, *The Viper on the Hearth: Mormons, Myths, and the Construction of Heresy* (New York: Oxford University Press, 1997), 97–152; Sarah Barringer Gordon, "A War of Words: Revelation and Storytelling in the Campaign against Mormon Polygamy," *Chicago-Kent Law Review* 78, no. 2 (2003): 739–72; Sarah Barringer Gordon, "'Our National Hearthstone': Anti-Polygamy Fiction and the Sentimental Campaign against Moral Diversity in Antebellum America," *Yale Journal of Law and the Humanities* 8, no. 2 (1996): 295–350; Talbot, *Foreign Kingdom*, 129–46.

31. For a discussion of the 1854 debate, see Stephen Eliot Smith, "Barbarians within the Gates: Congressional Debates on Mormon Polygamy, 1850–1879," *Journal of Church and State* 51, no. 4 (2009): 595–98.

32. Cong. Globe, 33d Cong., 1st Sess. 1112 (1854) (Rep. John Letcher of Virginia).

33. Cong. Globe, 33d Cong., 1st Sess. 1101 (1854) (Rep. Caleb Lyon of New York).

34. Cong. Globe, 33d Cong., 1st Sess. 1099 (1854) (Rep. Charles Ready of Tennessee).

35. Cong. Globe, 33d Cong., 1st Sess. 1111 (1854) (Rep. William Waters Boyce).

36. S. E. Smith, "Barbarians within the Gates," 597–98.

37. "Republican Platform," in *Proceedings of the First Three Republican National Conventions of 1856, 1860, and 1864*, ed. Charles W. Johnson (Minneapolis, MN: Harrison and Smith, 1893), 43; Thomas Hudson McKee, ed., *The National Conventions and Platforms of All Political Parties, 1789 to 1904*, rev. 5th ed. (Baltimore: Friedenwald, 1904), 98.

38. George A. Smith to Brigham Young, June 30, 1856, Brigham Young Collection, CHL.

39. Brent M. Rogers, *Unpopular Sovereignty: Mormons and the Federal Management of Early Utah Territory* (Lincoln: University of Nebraska Press, 2017), 136.

40. For a discussion of the Utah War, see Paul Bailey, *Holy Smoke: A Dissertation on the Utah War* (Los Angeles: Westernlore Books, 1978). For a more recent reevaluation of the war, which has been controversial among historians, see David L. Bigler and Will Bagley, *The Mormon Rebellion: America's First Civil War, 1857–1858* (Norman: University of Oklahoma Press, 2011).

41. Cong. Globe, 35th Cong., 1st Sess., app. 5 (1857).

42. Cong. Globe, 35th Cong., 1st Sess., app. 5 (1857).

43. Richard D. Poll and Ralph W. Hansen, "'Buchanan's Blunder': The Utah War, 1857–1858," *Military Affairs* 25, no. 3 (1961): 131.

44. An Act to punish and prevent the Practice of Polygamy in the Territories of the United States and other Places, and disapproving certain Acts of the Legislative Assembly of the Territory of Utah [Morrill Act], 12 Stat. 501 (1862); An Act in relation to the courts and judicial officers in the Territory of Utah [Poland Act], 18 Stat. 253 (1874).

45. Cong. Globe, 41st Cong., 2d Sess. 2147 (1870) (Rep. Austin Blair of Michigan).

46. For a discussion of these debates, see S. E. Smith, "Barbarians within the Gates," 600–615.

47. Cong. Globe, 36th Cong., 1st Sess. 1497 (1860) (Rep. Emerson Etheridge of Tennessee), 1515 (Rep. John B. Clark of Missouri), 1519 (Rep. Eli Thayer of Massachusetts); Cong. Globe, 41st Cong., 2d Sess. 3574 (1870) (Sen. Aaron H. Cragin of New Hampshire).

48. Cong. Globe, 36th Cong., 1st Sess. 1496 (1860) (Rep. Roger A. Pryor of Virginia).

49. Cong. Globe, 41st Cong., 2d Sess. 1373 (1870) (Rep. Shelby M. Cullom of Illinois).

50. Cong. Globe, 36th Cong., 1st Sess. 1519 (1860) (Rep. Eli Thayer of Massachusetts).

51. Cong. Globe, 41st Cong., 2d Sess. 3581 (1870) (Sen. Aaron H. Cragin of New Hampshire).

52. Cong. Globe, 41st Cong., 2d Sess. 3576 (1870) (Sen. Samuel C. Pomeroy of Kansas).

53. Cong. Globe, 36th Cong., 1st Sess. 1514 (1860) (Rep. John A. McClernand of Illinois).

54. Cong. Globe, 36th Cong., 1st Sess. 1522 (1860) (Rep. Joshua Hill of Georgia).

55. Cong. Globe, 36th Cong., 1st Sess., app. 202 (Rep. William E. Simms of Kentucky).

56. Cong. Globe, 41st Cong., 2d Sess. 2151 (1870) (Rep. Charles Pomeroy of Iowa).

57. Cong. Globe, 36th Cong., 1st Sess. 1500 (1860) (Rep. Emerson Etheridge of Tennessee).

58. See, e.g., Cong. Globe, 41st Cong., 2d Sess. 1518 (1870) (Rep. Thomas Fitch of Nevada), 1520 (Rep. Aaron A. Sargent of California), and 2145 (Rep. Robert C. Schenck of Ohio).

59. Some have maintained that no such agreement between the church and the federal government existed. See, e.g., Robert Joseph Dwyer, *The Gentile Comes to Utah: A Study of Religious and Social Conflict (1862–1890)* (Washington, DC: Catholic University of America Press, 1941), 112–13. However, the circumstances of the case suggest otherwise, and most observers have agreed that, at least initially, some form of arrangement between the church and the government must have been reached. See, e.g., Edward Brown Firmage and Richard Collin Mangrum, *Zion in the Courts: A Legal History of the Church of Jesus Christ of Latter-day Saints, 1830–1900* (Urbana: University of Illinois Press, 1988), 151; B. H. Roberts, *A Comprehensive History of the Church of Jesus Christ of Latter-day Saints: Century I*, 6 vols. (Salt Lake City, Utah: Deseret News Press, 1930), 5:469; and Orson F. Whitney, *History of Utah*, 4 vols. (Salt Lake City, Utah: George Q. Cannon and Sons, 1893), 3:46–47.

60. US Const., amend. 1: "Congress shall make no law respecting an establishment of religion, *or prohibiting the free exercise thereof*" (emphasis added to indicate free exercise clause). For the church's defense of plural marriage on constitutional grounds given at the 1852 announcement, see Orson Pratt, "Celestial Marriage: A Discourse Delivered in the Tabernacle, Great Salt Lake City, August 29, 1852," *Journal of Discourses* 1 (1854): 53–66.

61. Reynolds v. United States, 98 US 145, 166 (1878).

62. Taylor was officially instituted as president of the church in October 1880.

63. See, e.g., John Taylor, "Discourse Delivered at the General Conference, held in the Tabernacle, Salt Lake City, Oct. 6th, 1879," *Journal of Discourses* 20 (1880): 316–21; and George Q. Cannon, "Discourse Delivered in the Tabernacle, Salt Lake City, on Sunday Morning, July 20th, 1879," *Journal of Discourses* 20 (1880): 275–77. For a discussion of the civil disobedience campaign that lasted in some form from *Reynolds* until the Manifesto, see J. David Pulsipher, "'Prepared to Abide the Penalty': Latter-day Saints and Civil Disobedience," *Journal of Mormon History* 39, no. 3 (2013): 143–53.

64. 13 Cong. Rec. 28 (1881) (Sen. George F. Edmunds of Vermont).

65. 13 Cong. Rec. 28, app. 28 (1882) (Rep. Stanton J. Peelle of Indiana).

66. 13 Cong. Rec. 28, 1207 (Sen. Wilkinson Call of Florida); 13 Cong. Rec. 28, 1157 (Sen. George G. Vest of Missouri).

67. 13 Cong. Rec. 28, 1204–5 (Sen. Joseph E. Brown of Georgia).

68. 13 Cong. Rec. 28, 1217 (Senate), 1877 (House).

69. 13 Cong. Rec. 28, 2197; 22 Stat. 32.

70. An act to amend section fifty-three hundred and fifty-two of the Revised Statutes of the United States, in reference to bigamy, and for other purposes [Edmunds Act], 22 Stat. 30b (1883).

71. In bigamy prosecutions under the Morrill Act, prosecutors found it nearly impossible to obtain legally admissible proof that a man had entered into multiple marriages. Paper records were not generally available because church leaders either did not record the plural marriages they performed or kept such records well hidden. Even government records of first (legal) marriages were nonexistent because Congress had not required that the territories issue marriage licenses or keep a registry of marriages. Eyewitness testimony regarding plural marriages was not generally available because they were not public affairs (most were performed in the Endowment House in Salt Lake City, which was only accessible to faithful Latter-day Saints) and the officiator and witnesses were more likely to submit to contempt charges than provide testimony that would convict a fellow church member. A man's first wife usually had knowledge of his subsequent plural marriages, but even if she cooperated with prosecutors, under the common law a wife's testimony was inadmissible in a criminal prosecution of her husband.

72. Edmunds Act, sec. 3.

73. The offense called "bigamy" in the Morrill Act was renamed "polygamy" by section 1 of the Edmunds Act. Edmunds Act, sec. 8.

74. Sarah Barringer Gordon, *The Mormon Question: Polygamy and Constitutional Conflict in Nineteenth-Century America* (Chapel Hill: University of North Carolina Press, 2002), 155–56. For a full discussion, see Sarah Barringer Gordon and Kathryn Daynes, *Convictions: Mormon Polygamy and Criminal Law Enforcement in Nineteenth-Century Utah* (Urbana: University of Illinois Press, forthcoming).

75. John Taylor, "Discourse Delivered at the General Conference, on Sunday Afternoon, April 9th, 1882," *Journal of Discourses* 23 (1883): 67.

76. John Taylor, "Discourse Delivered in the Tabernacle, Salt Lake City, Sunday Afternoon, Feb. 1, 1885," *Journal of Discourses* 26 (1886): 155.

77. Gordon, *Mormon Question*, 159.

78. James B. Allen and Glen M. Leonard, *The Story of the Latter-day Saints*, 2nd ed. (Salt Lake City, UT: Deseret Book, 1992), 407.

79. Richard A. Van Wagoner, *Mormon Polygamy: A History*, 2nd ed. (Salt Lake City, UT: Signature Books, 1989), 125–26.

80. 15 Cong. Rec. 23 (1883).

81. 16 Cong. Rec. 7 (1884).

82. McKee, *National Conventions and Platforms*, 213–14.

83. Firmage and Mangrum, *Zion in the Courts*, 198.

84. Firmage and Mangrum, *Zion in the Courts*, 198.

85. 18 Cong. Rec. 592 (1887) (Rep. Lucien B. Caswell of Wisconsin).

86. 18 Cong. Rec. 592 (1887), app. 144. For Senator Wilkinson Call's similar objection, see 18 Cong. Rec. 592 (1900).

87. 17 Cong. Rec. 509 (1886) (Sen. John T. Morgan of Alabama).

88. 18 Cong. Rec. 590 (1887) (Rep. John T. Caine).

89. 18 Cong. Rec. 590 (1887), 594 (Rep. John Randolph Tucker of Virginia).

90. 18 Cong. Rec. 590 (1887), 1882 (House), 1904 (Senate). Due to an unusually large number of abstentions, the bill only garnered a plurality of the vote in the Senate: only 37 of 76 senators voted in favor of the bill.

91. Edmunds-Tucker Act, sec. 1. In practice, the effect of this change was minimal. Although the act made a legal wife competent to testify if she chose to do so, it also established that she was not a compellable witness without the consent of her husband, the accused. Most wives were not willing to testify against their husbands, and only in extraordinary circumstances would a husband permit his wife to be compelled to testify against him.

92. Edmunds-Tucker Act, sec. 9.

93. Edmunds-Tucker Act, sec. 20. Apparently, this was done on the theory that a plural wife submissively voted according to the dictates of her domineering husband. A notable quip of the day was that "woman suffrage in Utah means only woman suffering." Gordon, *Mormon Question*, 168.

94. Edmunds-Tucker Act, sec. 17. The act that incorporated the church was Ordinance Incorporating the Church of Jesus Christ of Latter-day Saints, Utah (Terr.) Laws, February 4, 1851, reprinted in Dale L. Morgan, "The State of Deseret," *Utah Historical Quarterly* 8, nos. 2–4 (1940): 223–25. Notably, section 3 of the territorial law granted the church the right to "solemnize marriage compatible with the revelations of Jesus Christ" and declared that its decisions with respect to the marriages of its members "may not be legally questioned." Section 2 of the 1862 Morrill Act had annulled any grant of corporate power that the territorial legislature may have given to the church which purported to permit the church to "establish, maintain, protect, or countenance the practice of polygamy," but nothing had been done to enforce this provision.

95. Edmunds-Tucker Act, sec. 13.

96. Edmunds-Tucker Act, sec. 17.

97. Edmunds-Tucker Act, sec. 15.

98. Van Wagoner, *Mormon Polygamy*, 133. The government estimated that the church had real estate and personal property valued in excess of $3 million. Leonard J. Arrington, *Great Basin Kingdom: An Economic History of the Latter-day Saints, 1830–1900*, new ed. (Urbana: University of Illinois Press, 2005), 365.

99. Thomas G. Alexander, "The Odyssey of a Latter-day Prophet: Wilford Woodruff and the Manifesto of 1890," *Journal of Mormon History* 17 (1991): 198.

100. Alexander, "Odyssey," 190.

101. White, *Utah State Constitution*, 10.

102. In the presidential election, the Republican Benjamin Harrison lost the popular vote but defeated President Cleveland in the Electoral College, and Republican majorities were elected to both houses of Congress.

103. An act to provide for the division of Dakota into two States and to enable the people of North Dakota, South Dakota, Montana, and Washington to form constitutions and State governments and to be admitted into the Union on an equal footing with the original States, and to make donations of public lands to such states, 25 Stat. 676 (1889).

104. Lyman, *Political Deliverance*, 107.

105. Walter B. Stevens, "Among the Mormons," *St. Louis Globe-Democrat*, October 10, 1889. In Utah, the interview was reprinted in the *Salt Lake Herald*, October 27, 1889.

106. Stevens, "Among the Mormons."

107. Stevens, "Among the Mormons."

108. Stevens, "Among the Mormons."

109. Late Corporation of the Church of Jesus Christ of Latter-day Saints v. United States, 136 US 1, 50 (1890).

110. Late Corporation of the Church of Jesus Christ of Latter-day Saints v. United States, 136 US 1, 50 (1890), 66–68, 44, 45.

111. For a discussion of the events leading up to the Manifesto, see Thomas G. Alexander, *Things in Heaven and Earth: The Life and Times of Wilford Woodruff, a Mormon Prophet* (Salt Lake City, UT: Signature Books, 1991), 235–59.

112. "The Mormons and Polygamy," *New York Times*, December 21, 1890.

113. *Annual Report of the Utah Commission* (Washington, DC: Government Printing Office, 1890).

114. Wilford Woodruff, "Official Declaration," *Deseret Evening News*, September 25, 1890, reprinted as "Official Declaration 1," in *Doctrine and Covenants*, 292.

115. Woodruff, "Official Declaration."

116. Coverage in the non-Mormon press within Utah was mixed. While some accepted the Manifesto at face value and regarded it as a significant development, others reacted with skepticism. See, e.g., "President Woodruff's Manifesto," *Salt Lake Times*, September 25, 1890; "Why the Devious Way?," *Salt Lake Tribune*, September 25, 1890; "That Manifesto," *Salt Lake Tribune*, September 26, 1890; and "The Manifesto Is All Right," *Salt Lake Herald*, October 4, 1890.

117. See, e.g., "Woodruff's Manifesto on Polygamy," *Los Angeles Times*, September 26, 1890; "Manifesto from the President of the Mormon Church," *San Francisco Call*, September 25, 1890; "A Mormon Manifesto," *Helena (MT) Independent*, September 25, 1890; and "The Mormon Church: The Practice of Polygamy Is Denied," *Arizona Republican* (Phoenix), September 26, 1890.

118. One exception is that a week after the Manifesto was issued, the *New York Times* commented that, although historically "Mormon leaders have shown themselves wily, . . . a fair representation of this proclamation is that it is made in good faith, and if so, its influence must be great." "The Doom of Polygamy," *New York Times*, October 3, 1890.

119. *President Woodruff's Manifesto: Proceedings at the Semi-Annual General Conference of the Church of Jesus Christ of Latter-day Saints* (Salt Lake City, UT: Church of Jesus Christ of Latter-day Saints, 1890), 3. The *New York Times* noted that the action of the general conference was "the most important step taken by the Church for more than a quarter of a century." "Polygamy and the Church: President Woodruff Forbids Plural Marriage to the Mormons," *New York Times*, October 7, 1890.

120. "The End of Polygamy," *New York Times*, October 7, 1890.

121. An Act to Punish Polygamy and Other Kindred Offenses, 1892 Utah (Terr.) Laws, chap. 7, secs. 1–2, codified as Utah Revised Statutes 1898, title 75, chap. 24, secs. 4208–9 (1898).

122. Committee on the Territories, Admission of Utah, HR Rep. 2337, at 7 (1893).

123. 26 Cong. Rec. 216–17 (1893) (Rep. Case Broderick of Kansas).

124. 26 Cong. Rec. 220 (House), 7251 (Senate). The Enabling Act passed with just two dissenting votes each in both the House and the Senate. Joan Ray Harrow, "Rawlins, Joseph L.," in *Utah History Encyclopedia*, ed. Allen Kent Powell (Salt Lake City: University of Utah Press, 1994); Verdoia and Firmage, *Utah*, 172; 28 Stat. 113.

125. Wilford Woodruff, journal entry, October 17, 1894, *Wilford Woodruff's Journal, 1833–1898: Typescript*, ed. Scott G. Kenney, 9 vols. (Salt Lake City, UT: Signature Books, 1983), 9:311.

Chapter 9. A Snake in the Sugar

1. Judson C. Welliver, "The Mormon Church and the Sugar Trust," *Hampton's Magazine* 29 (July 1910): 82, 86.

2. Kenneth L. Cannon wrote a detailed history of these articles, but his work does not mention Welliver's publications or the subsequent House of Representatives investigation it led to. Kenneth L. Cannon II, "'And Now It Is the Mormons': The Magazine Crusade against the Mormon Church, 1910–1911," *Dialogue: A Journal of Mormon Thought* 46 (Spring 2013): 1–63.

3. Glenn Porter, *The Rise of Big Business, 1860–1920*, 2nd ed. (Wheeling, IL: Harlan Davidson, 1992), 45–47.

4. Matthew C. Godfrey, *Religion, Politics, and Sugar: The Mormon Church, the Federal Government, and the Utah-Idaho Sugar Company, 1907–1921* (Logan: Utah State University Press, 2007), 18–19, 43.

5. Richard C. Brown, "The Muckrakers: Honest Craftsmen," *History Teacher* 2 (January 1969): 52–53; see also Josephine D. Randolph, "A Notable Pennsylvanian: Ida Minerva Tarbell, 1857–1944," *Pennsylvania History: A Journal of Mid-Atlantic Studies* 66 (Spring 1999): 216; and Louis Filler, *Muckraking and Progressivism in the American Tradition* (New Brunswick, NJ: Transaction, 1996), 247.

6. Filler, *Muckraking and Progressivism*, 248–51.

7. Quotations in Filler, *Muckraking and Progressivism*, 333; see also Brown, "Muckrakers," 53; and Cannon, "And Now It Is the Mormons,'" 5.

8. Cannon, "And Now It Is the Mormons,'" 4–5.

9. Frank J. Cannon, *Under the Prophet in Utah: The National Menace of a Political Priestcraft* (Boston, MA: C. M. Clark, 1911), 276. For information about the Smoot hearings, see Kathleen Flake, *The Politics of American Religious Identity: The Seating of Senator Reed Smoot, Mormon Apostle* (Chapel Hill: University of North Carolina Press, 2004); and Michael Harold Paulos, ed., *The Mormon Church on Trial: Transcripts of the Reed Smoot Hearings* (Salt Lake City, UT: Signature Books, 2008).

10. Alfred Henry Lewis, "The Viper on the Hearth," *Cosmopolitan Magazine* 50 (March 1911): 447.

11. Cannon, "And Now It Is the Mormons,'" 5.

12. Leonard J. Arrington, *Great Basin Kingdom: An Economic History of the Latter-day Saints, 1830–1900* (Cambridge, MA: Harvard University Press, 1958; repr., Salt Lake City: University of Utah Press, 1993), 392–400, 403–6; Thomas G. Alexander, *Mormonism in Transition: A History of the Latter-day Saints, 1890–1930* (Urbana: University of Illinois Press, 1986), 74–92.

13. Porter, *Rise of Big Business*, 3.

14. Frank Luther Mott, *A History of American Magazines*, 5 vols. (Cambridge, MA: Harvard University Press, 1968), 5:145–50.

15. "Writers and Their Work," *Hampton's Magazine* 23 (November 1909): 725–26.

16. Judson C. Welliver, "The Story of Sugar," *Hampton's Magazine* 23 (October 1909): 433–34.

17. Welliver, "Story of Sugar," 435–46.

18. Judson C. Welliver, "The Story of Sugar: Second Article—The Organization of the Sugar Trust," *Hampton's Magazine* 23 (November 1909): 648–58.

19. Godfrey, *Religion, Politics, and Sugar*, 20–21, 24–27; Welliver, "Mormon Church and the Sugar Trust," 87–88.

20. Welliver, "Mormon Church and the Sugar Trust," 82.

21. Godfrey, *Religion, Politics, and Sugar*, 43–47.

22. Godfrey, *Religion, Politics, and Sugar*, 10–11.

23. Welliver, "Mormon Church and the Sugar Trust," 82–93.

24. Richard Barry, "The Political Menace of the Mormon Church," *Pearson's Magazine* 24 (September 1910): 319 (emphasis in the original); Welliver, "Mormon Church and the Sugar Trust," 86.

25. Barry, "Political Menace of the Mormon Church," 319.

26. Richard Barry, "The *Mormon* Method in Business," *Pearson's Magazine* 24 (November 1910): 572, 575–76.

27. Cannon, *Under the Prophet in Utah*, 194–202; Cannon, "'And Now It Is the Mormons,'" 4, 8–9; Kenneth L. Cannon II, "'The Modern Mormon Kingdom': Frank J. Cannon's National Campaign against Mormonism, 1910–18," *Journal of Mormon History* 37 (Fall 2011): 62–74. Frank Cannon also repeated the assertion that Smith controlled the selection of congressmen in Utah and "many of the surrounding states." Cannon, *Under the Prophet in Utah*, 397.

28. Alfred Henry Lewis, "The Viper's Trail of Gold," *Cosmopolitan Magazine* 50 (May 1911): 823–33.

29. For a full examination of this congressional investigation, see Godfrey, *Religion, Politics, and Sugar*, 51–92.

30. US House, 62nd Cong., 1st Sess., "H.R. 157, A Resolution to Elect a Special Committee to Investigate the American Sugar Refining Co. and Others," *Congressional Record*, 1911, 47, pt. 2:143.

31. House of Representatives Special Committee, *Hearings Held before the Special Committee on the Investigation of the American Sugar Refining Co. and Others on June 12, 13, 14, 15, 16, 19, 20, 21, 22, 23, 24, and 26, 1911*, 62nd Cong., 1st Sess., H3 (1911).

32. "Magazine Slanders Confuted by the First Presidency of the Church," *Improvement Era* 14 (June 1911): 720; Cannon, "'And Now It Is the Mormons,'" 31–33.

33. "Testimony of Mr. Thomas R. Cutler," June 23, 1911, *Hearings Held before the Special Committee on the Investigation of the American Sugar Refining Co. and Others*, 787, 813–14.

34. Joseph F. Smith, "True Economy," *Deseret Evening News* (Salt Lake City, UT), December 16, 1893.

35. "Testimony of Mr. Joseph F. Smith," June 27, 1911, *Hearings Held before the Special Committee on the Investigation of the American Sugar Refining Co. and Others*, 1041.

36. "Testimony of Charles W. Nibley," June 27, 1911, *Hearings Held before the Special Committee on the Investigation of the American Sugar Refining Co. and Others*, 1092.

37. "Testimony of Mr. Thomas R. Cutler," June 23, 1911, *Hearings Held before the Special Committee on the Investigation of the American Sugar Refining Co. and Others*, 817. According to church doctrine, members of the church should give 10 percent of their annual increase to the church.

38. For an example of an article addressing the Latter-day Saint practice of tithing, see Barry, "*Mormon* Method in Business," 571–78.

39. "Testimony of Mr. Joseph F. Smith," June 27, 1911, *Hearings Held before the Special Committee on the Investigation of the American Sugar Refining Co. and Others*, 1040.

40. "Testimony of Mr. Thomas R. Cutler," June 23, 1911, *Hearings Held before the Special Committee on the Investigation of the American Sugar Refining Co. and Others*, 817.

41. "Testimony of Charles W. Nibley," June 27, 1911, *Hearings Held before the Special Committee on the Investigation of the American Sugar Refining Co. and Others*, 1097–98.

42. Barry, "*Mormon* Method in Business," 574.

43. "Testimony of Mr. Joseph F. Smith," June 27, 1911, *Hearings Held before the Special Committee on the Investigation of the American Sugar Refining Co. and Others*, 1044.

44. Welliver, "Mormon Church and the Sugar Trust," 86.

45. "Testimony of Mr. Joseph F. Smith," June 27, 1911, *Hearings Held before the Special Committee on the Investigation of the American Sugar Refining Co. and Others*, 1034, 1037–39.

46. Leonard J. Arrington, "Notes from the Utah Sugar Company Minutes, 1900–1907," Leonard J. Arrington Papers, Manuscript Series (MSS) 1, ser. 12: box 10, folder 1, Writings of Leonard J. Arrington, Leonard J. Arrington Historical Archives, Special Collections and Archives, Merrill Library, Utah State University, Logan, Utah.

47. "Testimony of Charles W. Nibley," June 27, 1911, *Hearings Held before the Special Committee on the Investigation of the American Sugar Refining Co. and Others*, 1097.

48. "Testimony of Mr. Thomas R. Cutler," June 23, 1911, 826–27; "Testimony of Mr. Joseph F. Smith," June 27, 1911, 1057, 1062–63; and "Testimony of Charles W. Nibley," June 27, 1911, 1104, 1106; all in *Hearings Held before the Special Committee on the Investigation of the American Sugar Refining Co. and Others*.

49. "Testimony of Mr. Thomas R. Cutler," June 23, 1911, *Hearings Held before the Special Committee on the Investigation of the American Sugar Refining Co. and Others*, 805–6, 810.

50. "Testimony of Mr. Joseph F. Smith," June 27, 1911, 1076–77; and "Testimony of Charles W. Nibley," June 27, 1911, 1107–8; both in *Hearings Held before the Special Committee on the Investigation of the American Sugar Refining Co. and Others*.

51. Claudius O. Johnson, *Borah of Idaho* (New York: Longmans, Green, 1936), 29.

52. Merle H. Wells, "Origins of Anti-Mormonism in Idaho, 1872–1880," *Pacific Northwest Quarterly* 47 (October 1956): 116.

53. Even President Theodore Roosevelt disparaged the notion of Latter-day Saint political influence in areas such as Idaho and Wyoming. Responding to allegations that Smoot and other church leaders had struck a bargain with Republicans to deliver

electoral votes in Idaho and Wyoming during the 1908 presidential election, Roosevelt said, "Neither Senator Smoot nor any other citizen of Utah was, as far as I know, ever so much as consulted about the patronage in the States surrounding Utah." See "Mr. Roosevelt to the Mormons," *Collier's*, April 15, 1911, 28.

54. For a full discussion of Smoot's tariff policies, see James B. Allen, "The Great Protectionist, Sen. Reed Smoot of Utah," *Utah Historical Quarterly* 45 (Fall 1977): 325–45.

55. Milton R. Merrill, *Reed Smoot: Apostle in Politics* (Logan: Utah State University Press, 1990), 287.

56. *Congressional Record*, 63rd Cong., 1st Sess., 1913, 50, pt. 3:2611.

57. Merrill, *Reed Smoot*, 340.

58. "Testimony of Sen. Reed Smoot," June 5, 1913, in Senate Subcommittee of the Committee on the Judiciary, *Maintenance of a Lobby to Influence Legislation: Hearings before a Subcommittee of the Committee on the Judiciary Pursuant to S. Res. 92*, 63rd Cong., 1st Sess. (1913), 451–52; Matthew C. Godfrey, "The Battle over Tariff Reduction: The Utah-Idaho Sugar Company, Senator Reed Smoot, and the 1913 Underwood Act," in *Utah in the Twentieth Century*, ed. Brian Q. Cannon and Jessie L. Embry (Logan: Utah State University Press, 2009), 188–92.

59. Alexander, *Mormonism in Transition*, 80.

60. "Testimony of Mr. Joseph F. Smith," June 27, 1911, *Hearings Held before the Special Committee on the Investigation of the American Sugar Refining Co. and Others*, 1042, 1057.

61. Alfred S. Eichner, *The Emergence of Oligopoly: Sugar Refining as a Case Study* (Baltimore, MD: The Johns Hopkins University Press, 1969), 316–24; Jeremiah Jenks and Walter E. Clark, *The Trust Problem*, 5th ed. (Garden City, NY: Doubleday, Doran, 1929), 357; "Cutler Talks of Sugar Trust Suit," *Salt Lake Tribune*, December 14, 1911; "Sugar Trust Files Answer to Charges," *Salt Lake Tribune*, February 5, 1912.

62. Godfrey, "Battle over Tariff Reduction," 188; Godfrey, *Religion, Politics, and Sugar*, 94.

63. *In the World: The Diaries of Reed Smoot*, ed. Harvard S. Heath (Salt Lake City, UT: Signature Books, 1997), 108.

64. According to Kenneth Cannon II, the magazine campaign against the church enabled church leaders to "learn the art of public relations" in their responses to the allegations leveled against them. This included utilizing the journalist Isaac Russell to write responses to the magazine articles, although the responses mostly involved the charges of the continuous practice of plural marriage. Cannon, "'And Now It Is the Mormons,'" 6; Kenneth L. Cannon II, "Isaac Russell: Mormon Muckraker and Secret Defender of the Church," *Journal of Mormon History* 39 (Fall 2013): 44–98.

65. Joseph F. Smith to Senator Reed Smoot, December 31, 1915, box 49 folder 8, MS 1187, L. Reed Smoot Papers, Tom Perry Special Collections and Archives, Harold B. Lee Library, Brigham Young University, Provo, Utah.

66. C. G. Patterson, *Cracking Nuts in Utah: Little Essays on Tender Subjects* (Salt Lake City, UT: n.p., 1922), 11.

67. For detailed discussions of these cases, see Godfrey, *Religion, Politics, and Sugar*, 127–97.

68. Council of Fifty, Minutes, April 11, 1845, in *The Joseph Smith Papers: Administrative Records; Council of Fifty, Minutes, March 1844–January 1846*, ed. Matthew J.

Grow, Ronald K. Esplin, Mark Ashurst-McGee, Gerrit J. Dirkmaat, and Jeffrey D. Mahas (Salt Lake City, UT: Church Historian's Press, 2016), 401.

69. C. G. Patterson, *Business, Politics and Religion in Utah*, 3rd ed. (Salt Lake City, UT: F. W. Gardiner, 1916), 15.

70. Bernard DeVoto, "The Centennial of Mormonism," *American Mercury* 19 (January 1930): 11, 13.

Chapter 10. "Rather Than Recognize This Wretched Imposture"

1. Cong. Globe, 31st Cong., 1st Sess. 86, 92 (1849–1850). Questions about whether Mormons were treasonable or loyal Americans, raised by petitions from rival Mormon factions, persisted well into the spring of 1850; see Cong. Globe, 31st Cong. 1st Sess. 413, 524.

2. For all this (and much more!), see Matthew Mason, *Apostle of Union: A Political Biography of Edward Everett* (Chapel Hill: University of North Carolina Press, 2016).

3. Edward Everett to Robert C. Winthrop, December 1, 1849, Za Letter File, Edward Everett Letters, Beinecke Rare Book and Manuscript Library, Yale University.

4. Robert C. Winthrop to Edward Everett, December 11, 1849, Edward Everett Papers, 1675–1910 (hereafter cited as Everett Papers), microfilm edition, Massachusetts Historical Society (hereafter cited as MHS); Everett to Henry A. Wise, January 8, 1852, Everett-Hopkins Papers, 1813–1921, MHS.

5. Benedict Anderson, *Imagined Communities: Reflections on the Origin and Spread of Nationalism* (London: Verso, 1991).

6. Everett to Daniel Webster, January 3, 1850, Everett Papers, MHS.

7. For a good history of this crisis, see Fergus M. Bordewich, *America's Great Debate: Henry Clay, Stephen A. Douglas, and the Compromise That Preserved the Union* (New York: Simon and Schuster, 2012).

8. Edward Everett, diary entries, December 26, 1849, January 29, February 17, August 24, 2 (quotation), November 15, 1850, and February 12, 1851, Everett Papers, MHS.

9. Everett to Webster, January 3, 1850, Everett Papers, MHS; Everett to Winthrop, August 13, 1850, Winthrop Family Papers, microfilm edition, MHS.

10. Winthrop to Everett, December 11, 1849, Everett Papers, MHS.

11. Cong. Globe, 31st Cong., 1st Sess. 94, 99–100, 166–68, 211–13, 1413–16, 1418–23, 1773 (1849–1850).

12. For an instant-classic exploration of these themes throughout the antebellum era, see Daniel Walker Howe, *What Hath God Wrought: The Transformation of America, 1815–1848* (New York: Oxford University Press, 2007).

13. Everett to Webster, January 3, 1850, Everett Papers, MHS.

14. J. Spencer Fluhman, *"A Peculiar People": Anti-Mormonism and the Making of Religion in Nineteenth-Century America* (Chapel Hill: University of North Carolina Press, 2012).

15. Edward Everett, diary entries, January 31, 1847, and November 10, 1850, Everett Papers, MHS.

16. Everett to Webster, January 3, 1850, Everett Papers; Everett, diary entries, February 22 and March 4, 1850, Everett Papers; Everett to Winthrop, August 13, 1850, Winthrop Family Papers; all at MHS.

17. Everett to Messrs. Gales and Seaton, February 22, 1850, Everett Papers, MHS.

18. *Daily National Intelligencer* (Washington, DC), February 27, 1850.

19. This is so true that Daniel Walker Howe dedicated *What Hath God Wrought* to Adams!

20. David Waldstreicher and Matthew Mason, eds., *John Quincy Adams and the Politics of Slavery: Selections from the Diary* (New York: Oxford University Press, 2017), 59–61.

21. Eric Burin, *Slavery and the Peculiar Solution: A History of the American Colonization Society* (Gainesville: University Press of Florida, 2005).

Chapter 11. Ambiguous Allegiances and Divided Sovereignty

1. Kevin T. Barksdale, *The Lost State of Franklin: America's First Secession* (Lexington: University Press of Kentucky, 2009); Andros Linklater, *An Artist in Treason: The Extraordinary Double Life of General James Wilkinson* (New York: Walker, 2009), 76–78.

2. John Mack Faragher, *Daniel Boone: The Life and Legend of an American Pioneer* (New York: Holt, 1992); Gregg Cantrell, *Stephen F. Austin: Empresario of Texas* (New Haven, CT: Yale University Press, 1999).

3. Thomas Richards, "The Texas Moment: Breakaway Republics and Contested Sovereignty in North America, 1836–1846" (PhD diss., Temple University, 2016).

4. Illinois Legislature, "An Act to Incorporate the City of Nauvoo," November 16, 1840, MS 3404, Church History Library, Church of Jesus Christ of Latter-day Saints, Salt Lake City, Utah.

5. Robert Bruce Flanders, *Nauvoo: Kingdom on the Mississippi* (Urbana: University of Illinois Press, 1965), 92–99.

6. Flanders, *Nauvoo*, 100.

7. David L. Bigler, *Forgotten Kingdom: The Mormon Theocracy in the American West, 1847–1896* (1998; repr. Spokane, WA: Arthur H. Clark, 2005), 28; Flanders, *Nauvoo*, 110–14.

8. Richard Lyman Bushman, *Joseph Smith: Rough Stone Rolling; A Cultural Biography of Mormonism's Founder* (New York: Vintage Books, 2007), 384–85.

9. "Volume Introduction: The Council of Fifty in Nauvoo, Illinois," in *The Joseph Smith Papers: Administrative Records; Council of Fifty, Minutes, March 1844–January 1846*, ed. Matthew J. Grow, Ronald K. Esplin, Mark Ashurst-McGee, Gerritt J. Dirkmaat, and Jeffrey D. Mahas (Salt Lake City, UT: Church Historian's Press, 2016), xxiii, xxxiv (hereafter cited as *JSP: Council of Fifty, Minutes*).

10. The term "shadow government" is ubiquitous. See Bushman, *Joseph Smith*, 521; Flanders, *Nauvoo*, 292; David Vaughn Mason, *Brigham Young: Sovereign in America* (New York: Routledge, Taylor and Francis Group, 2015), 49.

11. *JSP: Council of Fifty Minutes*, xxiii.

12. See, for instance, Sidney Rigdon's speech in *Times and Seasons* (May 1, 1844): 524.

13. *JSP: Council of Fifty Minutes*, xxxvi.

14. George Miller, *Correspondence of Bishop George Miller with the Northern Islander* (N.p.: n.p., 1855), 20.

15. Richards, "Texas Moment"; Andrés Reséndez, *Changing National Identities at the Frontiers: Texas and New Mexico, 1800–1850* (New York: Cambridge University Press, 2005); Anne Hyde, *Empires, Nations, and Families: A History of the North American West, 1800–1860* (Lincoln: University of Nebraska Press, 2011); Pekka Hämäläinen, *The Comanche Empire* (New Haven, CT: Yale University Press, 2008).

16. Michael Scott Van Wagenen, *The Texas Republic and the Mormon Kingdom of God* (College Station: Texas A&M Press, 2002), 3.

17. Joseph Smith, Memorial to Congress, March 25, 1844, House Committee on Public Lands file for the 44th Cong., 1st Sess. (1844), RG 233, National Archives, Washington, DC. My thanks to Brent M. Rogers for passing along a copy of this source.

18. Orson Hyde to the Council of the Church of Jesus Christ of Latter Day Saints, April 25, 1844, in MS 1511, box 3, folder 6, Joseph Smith Collection, Church History Library, Church of Jesus Christ of Latter-day Saints, Salt Lake City, Utah (hereafter cited as Joseph Smith Collection, CHL), accessed August 19, 2017, http://www.josephsmithpapers.org/paper-summary/letter-from-orson-hyde-25-april-1844/1.

19. Joseph Smith, journal entry, February 20, 1844, in *The Joseph Smith Papers: Journals*, vol. 3., *May 1843–June 1844*, ed. Andrew H. Hedges, Alex D. Smith, and Brent M. Rogers (Salt Lake City, UT: Church Historian's Press, 2015), 180.

20. Lyman Wight to the First Presidency and the Quorum of the Twelve Apostles of the Church of Jesus Christ of Latter-day Saints, February 15, 1844, MS 155, box 3, folder 6, Joseph Smith Collection, CHL.

21. Council of Fifty, Minutes, March 11, 1844, in *JSP: Council of Fifty, Minutes*, 40.

22. Orson Hyde to the Council of the Church of Jesus Christ of Latter Day Saints, April 25, 1844, MS 155, box 3, folder 6, Joseph Smith Collection, CHL, accessed August 19, 2017, http://www.josephsmithpapers.org/paper-summary/letter-from-orson-hyde-25-april-1844/6.

23. For a description of the events leading up to Joseph Smith's death, see Bushman, *Joseph Smith*, 540–50.

24. John G. Turner, *Brigham Young: Pioneer Prophet* (Cambridge: Belknap Press of Harvard University Press, 2012), 116–17; Mason, *Brigham Young*, 50–51.

25. J. C. Little to the president, June 1, 1846, from a copy by George Q. Cannon in the Brigham Young Collection, Archives of the Historical Department of the Church of Jesus Christ of Latter-day Saints, Salt Lake City, Utah, as reprinted in David L. Bigler and Will Bagley, eds., *Army of Israel: Mormon Battalion Narratives* (Logan: Utah State University Press, 2000), 34.

26. J. C. Little to the president, June 1, 1846, 34.

27. Milo Milton Quaife, ed., *The Diary of James K. Polk during His Presidency, 1845 to 1849*, 4 vols. (Chicago: A. C. McClurg, 1910), 1:443–50, as reprinted in Bigler and Bagley, *Army of Israel*, 36.

28. Bigler and Bagley, *Army of Israel*, 37.

29. Bigler and Bagley, *Army of Israel*.

30. Bigler and Bagley, *Army of Israel*, 22–29.

31. Richards, "Texas Moment," 339–410; John Mack Faragher, *Eternity Street: Violence and Justice in Frontier Los Angeles* (New York: W. W. Norton, 2016), 69; Albert L. Hurtado, *John Sutter: A Life on the North American Frontier* (Norman: University of Oklahoma Press, 2008).

32. Howard Roberts Lamar, *The Far Southwest, 1846–1912: A Territorial History* (New Haven, CT: Yale University Press, 1966); Richard White, *It's Your Misfortune and None of My Own: A History of the American West* (Norman: University of Oklahoma Press, 1991); Faragher, *Eternity Street*; Kent D. Richards, *Isaac I. Stevens: Young Man in a Hurry* (Pullman: Washington State University Press, 1993).

33. Brent M. Rogers, *Unpopular Sovereignty: Mormons and the Federal Management of Early Utah Territory* (Lincoln: University of Nebraska Press, 2017).

34. As Brent M. Rogers has emphasized, Mormons were particularly attuned to the importance of states' rights because of federal officials' repeated refusal to intervene to protect Mormons from state authorities in Missouri and Illinois. Rogers, *Unpopular Sovereignty*, 25–29.

35. David L. Bigler and Will Bagley, *The Mormon Rebellion: America's First Civil War, 1857–1858* (Norman: University of Oklahoma Press, 2011), 35–36; Jeffrey Ogden Johnson, "Deseret, State of," in *Encyclopedia of Mormonism*, vol. 1, *The History, Scripture, Doctrine and Procedure of the Church of Jesus Christ of Latter-day Saints*, ed. Daniel H. Ludlow (New York: Macmillan, 1992), 371.

36. Rogers, *Unpopular Sovereignty*, 39; Richards, "Texas Moment," 411–72.

37. John F. Burns, "Taming the Elephant: An Introduction to California's Statehood and Constitutional Era," in *Taming the Elephant: Politics, Government, and Law in Pioneer California*, ed. John F. Burns and Richard J. Orsi (Berkeley: University of California Press, 2003), 6–7.

38. Allan Kent Powell, "Utah Territory," in *Encyclopedia of Mormonism*, vol. 1, 1503.

39. Bigler, *Forgotten Kingdom*, 50.

40. Bigler and Bagley, *Mormon Rebellion*, 33–34.

41. Bigler and Bagley, *Mormon Rebellion*, 43.

42. "Report of Messrs. Brandebury, Brocchus, and Harris, to the President of the United States," December 19, 1851, in H.R. Ex. Doc. 25, "Message from the President of the United States, transmitting information in reference to the condition of affairs in the Territory of Utah," 32nd Cong, 1st Sess., January 9, 1852, 11.

43. Rogers, *Unpopular Sovereignty*, 46–48, 100.

44. Turner, *Brigham Young*, 262; Faragher, *Eternity Street*; Nancy J. Taniguchi, *Dirty Deeds: Land, Violence, and the 1856 San Francisco Vigilance Committee* (Norman: University of Oklahoma Press, 2016); Susan Lee Johnson, *Roaring Camp: The Social World of the California Gold Rush* (New York: W. W. Norton, 2000).

45. Rogers, *Unpopular Sovereignty*, 97–134.

46. Brendan C. Lindsay, *Murder State: California's Native American Genocide* (Lincoln: University of Nebraska Press, 2012); Benjamin Madley, *An American Genocide: The United States and the California Indian Catastrophe, 1846–1873* (New Haven, CT: Yale University Press, 2016).

47. Andrés Reséndez, *The Other Slavery: The Uncovered History of Indian Slavery in America* (New York: Houghton, Mifflin, Harcourt, 2016), 277–84.

48. Ari Kelman, *A Misplaced Massacre: Struggling over the Memory of Sand Creek* (Cambridge, MA: Harvard University Press, 2013); Karl Jacoby, *Shadows at Dawn: A Borderlands Massacre and the Violence of History* (New York: Penguin Press, 2008).

49. Richards, *Isaac I. Stevens*; Lamar, *Far Southwest*.

50. Brigham Young to the president, September 29, 1851, in H.R. Ex. Doc. 25, "Message from the President of the United States, transmitting information in

reference to the condition of affairs in the Territory of Utah," 32nd Cong, 1st Sess., January 9, 1852, 30.

51. Mason, *Brigham Young*, 101.

52. Eric H. Walther, *The Fire-Eaters* (Baton Rouge: Louisiana State University Press, 1992); Eric H. Walther, *William Lowndes Yancey and the Coming of the Civil War* (Chapel Hill: University of North Carolina Press, 2006); Jon L. Wakelyn, *Southern Pamphlets on Secession, November 1860–April 1861* (Chapel Hill: University of North Carolina Press, 1996).

53. See, for instance, Cong. Globe, 36th Cong., 1st Sess., pt. 1, April 16, 1860, 1728; *Sacramento (CA) Daily Union*, December 13, 1860, 2; Winfield J. Davis, *History of Political Conventions in California, 1849–1892* (Sacramento: California State Library, 1893), 129–30; Joseph Ellison, "Designs for a Pacific Republic," *Oregon Historical Quarterly* 31, no. 4 (December 1930), 319–37; Dorothy Hull, "Movement in Oregon for the Establishment of a Pacific Coast Republic," *Oregon Historical Quarterly* 17, no. 3 (September 1916): 177–200.

54. "Republican Platform of 1856," June 18, 1856, American Presidency Project, accessed July 11, 2015, http://www.presidency.ucsb.edu/ws/?pid=29619.

55. "Instructions to General W. S. Harney," June 29, 1857, reprinted in *Mormon Resistance: A Documentary Account of the Utah Expedition, 1857–1858*, ed. Leroy R. Hafen and Ann W. Hafen (1958; repr., Lincoln: University of Nebraska Press, 2005), 30.

56. James Buchanan, "First Annual Message to Congress," December 8, 1857, in *The Works of James Buchanan, Comprising His Speeches, State Papers, and Private Correspondence*, ed. John Bassett Moore, 12 vols. (New York: Antiquarian Press, 1960): 10:129–63, as excerpted in William P. MacKinnon, ed., *At Sword's Point, Part 1: A Documentary History of the Utah War to 1858* (Norman, OK: Arthur H. Clark, 2008), 483.

57. Brigham Young to the officer commanding the forces now invading Utah Territory, September 29, 1857, in H.R. Ex. Doc. 71, 35th Cong., 1st Sess., February 26, 1858, 33.

58. "Proclamation of the Governor," included in Brigham Young to the officer commanding the forces now invading Utah Territory, September 29, 1857, in H.R. Ex. Doc. 71, 35th Cong., 1st Sess., February 26, 1858, 34.

59. "Proclamation of the Governor," 34. See also Bigler and Bagley, *Mormon Rebellion*, 184.

60. For the Mountain Meadows Massacre, see David L. Bigler and Will Bagley, eds., *Innocent Blood: Essential Narratives of the Mountain Meadows Massacre* (Norman, OK: Arthur H. Clark, 2008); Juanita Brooks, *The Mountain Meadows Massacre* (Stanford, CA: Stanford University Press, 1950); Will Bagley, *Blood of the Prophets: Brigham Young and the Massacre at Mountain Meadows* (Norman: University of Oklahoma Press, 2002); and Ronald W. Walker, Richard E. Turley Jr., Glen M. Leonard, *Massacre at Mountain Meadows: An American Tragedy* (New York: Oxford University Press, 2008).

61. "Diary of Captain Phelps," in Hafen and Hafen, *Mormon Resistance*, 102, 111; Charles R. Morehead, "Recollections," 1907, app. C, *Doniphan's Expedition and the Conquest of New Mexico and California* (Topeka, KS: Crane, 1907), reprinted in MacKinnon, *At Sword's Point, Part 1*, 187–89; Hafen and Hafen, *Mormon Resistance*, 18–19.

62. Alfred Cumming to Lewis Cass, May 2, 1858, reprinted in Hafen and Hafen, *Mormon Resistance*, 308; see also 305–6.

63. Bigler and Bagley, *Mormon Rebellion*, 344–45.

64. W. P. Mack, "Utah Expedition of 1857–58, or Utah War," in *The New Encyclopedia of the American West*, ed. Howard Roberts Lamar (New Haven, CT: Yale University Press, 1998), 1150.

Chapter 12. Mormons at Midcentury

1. Matt Fitzgerald, "Chasing Beauty, Finding Grace: An Interview with David Brooks," *Christian Century*, February 1, 2017, 30.

2. Peter Novick, *That Noble Dream: The Objectivity Question and the American Historical Profession* (Cambridge: Cambridge University Press, 1988), 333: "'Consensus' became the key word in postwar attempts to produce a new interpretive framework for American history, focusing attention on what had united Americans rather than what had divided them." Novick thoroughly examines the turn to "consensus history" in his chapter which is tellingly titled, "A Convergent Culture," 320–60. For a helpful, concise discussion of the optimism of the 1950s—as well as the under-recognized challenges to that optimism during the decade—see the introduction to *The 1950s*, by William H. Young, with Nancy K. Young, American Popular Culture through History series (Westport, CT: Greenwood Press, 2004), xi–xiv.

3. On the "long fifties," see Kenneth L. Woodward, *Getting Religion: Faith, Culture, and Politics from the Age of Eisenhower to the Era of Obama* (New York: Convergent Books, 2016), 36–37; Young, *1950s*, xi. On the "golden era of Mormonism," see Bruce L. Olsen, interview by Jonice Hubbard, September 8, 2006, transcript included in Hubbard, "Pioneers in Twentieth Century Mormon Media: Oral Histories of Latter-day Saint Electronic and Public Relations Professionals" (master's thesis, Brigham Young University, 2007), 121; accessible online at scholarsarchive.byu.edu/cgi/viewcontent.cgi?article=2255&context=etd. Olsen retired in 2008 as the managing director of the church's Public Affairs Department. See also Matthew Bowman, *The Mormon People: The Making of an American Faith* (New York: Random House, 2012), 154: "In seeking common ground with Progressive America, Mormons drained from their faith the apocalyptic utopianism of the dusty Great Basin frontier and made of it a church more American, but also no less Mormon. They did not understand themselves to be compromising or assimilating their faith; rather, they believed that what they found in America gave them new ways to express its possibilities. That they became in the fifty years after the Manifesto a model American minority was a happy side effect."

4. See Woodward, *Getting Religion*, 36–64. Compare William Chafe's argument that the 1950s are best characterized by the complexities of the paradoxes of the age. See Chafe, "The Paradox of Change: American Society in the Postwar Years," in *The Unfinished Journey: America since World War II* (New York: Oxford University Press, 1999), 111–45.

5. The two quotes come from "This Is the Place," *Newsweek*, July 28, 1947, 73; and "This Is the Place," *Christian Science Monitor*, July 24, 1947, 18.

6. Novick, *That Noble Dream*, 321.

7. Chafe, *Unfinished Journey*, 77–78. Public opinion about the Soviet Union changed—and crystallized—very quickly in the months surrounding the announcement of the Truman Doctrine. Chafe writes: "In late 1946 and early 1947 the

American people were still divided over the possibility of seeking an accommodation with the Soviet Union. Over 70 percent, according to a Gallup Poll, supported Harry Wallace's call in September for pursuing more friendly policies toward the Russians. Another Gallup Poll, taken a year later, showed that 76 percent of the nation believed that Russia was out to rule the world, and that 63 percent expected a full-scale war within the next twenty-five years" (109). Chafe also quotes a prayer offered by FBI director J. Edgar Hoover that "the Supreme architect will give us the strength, wisdom, and guidance to triumph against the onrush of Red fascism and atheistic communism" (109). Compare also Patrick Allitt, *Religion in America since 1945: A History* (New York: Columbia University Press, 2003), especially his section "Fighting Godless Communism," 21–26.

8. For a helpful sampling of contemporary writings by prominent religious voices in the 1950s that speak to national apprehensions about communism, see "Mainline Religion and the Cold War," in *The Columbia Documentary History of Religion in America since 1945*, ed. Paul Harvey and Philip Goff (New York: Columbia University Press, 2005), 3–40.

9. Patrick Henry, "'And I Don't Care What It Is': The Tradition-History of a Civil Religion Proof-Text," *Journal of the American Academy of Religion* 49, no. 1 (1981): 35–47. Compare Woodward, *Getting Religion*, 45.

10. Mark A. Noll, *A History of Christianity in the United States and Canada* (Grand Rapids, MI: William B. Eerdmans, 1992), 437.

11. Edwin Gaustad and Leigh Schmidt, *The Religious History of America*, rev. ed. (San Francisco, CA: HarperSanFrancisco, 2002), 335.

12. Woodward, *Getting Religion*, 44.

13. Robert D. Putnam and David E. Campbell, *American Grace: How Religion Divides and Unites Us* (New York: Simon and Schuster, 2010), 82–83, 88.

14. Harvey and Goff, *Columbia Documentary History of Religion in America since 1945*, 4–5.

15. Putnam and Campbell, *American Grace*, 82–83, 88.

16. Harvey and Goff, *Columbia Documentary History of Religion in America since 1945*, 5–6. Harvey and Goff also note another example of the far-reaching impact of the convergence of religion and anticommunism in the period: "The rapid rise of evangelicalism and Pentecostalism is clearly connected to American fears surrounding the Cold War. Billy Graham, the foremost global evangelist of the twentieth century, earned his worldwide fame by catching the attention of virulently anticommunist publisher William Randolph Hearst through his attacks on communism's spiritual bankruptcy. Hearst instructed his editors to 'puff Graham,' and soon the North Carolina preacher's face covered *Time* magazine and other national publications" (3). On Billy Graham's anticommunism, and Hearst's publicity efforts, see also Grant Wacker, *America's Pastor: Billy Graham and the Shaping of a Nation* (Cambridge, MA: Belknap Press of Harvard University Press, 2014), 72–75, and 231–34.

17. Woodward, *Getting Religion*, 45.

18. Kevin Schultz, *Tri-Faith America: How Catholics and Jews Held Postwar America to Its Protestant Promise* (New York: Oxford University Press, 2011).

19. Colleen McDannell, *The Spirit of Vatican II: A History of Catholic Reform in America* (New York: Basic Books, 2011), 31.

20. See Allitt, *Religion in America since 1945*, 44–47.

21. St. Clair Drake and Horace R. Cayton, "The Churches of Bronzeville," an excerpt from *Black Metropolis: A Study of Negro Life in a Northern City*, reprinted in *African American Religious History: A Documentary Witness*, ed. Milton C. Sernett, 2nd ed. (Durham, NC: Duke University Press, 1999), 435–37.

22. Schultz, *Tri-Faith America*, 8.

23. Michael Battle, *The Black Church in America: African American Christian Spirituality* (Malden, MA: Blackwell, 2007), 127.

24. See Edward Blum on the work of the historian Taylor Branch, in Blum's historiographical essay, "Religion, Race, and African American Life," in *The Columbia Guide to Religion in American History*, ed. Paul Harvey and Edward J. Blum (New York: Columbia University Press, 2012), 231. For a nuanced view—and corrective—about proponents of the social gospel being attentive to issues of racial inequality, see Paul Harvey, *Bounds of Their Habitation: Race and Religion in American History* (Lanham, MD: Rowman and Littlefield, 2017), 141–42, 159–60.

25. Martin Luther King Jr.'s "Letter from Birmingham Jail—April 16, 1963," is reprinted in Sernett, *African American Religious History*, 519–35.

26. Compare Thomas F. O'Dea, "Sources of Strains and Conflict," in *The Mormons* (Chicago: University of Chicago Press, 1957), 222–57, with this follow-up essay: Thomas F. O'Dea, "Sources of Strain in Mormon History Reconsidered," in *Mormonism and American Culture*, ed. Marvin S. Hill and James B. Allen (New York: Harper and Row, 1972), 147–67. The bulk of O'Dea's later essay dealt with mounting national attention and criticism—and internal church discussion—of the Latter-day Saints' race-based restrictions for temple and priesthood participation. The contrast in O'Dea's two works speaks, too, to changes in the general American consciousness around civil rights in the decade and a half that separated the two publications.

27. See Allit, *Religion in America since 1945*, 59: "African American activists in the 1950s and early 1960s used their religion to support their claim to first-class citizenship. American Mormons, by contrast, had endured a long struggle to establish the principle that they were entitled to first-class citizenship *despite* their religion. Their religion was exactly what most other Americans hated, especially in the nineteenth century. Nevertheless, by the mid-twentieth century, the Mormons had found a way to reconcile their faith with wholehearted participation in American life." For crucial analysis of the development and explication of race-based aspects of Latter-day Saint theology and practice, as well as analysis of how Latter-day Saints were integrated into the mainstream of white America after their nineteenth-century struggles over such acceptance, see W. Paul Reeve, *Religion of a Different Culture: Race and the Struggle for Whiteness* (New York: Oxford University Press, 2015).

28. Schultz opens his book with a retelling of the *Dorchester* episode and its impact in American popular culture—and its later connection to religious opposition to John F. Kennedy's presidential campaign. See *Tri-Faith America*, 3–7.

29. Putnam and Campbell, *American Grace*, 88. Compare Woodward, *Getting Religion*, 45.

30. The sociologist Herbert Gans was studying suburban Levittown, New Jersey; he is quoted in Schultz, *Tri-Faith America*, 101.

31. See Neil J. Young, *We Gather Together: The Religious Right and the Problem of Interfaith Politics* (New York: Oxford University Press, 2016), 9–13, for an overview of

how Mormons, Catholics, and evangelical Christians often remained disinterested in ecumenical moves in the 1940s and 1950s.

32. Schultz, *Tri-Faith America*, 8.

33. This was the title of a letter that Daniel Poling wrote to honor his son, one of the four fallen chaplains, and his fellow chaplains. In Schultz, *Tri-Faith America*, 4.

34. "This Is the Place," *Newsweek*, July 28, 1947, 72.

35. Schultz, *Tri-Faith America*, 178; see also Young, *We Gather Together*, 10.

36. "This Is the Place," *Christian Science Monitor*, July 24, 1947, 18.

37. "This Is the Place," *Newsweek*, July 28, 1947, 72. Compare Fawn M. Brodie, "Polygamy Shocks the Mormons," *American Mercury* (April 1946): 399–404. The focus of the lengthy article was the degree to which the Church of Jesus Christ of Latter-day Saints had officially distanced itself from polygamy, illustrated starkly for Brodie by strong Mormon support for the conviction of fifteen fundamentalist polygamists in Salt Lake City in June 1944.

38. "What It's Like to Be Mormon," *Los Angeles Times*, July 20, 1947, 21.

39. For another example, only a few years earlier, of downplaying Mormon theological distinctiveness (in this case, polygamy) in favor of highlighting contemporary American values, see James D'Arc, "Darryl F. Zanuck's *Brigham Young*: A Film in Context," *BYU Studies* 29, no. 1 (Winter 1989): 5–33. D'Arc's thoughtful contextualization of this landmark 1940 Hollywood film shows that both church president Heber J. Grant and film critics nationwide praised the film, primarily for the way it spoke to contemporary issues, especially the importance of religious liberty. One review, cited by D'Arc, said: "It is difficult for us to believe that they [Mormons] were persecuted in Missouri and Illinois with the savage bigotry of present-day Nazism, but such was the case" (26). The *New York Mirror*'s review of the film recommended that "those officials of various towns who have been chasing out that fantastic sect known as 'Jehovah's Witnesses'" should watch "Brigham Young's defense speech at Joseph Smith's trial for treason. It's the kind of Americanism that some of us are sometimes inclined to forget" (27). Polygamy made its appearance in the film, but it was intentionally a minor plotline. D'Arc notes that Zanuck was initially worried that polygamy would make the film an impossibility because government censors would not allow that subject to appear in a movie at all. Yet, in the end, D'Arc concludes, "the matter of polygamy seemed to be an insuperable obstacle, even to Zanuck, until he was convinced that another element—the theme of religious or racial tolerance—outweighed the liabilities" (28).

40. Ruth H. Chadwick, "Children's Arts and Crafts Honor Pioneers of North America," *School Arts*, October 1947, 57.

41. Noll, *A History of Christianity in the United States and Canada*, 440. Matthew Bowman, in *Mormon People*, 186, noted that church president David O. McKay published the book *Secrets of a Happy Life* in 1960—and "it was no mistake that all these men wrote books with basically interchangeable titles."

42. Harvey and Goff, *Columbia Documentary History of Religion in America since 1945*, 40.

43. Matthew S. Hedstrom, *The Rise of Liberal Religion: Book Culture and American Spirituality in the Twentieth Century* (New York: Oxford University Press, 2013), 212.

44. "What It's Like to Be Mormon," *Los Angeles Times*, July 20, 1947, 5.

45. Thomas G. Alexander, *Mormonism in Transition: A History of the Latter-day Saints, 1890–1930*, Illini Books ed. (Urbana: University of Illinois Press, 1996), 307.

46. Jan Shipps, "From Satyr to Saint: American Perceptions of the Mormons, 1860–1960," in *Sojourner in the Promised Land: Forty Years among the Mormons* (Urbana: University of Illinois Press, 2000), 68–70.

47. On the "anti–New Dealer's sweetest dream," see "Tithes and Security," *Time*, August 1, 1938, 26.

48. "What It's Like to Be Mormon," *Los Angeles Times*, July 20, 1947, 5.

49. For a retelling of Capehart's statement in the context of the time—the same month as Joseph McCarthy's initial anticommunism speech in Wheeling, West Virginia, in February 1950—see Haynes Johnson, *The Age of Anxiety: McCarthyism to Terrorism* (New York: Harcourt, 2005), 14. In elections later that year, Republicans would gain five Senate seats, campaigning against what they saw as Democratic efforts to promote socialism.

50. "What It's Like to Be Mormon," *Los Angeles Times*, July 20, 1947, 5.

51. "A Peculiar People," *Time*, July 21, 1947, 18, 20.

52. "Peculiar People," 19.

53. "Peculiar People," 20–21.

54. "Peculiar People," 18, 21.

55. "What It's Like to Be Mormon," *Los Angeles Times*, July 20, 1947, 5.

56. See Kathleen Flake's study of the broad implications of the Reed Smoot episode, *The Politics of American Religious Identity: The Seating of Senator Reed Smoot, Mormon Apostle* (Chapel Hill: University of North Carolina Press, 2004).

57. Thomas Ford and Thomas Sharp are both quoted in Richard Lyman Bushman, *Joseph Smith: Rough Stone Rolling; A Cultural Biography of Mormonism's Founder* (New York: Alfred A. Knopf, 2005), 428–29, 509.

58. For a helpful overview of the religious and political philosophy behind Joseph Smith's notion of "theodemocracy," as well as the ways that philosophy was embodied organizationally in the Council of Fifty, see "Volume Introduction: The Council of Fifty in Nauvoo, Illinois," in *The Joseph Smith Papers: Administrative Records; Council of Fifty, Minutes, March 1844–January 1846*, ed. Matthew J. Grow, Ronald K. Esplin, Mark Ashurst-McGee, Gerrit J. Dirkmaat, and Jeffrey D. Mahas (Salt Lake City, UT: Church Historian's Press, 2016), xxiii–xlv.

59. Alexander, *Mormonism in Transition*, 16.

60. For important discussion about the stops and starts, especially behind the scenes, as Latter-day Saint church officials navigated the change from open political involvement to a more pronounced political neutrality, see the first three chapters of Alexander, *Mormonism in Transition*, 3–59; also D. Michael Quinn, *The Mormon Hierarchy: Extensions of Power* (Salt Lake City, UT: Signature Books, 1997).

61. This excerpt from the *Springfield (MA) Union* is quoted in Dean L. May, *Utah: A People's History* (Salt Lake City: University of Utah, 1987), 127. The article was apparently reprinted in the February 15, 1885 edition of the *Salt Lake Tribune*.

62. Fawn M. Brodie, "'This Is the Place'—and It Became Utah," *New York Times Magazine*, July 20, 1947, 14; italics mine.

63. Carey McWilliams, "Memo on the Mormons," *Nation*, January 26, 1946, 97–98. There were even subtle signs in this era that Latter-day Saints generated

less concern in some public opinion quarters than did Roman Catholics. A number of factors were certainly at work here. In 1950 there were thirty times as many Catholics in the United States as there were Mormons. The vast majority of Mormons lived in the Intermountain West. Sheer size and demographic distribution made the Catholic presence—and potential for power—far more visible, and thus, in some minds, more menacing. Importantly, though, many Americans saw Roman Catholicism as an immigrant church, with Catholic loyalty to a foreign pope as a threat to American sovereignty. Issues of race and ethnicity surrounded Catholics in a way that no longer seemed to be the case for Mormons, despite their nineteenth-century struggles over such acceptance. For Mormonism's twentieth-century place in American racial conceptions, see the concluding chapter of Reeve, *Religion of a Different Culture*, 247–72. In this new post–World War II "tri-faith America," Catholics were certainly enjoying social and cultural prominence in the United States as never before. Yet Norman Vincent Peale, one of America's most influential Protestant ministers, was outspoken in his opposition to the presidential candidacy of John F. Kennedy, a Catholic, on religious grounds—as were many of Peale's Protestant colleagues. No Mormon ran for president in this "long fifties" era, so it is impossible to know if such a candidate would have generated comparable opposition. Still, Norman Vincent Peale did not express any similar concerns about Mormons. In fact, he paid public tribute to church president David O. McKay. See Mary Jane Woodger, *David O. McKay: Beloved Prophet* (American Fork, UT: Covenant, 2004), 228–32, for quoted tributes from Peale and others. The prominence of personal and family religiosity in the public profile of Latter-day Saint apostle Ezra Taft Benson during his years as secretary of agriculture in the Eisenhower cabinet suggests that there seemed to be little public discomfort vocalized against Mormonism. See Sheri L. Dew, *Ezra Taft Benson: A Biography* (Salt Lake City, UT: Deseret Book, 1987), 297–98, for reaction to the Benson's "family home evening" on the Edward Murrow show, *Person to Person*, in 1954. Benson's wife, Flora, told Murrow: "We have daily prayer—individual and together—because we feel that a family that prays together stays together. I feel that's true of the nation." Dew reports that "Eisenhower told Ezra: 'Besides all the rest of it, it was the best political show you could have put on.'" Benson received a letter that speaks, perhaps, to this sense of persistent anti-Catholicism. The writer said: "May a Catholic priest tell you and your family how inspiring and wholesome your visit was via television tonight? I never expect to live to see one of my own faith elected President. I would like to see candidates of your timber, and indeed you would be assured of my vote" (Dew, *Ezra Taft Benson*, 298). George Romney, a Latter-day Saint, did run for president in 1967–68, and there was very little opposition to his candidacy on the grounds of his Mormonism. It is likely that one effect of Kennedy's election was to diminish the public appetite—and approval—for open opposition to presidential candidates based on their religious identity. On the role of religion in presidential politics—including the opposition to John F. Kennedy on the part of Peale, W. A. Criswell, Paul Blanshard, and others—see Randall Balmer, *God in the White House: A History; How Faith Shaped the Presidency from John F. Kennedy to George W. Bush* (New York: HarperOne, 2008), 10–12, 25–32. See also Allitt, *Religion in America since 1945*, 65: "Anti-Catholicism was widespread in America during the 1940s and 1950s, and socially respectable too." For the reaction to George Romney's presidential campaign, see chapter 2 of J. B. Haws, *The Mormon Image in the American Mind: Fifty Years of Public Perception* (New York: Oxford University Press, 2013), 12–46.

64. "Peculiar People."

65. Brodie, "'This Is the Place'—and It Became Utah," 14.

66. "This Is the Place," *Newsweek*, July 28, 1947, 73.

67. On the increase in expressed anxiety about the potential for Mormon political power during the campaign for the Equal Rights Amendment in the 1970s, as well as a public resurgence of anti-Mormonism from conservative Christians in the 1980s, see chapters 4 and 5 of Haws, *Mormon Image in the American Mind*.

68. On Chiung Hwang Chen and Ethan Yorgason's important survey, see "'Those Amazing Mormons': The Media's Construction of Latter-day Saints as a Model Minority," *Dialogue: A Journal of Mormon Thought* 32, no. 2 (Summer 1999): 107–28.

69. Armand L. Mauss, *The Angel and the Beehive: The Mormon Struggle with Assimilation* (Urbana: University of Illinois Press, 1994), ix–xiii; Terryl Givens on part two of *The Mormons*; transcript accessible at http://www.pbs.org/mormons/interviews/givens.html.

Chapter 13. The Historic Conflicts of Our Time

1. Wallace F. Bennett, "The Story behind the Attacks on Secretary Benson," speech delivered to Salt Lake Rotary Club, October 27, 1953, 9, J. Reuben Clark Papers, L. Tom Perry Special Collections, Harold B. Lee Library, Brigham Young University (hereafter cited as Perry Special Collections, Lee Library, BYU).

2. Benson appeared on the cover of *U.S. News and World Report* on March 6, 1953, *Newsweek* on November 30, 1953, and *Time* on April 13, 1953, and May 7, 1956.

3. See Ezra Taft Benson, *Cross Fire: The Eight Years with Eisenhower* (Garden City, NJ: Doubleday, 1962).

4. See Jan Shipps, "From Satyr to Saint: American Perceptions of the Mormons, 1860–1960," in *Sojourner in the Promised Land: Forty Years among the Mormons* (Urbana: University of Illinois Press, 2000), 51–97; and Shipps, "Mormon Ethnicity as Reality and Metaphor," in *Directions for Mormon Studies in the Twenty-First Century*, ed. Patrick Q. Mason (Salt Lake City: University of Utah Press, 2016), 40–42.

5. See Armand L. Mauss, *The Angel and the Beehive: The Mormon Struggle with Assimilation* (Urbana: University of Illinois Press, 1994).

6. See Robert D. Putnam and David E. Campbell, *American Grace: How Religion Divides and Unites Us* (New York: Simon and Schuster, 2010), chaps. 3–4.

7. David Sehat, *The Myth of American Religious Freedom* (New York: Oxford University Press, 2011), quote on 5.

8. On this period in Mormon history, see Gregory A. Prince and William Robert Wright, *David O. McKay and the Rise of Modern Mormonism* (Salt Lake City: University of Utah Press, 2005); and Matthew Bowman, *The Mormon People: The Making of an American Faith* (New York: Random House, 2012), chap. 7.

9. David H. Smith, "World Religious Leader Asks Preparation for God's Reign," *Argus-Leader* (Sioux Falls, SD), September 14, 1951, 3; "Latter Day Saints Meet in Marianna Tuesday Evening," *Panama City (FL) News-Herald*, November 25, 1951, 13.

10. "Latest Cabinet Choice Is Mormon Leader and Former Executive of National Farm Co-Op Council," *St. Louis (MO) Post-Dispatch*, November 24, 1952, 1; "Utah Man Gets Agriculture Secretary Job," *Fresno (CA) Bee*, November 24, 1952, 1; "Rumor Cabinet Post for Benson in United States," *Lethbridge (AB) Herald*, November 24, 1952, 10.

11. Harold H. Martin, "Elder Benson's Going to Catch It!," *Saturday Evening Post*, March 28, 1953, 22–23, 110–13.

12. "Apostle at Work," *Time*, April 13, 1953.

13. Louis Bromfield, "Benson Appointment Is Boon to Country," *Cincinnati (OH) Enquirer*, December 14, 1952, 84.

14. "New Secretary of Agriculture Defender of Free Enterprise," *Times Standard* (Eureka, CA), December 30, 1952, 7.

15. The secretary of agriculture was placed seventh in the 1947 Presidential Succession Act.

16. The Utah state legislature sent Reed Smoot, a junior member of the church's Quorum of the Twelve Apostles, to Washington as a US senator in 1903 (the Seventeenth Amendment, providing for the direct election of senators, was not ratified until 1913). Smoot's election prompted a firestorm of controversy from people across the nation who were still suspicious of Mormonism. The Senate hearings, which lasted for four years, once again shone a national spotlight on Mormon political power, temple ceremonies, and the continuation of secret plural marriages. As a result, the church president Joseph F. Smith issued a second "Manifesto" putting an end to plural marriage, two intransigent apostles were removed from their offices (one was excommunicated), and the church affirmed its commitment to civic loyalty and democratic politics. The Senate confirmed Smoot's election in 1907. See Kathleen Flake, *The Politics of American Religious Identity: The Seating of Senator Reed Smoot, Mormon Apostle* (Chapel Hill: University of North Carolina Press, 2004).

17. On the development of twentieth-century First Amendment jurisprudence, see Sarah Barringer Gordon, *The Spirit of the Law: Religious Voices and the Constitution in Modern America* (Cambridge, MA: Belknap Press of Harvard University Press, 2010). On religion and public life in the Eisenhower era, see Kevin M. Kruse, *One Nation under God: How Corporate America Invented Christian America* (New York: Basic Books, 2015).

18. "Appointment to Cabinet Unexpected, Benson Says," *Los Angeles Times*, November 25, 1952, 9; see also Doctrine and Covenants 101:80.

19. See Ethan R. Yorgason, *Transformation of the Mormon Culture Region* (Urbana: University of Illinois Press, 2003), chap. 4.

20. See "The Mormons," *Democrat and Chronicle* (Rochester, NY), August 8, 1953, 6; and Frank White, "Salt Lake Mormon Temple Is Popular," *Franklin (IN) Evening Star*, August 5, 1958, 1.

21. Arnold Mulder, "Library Adventures," *Holland (MI) Evening Sentinel*, May 3, 1958, 12. On the notion of twentieth-century Mormon scattering and its impact on public perceptions, see Shipps, *Sojourner in the Promised Land*, 98–99.

22. "Apostle at Work," *Time*, April 13, 1953.

23. *New York Daily News*, May 24, 1954.

24. Rev. M. L. Oswalt, *Pen Pictures of Mormonism* (Philadelphia, PA: American Baptist Publication Society, 1899), 8; "The Course to Pursue," *Atlanta (GA) Constitution*,

February 16, 1900. See Patrick Q. Mason, *The Mormon Menace: Violence and Anti-Mormonism in the Postbellum South* (New York: Oxford University Press, 2011), esp. 62–68; and Christine Talbot, *A Foreign Kingdom: Mormons and Polygamy in American Political Culture, 1852–1890* (Urbana: University of Illinois Press, 2013), esp. chap. 4.

25. Grant Salisbury and Warren K. Leffler, "A Church Service in Soviet Russia," *U.S. News and World Report*, October 26, 1959, 76. See also Reid L. Neilson, "A Light in the Darkness: Apostle Ezra Taft Benson's 1959 Sermon at Moscow's Central Baptist Church," in *The Worldwide Church: Mormonism as a Global Religion*, ed. Michael A. Goodman and Mauro Properzi (Provo, UT: Religious Studies Center and Deseret Book, 2016), 165–84.

26. Mauss, *Angel and the Beehive*, 77, 79.

27. Jan Shipps, "Surveying the Mormon Image since 1960," in *Sojourner in the Promised Land*, 100.

28. J. B. Haws, *The Mormon Image in the American Mind: Fifty Years of Public Perception* (New York: Oxford University Press, 2013), 10–11.

29. See Lisa McGirr, *Suburban Warriors: The Origins of the New American Right* (Princeton, NJ: Princeton University Press, 2001); and Darren Dochuk, *From Bible Belt to Sun Belt: Plain-Folk Religion, Grassroots Politics, and the Rise of Evangelical Conservatism* (New York: W. W. Norton, 2011).

30. See Neil J. Young, *We Gather Together: The Religious Right and the Problem of Interfaith Politics* (New York: Oxford University Press, 2015); and Matthew Bowman, "The Evangelical Countercult Movement and Mormon Conservatism," in *Out of Obscurity: Mormonism since 1945*, ed. Patrick Q. Mason and John G. Turner (New York: Oxford University Press, 2016), 259–77.

31. "Benson-Birch Tie Disturbs Utahans," *New York Times*, November 4, 1962; Ezra Taft Benson, "An Internal Threat Today," box 165, folder 3, Ernest L. Wilkinson Papers, Special Collections, Lee Library, BYU, 17; "Benson Calls Birch Society a Leader in Fight on Reds," *New York Times*, January 16, 1966; Ezra Taft Benson, "Stand Up for Freedom," address given at Assembly Hall, Temple Square, Salt Lake City, Utah, February 11, 1966, Perry Special Collections, Lee Library, BYU, 13.

32. See Gregory A. Prince, "The Red Peril, the Candy Maker, and the Apostle: David O. McKay's Confrontation with Communism," *Dialogue: A Journal of Mormon Thought* 37, no. 2 (Summer 2004): 37–94; and D. Michael Quinn, "Ezra Taft Benson: A Study of Inter-Quorum Conflict," in *The Mormon Hierarchy: Extensions of Power* (Salt Lake City, UT: Signature Books, 1997), 66–115.

33. "Benson-Birch Tie Disturbs Utahans," *New York Times*, November 4, 1962; *Statesman Journal* (Salem, OR), March 19, 1966, 4; "Birch Dinner in Salt Lake City Vexes Mormons," *New York Times*, April 8, 1966.

34. "Birch Society Aim Hailed by Benson," *New York Times*, September 24, 1963.

35. Drew Pearson, "Mormon Elders Said Disavowing McKay Liberalism," *Orlando (FL) Sentinel*, October 16, 1966, 8.

36. Ralph Harding, "Ezra Taft Benson's Support of John Birch Society Is Criticized," September 25, 1963, *Congressional Record: Proceedings and Debates of the 88th Congress, First Session* (Washington, DC: Government Printing Office, 1963); "Mormon Mulligan," *Idaho State Journal* (Pocatello), September 30, 1963; "Ike and Mormons Slap Benson's Birch Views," *Kansas City (MO) Times*, February 21, 1964, 29.

37. "Benson Is Sought for Ticket in '68," *New York Times*, May 8, 1966.

38. Wallace Turner, "Liberals Seek Voice in Growing Mormon Church," *Kansas City (MO) Times*, December 31, 1965, 26; Charles O. Gridley, "Will Church Involve GOP?," *Lawton (OK) Constitution*, August 17, 1966, 12.

39. Arlen J. Large, "Mormons and Politics," *Wall Street Journal*, August 8, 1966, 1.

40. "Integration Foes Booming Wallace," *New York Times*, September 5, 1971.

41. "Support for Candidate Possible Some Day, LDS Apostle Says," *Salt Lake Tribune*, February 22, 1974.

42. Russell Chandler, "Mormons: New Test of Their Faith," *Los Angeles Times*, June 26, 1983.

43. "Bleak Future Seen as Mormonism Grows," *Chicago Tribune*, November 7, 1984, 35.

44. Muriel Dobbin, "Conservative Seeking Leadership Worries Some Mormons," *Baltimore Sun*, December 11, 1983.

45. Vern Anderson, "Many Fear Benson as Mormon Chief," *Nashville Tennessean*, November 10, 1985, 17.

46. See David E. Campbell, John C. Green, and J. Quin Monson, *Seeking the Promised Land: Mormons and American Politics* (New York: Cambridge University Press, 2014), 80–86.

47. Daniel T. Rodgers, *Age of Fracture* (Cambridge, MA: Belknap Press of Harvard University Press, 2011).

48. Speech by George Putnam, Salt Lake City, UT, 15 Dec. 1963, Box 214, Folder 1, Ernest L. Wilkinson Papers, Perry Special Collections, Lee Library, BYU.

49. Pew Research Forum, "Views of the Mormon Religion," November 23 2011, http://www.pewforum.org/2011/11/23/romneys-mormon-faith-views-of-the-mormon-religion.

50. Ezra Taft Benson, "Fourteen Fundamentals in Following the Prophet," *Liahona* (June 1981), accessed February 18, 2017, https://www.lds.org/liahona/1981/06/fourteen-fundamentals-in-following-the-prophet?lang=eng.

About the Contributors

Keith A. Erekson is a writer, speaker, and public historian who currently serves as director of the Church History Library of the Church of Jesus Christ of Latter-day Saints. He earned a PhD in history from Indiana University and attained the rank of associate professor of history at the University of Texas at El Paso. He is the author of *Everybody's History: Indiana's Lincoln Inquiry and the Quest to Reclaim a President's Past* (Amherst: University of Massachusetts Press, 2012) and the editor of *Politics and the History Curriculum* (New York: Palgrave Macmillan, 2012) and *Mormon Women's History* (Madison, NJ: Fairleigh Dickinson University Press, 2017).

Matthew C. Godfrey is a general editor and the managing historian of the Joseph Smith Papers. He holds a PhD in American and public history from Washington State University and is the author of *Religion, Politics, and Sugar: The Mormon Church, the Federal Government, and the Utah-Idaho Sugar Company, 1907–1921* (Logan: Utah State University Press, 2007), which was a cowinner of the Mormon History Association's Smith-Petit Award for Best First Book.

Amy S. Greenberg is the Edwin Erle Sparks Professor of History and Women's Studies at Penn State University. She is the author of four books, including *A Wicked War: Polk, Clay, Lincoln, and the 1846 Invasion of Mexico* (New York: Knopf, 2012), *Manifest Manhood and the Antebellum American Empire* (New York: Cambridge University Press, 2005), and *Cause for Alarm: The Volunteer Fire Department in the Nineteenth-Century City* (Princeton: Princeton University Press, 1998). She is currently writing a biography of Sarah Childress Polk.

J. B. Haws is associate professor of church history and doctrine at Brigham Young University and the author of *The Mormon Image in the American Mind: Fifty Years of Public Perception* (New York: Oxford University Press, 2013).

Adam Jortner is the Goodwin-Philpott Professor of Religion in the history department at Auburn University. He is the author of *The Gods of Prophetstown:*

The Battle of Tippecanoe and the Holy War for the American Frontier (New York: Oxford University Press, 2012) and *Blood from the Sky: Miracles and Politics in the Early American Republic* (Charlottesville: University of Virginia Press, 2017).

Matthew Mason is professor of history at Brigham Young University. He is the author or editor of several books including *Apostle of Union: A Political Biography of Edward Everett* (Chapel Hill: University of North Carolina Press, 2016) and *John Quincy Adams and the Politics of Slavery: Selections from the Diary* (New York: Oxford University Press, 2017).

Patrick Q. Mason is Leonard J. Arrington Chair of Mormon History and Culture at Utah State University. He is the author or editor of several books, including, most recently, *Mormonism and Violence: The Battles of Zion* (New York: Cambridge University Press, 2019) and *What Is Mormonism? A Student's Introduction* (New York: Routledge, 2017).

Spencer W. McBride is a historian and documentary editor of the Joseph Smith Papers and the author of *Pulpit and Nation: Clergymen and the Politics of Revolutionary America* (Charlottesville: University of Virginia Press, 2016). He is currently researching and writing a book on Joseph Smith's 1844 presidential campaign.

Benjamin E. Park is assistant professor of history at Sam Houston State University. He is the author of *American Nationalisms: Imagining Union in an Age of Revolutions* (New York: Cambridge University Press, 2017) and *Kingdom of Nauvoo: The Rise and Fall of a Religious Empire on the American Frontier* (New York: W.W. Norton/Liveright, 2020), and is currently the co-editor of *Mormon Studies Review*.

Thomas Richards Jr. is the author of *Breakaway Americas: The Unmanifest Future of the Jacksonian United States* (Johns Hopkins University Press, 2020), as well as several articles and essays on expansion in the Jacksonian era. He was the 2017–18 David S. Weber Fellow at the Clements Center for Southwest Studies, and he has also received fellowships from the McNeil Center for Early American Studies, the Bancroft Library, the Huntington Library, and the Charles Redd Center for Western History. He received his PhD from Temple University in 2016, and is currently a history teacher at Springside Chestnut Hill Academy in Philadelphia.

Brent M. Rogers is associate managing historian of the Joseph Smith Papers. He holds a PhD from the University of Nebraska–Lincoln and is the author of *Unpopular Sovereignty: Mormons and the Federal Management of Early Utah Territory* (Lincoln: University of Nebraska Press, 2017).

Natalie K. Rose is a graduate of the Michigan State University history doctoral program. Her dissertation, "'Our Utah Girls': Girls and Young Women in the Transitional Mormon Church," focuses on the intersection of girlhood, religion, and modernity around the turn of the twentieth century. Her article "Courtship, Marriage, and Romantic Monogamy: Young Mormon Women's Diaries at the Turn of the Twentieth Century" was published in the *Journal of Mormon History* (January 2016). Her next two projects explore questions of politics, gender, and religion. She is writing an article about women's political activism and religiosity in Michigan during the campaign for the Equal Rights Amendment. Rose has won fellowships and awards from the Charles Redd Center for Western Studies and the Graduate School at Michigan State University. Most recently, she has taught gender history and history of religion courses at MSU.

Stephen Eliot Smith has been a member of the Faculty of Law at the University of Otago in Dunedin, New Zealand, since 2006. Raised in Alberta, Canada, he received degrees from the University of Alberta, Queen's University, and Harvard Law School. He was a law clerk for the judges of the Court of Queen's Bench and Court of Appeal of Alberta, was admitted to the bar in Alberta, and has been a visiting professor of international and comparative law at the University of Oklahoma. His areas of academic interest include legal history, criminal law, international law, and church and state relations.

Rachel St. John is a native of California and is associate professor of history at the University of California, Davis, where she joined the faculty in 2016. She is the author of *Line in the Sand: A History of the Western U.S.–Mexico Border* (Princeton: Princeton University Press, 2011). Her current book project, *The Imagined States of America: The Unmanifest History of Nineteenth-Century North America*, explores the diverse range of nation-building projects that emerged across the continent in the nineteenth century.

INDEX

Page numbers in italics indicate figures

CPSIA information can be obtained
at www.ICGtesting.com
Printed in the USA
LVHW051353190620
658368LV00006B/425